Prisoner Litigation

PRISONER LITIGATION

The Paradox of the Jailhouse Lawyer

Jim Thomas

Rowman & Littlefield
PUBLISHERS

ROWMAN & LITTLEFIELD

Published in the United States of America in 1988
by Rowman & Littlefield, Publishers
(a division of Littlefield, Adams & Company)
81 Adams Drive, Totowa, New Jersey 07512

Copyright © 1988 by Rowman & Littlefield

Library of Congress Cataloging-in-Publication Data

Thomas, Jim, 1941–
  Prisoner litigation : the paradox of the jailhouse lawyer / Jim Thomas.

  Bibliography: p. 273
  Includes index.
  ISBN 0–8476–7477–0
  1. Prisoners—Legal status, laws, etc.—United States.   I. Title.
KF9731.T48   1988
344.73'0356—dc19
[347.304356]   87–19870
                                                           CIP

90 89 88
7 6 5 4 3 2 1

Printed in the United States of America

Contents

Tables

Acknowledgments

T HE GENESIS OF THIS PROJECT WAS NONE OF MY DOING. I was content as a potential social theorist until Shubie Moore put me in prison, Ra Rabb Chaka introduced me to prison law, and Edmund Clemons, in his gentle way, planted and nurtured the notion of an ambitious project. It is not clear whether they should be condemned or thanked, but their role is acknowledged and their support has been unwavering. Mylon (Milo) Cross also had a lot to do with suggesting ideas and data sources. I don't see Shubie or Ed much, now that they've moved on to another phase of their life, but Ra and Milo have journeyed with me through the final chapter.

Acknowledgments are not necessarily self-indulgent. They are "thank yous" to those who consistently subordinated their own needs, often with some sacrifice, to assist in an endeavor not their own. Many friends, and even sympathetic critics, have contributed to this project in various ways. Elijah Baptist, Michael Clark, Robert Curtis, Doug Gates, Bob Johns, Johnnie Lane, Alex Neal, John Shannon, Reggie Smith, David Stribling, and many others helped me do prison time "on the installment plan." If I have omitted any names, it is an oversight, not a slight. Numerous jailhouse lawyers patiently shared their knowledge and experiences. Among them were Frank Alerte, Michael Antonelli, Michael Green, Richard Homans, Aaron Snowden, Artur (Rico) Stringer, Kenneth Thompson, Howard Williams, and many others who prefer anonymity. I am also grateful for the assistance of James Newsome and Joe Woods, two of the best jailhouse lawyers in the state, although Ahmad and Rico are also counted among the best. I am also heavily indebted to Ruthie Carbona, Rebecca Fuller, and Pat Wheeler. Most are back on the streets, some are not, but all remain committed to prison reform.

Federal court personnel were of immense help and provided useful off-the-record information. They prefer to remain anonymous. I owe a considerable debt to the Illinois Department of Corrections (IDOC) for allowing access to prisoners and for authorizing interviews to be tape-recorded. To my pleasant surprise, I found IDOC administrators and staff to be helpful and forthright, for which I am most appreciative. They cooperated by providing another perspective; hopefully, they are not disappointed.

Friends and colleagues active in the John Howard Association, the Illinois prison system's watchdog agency, especially Jeanette Musengo and Jerome Blakemore, shared their years of experience and helped obtain otherwise unobtainable data. Attorneys and legal researchers also kept their sense of humor while I pestered them with endless questions and usurped much time that they would otherwise use to advocate prisoner rights. Ruthanne DeWolfe, Lonna Radunski, and Jan Sussler were especially helpful. Theodore Eisenberg provided useful ideas and data, and his research on civil rights litigation has influenced much of my own thinking. Monica Hardesty's touch permeates the latter chapters. I also acknowledge the willingness of James McCafferty of the Administrative Office of the United States Courts to allow indirect release of computerized federal court data. Richard Doherty, Joni Hickman, Devin Keeler, Virginia Kroncke, Melissa Melton, David Moton, Kathy Harris, Sue Los, Norman Guzman, Valery Holloway, Clarissa Palermo, Brad Slavin, and George Wheetly also helped in their own individual ways.

Northern Illinois University provided release time, a sabbatical, summer funding, late afternoon classes, and other useful amenities. The computer staff at Northern Illinois University, luckily, takes pride in problem-solving, and this project tested their sense of humor, which they never lost. Rick Tarulis and Chris Wagner tolerated my late calls and kept things running. To John Austin, Anmarie Aylward, Jim Marquart, Harry Mika, Bill Minor, Bob Suchner, Francis Cullen, Pam Crawford, Chenko Caninovitch, Chris Vanderpool, and John Van Maanen I also owe a debt. The sociology department secretaries, Joanne Russell and Barb Rink, were invaluable in assuring that my departmental obligations did not suffer excessively during periods of overload. My students deserve more acknowledgment than can be given here; they tolerated eccentricities with relatively good humor. Several readers provided detailed suggestions and criticisms, especially Spencer Carr and Gabriele Strohschen. David Luckenbill's assistance in "moving cookies to a lower shelf" was also helpful. Rhonda Nirva devoted many hours in helping make the first chapters generally more readable and offered numerous suggestions before searching for an Arizona rainbow. Jennifer Findlay's warmth, humor, and chili smoothed many rough edges.

This project benefited from the late Ed Sagarin's intellectual critiques as well as his many active years as a prison reformer. He was supportive to his final hour. If Peter Manning's years of friendship and guidance have not produced the product they deserved, hopefully his sense of humor and subheads have. New beginnings occur in strange places. With Barbara, it has begun where the final chapter of this volume concludes.

1

Introduction: Prisoners, Litigation, and the Law

Find out just what people will submit to, and you have found out the exact amount of injustice and wrong which will be imposed upon them; and these will continue till they are resisted. The limits of tyrants are prescribed by the endurance of those whom they oppress (Fredrick Douglass, 1857).

But though his rights may be diminished by the needs and exigencies of the institutional environment, a prisoner is not wholly stripped of Constitutional protections when he is imprisoned for crime. There is no iron curtain drawn between the Constitution and the prisons of this country (Justice Byron White, *Wolff v. McDonnell*, 1974).

Digger believed that a man's cell was his castle; in the summer heat especially, he preferred the comfort of jockey briefs to uncomfortable prison clothes. The problem was, his attire, or lack of it, made the female counsellor uncomfortable when she talked to him through the bars of his cell. She also disapproved of all the pictures of naked women pasted on his wall. She decided that he was some kind of "sex nut," and placed her conclusion in his prison file. There are few secrets from those well placed in the prison culture, and Digger soon learned of her "diagnosis," which would not only decrease his opportunities for rewards but could jeopardize his chances for transfer or release as well. In retaliation, he threatened a civil rights lawsuit, but a compromise was reached, and he was transferred to a more favorable environment. For Digger, law, or the threat of invoking it, was successful, and his experience typifies the many grievances that impel prisoners to turn to the courts to resolve problems.

THE ISSUES SIMPLY STATED

There are many social and legal issues underlying prisoner litigation, but they can be grouped under four broad categories.[1] The first issue revolves around the role of the federal courts in reviewing the constitu-

1

tionality of state activity and the tension between states' rights and federalism. Should states be relatively free from federal intervention, or should the federal government attempt to establish between states uniform procedures and behavior consistent with Constitutional norms? How far should federal courts go in intervening into the domain of state officials? Are expanded civil rights a consequence of "sociology majors on the bench?"

The second issue is the meaning of rights articulated in the Constitution. Are the definitions of individual liberty "built into" the literal language of the Constitution? Does (or should) the federal judiciary have the power to reinterpret the literal text of the document in a manner more in line with changing social conditions, attitudes, and norms? What were the "original intents" of the Framers? As one conference critic glibly argued, "Show me where in the Constitution it says that prisoners have the right to toilet paper!" Lacking an explicit court intent, so the logic runs, there is no reason to translate an abstract claim of rights into specific legal remedy.

The status of prisoners as legal subjects is the third issue. One argument holds that those who have been convicted of abusing the law should be restricted from further access to it in noncriminal cases until their social debt is paid by incarceration. The "civil death" doctrine, in which prisoners possess no more legal rights than a "dead man," long prevailed. As late as 1973, a few states clung to this doctrine, even though it had been ruled unconstitutional (e.g., *Delorme v. Pierce Freightlines Co.* 353 F.Supp. 258, 1973). What Constitutional rights, then, should prisoners possess? If they possess rights, how are they to be protected? By the courts, by the states, or by prison adminstrators?

The fourth issue centers on social ideology and the relationship between freedom and control, natural and positive law, the philosophy of justice and its implementation, and social change and social stability. How much freedom do we allow persons who have been deprived of freedom? How should legal change occur? What are the principles of justice to which we, as an "enlightened society," are bound, and how ought we express these principles? How far should we go in expanding prisoners' rights?

Each of these issues requires a social approach to the study of prisoner litigation. Above all, we must recognize that law is a form of social action, and just as law changes, so too does the manner in which it is employed by those seeking redress of real or imagined grievances.

PROLOGUE

Discussions of the world of prisoner litigation often resemble the tales of Marco Polo returning from the orient: there are fabulous descriptions, incoherent tales, and lack of common words and experiences create disbelief, suspicion, and hostility. One too sympathetic toward the prisoner culture risks being ignored as a naive romantic; one too hostile is dismissed as insensitive to cultural nuances of meaning. One means of displaying the contours of the litigation landscape might be to invite others to participate in a guided tour, a travelogue. I, the tour guide, will lead us through the complex history by which prisoners' rights have evolved and display the changing topography of litigation trends. En route, we will visit some of the denizens of prisons, courts, and corrections and listen to their tales.

Lifting the haze obscuring the litigation scene requires a step-by-step journey in which we identify selected landmarks, primary points of interest, and chat a bit with key players in the litigation game. As with any journey, we cannot visit everything or everyone, but we can obtain a flavor of the culture and, with luck, come away with a stronger understanding of and appreciation for this alien world. Each chapter is a tour stop, and each stop will provide answers to questions, dispel misconceptions, and illuminate issues that are too often addressed with little fact or insight.

MAPPING THE TERRAIN

The social practices and relationships of law are not to be found in law books or case annals, and many of the conventional paradigms for interpreting these relationships are breaking down (e.g., Nelken, 1986). Understanding prisoners' use of law requires a grounding in the history, litigation trends and social processes that generate their litigation. Critics of prisoners' access to law, and they seem to be an overwhelming and strident majority, lack this grounding and view these suits as an abuse of the legal system. But as Engel has observed:

> Criticism of what is seen as an overuse of law and legal institutions often reveals less about the quantity of litigation at any given time than about the interests being asserted or protected through litigation and the kinds of individuals or groups involved in cases the courts are asked to resolve (Engel, 1984: 552).

The rights protected by criminal and civil law do not arise *de novo*, but are context bound and located in the social acts and attitudes of a given historical moment. Through their social activity, people create belief systems that define rights. They then make laws to protect them. Other people then attempt to scurry under the panoply of protections these laws have created. But law, in its precision, may not always recognize the rights of newcomers, and the struggle for rights begins anew (Roby, 1969).

My concern in this volume is civil rights, where these rights are located, how the law protects them, what access there is, how rights have broadened in recent decades, and how this broadening has occured. My window into this world is prisoner litigation, which raises all of these issues, though not with equal force. Our window holds a double prism. The first reflects the trends of prisoners' filings through the objective lens of filing data, the same data that critics use to dismiss the enterprise, to obtain a more accurate image than currently exists (Thomas, Harris, and Keeler, 1987). The second reflects the process of litigation as seen by those who have created it, primarily prisoners, in order to better understand the social and empirical context out of which the use of courts arises. Despite the discourse of revelation, the intent is interrogatory, and descriptions should be interpreted as questioning the social sources and political ideology of and resistance to our thinking about the evolution of rights in general and prisoners' rights in particular.

What began as a short day trip into the world of jailhouse lawyers assumed a dynamic of its own, and I lost control of the tour. What there was to see and understand required additional trips, extended visits, and fuller immersion into the historical location of prisoners' rights, litigation trends and patterns, judicial processes, prison existence, and the culture of the jailhouse lawyer. The story of the jailhouse lawyer cannot be told without first providing a massive prologue; this is the function of this work. As jailhouse lawyers told their story, dramatic discrepancies quickly appeared between their views and the views of their critics, discrepancies in the reasons for filing, the substantive merit of suits, the judicial outcomes, the methods of processing, and the environment and motivations of those litigating. Before their story could be told, a fundamental clarification of prisoner litigation first seemed necessary. Tracing the history of the development of rights, identifying distinctions in filing patterns, and describing the nature of suits, procedures of processing and environment from which suits emerge, furnishes the necessary preliminary framework. A separate story of the jailhouse lawyer will later be told.[2]

Who Cares?

Why, some have asked, should anybody care about prisoner litigation? One reason lies in our country's unique system of laws. The United States is the only country in the world that provides convicted prisoners with the right to petition *directly* to the judiciary to redress grievances concerning either their original conviction (habeas corpus) or complaints of treatment or conditions (civil rights). Other nations may allow indirect access to the courts through intermediaries such as lawyers or their equivalent, but none provide and protect a formal channel for prisoners *themselves* to petition directly to the courts. None require the courts to provide a flexible and sympathetic interpretation of prisoner complaints, and none have ordered reasonable availability of resources to allow unfettered access to initiate complaints. Such direct access to law has had a dramatic impact on state and federal fiscal resources, prison administration, judicial proceedings, and prison conditions.[3] Despite the claims of critics and skeptics, these suits have had substantial impact on fiscal policies, prison administration, court operations, and prison social order. Prisoner litigation has also contributed to the development of individual liberty by expanding Constitutional protections of a variety of rights. Perhaps more than any other single mechanism, prisoner litigation has contributed to prison reform, and even when a suit is lost, litigation opens the windows of prisons just a bit wider to make their historically dark interiors just a bit more visible to those on the outside.

The Genesis of Litigation

The roots of prisoner litigation extend back to pre-Norman common law, but the contemporary beginnings are more recent. The Fourteenth Amendment and post-Civil War legislation provide the basis for both habeas corpus and civil rights litigation. These bases have been expanded by recent interpretations of individual rights and shaped by the civil rights and other activist movements in the 1960s. Black Muslims were particularly astute in recognizing these changes, and after protracted court battles, they won a series of political victories for religious recognition. Their successes, and even some failures, provided precedents that established the broader rights of prisoners.

Viewing the 1960s as the watershed of prisoners' rights, however, is misleading. Prisons in the United States have historically been personal fiefdoms, generally closed to outside inspection. In the 1950s, prison riots, changes in prison governance, and shifting definitions of humane treatment contributed to the translation of prisoner privileges into rights.[4] The 1950s were also the beginning of more active federal intervention into the affairs of states, and the Supreme Court began reviewing state practices alleged to violate federal or Constitutional principles. A decade of political, penal and social change in the 1950s thus eased the way for expansion of prisoner rights in the next decade. Together, prison changes, old law, and new judicial interpretations have given birth to a phenomenon that has generated considerable controversy among criminal justice practitioners, lawyers, and civil libertarians. In the past quarter century, state and federal prisoners have filed nearly a half-million suits in federal district courts, constituting a substantial portion of all federal litigation.

The Trouble with Prisons

Prisoners sue primarily because they object to the conditions of their confinement. Literature on prison life, overwhelming in its abundance, provides rich descriptions of the conditions faced by inmates. Since the eighteenth-century work of John Howard, descriptions of prison life in the United States by de Beaumont and de Toqueville (1970/1833), the mid-eighteenth-century revelations of the Prison Discipline Society of Boston (1972), and the later studies of Clemmer (1958) and Sykes (1958), analyses of prisoner social order and existence have revealed many of the problems prisoners and staff must confront daily. Among the most common contemporary problems include prisoner violence (Abbott, 1981; Colvin, 1981, 1982; Ekland-Olson, 1986; Granger, 1977; Marquart and Crouch, 1984; Sylvester et al., 1977; Useem, 1985), guard violence (Cohen and Taylor, 1972; Marquart, 1986a; Possley, 1981), psychological degradation (Cloward, 1960; DeWolfe and DeWolfe, 1979; Goffman, 1961; Menninger, 1978), sexual predation (Lockwood, 1980; Wooden and Parker, 1982), street gangs (Camp and Camp, 1985a; De Zutter, 1981; Jacobs, 1974a, 1977; Stastny and Tyrnauer, 1983), racial conflict (Carroll, 1974, 1977a, 1977b; Jacobs, 1982), unfair disciplinary procedures (Jacobs, 1983; Thomas, Aylward, Mika, and Blakemore, 1985), and general conditions (Braly, 1977; Cardozo-Freeman, 1982; Irwin, 1962, 1970; Thomas, 1984b). Some of these characteristics are inherent in the nature of prisons, but many are not, and are created by the arrogance, abuse, and indifference of correction officials.

Prisoners have responded to these problems in various ways. In the early nineteenth-century prisons, especially in Philadelphia's isolation model, psychological disintegration was one, albeit involuntary, response. In our contemporary prisons, "burn-out" still occurs in more subtle forms characterized often by heavy drug use, behavioral passivity, and psychological withdrawal. "Ghosting," or avoiding work or interaction with others, remaining unassigned to work details, and skipping meals is another way some prisoners cope with a hostile environment. Another form of response is actual or threatened physical retaliation. Several prisoners interviewed for this project expressed considerable pride in their use of violence against guards or other inmates as a means of dispute resolution. Still others "put on their mask," a frontstage persona of aloof indifference, to "skate through" their time. In Illinois prisons, most prisoners (estimated as high as 75 percent by some correctional officials) affiliate with street gangs as a means of obtaining resources and protection against the predations of others.[5]

Some prisoners, however, are neither passive nor violent. When confronted with extreme problems from either staff or other prisoners, they have their own way of retaliating. Sometimes their problems arise from apparently minor incidents, such as maliciously being denied toilet paper by staff. At other times, the issue is quite serious, involving life-or-death matters of physical protection, health care, or guard violence. However, rather than unblock "information feedback loops" by pushing a guard off a four-level tier to initiate dialogue with the administration, a more peaceful and productive strategy is found. Whence comes the jailhouse lawyer.

Understanding Prisoner Litigation

Jailhouse law is a form of dispute resolution by which prisoners attempt to bring conditions of existence closer to their liking. Litigation alerts staff that guard complicity with street gangs is inappropriate, that ignoring potentially critical safety hazards may mean liability, and that ignoring pleas for help during a gang-rape are not to be tolerated. Litigation also creates and expands rights and expectations of prisoners during captivity, and although staff are often able to subvert these rights, their incremental expansion is undeniable (e.g., Jacobs, 1982). More simply, jailhouse law has become a means of using the legal system for the purpose for which it has been designed, that of social mainte-nance.[6] But for prisoners, social maintenance possesses a different meaning than for the public or for corrections' officials. As a conse-quence, critics see cynical manipulation of the law where prisoner advocates perceive peaceful conflict resolution.

Lawyers attempt to understand law by examining what is or has been adjudicated, the formal processes involved, or the cases that have emerged. However, these issues are meaningless when stripped from their social context. Litigation does not occur until there is, first, a dispute, and second, the recognition of law as a means of resolution. An understanding of prisoner litigation cannot be understood in isolation from such broader social factors as "justice," ideology, the changing role of the Constitution as the basis for acquiring or defending rights, the changing function of the state in implementing them or the litigants who make it happen. Hence, the organizing theme of this work is sociological. Discussions of case law have been omitted except where directly relevant.[7] Understanding prisoner litigation also requires an understanding of prison life, social control strategies, prison conditions and administration, civilian litigation, and the recent history of federal law. It is not possible to fully address all of these topics here, or even to treat them equally because of lack of available data and of the complexity of the issues. As if performing an "ethnographic biopsy," I have at-tempted to take a slice from the most accessible layers of the topic's body in order to study the origins and processes of prisoner litigation. Some topics are presented with broad brushstrokes; others, especially those that have received scant attention elsewhere, are filled in with more detail.

One overriding question dominates discussions of prisoner litigation: is it really an apocalyptic "explosion" of "epidemic" proportions? Galanter (1983) has borrowed the term *hyperlexis* (from Manning, 1977) to challenge the belief that the United States is an excessively litigious society. This work focuses on one viewpoint of litigation, that of the prisoners, and expands upon Galanter's argument that litigation is not a form of "legal pollution" but arises from legitimate complaints endemic in the nation's prisons. The organizing principle of this work is that prisoner litigation is a form of resistance to the deprivations of prison life. It comes about because one group of people, prisoners, has invoked the law to stimulate another group of people, lawyers and court personnel, to respond to the injustices created by a third group, corrections' officials.

Conceptualizing Prisoner Litigation

The term "prisoner litigation" is ambiguous. It typically connotes civil rights complaints or habeas corpus suits filed by incarcerated persons.[8] In practice, however, prisoners' suits may be filed by lawyers, rather than by prisoners themselves, or by persons not incarcerated who are attempting to avoid prison. Further, suits classified in federal reports as "state prisoner litigation" may be filed by persons in county jails, by guardians of juveniles, by persons in nonprison facilities, such as mental health hospitals, or by private citizens. As a consequence, the term "prisoner litigation" encompasses a variety of complaints and disparate categories of persons who have a grievance against the state or federal criminal justice system.

The term "prisoner litigation" technically includes litigation filed in both state and federal courts. Conventional usage, however, tends to restrict the term to *federal* litigation, and this volume remains limited to federal filings. Most states have some protection against abuses of Constitutional rights of prisoners. When filing habeas corpus petitions, prisoners must normally first exhaust all state remedies prior to filing. When filing civil rights complaints, however, they may file in federal courts without first exhausting state remedies, and thus state courts are often bypassed for civil complaints.[9] This occurs because federal courts are perceived to be more sympathetic to civil rights, and because prisoners need not exhaust state remedies prior to filing a federal claim. Federal courts are also more powerful than state courts, so their decisions have more impact on society, prisons, and state law. This work emphasizes civil rights litigation. This is partly because they are the most common, the most dramatic, and the most interesting. But more impor-

tantly, civil rights complaints filed by state prisoners illustrate the transformations in the ideas and practices of rights, law, and society.

THE SOCIAL CONTEXT OF PRISONER LITIGATION

Distinctions between groups of legal subjects, those persons upon whom
rights are conferred, are a function of the public grace, which at any
given historical moment defines the substance of these changing values.
Courts, as Fiss (1979) has cogently argued, exist not so much to resolve
disputes, but to procedurally mediate and implement these values. The
extension of rights to convicted offenders is an example of changing
public values in which harsh codes guiding social response to and control
of prisoners are breaking down. Courts have become one conduit for
diverting changes from abstract ideas into social practice. Legal reforms
have been triggered by the increased importance of civil society, by the
increasing importance of individual rights, and by the willingness of
individuals or groups to establish new case law that ultimately expands
the rights of other groups as well. Other factors inducing legal changes
include the subordination of punishment to external monitoring, the
use of law as an instrument in social change, and the role of the state in
protecting and expanding rights of citizens. Prisoner litigation has both
benefited from and contributed to these changes as prisoners have used
law to peacefully oppose what they perceive to be a denial of Constitutional protection.

One source of social change is social conflict. Those with power and
rights wish to preserve them; those who lack power and rights wish to
obtain them. Historically, many social groups have been systematically
excluded from the full protection of rights to which they are perceived
to be entitled. But as Robinson (1984: 10) reminds us, there has never
been a social system in which masters had all the rights and slaves had
none. The master cannot exist without the slave, and resistance to
domination by the latter requires concessions or changes by the former.

As societies change, so too do the corresponding methods of maintaining social order. Durkheim observed that in so-called "primitive" societies, social order is ostensibly consensual and reflects dominant norms
and beliefs. Consensual obligations are not as useful in providing guidelines for pluralistic societies, in which disagreements over definitions
and rights may more easily arise. In societies with complex legals
systems, social change contributes to changes in the content and application of law, as well as to the refinement of the definitions and
applications of rights and who is to receive or be denied them. There
often arises a tension between established rules that guide social behavior, such as norms, laws or values, and changing practices that seem to
challenge or violate them. Prisoner litigation is one example of such a

tension. In our society, prisoners have traditionally been accorded the minimum rights to food, shelter, and other necessities defined by standards of the time as "humane." But the assertion of prisoners to their rights provides both the rationale and legal basis for subsequent expansion of Constitutional rights as well.

The Irony of Prisoner Litigation

That imprisoned offenders are able to employ the law as a weapon against their keepers is an *irony*. That convicted offenders are able to use the law to enforce compliance with Constitutional protections is a *paradox*. That the *object* of law, those persons or things upon whom legal force and corresponding practices are brought to bear, becomes the *subject* of law, those upon whom legal rights and obligations are conferred, is a *contradiction*. *Irony*, the heart of dialectics, means simply that "A goes forth and returns as *non-A*." Irony is a form of *peripity*, a sudden and unexpected turn of events (Burke, 1969: 517). The irony that prisoners can shape, and often improve, both the criminal justice system and the wider society through their legal struggles has created a *dialectical* process, a process by which the social world, law or prisons, is transformed by those who would themselves be transformed by it.

The relationship between freedom and law is itself dialectical. Although law is used to oppress as well as liberate, it has historically served to liberate to a greater extent than it has not. One outcome of the liberating capacity of law is that it can be used by persons or groups who have been socially, although not necessarily legally, excluded from its utility and protection. The most obvious example of legal protections that have not resulted in corresponding social protection is civil rights. Ethnic groups, gays, and women, for example, are protected under numerous state and federal statutes, but this legislation has not resulted in full equality or freedom from social domination for which such laws were intended. Further, access to law in both criminal and civil procedures, although a Constitutional right, is accorded primarily to those with sufficient motivation and resources to pursue it. Law and rights, then, are an outcome of struggles for freedom and of conflicts over the resources by which to attain it.

Law as Social Action

Law specifies many of the essential social rules by which we live. But rules are not an end in themselves; they are temporary guidelines that provide cohesion, control, and communication between social groups and between groups past and present:

> Man is as much a rule-following animal as a purpose-seeking one. And he is successful not because he knows why he ought to observe the rules which he does observe, or is even capable of stating all these rules in words, but

because his thinking and acting are governed by rules which have by a process of selection been evolved in the society in which he lives, and which are thus the product of the experience of generations (Hayek, 1973: 11).

The "experience of generations" of which Hayek spoke contributes to continual formulation of new rules. In the past two decades, our legal system has undergone fundamental changes in expanding and protecting rights. Do legally mandated changes fall within the ambit of "original intents?" In arguing for a "jurisprudence of original intention" in which the Constitution and early law is taken literally, Attorney General Edwin Meese would eliminate the role of changing social conditions from the interpretation of law (Meese, 1985a, 1985b). This reduces interpretations of law to *legal fundamentalism*. In this view, it is not the spirit of a given law but the literal language of a statute and the "original intents" of those who wrote it that should determine how law is to be interpreted and applied. Legal fundamentalists are among the most strident opponents of prisoner rights and litigation. In their view, judicial decisions should be deduced by contemporary lawmakers from the literal terminology of earlier statutes. They recognize the "rule following" while failing to see the "purpose seeking" character of human activity. As a consequence, the historical changes by which prisoners have come under increasing the protection of the Constitution is ignored.

Legal Fundamentalism and "Living Law"

Legal fundamentalism should not be confused with *antiquarianism*, despite apparent similarities. Antiquarianism is primarily a legal philosophy and advocates emphasize *stare decisis*, or adherence to past judicial decisions to guide contemporary legal interpretations. *Stare decisis* is the basis of common law by which decades, even centuries, of case law provide the foundation for the meaning and procedures for judicial decision-making. Antiquarians also recognize and respond to the necessity to bring established traditions in line with contemporary needs; they prefer, however, gradual and incremental changes rather than dramatic and sweeping reversals. The advantage of the antiquarian perspective is the stability, consistency, and continuity it provides in legal intepretations. Legal fundamentalism, by contrast, is primarily a political ideology by which existing power hierarchies and political policies are justified by appeal to the legal purity of implied intents of the Constitution's Framers. Legal fundamentalists, while often using the rhetoric and discourse of antiquarian philosophy, are not loath to dramatically change case law when it serves their goals. Contemporary legal fundamentalists, for example, have criticized federal court decisions such as *Miranda* or *Roe v. Wade* and have actively sought to overturn them (Meese, 1985a, 1985b, 1985c). Legal fundamentalism, then, is not so much a legal philosophy as a doctrinal stance in a struggle for power. At stake is the claim to mastery of a text, and those who control textual interpretations control its use. That use should not, in this view, be extended to protect prisoners.

One alternative to legal fundamentalism is the "living law" perspective. In this view, law is a process, a dialectical relationship between social beings. Law is a set of behavior-guiding symbols shaped both by social structure and by an internal "logic" that organizes with some continuity the law's content, the procedures by which it is applied, and the social philosophy rooted in that continuity. Law is seen as the reflection of intellectual, political, and economic activity involved in the process of goal-oriented selection by conscious actors who assess, interpret, and choose particular courses of action in creating social existence. In this view, law can be a means for social reform. Adherents recognize that law is the embodiment of power relations, social and historical experience, world views and ideology; law guides social formation according to preconceived definitions of appropriate social order.

When law becomes the center of political struggle in which one group uses it for empowerment, those who lose power respond. Prisoners' rights have triggered resistance from many groups, and when one right is protected, it might quickly be subverted through counterploys (Thomas, Aylward, Mika, and Blakemore, 1985). For example, when prison staff lose the absolute right to punish prisoners, they can assert their power in alternative ways not yet legally proscribed. Hence, there are winners and losers in the enactment and implementation of law, and in our society, both civil and criminal law provide prescriptions and proscriptions of behavior that are, at least ostensibly, based on right and wrong. Hence, "The Law" is not sacrosanct, but subject to the same accountability and need for change as any other social institution.

The concepts of legal fundamentalism and "living law" are analytic categories, useful for sorting out the positions and issues in the debate over prisoner litigation. Legal fundamentalists do make some concessions to the changing needs of society and the concept of living law, and adherents of living law do make some concessions to the need for precedent. In practice, however, each reflects a different way of viewing the relationship between law and society, and of interpreting the relationship of the state and the Constitution to the preservation of social order. For adherents of the "living law" view, law cannot be reduced simply to a set of codified prescriptions and proscriptions or the logic of case law, as sociological jurisprudence suggests. Nor is law simply an instrument of repression, domination, or control, as many conflict theorists and deterministic Marxians argue. Beneath its formal language, law constitutes a system of behavioral signposts engendered by human activity.

LAWS, SIGNS, AND HUMAN ACTIVITY

Law as Signs

Law, above all, is a type of sign system, or code. Code, as used here, does not refer to codified statutes. It is used in its literary sense as a set of symbols that provides a text connoting a meaning-laden structure and indicating possibilities for social action. As a sign system, law embodies those symbols that provide order, establish and protect hierarchy, confer legitimacy, convey appropriate definitions of social structure and interaction, and indicate sanctioned methods for dispute resolution. For prisoners, the expectation of certain rights to reasonable treatment derives from the legal text that provides consistent signposts distinguishing what is proper treatment from what is not. For prison administrators, the legal text signals obligations and clarifies mandates.

As a code, law changes in that the signs (specific legal statutes or sanctions) are modified as the ideological character (e.g., equality, due process) changes. But signs and their meanings do not exist apart from the activity of those who create, interpret, and use them. As a consequence, the symbolism of law requires continuous social reproduction. Like Thales' river, the general contours may appear constant, but the contents do not remain the same. By viewing law primarily as statutes and procedures, we gloss over the social relations it symbolizes. Arguments for legal fundamentalism, whatever other merits they might possess, miss this connection between law as connoter of social meaning, and emphasize instead law as denoter of precise prescriptions and proscriptions.

As a symbolic text, law has a history, an audience, and above all, an author. This authorship suggests the second element of law—*human activity*.

Law and Human Activity

Law, despite its occasionally autonomous character, does not exist independently of other forms of social action. Its emergence and alterations do not occur as part of some external master plan or "spirit," as Hegel has suggested; nor is it simply part of a grand evolutionary process of social development. *People* behave in usually intelligible ways in their on-going process of producing and reproducing social existence. As with history, people make law, but not always within the conditions of their choosing. Legal concepts, theories, and principles emerge, are modified, or pass out of existence as a response to changing social factors and interpretations of order, right, and obligation. The symbolic and practical aspects of law are thus patterned by *historical, phenomenological,* and *structural* factors.

The Historicity of Law

Historicity refers to those patterns of events that individually or cumulatively shape social structure, culture, or thought. Law is the historical consequence of human activity that goes beyond mundane social practices in ways that dramatically transform it. Structural factors are those preexisting taken-for-granted institutions, cultural beliefs and expectations, power and economic arrangements and ideologies that provide the conceptual and operative machinery for everyday life. Social structure creates relatively invariant and predictable social relationships. It is through social structure that our rules emerge, that battles are fought to attain a better position in the social hierarchy, and that systems of cultural—including legal—meanings are produced as we create and resolve our social problems. Prisoner litigation, for example, is affected by the structure of the criminal justice system, including criminal procedures, punishment, the power and organization of the state and social attitudes toward "justice."

The Phenomenology of Law

Phenomenological patterns of law refer to the manner in which people experience and interpret law, the ways law becomes accepted as a legitimate social control mechanism, the manner in which it is used to create order in everyday existence. Prisoner litigation, for example, is based on broader historical judicial principles of habeas corpus, individual liberty and civil rights, all of which shape how prison is experienced by prisoners, by administrators, and by society. Prisoner litigation embodies not only the history of struggles for rights, but the attempts to recreate a social existence more compatible with "enlightened" conceptions of social organization and order. More simply, it is an attempt to bring experience in line with ideals. Just as prisons have moved from the penitence and medical models of the nineteenth century to the human management models of the late twentieth, so too have demands for prisoners' rights shifted to correspond to these models. This shift has influenced how prisons are experienced, which in turn changes the relationship between prisons, prisoners, society, and law.

There is a broader aspect of how prisons are experienced. Society, too, "experiences" prisons, and the consequences reverberate across a variety of social levels. Expenditures to bring prisons to acceptable standards or to pay substantial settlements place a burden on scarce fiscal resources, perceptions of and feelings about crime are intimately connected to feelings about prisons, and taxpayers experience a sense of resentment when they are forced to fund "country club" prisons. This, in turn, may lead to public backlash against prison reform, against tax increases, or against politicians who publicly advocate public expenditures for prisons. In short, a single successful suit may ripple across the social stream creating waves of political resistance as it swells.

Law and Social Praxis

Prisoner rights do not become a significant legal issue until an awareness of the possibility of using law as a form of *social praxis*, as distinguished from *social practice*, exists. Social practices are those daily activities in which we engage as matter-of-fact routines and by which we unreflectively reproduce social relations. Common forms of social practice include use of language, going to work at the accustomed time, or participating in conventional eating rites (dinner at six, meat and potatos).

Social praxis, by contrast, refers to those activities by which we transform our symbolic and material world. Social praxis may be an individual or group affair. Examples include war, social activism, technological, and scientific innovation, obtaining an education in order to obtain secure employment, or prisoner litigation. An employee, when angry at the boss, may complain to co-workers, and then go out drinking and go home and kick the cat. This is social practice. Another employee may become angry, but instead files a complaint or engages in covert workplace sabotage. This, as Aronowitz (1973) has suggested, may be a form of social praxis. Similarly, one prisoner may escape monotonous prison routine by withdrawing into drugs, a common social practice. A second prisoner may challenge the lack of meaningful work assignments or lack of programs by filing lawsuits.

It is through social praxis that law changes. Prisoner litigation, for example, has had a profound impact upon civil rights litigation by opening up new avenues for civilian litigation. It was, after all, a prisoner-related suit, *Monroe v. Pape*, (365 U. S. 167, 1961), that resurrected nineteenth-century civil rights law, incorporated into U.S.C. 42 Section 1983, which in turn has provided the legal theory underlying much contemporary civil rights struggles.

A Conceptual Integration

The concepts of structure, phenomenology, and praxis provide three paths by which to explore the boundary processes and social transactions out of which prisoner litigation emerges and by which it is accomplished. Tracing the history of law offers one window into the structure that makes litigation possible and a context in which it "makes sense." The trends of litigation provide insights into how and the extent to which it is experienced by courts and prisoners. These insights are further supplemented by examining the actual experiences of those engaged in prisoner litigation. Finally, Black's (1976) typology of law indicates that prisoner litigation reflects a *conciliatory* style of response, or a form of self-help.[10] Law does not itself "behave," but is invoked by persons in need. Court officials do not proactively respond to prisoner needs but, instead, react to invocation of their services. By examining how prisoners invoke and how the organizational personnel of courts respond, the link between social praxis and legal structure and experience takes on sharper focus.

To understand prisoner litigation, we must understand how these three aspects, the historical, phenomenological, and structural, as products of human activity, have combined to provide the symbolic text that guides and changes the theory and practice of a legal system that allows convicted felons to employ the law against their keepers. These three aspects correspond to historical developments and litigation patterns, filing processes and the reasons that impel prisoners to sue, and the structural impact of prisoner litigation.

Prisoner litigation represents a new form of social action embodied in changing social conceptions of choice. Despite prevailing popular views to the contrary, prisoner litigants do not automatically hate their keepers, and suits cannot be easily explained simply as cathartic hostility. While there exists a definite adversarial relationship between prisoners and their keepers, petitions tend to use personal issues as a means of addressing broader problems endemic in the nation's prisons. Taken as a whole, prisoner petitions symbolize a common trend, namely that of resistance to the problems of prison existence.

A THEORETICAL OVERVIEW

The organizing framework of both the research and conceptualiztion derives from critical theory and interactionism. The discourse, however, has been purged of the esoteric buzzwords normally associated with these positions. Readers familiar with the traditions should be able to recognize the inferences. Others should be aware of the following premises implied throughout.

First, despite its formality, the law provides a mediating link between those who control and those who are controlled. The power of the state to enforce its will is mandated by law, but it is also mediated by what the law will allow. A form of "loose coupling" exists between control and those controlled, and law is one means by which slippage can occur. When one group chooses to resist, law may become one strategy for resistance. The ability of law to mediate and transform social existence occurs in many ways, and prisoner litigation is one (Thomas, 1984a).

Second, in addition to its coercive function, law also possesses an ideological function. It contains assumptions of contemporary values of "good and evil" and "right and wrong." Ideology, the taken-for-granted conceptual machinery that guides daily life, conveys assumptions and justifications for the "proper state of things." Legal matters thus become ideological matters in that they "name the world" by providing definitions of value and obligation. For example, current debates over the proper role of judicial review represent, in part, an ideological battle in that at stake are beliefs of proper social order, power sharing and decision-making. Prison policies of punishment and conditions reflect both administrative and social ideology in that exercise of power is justified on appeal to broad principles regarding the nature of offenders and the role of social order. As ideology, prisons and prison policies become a mechanism to explain certain occurrences and disclaim others (Berkman, 1979: 23). Prisoner litigation provides one means of mediating this ideology, and if not changing it, at least limiting the absolute power to define staff behavior as "correct."

A final premise, derived from interactionism, holds that human behavior, including official rule making, is situated in multiple contexts. To understand prisoner litigation, one must also understand the contexts from which it arises, by which it is processed, and in which it is done. Prison structure creates deprivations for both staff and prisoners, which may lead to complaints that require resolution. Courts process these complaints guided by formal rules, but the processers also carry additional baggage that influences processing. As a consequence, prisoner litigation entails a myriad of sequenced acts, each reflecting different needs and goals.

These three premises imply a dialectical tension between the *form* of litigation (documents, courts and decisions) and an *act* of litigation, which is situated human activity. Prisoner litigation should be recognized as an unfolding of structure, behavior, ideas, values, and consequences, each altering the other, and each affecting the larger society. Different observers perceive the same phenomena through their own subjective frames of reference, which are mediated by ideology, personal experience, and interests. These implicit premises have patterned my own seeing and telling.

THE DATA

Both quantitative and qualitative data have been gathered from a variety of sources. Summary statistics from government records and documents on national filing trends and files from Illinois' Northern District provided detailed information on filings. Qualitative data were obtained from interviews with court personnel and participant observation data from prisons.

The Quantitative Data

Quantitative data bring together precise information on filing trends that most observers only allude to in broad generalizations. For example, when critics claim that prisoners sue for release, they, to my knowledge, have never provided any substantive figures to corroborate the statement. I have attempted to organize discussions in a way that provides broad outlines of the changing trends of prison suits to enable a more accurate assessment of national, state, and Illinois filings. Although the quantitative data have been analyzed with a variety of statistical procedures, their use here is limited to percentage tables or frequency charts. The goal is to show general trends, and little is lost by the omission of more sophisticated procedures. Those interested in logit regression and similar statistical techniques should refer to previous works (e.g., Suchner et al., 1986; Thomas, 1987).

Ethnographic Research

The bulk of this work falls within the ethnographic tradition of research in which one journeys into an alien culture. Ethnography, the study of cultures from the participant's point of view, can be tricky for outsiders, especially in cultures in which outsiders are viewed with considerable suspicion, if not hostility. Several years may be required to negotiate access to sufficiently informed persons to make a study worthwhile, and several more years may be required before sufficient trust exists to mine the wealth of information that the insiders guard. This research was no exception, but trust, double-edged as it is, must be shared. It is difficult to trust persons without sharing, and one does not share openly without close affinity. Affinity leads to friendship, or at least close acquaintanceship, and once this has developed, the researcher risks the charge of "joining the other side." I probably am guilty of this charge, because I am writing for and about friends and acquaintances. As Van Maanen (1988) has observed, ethnography is a story told from *somebody's* perspective, but, then, what research is not? The questions posed and the answers given could probably not have been otherwise obtained, and I have tried to announce and identify my biases throughout.

The style of my telling proceeds from what Van Maanen (1988) has described as "the impressionist tale" in that, like a nineteenth-century painter, I attempt:

> to capture a worldly scene in a special instant or moment of time. The work is figurative, although it conveys a highly personalized perspective. What a painter sees, given an apparent position in time and space, is what the viewer sees.

My goal, as Van Maanen would argue, is one of *evocation,* and the selection of themes and illustrations invites the reader to *feel* in a way that "startles complacent viewers accustomed to and comfortable with older forms":

> The magic of telling impressionist tales is that they are always unfinished. With each retelling, we discover more of what we know. Because of their form and audience dependency, meaning will be worked on again and again. By telling our stories and telling them over in different ways, we are admitting to those we trust that our goals are not necessarily fixed, that we are never free of doubt and ambiguity, that our strategic choices in the fieldwork are often accidential (guided more by inchoate lore than by a technical logic), that our data, to be meaningful, require development over time, and that we are far more dependent on the people we study than we can know or say (Van Maanen, 1988).

I am confident that the data are accurate, I am certain that the story is the prisoners,' but I have undoubtedly mediated their telling with my interpretation and writing. My tellings are not intended to provide a definitive picture, but to begin a rough outline and fill in some color. Perhaps these are both the limits and the strengths of all research.

Data Collection and Caveats

Several methodological difficulties obstruct analysis of prisoner litigation, prompting several caveats. First, there are currently little accessible data available on the details of prisoner petitions. Federal courts are just beginning to computerize such information, which when possible, has been utilized. Detailed civil rights data exist only from the early 1970s, and occasional computational errors or changes remain in their statistics. Nonetheless, federal figures remain sufficiently accurate if used with caution.

Second, interviews, conversations and correspondence with jailhouse lawyers and other litigants are drawn from all four of the state's maximum security prisons, the women's institution, and two medium and one minimum security institutions. The Illinois Department of Corrections allowed tape recorded interviewing and observation, which provided the opportunity to tape accounts of prisoners and staff. Researching prisons is not like tenting with Malinowski. Prisons not only keep insiders in; they also keep outsiders out. Laws and policies can inhibit research, but through a variety of activities, I have been in constant personal contact with prisoners since 1980. Other interviews were conducted with federal judges, corrections administrators and personnel, Illinois Department of Corrections officials, and federal court personnel. I have also drawn from visitations since 1981 with the John Howard Association, Illinois' prison monitoring group. Taped and untaped interviews were collected, and when used, they are presented unedited.[11]

Third, like all official records, court filing statistics are social constructs, and thus are subject to discretionary interpretation and classification by those who collect, process, and classify them (Hindness, 1973). While this does not present a significant problem in ascertaining general trends, it can make analysis difficult for those attempting precise statistical analysis. Further, as with official crime statistics, different definitions and classification methods may be used by various jurisdictions or within the same jurisdictions at different times. Federal statistics classify prisoner suits into "United States" and "private," with the former usually indicating that the suits are from federal prisoners. The data actually mean, however, that the *defendant* is a federal official, even though most suits are, in fact, filed by federal prisoners. Some federal prisoners sue state or private officials, and their suits are classified as private, while state and other prisoners may sue federal agents, and their suits are thus classified as United States. Hence, filings do not necessarily reflect the status of the prisoners who file, but the status of the defendant. They are usually identical, but this technical point should not be overlooked.

In addition, in some jurisdictions, prisoner litigation may be classified only as those cases that are filed *in forma pauperis* (IFP), and others may include all prisoner petitions, even when filed by attorneys. IFP petitions are suits that are filed without the customary filing fee, because the plaintiff (the person filing) has requested permission to proceed as a "poor person." In Illinois' Northern District, however, all suits filed by prisoners are tabulated separately, and IFP decisions constitute over 89 percent of all prisoner petitions. Classification precision may also be hampered when lawyers file directly for prisoners. Federal procedures require completion of a Civil Cover Sheet on which the category of the case is indicated, and lawyers have the discretion to indicate whether the suit is other than a prisoner petition, or they may misclassify by error. In most districts, lawyers are appointed after it has been established that a case has judiciable merit, and it is rare for lawyers to file the initial petition on a prisoner's behalf. If they do, they usually routinely identify prisoner petitions on filing forms. This may not be the case in other districts, however, and researchers should be alert for possible misdesignation. Nonetheless, this is one reason why federal listings, accurate as they are for general statistical purposes, may not precisely match data obtained from other sources.

Fourth, not all prisoner suits are classified as such. For example, some cases may be filed as torts or as contractual violations in state and federal courts. Especially when prisoners retain a private attorney, there is no way to retrieve this information, because they are not listed as "prisoner cases." Available evidence indicates that such suits in the Northern District are rare, and thus are not sufficiently numerous to distort analysis. Such suits tend to be suits against private individuals (former landlords or employers) rather than against criminal justice personnel and are not relevant to this study.

Fifth, some federal records are kept by fiscal year, while others are kept by calendar year. Although this dual method of record keeping does not directly affect these data, readers may notice that some figures here may seem inconsistent with those found in other government publications in which annual data are classified by different categories. For nationwide data, I have relied on annual court reports from the Administrative Office of United States Courts and on Department of Justice documents through 1986. For data from the Northern District, I have calculated data obtained directly from court records. Because of cross-checking of individual cases, I consider the Northern District data most accurate. In addition, because of changes in federal terminology, and because the federal system continually updates and corrects data from previous years, the data used here, drawn from latest available tables, may not match figures published in earlier publications.[12]

Sixth, although suits are classified as "state prisoner petitions" by the federal government, the label is somewhat misleading. Not all petitions are from state or federal prisons; many litigants are in county jails, are not in custody, or are nonoffenders filing on behalf of others. State prisoners file about three-quarters of all prisoner suits in Illinois' Northern District, a rate presumably comparable to other districts. This subtly inflates the total litigation figure, and should be taken into account. Chapter 7 provides a breakdown of nonprison categories.

Seventh, it is often difficult to assess the meaning of some legal decisions, and classifying them as "won" or "lost" can often be misleading. A criminal case "won" by a prisoner at the district level may be appealed by state defendants and remanded to an inferior court where it is then lost by plaintiffs. Conversely, a civil rights case ostensibly lost may contain sufficient merit that, despite a negative decision, it may be relitigated in superior courts and won. It is also possible that a case that is lost may contain some legal issues that have been allowed to stand, thus providing a partial victory for either plaintiffs or defendants, or the legal basis for related subsequent suits by other litigants. This suggests that one should be careful when claiming that a suit is lost, or that prisoner litigation is ineffective. Casey Stengel's observation, often attributed to Yogi Berra, remains true: "It ain't over 'til it's over!"

Eighth, some readers have interpreted my discourse as proprisoner and have wondered why there is not more data from prison wardens and staff.[13] The answer is simple: this work is about prisoners and *their* litigation. Ample accounts exist elsewhere from the perspective of criminal justice personnel. Since prisoners far outnumber prison staff or judicial personnel, there is also a wider pool from which to draw data. Prisoners are also more eager to provide information, and the usual reliability and cross-checks indicate that they are exceptionally accurate, able to provide additional sources by which to confirm their accounts; they occasionally have even identified and introduced me to prison personnel willing to provide information.[14] Although some responses were self-serving, in the main, prisoners were objective, critical, and sensitive to the need for precision and were able to document claims with hard data.

Finally, lawyer friends sometimes complained that my use of some terms did not always correspond with their own legalistic definitions. Some, such as "complaint," "relief," "petition" or "grounds," connote lay meanings that differ from technical legal meanings. In this volume, lay usage has taken precedence over legal terminology.

The Ethics of Prison Research

Ethnographic research entails many ethical questions, dilemmas, and responsibilities, and some readers have asked the inevitable "ethical" question: "Did you have the permission of the prisoners to research them?" The so-called "professional ethics" underlying research in problem settings have been addressed elsewhere (Thomas and Marquart, 1987), and the difficulties of doing research in maximum security prisons have also been adequately discussed elsewhere (e.g., Carroll, 1980; Jacobs, 1974b; Marquart, 1986b). My interest in prisons was never hidden from prisoners; those prisoners I did not know were informed in advance both by myself and by those who introduced me that I was working on a prisoner litigation project. Key informants read at least one paper and draft chapters and were invited to provide critique. Chapters of this project were distributed to prisoners who assisted so they could see how their information was used. They did not always agree with my interpretations and occasionally indicated that some passages were too revealing. All readers, however, without exception, put the needs of "science" above the needs of their own self-interest. "Dirty data," discrediting information that would place prisoners or staff in jeopardy or would incriminate a specific individual, were excluded. I have not used unsolicited compromising information given by persons unaware of my research. Court personnel, too, were aware of my project and had the same opportunity to read this material. As argued elsewhere (Thomas and Marquart, 1987), prison research may require ethical choices that do not always correspond to the canons of established professional norms, but the primary obligation of fieldwork is to protect the integrity of inquiry and to protect those who give us information. I have, I hope, done both.

Such methodological problems affect most social analysis. They are recounted here in part to alert researchers to methodological difficulties, in part to make readers aware of apparent discrepancies between data bases, and to clarify how procedural decisions were made. If caution is used, it remains possible to pull together an accurate picture of prisoner litigation.

SCOPE

What needs to be said about prisoner litigation would fill many large volumes. In this one, I have been content to limit the focus to a general clarification of the fundamental issues. I have not attempted an analysis of litigation's impact, nor have I gone into excessive detail on the "causes," broad impact, legal outcomes, or trends in case law.

Our tour begins in Chapter 2, where we trace the emergence of legal rights in general from English common law through court decisions of the 1970s. We find that the expansion of rights is not recent, but has evolved over many centuries.

In the next stop, Chapter 3, we describe the lay of the land by identifying, then removing, selected misconceptions that blot the scenary.

Chapter 4 describes the genesis of the two legal theories—habeas corpus and civil rights—on which prisoners normally justify their filings. I conclude that prisoners' rights are but a moment in a long phase of legal and Constitutional transformation, and their locus derives from a social, rather than legal, context.

If the history of habeas and civil rights law differs we would expect the filing patterns of each to differ as well. In Chapter 5, the most cluttered locale on our itinerary, we pause long enough to collect basic information on filing patterns between these two legal theories. Here, we discover considerable diversity in trends that cuts across years, states, and grounds of filing, such that we cannot speak of prisoner litigation without also being aware of filing variations.

All tours should provide an opportunity to mingle with the natives, and in Chapters 6 through 9, we visit with those who do litigation. Not all readers read prisoner stories in the same way, and how stories are keyed and how readings are framed differs dramatically. Chapter 6 presents the nature of prisoner cases as impressionist stories, and includes a typology of narrative styles through which prisoners communicate their complaints.

Litigation involves a multi-phased drama in which numerous players enter and exit. Chapter 7 provides the opportunity for us to meet with judicial and other players, and listen as they narrate their involvement. We discover that processing itself is not a simple task, and it involves interactions between numerous personnel, and often creates intraorganizational tensions and other problems for processors.

The complex culture of prison law, out of which the prisoner tale emerges, tends to be ignored by both critics and advocates alike. In Chapter 8, jailhouse lawyers and other prisoners describe their careers, problems and motivations. We are given a behind-the-scenes look at prison life and view the career development and daily practices of litigants.

Chapter 9 describes how jailhouse lawyers practice their craft, the problems this practice may cause, and the role of law in resolving prison problems.

The concluding chapter integrates the three themes of history, trends, and processes by arguing that prisoner litigation reflects a form of social resistance, even if it often triggers countermeasures by those being resisted. The multiple ironies of law are used to illustrate the dialectical nature of prisoner rights and to argue that, despite the lack of fundamental changes, prisoner litigation remains a boon to prisoners and prison reformers.

NOTES

1. Bedau (1981) has cogently argued that there are no simple ways to discuss prisoners' rights and has identified over two dozen issues that require clarification. Some of these have been given broader treatment elsewhere, particularly Berkman (1979); Jacobs (1983: 34–47); Mika and Thomas (1987); Rothman (1980); and Thomas (1987).
2. The second volume of this project, *The Jailhouse Lawyer: Scaling the Walls*, is in progress.
3. For fuller discussion of the impact of prisoner litigation, see Jacobs (1982: 51–60) and Hardesty and Thomas (1986).
4. For excellent discussions of the historical or political roots of prisoner litigation, see especially Berkman (1979), Jacobs (1977), and Rothman (1979).
5. In Stateville, street gangs provide numerous services, including food, recreation, safety, discipline, social welfare and, for those well placed, even bail.
6. Contrary to the interpretation of one critic (Mandel, 1986: 84) of a previous work (Thomas, 1984a), I certainly do not proceed from an "idealist" position, either philosophic or moral, and an alleged "wild enthusiasm" for prisoner litigation does not derive from a view that it alone is the solution to the prison crisis (see, e.g., Thomas et al., 1981). Prisoner litigation remains useful for prisoners in some instances, and it has brought some relief, but I am in absolute agreement with Jacobs (1982) that the solution to the so-called "prison crisis" requires social and political action. Legal reform, by contrast, is short-term, often temporary and at best, generally leads to discrete changes and heightened visibility of problems.
7. There are several excellent summaries of case law, the development of prison-related civil rights and habeas law, and summaries of legal trends. The interested reader should refer to Bronstein (1979); Hoffman (1981); Palmer (1985); and Turner (1979) for excellent discussions. Other helpful

source books include Bronstein and Hirschkop (1979); Gobert and Cohen (1981); Haft and Hermann (1972); and Singer and Statsky (1974). For a useful overview of prisoner law and corrections personnel, see Robinson (1984), and for description of prisoners' rights as a political movement, Berkman (1979).

8. Civil rights suits are properly called "complaints," and habeas corpus suits are "petitions." In common discourse, however, strict legal terminology is often ignored. The strict legal usages generally will be retained in this volume.

9. Since the early 1980s, however, federal court decisions have increasingly required state prisoners to pursue their grievances in state courts prior to litigating in federal court, especially in tort claims.

10. For related arguments, see especially Black (1983), and the corpus of Alpert's works (1982, 1978a, 1978b, 1976); Alpert and Huff, (1981); Alpert et. al. (1978); and Alpert and Wiorkowski (1977).

11. Punctuation is intended to communicate a sense of the flow of discourse rather than publishers' style, and such vocabulary as "blah, blah, blah," and other particularistic expressions are retained. Pauses, successive "ahs," and similar extraneous bridges were removed, however. Some readers have wondered whether prisoner interviews were not modified because of the often highly articulate and precise responses; they are not. Jailhouse lawyers, with rare exceptions, tend to be exceptionally bright and articulate, well-read, and reflective.

12. One typical example is the category of civil rights United States filings published for 1973. The published figure of 414 does not correspond with the complaints calculated by individual states (423), and the incorrect figure has remained unnoticed and used by researchers for 13 years. When discrepancies were found, I relied on my own computations, after first checking with the appropriate federal agency. Hence, these data should be more accurate than federal data. In addition, prison population data are revised annually as previous years' figures are updated, creating discrepancies between annual figures for identical categories.

13. I am not proprisoner any more than I am proprofessor. The study of cultures requires getting "inside the culture," and this I have attempted to do. Readers of this and previous works who have identified the perspective as "pro" perhaps recognize a bias toward and respect of human rights. I have developed a deep appreciation for the problems faced by both staff and prisoners, and advocating rights for one group implies expanding and protecting rights for all.

14. Factual claims of prisoners and staff were verified by a variety of cross-checking strategies. The most common methods included comparing prisoner or staff accounts against transcripts or other official documents, multiple corroboration between informants unknown to each other, and personal observation. Quotes that provide erroneous information are so indicated by a qualifying footnote in the text.

2

Historical Roots

The greatest of all legal fictions is that the law itself evolves, from case to case, by its own impartial logic, true only to its own integrity, unswayed by expedient considerations (Thompson, 1975: 250).

It is our belief that only "the sense in which the Constitution was accepted and ratified by the nation," and only the sense in which laws were drafted and passed provide a solid foundation for adjudication. Any other standard suffers the defect of pouring new meaning into old words, thus creating new powers and new rights totally at odds with the logic of our Constitution and its commitment to the rule of law (Attorney General Edwin Meese, 1985a: 18).

T HE CONSTITUTIONAL ISSUES SURROUNDING CIVIL RIGHTS, the administrative problems of abuse, arrogance, or incompetence that contribute to litigation, and the strategies by which litigation can be reduced tend to be ignored in the sound and fury of demagogic harangues against prisoners' "abuse of courts." Many of the criticisms begin with the assumption that prisoners' rights reflect something legally unique and socially recent. Before travelling further, we should stop temporarily to examine these claims. In this chapter, we shall see that the fundamental legal bases of prisoner litigation reflect one direction on the lengthy path of legal change. This path, beginning in Roman and Anglo-Saxon Law, has been shaped and reshaped by centuries of social and political struggle (Thomas, 1988). The direct antecedents, however, lie in Constitutional law as mediated by changing social needs.

Especially since the mid–1960s, critics of civil rights expansion have observed an "erosion" of fundamental Constitutional principles by activist judges who would rather "set policy" than interpret established law (Morgan, 1984; Meese, 1985a). Some, especially judicially conservative legal fundamentalists, claim this expansion violates the original intents of the Constitution. United States Attorney General Edwin Meese has expressed hope "for a day when the court returns to the basic principles of the Constitution." His concern, common among judicial conservatives, is over:

an inaccurate reading of the text of the Constitution and a disregard for
the Framers' intention that state and local governments be a buffer against
the centralizing tendencies of the national Leviathan (Meese, 1985a: 6).

In opposing what he calls "a jurisprudence of idiosyncracy," Meese
has appealed to a view of law in which the judiciary gives priority to
eighteenth-century juridical concepts, rhetoric, and practices, and halts
judicial meddling in the affairs of states. Chief Justice Warren Burger
has also expressed the view that current federal judicial decisions,
especially in the areas of civil liberties, rights of suspects and convicted
offenders, represent "bad law." He has asked: "If it doesn't make good
sense, how can it make good law?" (Duscha, 1969) Given this antipathy
toward expanding judicial review of matters previously within the sole
domain of the states, the question arises: How is it that, after nearly two
centuries of quiescence, prisoners' rights have expanded?

The history of law is the history of attempts to resolve through legal
means those disputes for which alternative resolutions are not as viable.
Struggles over who shall receive resources and who shall not, who
possesses legal rights and who does not, which laws shall be enacted and
who shall be targets of enforcement, and what role law shall play in
maintaining social and political order are typical of social conflicts
fought out in the judicial arena. As Robinson (1984: 16) has lucidly
observed, when existing social relationships do not fit within existing
social structures, they appear to contradict fundamental principles, and
appear "irrational, illegal, or unconstitutional." Systematic deprivation
of the rights of societal "out-groups" would appear to contradict the
fundamental Constitutional premise that all persons are entitled to equal
protection. However, prisoners' appeals to Constitutional principles to
secure freedom also strike some as irrational, because they are imprisoned as punishment, not to pester the courts.

The general right to seek release from unlawful confinement (habeas
corpus) is grounded in English common law and dates at least from the
Magna Carta. The specific right to seek relief from warders' abuse of
power or from substandard conditions (civil rights) derives from seventeenth-century theories of individual liberty, and more recently from
mid-twentieth-century interpretations of freedom and the role of the
state in mediating social conflict. This English legacy forms the basis of
our own Constitutional heritage of rights.

THE ENGLISH ROOTS

The development of English theories of rights was uneven and episodic.
Some epochs were marked by structural tensions and social conflicts out
of which these rights grew; others were characterized by repression and
retrenchment that suppressed rights. But all are interrelated in that

they gave rise to ideological, juridical, and philosophical transformations that contributed to legal changes.

The direct substantive antecedents of our own legal system, that part of which derives from English jurisprudence, arguably took shape prior to the Magna Carta. At the time of the Norman invasion (1066), the laws of the land served primarily to establish the security of the king and the feudal structure of land tenure, and such rights as were protected were limited to the nobility. The rights of the rest of the population were bound in custom and guaranteed only to the extent that manor lords were willing to recognize them, or insofar as commoners could coerce adherence, either through persuasion or threat of violence. The laws of this period have been described as "mere sermons preached to a disobedient folk" (Maitland, 1968: 29). Jurisdiction often overlapped or conflicted, and conflict often erupted over who possessed the right to hear particular cases. In serious offenses, courts often became an arena for working out broader territorial and other political disputes at least as often as they were forums of justice.

Legal change occurs when social formations generate structurally insoluble problems. Such problems become fundamental when "individuals or groups repeatedly confront one another with claims and intentions that are, in the long run, incompatible" (Habermas, 1975: 27). We call this a *structural contradiction*. In Norman England, there existed such a contradiction between the emerging centralization of royal control on one hand and the increased power of manor lords over local affairs on the other. When William the Conquerer assumed the English throne in 1066, one of his first tasks was consolidation of his power. One strategy, only marginally successful, was centralization of law. Although his system temporarily strengthened and stabilized the structure of the crown and judicial powers, it also made it more brittle. The increasing complexity of society made it impossible to deal effectively with new problems arising on the local level, and the existing legal and political systems were not able to adequately deal with problems of order, let alone new problems that were emerging. Centralization of royal authority required expanding the power of barons, and this in turn contributed to more powerful and better-organized forces of opposition to the crown. The result was the statutory development of feudal law defining reciprocal duties and obligations between crown and nobles, and creating the corresponding political apparatus to administer them. The major cornerstone of rights remains the Magna Carta.

The Magna Carta

Faced with the need to collect revenue and mollify querulous nobles, the twelfth-century English Kings, Henry I and Henry II, recognized the need to reform the legal system and consolidate their power more fully. Both Henry I and Henry II were successful in restructuring and streamlining the legal system and using it to establish their authority and unite disparate regional and local customs within a national system. But the sons of Henry II, Richard and John, lacked their father's fiscal and administrative ability. Following Richard's death in a petty quarrel in France, John was able to resume his goal of reconquering his lost Norman kingdoms and, in attempting to retrieve them, burdened his nobles with fiscal obligations that they refused to honor. The ensuing confrontation resulted in the signing of the Magna Carta at Runnymede (1215) and the beginning of the sovereignty of law.

The text of the Magna Carta was influenced by the twelfth-century juridical practices of Henry I and Henry II, and romanticized the legal procedures of Edward the Confessor of two centuries earlier. The key chapters included protections against arbitrary taxation, the establishment of basic judicial procedures, including trial by jury, protections against arbitrary punishment, and above all, adherence to the "law of the land," at that time meaning recognition of Edward the Confessor's laws as embodied especially in the statutes of William I. These basic protections not only consolidated existing judicial protections, but reaffirmed basic rights of medieval peers.

The Medieval Transition

Medieval law was not so much a tool employed to "suppress the masses," for this occured more effectively through military force and cultural domination. Law was rather a means of mediating interclass conflict among the aristocracy as various groups vied for political or economic power (which in mid-medieval England was often the same thing). The so-called "Tudor Revolution" of the sixteenth century, a dramatic reform of religion, government, and social structure, was a revolution by statute. Law was intended to suppress opposition, regulate social life—especially employment and religion—and increase royal power. By the seventeenth century, however, law became a two-edged sword that enabled the crown's opposition to expand individual liberty by appealing to principles of common law and the Magna Carta. It was under the seventeeth-century Tudor kings that the principle of individual liberty, especially the protection of the writ of habeas corpus, became more fully developed. In response to continual abuses of arrest powers and suppression of political and religious thought (which often coincided), several important acts were passed. These included the Petition of Right (1628), which prohibited the crown from raising revenue through forced loans or without the consent of parliament; The Habeas Corpus Act (1640), which abolished the oppressive Star Chamber and similar courts and stipulated that anyone imprisoned by the king or his council be quickly brought to trial and the cause of imprisonment shown; and the English Bill of Rights (1689), imposed upon William of Orange as a condition of his coronation, which curtailed the power of the sovereign and established numerous protections, many of which were later written into the United States Constitution.

The growth and development of English law emerged, then, not simply from its own inherent "logic." The form and content of law were shaped by tensions between political rivalries and changing social conditions in which old forms of legal practice became inappropriate. To paraphrase Thompson (1975: 260), the old legal forms were bent in order to legitimize the status of new land-owning and commercial interests.

Although the law was used to solidify the power of the sovereign, and later the state, it was also used by other groups to challenge state power. Marxians would call this a dialectical relationship between law and the state: law became the mechanism used to establish and protect sovereign authority and power, but it also was a means of successfully challenging this power. Beginning with the Barons who drafted the Magna Carta, both the content (what the law says) and procedures (how law is applied) of the legal system were used to limit autonomous power of the crown, but as these practices became a political force, the underlying ideology became a means to justify and rationalize state decisions.

The history of English law reveals that the appearance of a unified medieval law is a myth. This was a period of continual progress (or process) in which law was a useful tool for attempting to create, maintain, or alter power and privilege. The transformation from feudalism to mercantilism to an industrial society created a myriad of groups opposing existing social or political relations. In this manner, the fluid, mediating and double-edged character of law evolved and changed— and was changed by—England's industrial revolution.

THE CONSTITUTIONAL FOUNDATION

Contemporary judicial critics who perceive "intrusion" of federal courts into the state domain often argue that such action is actually unconstitutional and allows judges to vote their personal predilections rather than deduce legal principles (Berger, 1977; Bloch, 1958; Glazer, 1975a, 1975b; Morgan, 1984; Meese, 1985a). This criticism would seem to apply particularly to prisoner litigation in that many judicial decisions seem, in the eyes of some, to expand prisoners' rights far beyond any literal wording justified by the Constitution. But these criticisms ignore the early history of our legal traditions.[1] Our own concept of rights derives directly from a long legal tradition that itself went through substantial transformations. The Framers of our Constitution drew expressly from this tradition, and it was their intent, as their debates reveal, to ground our Constitution upon this legacy. To speak, then, of "original intents" while ignoring this tradition is to distort the basis of legal rights and further reduce their significance. Further, the so-called "intrusion" of judicial activism is not new. The history of judicial intervention began immediately following ratification of the Constitution and the enactment of the Judiciary Act of 1789. There have, however, been periodic cycles in which courts waxed and waned in their willingness to intervene in the legislative and judicial affairs of states. These cycles began in the colonial period.

The Colonial Period

Early colonial law did not directly reproduce English law. Concepts of rights during the colonial period were shaped by two main sources, English and enlightment philosophy, and the requirements for carrying out commerce and industry. To speak of a homogeneous law in the early American colonies is somewhat misleading, however, because the Dutch, French, Spanish, and English each brought their own customs with them as they settled the new land. As Friedman (1975) has argued, there were as many "colonial systems" as there were colonies, and many of the problems of colonial unification centered on the problem of integrating legal systems. Systems of justice began simply and gradually grew more complex, slowly drawing more from the English system as economic and political interdependence grew, and as an expanding population of English settlers were assimilated into what was becoming an increasingly common culture.[2]

Faced with uncertainty and the need for structure, one of the first tasks of the new colonies was drafting their governing charters. These charters did not create new rights, but rather reaffirmed in written form existing notions of freedom. All shared one common feature: they established statutory safeguards to individual liberty that were felt to be the basis of English law, even if not fully extended to all subjects in England. Charter provisions included religious freedom (e.g., Charter of Rhode Island, 1663), basic safeguards in criminal procedures such as trial by jury, liberty of conscience, "fair" trials (Concessions and agreements of West New Jersey, 1677), bail (Frame of Government of Pennsylvania, 1682), and right to counsel (Pennsylvania Charter of privileges, 1701).

The Constitution

The need for economic freedom in commerce, industry, and trade required autonomy from the restrictive laws that English kings passed in the seventeenth and eighteenth centuries in attempts to secure economic advantage. Economic repression by the English led to the convening of the First Continental Congress, which drafted The Articles of

Association (1775). The Articles called for civil disobedience to British law and declared that English crown had extended its powers beyond their ancient limits by depriving subjects of such rights as trial by jury (Carson, 1971: 37). This led to the Declaration of Independence (1776) and the Articles of Confederation (1777) declaring a "perpetual union."

The Articles of Confederation signified a shift from the colonial to the state system, and were written to protect states from the abuses of centralized power. The Articles created administrative procedures that did not specify rights, but rather established broad working arrangements between the separate states. In some ways, the Articles were an antiquated set of principles politically more appropriate to seventeenth-century post-feudal fiefdoms and regionalism that protected private interests rather than promoted national stability and economic growth. They did not provide a useful political philosophy by which to unify or guide diverse groups possessing often incompatible needs, policies, or goals. Nor did they provide for a central executive department, a federal judiciary, the power to regulate commerce or to prevent discriminatory trade practices, and there was no mechanism to generate revenue. The failure of the Articles prompted a move to draft a new Constitution based on a stronger federal system.

The Constitutional Convention met in Philadelphia in 1787 and adopted the new Constitution. The Articles of Confederation had generally reflected the philosophy, later espoused by nineteenth-century advocates of states' rights and their twentieth-century epigones, that the primary protection of liberties would be undertaken by individual state governments rather than a centralized judiciary. The Constitution, by contrast, was a fundamental shift away from the regionalism and local autonomy provided for in the Articles. It created an estate system with the executive, judiciary, and legislature in equal partnership. Article III of the Constitution placed judicial power in a single "Supreme Court" and extended this court's authority to all cases "in law and equity" arising under the Constitution. The principles of federalism dominated the language and implementation of the Constitution, but the document nonetheless represented a compromise between states' rightists and nationalists (Richardson and Vines, 1970: 22).

The original Constitutional powers of federal courts were ambiguous, but were clarified somewhat by the Judiciary Act of 1789 (1 Statutes at Large, 72). Shaped by the same philosophy that created the Constitution, the Act provided the mandate for judicial review of state action by federal courts, and the power to review and act upon the decisions of state courts by the Supreme Court, and authorized all federal courts to issue various writs, such as habeas corpus. As a concession to those who wanted assurances that state and regional law would be preserved, district courts were established within each state.

The rights and procedures articulated in the Constitution established a number of basic principles, including the following:

1. the idea of a fundamental law, the "law of the land," to which all official and governmental action was bound to conform, which law was to be applied by the courts in the course of orderly litigation according to the common law, and could be invoked against officials by anyone aggrieved; 2. the idea of immemorial rights of Englishmen, secured by the law of the land, and of the common law in which they were recognized as the birthright of Englishmen and so of American . . . 3. the idea of authoritative declarations of these rights in charters and bills of rights . . . 4. the idea of an independent judiciary, as set forth in the English Bill of Rights of 1688, to administer the fundamental law, and of lawmaking by a body distinct from the executive; 5. the idea of courts refusing to apply statutes in contravention of fundamental law (Pound, 1975: 61–62).

Judicial theorists assumed that state courts could be relied on for federal law enforcement. Such reliance was a failure. The incompatibility of the labor and social systems between various sectors of the nation, and the geographic and philosophical distance between federal and state courts, contributed to this failure. The result was a slow curtailment of state court power (Gibbons, 1984: 452). Hence, the expansion of federal power into "originally" state matters was, in part, a judicial response to problems created by the inadequacy of the original federal apparatus to implement the principles of the Constitution.

Recognititon of these fundamental principles did not reduce the tensions between those favoring and those opposing a strong central system. The question of balance between states' rights and nationalism remained then, as today, a divisive national issue. The stakes in the states' rights debate were political power rather than juridical principle, and the southern states especially argued for state supremacy because of their politically weaker position in relation to the North. The South was solidly agricultural, while the North was developing a strong infrastructure based on industry, finance, and commerce. The federalists dominated the judiciary and the legislature, and southern states perceived themselves as politically subservient to their northern neighbors. The judiciary, as a consequence, was balanced between the Scylla of judicial principle and the Charybdis of political expediency, a tension which led to cycles of judicial expansion and retrenchement.

CYCLES OF JUDICIAL CHANGE

Following Goldman and Jahnige (1985: 231), we can trace five broad historical cycles in United States political and judicial history. These were 1) the Federalist-Jeffersonian (1789–1828); 2) the Jacksonian (1828–1860); 3) the First Republican (1860–1896); 4) the Second Republican (1896–1933); and 5) the New Deal era through the Warren court. A sixth, the Retrenchment Era, began with the election of Richard Nixon in 1968 and his appointment of Chief Justice Burger, and has been more fully implemented in the 1980s by the Reagan administration. Each of these periods was shaped by broad social and political forces, and each illustrates shifts in the role and function of the court and helps clarify the emergence of prisoner litigation.

The Federalist-Jeffersonian Period (1789–1828)

Current Constitutional activity reflects a long process in the transformation of legal theory, and this transformation began immediately following the Constitution's ratification. The Federalist-Jeffersonian era contains, as Goldman and Jahnige (1985: 231) have observed, two distinct subphases. First was a period of consolidation as the Supreme Court cautiously defined its jurisdiction and the scope of its legal and political powers. The guiding theories of such early Constitutional theorists as James Wilson and John Marshall held that the relationship between states and the federal judiciary was based on the federalist theory of separation and balance of powers and upon the distribution of power among three coequal components. The second phase, 1800–1828, was that of Jeffersonian democracy. Guided by the Federalist Chief Justice John Marshall, the courts consolidated judicial power—and thus the Constitution—as the supreme law of the land.

In both phases, the Supreme Court faced the problem of defining the scope of the powers of the new federal government, as well as the relationship of its own power and goals to the national executive and legislative branches and to the new states on the other. Banks, transportation companies, and other enterprises that operated between states raised numerous legal and federally related questions that had never been encountered previously. Could a corporation based in one state but operating in several be taxed by those states, or only by the host state? Could the federal government intervene in interstate commerce? Could corporations or states enact policies or laws that would effectively put the federal government in a subordinate position to corporations? The judiciary resolved virtually all of these issues in a way that assured strong federal control and a social and political environment conducive to national commercial interests.

Three early decisions typify how the Supreme Court helped solidify federal power. *Marbury v. Madison* (5 U.S. (1 Cranch) 137, 1803), established the principle of judicial review; *Fletcher v. Peck* (10 U.S. (6 Cranch) 87, 1810) established the inviolability of contracts, placing them beyond the reach of state courts; and *McCulloch v. Maryland* (17 U.S. (4 Wheat.) 316, 1819) affirmed the doctrine of precedence of federal rights. Through judicial means, the federal government slowly established supremacy over the states by adapting the Framers' original philosophy and intents to the needs of a growing economic and political system. When seen in this light, the legal theories on which federal courts base their intervention in prison affairs is not merely the result of civil rights activists or "idiosyncratic law," but has deep roots in our early Constitutional history.

The Jacksonian Period (1828–1860)

The Jacksonian period represented both a dramatic social upheaval and a major transformation in the relationship of the federal to the state system. The Era of Good Feeling following conclusion of hostilities with the British was spawned by nationalist pride, promoted by federal politicians, and served the interests of the growing economic groups of the northeast. But after fifteen years of growing nationalism, a backlash occured. In 1828 the Democrats elected popular war hero Andrew Jackson to the first of his two terms as president. A political pragmatist rather than a doctrinaire ideologue, Jackson campaigned against Jeffersonian democracy, and led an attack on national institutions, especially banks and the Supreme Court, which he felt were tools by which the powerful minority maintained its position. Although Jefferson had opposed unrestrained centralized power as inimical to democracy, he and his followers nonetheless believed in, and created the political structure for, a strong national authority as a means to develop commerce and finance. Jackson, by contrast, developed policies based on expanding land values, diversified agriculture, and speculative opportunities:

> To Jackson, the federal government was not simply a policeman to keep order, but a parent who gave a helping hand when it was needed—but only when the citizen asked for it. The Jacksonian did not want the government to control his affairs except to the degree that he requested it to do so. He was never loath (nor were the Grangers and Populists later) to call on Washington for assistance, for roads, canals, credit or subsidies; yet at the same time he fiercely resented any intrusion of federal power into his own domain of authority (Nye and Morpurgo, 1970: 384).

The Jeffersonian-Federalist era had been dominated by Chief Justice Marshall and was characterized by decisions that strengthened both the federal government and the judiciary; Jackson reversed this. During his eight years, Jackson was able to appoint five of the then-sitting seven justices, including elevation of his friend Roger T. Taney to the position of Chief Justice. Although not judicially timid, Taney guided the court to a middle-of-the road position, and tended to side with Southern states on states' rights issues, particularly slavery and commerce.

To some, the Taney court was archetypically conservative because of its support of business interests and willingness to stamp approval upon legislative and executive policy. Others have viewed it as an activist court for its decisions, which extended long-term judicial power. The most significant of these was the Dred Scott decision (*Scott v. Sandford*, S.C. 19 Howard, 393, 1857). The case involved issues of legislative jurisdiction and judicial power as well as the subject status of slaves and the Constitutional rights such a status conferred (Fehrenbacher, 1978; Lewis, 1965). The decision was an attempt to resolve political tensions created by the Missouri Compromise (1820), which was repealed in 1854. The constitutionality of the 1820 act remained in doubt, and the Scott case provided the opportunity to address several political issues at once. The Court ruled that Congress did not have the power to prohibit slavery from territories, and that blacks could not be U.S. citizens and therefore were not entitled to full Constitutional protections. This decision reaffirmed the supremacy of judicial power even while promoting, in the short run, states' rights. Taney's legal logic in writing the majority opinion has often been questioned, but the significance of the outcome should not be overlooked. For the first time, the Supreme Court arrogated to itself (and to every other federal court) the right to settle sociopolitical conflicts by judicial decision, thus dramatically increasing the political power of the judiciary (Boudin, 1968: 3).

The First Republican Period (1860–1896)

The Civil War era marks the beginning of a dramatic shift in the political and judicial history of civil rights. By 1860, political and regional conflicts had shattered former party alliances, and the once-dominant Whigs and Democrats suffered internal tensions and were no longer an effective political force. The election of Republicans, as representatives of Northern political and economic interests, led to the final breach in the Union, and ultimately to secession of the Southern states. For the next quarter century, the Republicans solidified their national power and dominated the Supreme Court. During the Civil War, the federal judiciary had stayed out of the way of the federal legislative and executive branches (Miller, 1982: 73), and the Supreme Court was relatively quiescent, limiting itself primarily to review of war related cases.

The decade following the war has been called the "zenith of federalism" (Carson, 1971: 501). Among the issues brought before the court during this period were property and voting rights, interstate commerce, and the seemingly never-ending question of the status and rights of business. One function of the postwar federal government was to steer the social system through potentially disruptive conflicts that threatened the delicate harmony of reconstruction. The federal government used its status as military victor to politically reunite the states and define and implement a national agenda. The judiciary made it clear that it had exclusive authority to review the constitutionality of state policy on national issues. Two issues dominated the reconstruction judiciary. The first was civil rights. The civil status of former slaves and of Northern free blacks in Southern territory, the dissolution of the Southern system of agricultural labor and the relationship of all blacks to the Constitution demanded immediate attention. The second problem was the regulation of commerce and industry. This issue centered on whether the Constitution permitted government to counter the growing political and economic power of increasingly large businesses (trusts).

The Republicans were divided on Reconstruction policy; the Radical Republicans favored harsh penalties and corresponding legislation, and the moderates, led by President Johnson, favored a more lenient policy. The advocacy of minority rights to which Radical Republicans adhered, however, was not motivated by broad philosophic concerns, but by political expediency. Further, in the areas of commerce, individual rights, and other issues, they were not significantly distinguishable from their colleagues.

Reconstruction Law

The contemporary legal framework of civil rights litigation was laid in post-Civil War legislation. In 1866, the Ku Klux Klan had been secretly formed to preserve the "white race" by terrorizing blacks. It was thus judged by Northern politicians that legislation and Constitutional amendments would be useful to expand Constitutional rights to blacks. The most important piece of legislation, entitled "Act to Protect all Persons in the United States in their Civil Rights (1866)," was intended to protect freed slaves from potential civil rights abuses. Shortly after the ratification of the Fourteenth Amendment (1868), which extended Constitutional protections to the states, the last significant civil rights enactment of the reconstruction era was passed in 1871. This so-called "Ku Klux Klan Act" survives today as 42 U.S.C. Section 1983, and although it did not create rights, it provided civil cause of action enforceable in federal courts against any state official found to be violating rights "under color of law." The Act was modified and renewed several times in the next ten years, but the relevant language of the original civil rights legislation today remains essentially unchanged.

Post-War Amendments

In addition to legislative acts, three amendments were added to the Constitution. The first was the Thirteenth Amendment (1865). Its first section held that:

Neither slavery nor involuntary servitude, except as a punishment for crime whereof the party shall have been duly convicted, shall exist within the United States, or any place subject to their jurisdiction.

The Thirteenth Amendment was significant not only for its substance, but for the new political philosophy it reflected: the federal government assumed responsibility for guaranteeing liberty by nationalizing the right to freedom and enforcing this right through "appropriate legislation," a term inserted into the Constitution for the first time. But the Thirteenth Amendment did not fully abolish slavery for prisoners, and there is considerable evidence indicating a wide-spread practice, primarily in the south, of rounding up persons on "vagrancy" or similar laws and reenslaving them in the private sector.

The policies of reconstruction were necessarily lenient, thus allowing former slave-holding states opportunity to impose restrictive segregationist laws, which circumvented the intents of the amendment. Fearing that additional protections were required to protect rights, Congress passed the Fourteenth Amendment in 1868. The most significant of the civil rights amendments, it not only defined citizenship and prohibited states from enacting laws that abridged Constitutional rights, but also extended federal authority into what had previously had been nonfederal jurisdiction.

Prior to the civil war, it had been settled that the federal government lacked the power to apply federal Bill of Rights standards to individual states. The Supreme Court had earlier established in *Barron v. Baltimore* (7 Pet. 243, 1833) that these provisions were limited to the federal government only. Subsequent attempts to expand Constitutional protections to state actions through, for example, the "due process" clause of the Fifth Amendment, repeatedly failed. Failure prompted remedy, and additional legislation was required in order to provide the federal judiciary with explicit powers to enforce federal law in the states.[3]

The language of the Fourteenth Amendment was broad, and contained no reference to slavery or to any specific protected category. Consequently, it has been invoked by disparate groups to secure their rights:

> All persons born or naturalized in the United States, and subject to the jurisdiction thereof, are citizens of the United States and of the State in which they reside. No State shall make or enforce any law which shall abridge the privileges or immunities of citizens of the United States; nor shall any State deprive any person of life, liberty, or property, without due process of law; nor deny to any person within its jurisdiction the equal protection of laws.

The first sentence of Section One of the Fourteenth Amendment has become known as the "citizenship clause." It provided not only the definition of citizenship which justified extension of Constitutional rights to blacks but implicitly extended these rights to other ethnic groups as well. The second sentence, the "due process" (or equal protection) clause, remains controversial. In essence, it extended the Bill of Rights provisions to states by granting to all citizens Constitutional safeguards—in principle, at least—against discriminatory law, although this interpretation remained undeveloped for several decades.

The last amendment of the reconstruction period was the Fifteenth (1870), which was intended to protect voting rights:

> The right of the citizens of the United States to vote shall not be denied or abridged by the United States or by any State on account of race, color, or previous condition of servitude.

These amendments and legislation were sound in theory, but ineffective in practice, and any immediate gains were shortlived. There was no explicit extralegal machinery created to protect the rights, because it was erroneously assumed that the judicial enforcement of legislation and amendments would suffice for the task. State courts continued to affirm regional discriminatory social practices, and federal district courts were hesitant to review state practices. Even when they did, they tended to ignore blatant state violations of civil rights. By the end of the 1870s and the reemergence of the successionist states to grace, little attention was given to Constitutional rights, and by the next Constitutional period, the gains obtained immediately after the war were considerably diminished by Southern Black Codes, "Jim Crow" laws, and federal quiescence in acting on civil rights violations.[4]

Post-Reconstruction Law

By the early 1870s, the overcentralization of federal power necessitated by the war was in temporary decline, and courts and Congress moved toward a new federal-state equilibrium. This balance was brought about in part by reinterpretation of law. Within a decade after passage of the Fourteenth Amendment, conservative Supreme Court decisions had effectively denied the federal government the mandate to invade the sovereignty of individual states in order to create a federal code for regulation of private rights (Collins, 1974: 23). But this did not end the influence of the Fourteenth Amendment in expanding rights.

In the late nineteenth century, businesses played much the same role in expanding Constitutional legal theory as civil rights groups have done since the 1960s, and with the same result: the law of the land was brought in line with the times, and legal models were created by which to resolve those social problems that other forms of dispute resolution could not. Railroads, for example, played a crucial role in expanding the scope of the Fourteenth Amendment:

> In order to successfully convert the Fourteenth Amendment into such a shield for railroad interests, lawyers had to convince the Court to change the meaning of due process so that it encompassed both substantive rights

and corporate interests. The railroad lawyers were eminently successful on both counts (Cortner, 1981: 280).

Corporations thus became "persons."

The Slaughter-House Cases (16 Wallace 36, 1872), the first litigation brought under the Fourteenth Amendment to reach the Supreme Court, provided the most dramatic example of this process. These cases challenged the right of a state to legislatively provide a business with exclusive operating rights. The decisions provided a narrow interpretation of the Fourteenth Amendment, which functioned to weaken much of the Reconstruction legislation. But they also had three long-range consequences for subsequent judicial theory. First, despite the apparently narrow interpretation, the decision effectively created a new category of litigants to whom the concept of due process would apply. This implicitly reaffirmed federal power to bring new legal subjects under Constitutional protection. Second, the decision expanded the legal status of business by granting them the same status as "persons." By extending Constitutional protections to corporate entities, the definition of citizenship was dramatically expanded. Hence, the inclusion of new groups to be protected by the Constitution is hardly a recent development of "activist judges." Finally, the *Slaughter House Cases* established one source of federal power to control private conduct (Barrett and Cohen, 1985: 1016). This conservative decision by a conservative court was intended to limit federal intervention into the social sector, even while expanding it in the economic realm.

A decade later, a series of decisions known as the *Civil Rights Cases* (109 U.S. 3, 1883) further circumscribed the expansion of rights when the Court sustained a narrow interpretation of previous civil rights legislation and Constitutional amendments, and effectively struck down the public accommodations section of the Civil Rights Act of 1875. *The Civil Rights Cases* passed the political power from the federal government back to the states, and especially in the south, an apartheid system became a fundamental part of the social structure. Other federal decisions of the post-Reconstruction era upheld discriminatory capital punishment based on an offender's race, the exclusion of blacks from juries and restrictive voting practices. By 1890, most southern and some northern states had restrictive laws against blacks and the civil rights legislation of the postwar decade had become inoperative. A spate of decisions held that racial discrimination in employment, exclusion on juries, disparate sentencing in criminal offenses and in public accommodations were either not necessarily unconstitutional or not within the domain of federal jurisdiction. By the close of the century, the Fourteenth Amendment had failed to restrain states from discriminatory practices, leaving its utility in considerable doubt.

The Subversion of Rights

Several factors contributed to the subversion of the Fourteenth Amendment's power to expand rights. First, the rise of Jim Crow laws and lynch laws in the South were ignored by federal courts. This allowed emergence of a dual system of justice distributed according to race. Second, the decline of the abolitionist movement after the Civil war removed a critical social voice and political force underlying expansion and protection of the rights of blacks. There was no corresponding social movement until the civil rights activism of the 1960s. Finally, the doctrine of states' rights prevailed, which allowed individual states to regulate affairs as they wished, without federal intervention.

Any doubts that the Supreme Court had little interest in expanding the rights of blacks were erased by *Plessy v. Ferguson* (163 U.S. 537, 1896). In writing the majority opinion in which only Justice Harlan dissented, Justice Brown argued that races cannot be "put on the same plane" by judicial fiat:

> Legislation is powerless to eradicate racial instincts, or to abolish distinctions based upon physical differences, and the attempt to do so can only result in accentuating the difficulties of the present situation. If the civil and political rights of both races be equal, one cannot be inferior to the other civilly or politically.

But if this decision marked the end of one phase of the struggle for expanded civil rights, another phase was about to emerge.

The Second Republican Period (1896–1933)

Between 1860 and 1900, twelve new states were added to the union, and the population more than doubled from the 1860 total of 31,500,000. By 1896 the nation was still rural, but the urban population was increasing rapidly. The country was in the middle of its industrial revolution—200 years after that of England—and large corporations began to dominate the economy. By the 1890s, liberal thinkers judged government to be controlled by a privileged few who ran it for the benefit of businesses, banks, railroads, and large industry.

The growth of national industry and the need for a corresponding set of laws and regulations demanded consistent legal policies and practices, and the courts were used to challenge those laws that stifled economic freedom. Through Constitutional interpretation and enforcement, the federal judiciary consistently voided state laws that stifled the growth of a national economy. Federal courts also enforced the right of contract as a Constitutional right, and the balance of power shifted from the states to the federal government. Thus began the Progressive Era in which the federal government took an increasingly prominent role in maintaining the stability and harmony of the social and economic order.[5]

In short, this was the era of "big business" and emerging monopoly capitalism, and the courts spent little time mulling over issues of individual rights or liberty. Neither were legislators, the judiciary, and other social institutions attentive to the changing social conditions, but the economic collapse of 1928 provided the opportunity for a change in legal philosophy. The ideal of equality during the Second Republican era had been kept alive by the ideal of occupational mobility (Aronowitz, 1973: 154), and it became increasingly clear that the ideology of opportunity was belied by the reality of class, exploitation, and general insensitivity by state and federal government to the problems of survival for an increasing portion of the population.

In retrospect, the 1920s marked the beginnings of a shift in the balance between federal and states' rights. The Supreme Court held that some rights were so fundamental—particularly First Amendment rights—that federal intervention was justified for their protection. Any ambiguity was removed in 1925, when the court explicitly made free speech applicable to the states under the "due process" clause (*Gitlow v. New York*, 268 U.S. 652, 1925). One particularly dramatic decision cracked judicial resistance to review of state trial proceedings. In the case of the "Scottsboro Boys" (*Powell v. Alabama*, 287 U.S. 45, 1932), eight blacks accused of raping a white female attracted world-wide attention and generated considerable social protest on behalf of the defendants, who were perceived to be victims of racially motivated prosecution. In ruling that state defendants were entitled to counsel in state criminal trials, the Supreme Court established a precedent guiding state prosecutions by extending rights to defendants under the "due process" clause of the Fourteenth Amendment. There were, however, no significant follow-up cases until the 1960s, and Bill of Rights protections generally remained limited to federal defendants. Federal judges were simply not inclined to expand Constitutional protections in criminal matters arising under the Fourth, Fifth, Sixth, and Eighth Amendments. As late as the 1940s, the Supreme Court refused in such key cases as *Betts v. Brady* (316 U.S. 455, 1942) and *Adamson v. California* (232 U.S. 46, 1947) to increase protections of state criminal defendants in, for example, right to counsel in noncapital offenses *(Betts)* or trial procedures *(Adamson)*.

The New Deal Era (1933–68)

If the second Republican period was one of mediating interclass conflicts in the realm of commerce and industry, the New Deal era was one of mediating social conflicts created by the Great Depression. National unemployment reached 15 million on the day of Roosevelt's inauguration (Greenberg, 1974: 105), and it became clear that the federal system, to preserve the capitalist structure, would be required to attack social ills as aggressively as it had mediated the economic problems in the Progressive Era. The federal machinery that had been used to create economic regulation in the business environment was now turned upon social regulation. Thus began the new cycle of federal intervention in the New Deal. This period was characterized by the emergence of the "welfare state" in which the federal government began to assume responsibility for maintaining social harmony. Using a variety of political and legislative stratagems, President Roosevelt took an aggressive role in national recovery. His social programs have been criticized as "creeping socialism," but they, in fact, staved off more dramatic social change by ameliorating the harsher conditions of the depression. To meet the Constitutional challenges to his recovery policies, Roosevelt recognized that a sympathetic judiciary was necessary. This led to his unsuccessful attempt in 1937 to expand and pack the Supreme Court with coideologues who would presumably rule in his favor on controversial cases.

During Roosevelt's "New Deal," the courts consistently limited Bill of Rights protections in criminal trials to federal defendants.

The Roosevelt legacy contributed to the expansion of rights in several ways. First, and most important, it established an operative ideology of social justice—albeit in rudimentary form—by creating the rationale for protection of "the little guy." The first civil rights acts, primarily intended to protect voting rights, were passed, providing the basis for subsequent federal legislation enforcing rights. Second, the federal judiciary, through narrow but explicit decisions, slowly chipped away at laws that repressed individual freedom. The NAACP was particularly active, but other groups also sought to redress social grievances through litigation. Third, the Supreme Court remained a Roosevelt court into the 1950s, thus providing a block of civil rights sympathizers that formed the backbone of the Warren court in the 1950s and beyond. Finally, and perhaps most important, Roosevelt's administration marked the beginning of aggressive federal intervention to mediate societal crises. To prevent disruption of the economic structure, Roosevelt recognized the need for centralization of power to resolve problems that threatened economic or social stability. This was done through New Deal legislation, reemergence of civil rights legislation, and above all, through translating social issues of poverty and public welfare to national policy problems. The courts became but one tool for the task of centralizing and legitimating federal power and policy.

The Warren Court

The election of President Eisenhower has been considered by many to represent a backlash to New Deal policies of his predecessors. This is only partially true, however, since the New Deal legacy remained intact and continued to provide the model for federal policy for the next fifteen years. President Eisenhower believed he could reverse the Court's philosophy when he appointed Earl Warren, a political conservative and judicial moderate, as the Court's chief justice in 1953. He was wrong. The Warren Court consolidated through judicial means the social reforms enacted by New Dealers. Almost immediately, the new chief justice established himself and his court as an advocate for social change. The first landmark decision, *Brown v. Board of Education* (347 U.S. 483, 1954), overturned *Plessy v. Ferguson,* and has been called, with ironic hyperbole, the "second reconstruction" because of its belated attempt to resurrect the broad language of the due process and citizenship clauses of the Fourteenth Amendment. Brown was not the first case to successfully challenge the Plessy decision, but was symbolic in that it was, to that time, the most dramatic and comprehensive civil rights decision of the century. It consolidated previous decisions by making explicit the legal theories underlying Constitutional guarantees. Writing the unanimous opinion,[6] Chief Justice Warren argued that using race as a criterion denied due process under the Fourteenth Amendment. More significantly, the decision explicitly ordered remedial action and established the federal government as the proper agent for carrying out the order.

The election of John F. Kennedy in 1962 reaffirmed the New Deal policies of government mediation of social and political problems. Kennedy's New Frontier entailed a series of policies aimed at garnering the support of groups previously excluded from political power. In developing programs to help minorities and the poor, Kennedy provided the structure and ideology for the civil rights movement for the next decade. During the eight years of the Kennedy/Johnson administrations, a flurry of legislative activity established protections for housing, voting, and employment (Antieau, 1980), and civil rights became a campaign issue in both national and local elections.

This period is particularly significant for decisions that extended Constitutional protections to the rights of criminal suspects. In 1963, the Supreme Court established the principle that indigent defendants were entitled to counsel in noncapital state trials (*Gideon v. Wainwright,* 371 U.S. 335, 1963). This decision not only overturned the *Betts* ruling of twenty years earlier, but more importantly, established that violation of the Fourteenth Amendment justified attack on conviction proceedings by direct appeal or by habeas corpus proceedings. Other landmark cases of the early 1960s included *Mapp v. Ohio* (367 U.S. 643, 1961), which expanded protection against illegal searches and provided the logic for the current "exclusionary rule" challenges to illegally obtained evidence in criminal trials; *Escobedo v. Illinois* (378 U.S. 478, 1964), which protected the rights of suspects during interogation; and *Miranda v. Arizona* (384 U.S. 436, 1966), which held that suspects must be read their rights and be provided with legal counsel when an investigation moves to the accusatory stage. These decisions gave the Warren Court the undeserved reputation of judicial permissiveness and excessive activism. They further nationalized civil liberties by challenging abusive criminal justice practices of states which appeared to run counter to Constitutional principles.

In 1963, the Warren Court also handed down its landmark decision in *Monroe v. Pate* (365 U.S. 167, 1961), which resurrected nineteenth-century civil rights legislation and provided the legislative justification for redressing state civil rights complaints in federal courts. A few years later, a federal appellate court extended to prisoners the First Amendment right to freely exercise their religion when it recognized the legitimacy of Black Muslims (*Cooper v. Pate*, 382 F.2d 518, 7th Cir., 1967). More importantly, the Cooper decision for the first time explicitly allowed state prisoners to file federal litigation under the Civil Rights Act.

These cases were not simply the result of changes in judicial thinking. The civil rights movement recognized the political utility of legal struggle, and concerted and increasingly sophisticated legal arguments were constructed to expand rights through the "due process" clause. In addition, the civil rights movement contributed to public tolerance of the expansion of rights, and there was less public backlash and opposition, making the "shorthand" doctrine of the Fourteenth Amendment politically and judicially more palatable. Equally important, this was an era of federal mediation of a variety of societal problems, typified by the "New Federalism" in which such problems as education, scientific research, poverty, crime, and social justice were seen as requiring national solutions. The combination of social recognition of the importance of fundamental rights and judicial willingness to intervene in state cases violating these rights led to a fundamental shift in the relationship between federal and state power in criminal and penal affairs.

Despite dramatic and highly visible decisions, the Warren Court did not so much create new rights as consolidate several decades of changing legal concepts and norms (Blasi, 1983). In this sense, it is incorrect to view the judicial activism of the 1960s as a juridical revolution or as a shift to a remarkably new period in judicial philosophy. Granted, the judicial players on Supreme Court acted out their legal dramas with flair, even ad-libbing when the occasion arose. But if the script of the legal play was altered somewhat, the genre was not; the Warren Court, with five of its members appointed by Eisenhower, and two later replaced by Kennedy, continued the ideological and philosophical roles that had been created decades earlier. It was with relief and optimism that conservatives welcomed Richard Nixon's inauguration in 1969, for it was believed that he would reverse the tide of perceived liberalism in the federal courts.

Retrenchment: 1969 and After

In some ways, the emergence of Nixon was reminiscent of Jackson's election in 1828: the country was ideologically split between nationalists and those of a more parochial view. A president was elected who, it was believed, would plug the dike and turn back the flood of federal intervention in matters considered by many to be private. President Nixon had boasted in 1968 that he would fill the federal courts with judicial conservatives to make the Constitution "more secure," and since 1969, judicial appointments have included consideration of whether the candidate was "soft on crime" (Goldman, 1975: 497).

Nixon appointed a Chief Justice, Warren Burger, and three associate justices to the Supreme Court, and his successor, Gerald Ford, appointed one associate justice. The Burger court thus became known as the "four plus one" court, and given that Nixon was meticulously careful about appointing coideologues, it was assumed that the interventionist judicial trend would be stemmed, if not actually reversed. Such was not the case. Although the Nixon "block of four" voted together on 54 of the 66 (82 percent) cases it heard in the 1972 term, none of the Warren Court decisions was overturned (Pollack, 1979: 307). In fact, it was under Nixon that one of the most dramatic prison law cases was decided. The Supreme court ruled in *Johnson v. Avery* (393 U.S. 483, 1969) that prisoners must be allowed proper legal materials for their work, and prison regulations could not bar prisoners from helping each other in litigating. Jailhouse lawyers could no longer be prevented from assisting less skilled inmates, and the availability of legal resources made access to courts easier. This expanded both the motivation and ability of prisoners to sue, and is for that reason perhaps one of the most influential decisions promoting prisoner suits.

By the mid–1970s, the momentum of the civil rights, anti-war and other social activist movements had waned, but the impetus for change remained. Hippies and yuppies moved from the streets and college campuses into the yuppie world of law and intrasystem change. The courts remained an arena for social struggle, and whatever their political ideology prior to enlistment on the bench, Supreme Court justices continued to expand individual rights. The Supreme Court continued to affirm New Deal and Warren Court decisions, but with little enthusiasm. Even those Burger court decisions attacking the Warren legacy tended to be narrow in scope, and they had little impact on reversing the civil rights trend. *Roe v. Wade* (410 U.S. 113, 1973), for example, overturned as unconstitutional state legislation prohibiting abortion, and symbolized the momentum of civil liberties. The case challenged Texas antiabortion statutes as unconstitutional under the concept of personal liberty embodied in the Fourteenth Amendment's Due Process

Clause, and under personal, marital, familial, and sexual privacy implied by the Bill of Rights.

The Roe decision has been criticized for "faulty legal logic," but this criticism is based on the Court's attempt to prescribe Constitutional guidelines for antiabortion state laws based on a trimester concept of prenatal life stages. Awkward as the Court's reasoning may have been, it was attempting to confront the definition of "person," which vague Constitutional language periodically required when new situations were confronted by old law. The Court was not making new law in this attempt; it was attempting to balance states' interests in protecting prenatal life with womens' right to choice over what was still a part of their bodies. The Court was faced with problems of legal definitions created by medical technology that changed conceptions of "life" and "citizenship," which had previously been relatively obvious. Nonetheless, the case generated considerable backlash for the next decade, and illustrates how a single decision can spawn movements, countermovements, and social protest through actions that are often more symbolic than substantive in their impact upon day-to-day existence.

Carter and Reagan

Contrary to some views, the administration of President Carter was not a reversal of Nixon's policies. In fact, as his plans for a potential second term have revealed, Carter's general political program was—if for different reasons—similar, if not identical, to that of his successor, Ronald Reagan. Further, Carter's stress on human rights did not translate into a resurgence of civil rights litigation in the courts, and there was no significant shift in legal policy during the Carter era.

It was under President Reagan that a direct broadside on "judicial activism" and civil liberties was levelled (Thomas, Doherty et al. 1987). Reagan pledged both during his first presidential campaign and after election to reverse the trend of "judicial liberalism." He delegated his Attorney General, William French Smith, the task of bringing the federal judiciary into ideological alignment with conservative principles:

> In October, 1981, Attorney General William French Smith launched a broadside attack on the federal courts for "subjective judicial policy-making." President Reagan, he said, would appoint new judges attuned to "the groundswell of conservatism evidenced by the 1980 elections." Mr. Reagan has done that (Taylor, 1984: E5).

Despite a number of narrow decisions circumscribing civil liberties, the ideological predilection of Reagan appointees has not produced a remarkable shift in the trend of judicial activism. The philosophy underlying Burger Court decisions has, as Howard (1980) observed, remained *ad hoc* and moderate, and to date the Roosevelt/Warren legacy remains intact. Burger rulings have generally weakened rights of suspects in criminal proceedings and strengthened states' rights, but there have been some suprises in which the court has ruled in favor of protecting individual liberties, including those of prisoners. Some evidence, in fact, suggests that Reagan appointees to the federal bench may be more liberal than their so-called "liberal" predecessors in preserving, if not actually expanding, rights (Suchner et al. 1986). The appointment of conservative William Rehnquist to Chief Justice and the addition of another conservative, Antonin Scalia, to the Court, did not immediately produce a dramatic shift in judicial philosophy, as the decisions rebuffing judicial conservativism indicate. As a consequence, there remains an uneasy but stable balance between those who would reduce federal protections of individual liberty and those who prefer more.

SUMMARY

This chapter began by asking the question: "Whence come expanded prisoners' rights?" The answer: they have come from centuries of evolving legal philosophy, from social and political change, and from more recent struggles of disempowered groups striving to obtain Constitutional protections from which they have been excluded. The use of courts in social struggle has its roots in the transition to an industrial economy during the closing decades of the nineteenth-century and the social transformations of the first decades of the twentieth. With the emergence of large, centralized industrialized bureaucracies, corporations began to acquire the status of *legal subjects*. This dramatically changed the conception of the legal subject in that entities other than individuals became bearers of rights and privileges, and could, in principle, engage as "equals" in litigation.

The transition from laissez-faire to monopoly capital also required transformations in the legal relations governing the productive and exchange structure between corporations. Legal relations were further mediated by labor struggles of the late nineteenth and early twentieth-century. The outcome was an expansion of rights—albeit in asymmetrical balance—for individuals, corporations (which acquired and strengthened their subject status), and the state itself (as it acquired increasing legal power and authority by which to intervene in mediating social existence). Although this increased subject status conferred a variety of rights, it also implied obligations in that legal subjects such as corporations and government agencies became potential targets for litigation, thus creating a new avenue for resolving social conflict under federal laws.

In examining the history of the development of law and the Constitution in the United States, several points become clear.

First, the relationship between the federal and state systems has always been a fragile one. From the inception of the Supreme Court, the debates over how much power should be extended to the federal realm have not subsided, nor should they. The tension between the two levels of government was part of the original intent.

Second, different social eras create different social issues, and this requires redefinition of legal concepts and legal subjects. The concept of punishment and prisons, for example, is based on an entirely different model in the 1980s than it was in the 1880s. As a consequence, the legal status of those incarcerated has also changed.

Third, law, as a sign system that indicates appropriate rules for social order, is mediated by numerous social factors that change how the code of law will be interpreted and applied. Social experiences, culture, political structure, and societal needs vary over time, and the laws that order social relations and define social intercourse are also subject to change. The meaning of the components of this sign system are not invariant, but continually change.

Finally, the changes in law, the philosophy of right and its application to social problems illustrate the manner in which law has retained, and more recently increased, its autonomy from a centralized and homogeneous state. Legal fundamentalism would, ironically, function to reunite the legal apparatus with the power of the state by rendering it subservient to political decisions. By recoupling law and the state, the slippage that currently allows for Constitutional checks by the federal judiciary on other branches of government would be tightened, and the courts would lose their primary function as protector of rights. The history of both English and U.S. law illustrates the manner in which this slippage has increased, and displays the role law has played in the gradual expansion of rights to, and redefinition of, new legal subjects.

Law, to borrow a metaphor from the seventeenth-century jurist Sir Matthew Hale (1971: 40), is like Jason's ship, the Argo. Although it appeared the same upon return as when it departed, during its long voyage virtually every part was replaced; despite the *appearance* of sameness, changes altered its *essence*. Law, too, is continually changing, such that we often fail to recognize that despite the illusion of permanency, it is continually transformed by powerful social forces that inexorably modify both its form and content. Prisoner litigation, although a small slice of the judicial pie, typifies one facet of a broader cycle of legal transition. By examining the Constitutional processes by which changes have occured, it becomes easier to understand prisoner litigation as an attempt to address through legal and quite peaceful means those grievances which, by law, may be unconstitutional.

NOTES

1. For an excellent review of and response to doctrinaire states' rights advocates and critics of Constitutional activism, see especially Miller, 1982.
2. For a brief but excellent history of English common law in the colonies, see especially Reinsch, 1967.
3. Collins (1974/1912: 7–12) has argued that the primary reasons for the passage of the Fourteenth Amendment were political. While acknowledging racial equality as one motivating factor, he adds that other functions included punishing the South, expanding and centralizing the power of the federal government, and enhancing control of the Republican party.
4. Jim Crow laws were laws specifically intended to maintain racial segregation. They functioned as current Apartheid law does in contemporary South Africa.
5. For excellent discussions of the political economy of the Reform Era, see especially Greenberg, 1974; Chandler, 1972, and Aronowitz, 1973.
6. The court included Justice Harlan, whose grandfather had been the lone dissenter in the Plessy decision.

3

Trends and Issues in Prisoner Litigation

All inmates are looking for the key to the front door. Law suits are the current vogue. Many serve to justify the existence of the new "camp followers," now that the Civil War is over and the civil rights battles have subsided. Inmates are the cannon fodder (Anonymous grant reviewer, National Institute of Justice, 1983).

CONTEMPORARY PRISONER LITIGATION

SINCE 1961, A COMBINED TOTAL of nearly 466,000 suits have been filed by state and federal prisoners in federal district courts. Over 186,000 have been filed between 1981 and 1986, representing approximately 40 percent of all federal prison suits filed since 1961. Prisoner litigation in 1986 alone accounted for 18 percent of all litigation filed in federal court in that year, significantly contributing to the judicial workload. This apparent swelling of litigation, some would argue, is symptomatic of "America's national disease" caused by an "overactive law-making gland" (Manning, 1977: 767), or the result of "sociopaths" abusing the courts (McGarr, quoted in Warren, Kelly, and Tybor, 1984). This alleged high rate of litigation, or *hyperlexis,* has been called "a heartworm that has literally fatal potential for the body politic of this country" (Manning, 1977: 770).

In providing an antidote to the hyperlexis view, Galanter (1983) has argued that we must strip away the misconceptions of litigation to examine the context in which it occurs. This chapter begins clarification of the concept of prisoner litigation, identifies salient issues, distinguishes private from U. S. litigation, and traces general filing trends over the past twenty five years. By heeding Galanter's warning, we find considerable diversity between state and federal prisoners, between prisoners in different states, and among the complaints prisoners identify.

CATEGORIES OF PRISONER LITIGATION

All *federal litigation* is divided into two basic categories. The first is called *U.S. cases,* and the second *private cases.* U.S. cases are suits in which the federal government is a defendant. In prisoner litigation, these are usually filed by federal prisoners against a federal agency or federal personnel. A private suit, by contrast, is one in which the federal government is not the defendant. Private prisoner litigation tends to be filed against state officials for violations of the prisoner's Constitutional rights. Technically, then, the classification of "U.S." and "private" refers to the status of the party being sued, not to the status of the party bringing suit. Because there are sufficiently few exceptions, the term "U.S." suits will be retained to refer to federal prisoner litigation, and "private suits" used to denote state prisoner litigation.

Types of Suits

Habeas Corpus Suits
There are two basic categories of *prisoner* litigation. The first are habeas corpus petitions, which challenge the fact of an inmate's detention. These usually address the proceedings, especially alleged irregularities, of the original case. The legal principle of habeas litigation dates back at least to the Magna Carta and English Common Law, but the modern legal theories for such suits stem from post-Civil War legislation expanding federal review of habeas corpus petitions by federal and especially state prisoners.

Civil Rights Suits
The second category of suits, civil rights complaints, derives from post-Civil War civil rights legislation, particularly the Fourteenth Amendment and various civil rights acts (surviving today as Title 42 Section 1983). In recent decades, there has also been an increased willingness of the federal judiciary to construct a strong body of case law justifying federal review of state civil rights practices based on the First, Fourth, Eighth, and Fourteenth Amendments, as these provide prisoner protections of, for example, religious expression, privacy, and liberty. It is these suits that have dramatically shaped prison policies and operations.

Other Suits
There are several other categories of prisoner suits that are classified separately from habeas or civil rights petitions. Federal prisoners file motions to vacate sentences, which are petitions requesting the court to reexamine the original sentence. Some of these suits, however, are filed after sentencing but prior to incarceration. As a consequence, this category is not as strong an indicator of prison conditions or policies as,

for example, habeas suits might be, but is more properly associated with the criminal proceedings of the original case. Because federal motions to vacate sentence challenge the fact of confinement, they are sociologically, if not legally, a functional equivalent of habeas corpus.[1] Federal (and less commonly state) prisoners also file *mandamus* petitions. A writ of mandamus, typically filed under the Mandamus Act (28 U.S.C. Section 1361), is a petition that seeks to compel a U.S. or state official to perform a duty owed to the plaintiff. Such complaints, however, are infrequent at the federal level, comprising about 5 percent of all suits by federal prisoners. Federal prisoner challenges to parole proceedings are also classified separately, but for state prisoners these tend to be filed as habeas actions.

Classification Problems

There are several problems with conventional discussions of prisoner litigation. First, despite federal classification distinctions, the categories of federal and state prisoners are commonly conflated, thus confounding the nature of filings. Second, civil rights and habeas cases tend not to be distinguished, thus distorting the filing differences among each group. For example, in recent years, most state filings have used Section 1983 as the legal theory on which to sue. Because the legislative wording of Section 1983 restricts its use to *state* prisoners, federal prisoners do not have Section 1983 available to them to challenge conditions of federal prisons. They may, however, employ this legal theory against nonfederal defendants. Some observers argue that federal prisoners may employ Section 1983 in conjunction with *mandamus* suits for the same purpose (e.g., Bronstein and Hirschkop, 1979: 120). Other observers, however, question whether such an indirect method of filing civil rights claims is necessary, because federal prisoners retain the full panoply of rights protected by the Bill of Rights (see, e.g., *Bivens v. Six Unknown F.B.I Agents*, (403 U.S. 388, 1971)). Federal prisoners thus tend to file similar complaints on somewhat different legal grounds than do state prisoners. Third, aggregating prisoner filings at the national level glosses over a number of significant differences between states. States with high prison populations tend to have proportionately higher civil rights suits filed than do those with lower prison populations. Fourth, the grounds of litigation by state and federal prisons have shifted over the years. Therefore, it becomes useful, even when aggregating at the national level, to distinguish between the various categories of prisoner suits.

By illustrating broad national trends in U.S. and private litigation separately, and by comparing these with civilian litigation rates, it becomes easier to explore the filing patterns and their implications.

NATIONAL FILING PATTERNS (1960–1986)

When observers speak of the "explosion" in the number of prisoner suits filed, they usually mean that the number of suits filed in recent years is remarkably higher than the number of suits filed two decades ago. The number of all prisoner suits filed in 1986, for example, is over 14 times greater than the number filed in 1960. This would seem to give some credence to the hyperlexis view by creating an image of prisoners flooding the courts with their claims. The figure is misleading, however. By distinguishing between the grounds of filing and who files which type, we can better understand Galanter's (1983: 61) claim that litigation occurs in a *social context* and is not simply a figure waiting to be passively counted. When we examine the average annual increase of suits by litigating prisoners and compare it with civilian litigation, a picture emerges that suggests we cannot interpret the increase in isolation from nonprisoner litigation. We also obtain a different view of litigation when we distinguish between federal and state prisoner filings.

Federal Prisoner Filings

As Table 3a shows, both the numbers and the nature of suits filed by federal prisoners have shifted since the 1960s. Federal prisoner petitions filed in 1986 have not quite tripled in twenty five years, and in 1986 were only 6 percent higher than the 1970 total. Despite modest fluctuations, the trend in federal suits is one of slow but rather steady decline since the peak filing year of 1974. In the past quarter century, the bulk of federal prisoner cases has been filed as motions to vacate sentence or as writs of habeas corpus. Taken together, both types of petitions are challenges to the fact of confinement, which consistently have accounted for approximately two-thirds to three-quarters of all federal prisoner suits, but there has been a dramatic shift in habeas and civil rights filings by federal prisoners, beginning about 1969. Civil rights suits increased steadily through the mid–1970s, but then decreased. Unlike state prisoners, civil rights claims have comprised a relatively small portion of all federal prisoners' suits, never exceeding 20 percent, and are usually much less. Habeas petitions, by contrast, decreased in the 1960s to a low of 29 percent of all filings in 1973, and have since begun a slow upward climb. Parole, classified as "other" after 1971, constituted less than 10 percent of annual filings through the 1960s. These suits are no longer classified separately, and federal legislation abolishing parole would presumably phase out this category completely.

The relative stability in the number of all federal prisoner filings since 1970 suggests that there has been neither an "avalanche" nor a rate of increase comparable to state filings. Lacking hard evidence, one can only suggest possible reasons for this relatively low growth of federal prisoner suits. First, it may be that federal courts are more aware of, and thus more closely follow, Constitutional procedures in criminal trials. Hence, there are fewer Constitutional grounds for challenging imprisonment. Second, it may be that federal appeals may be more quickly exhausted prior to imprisonment. By the nature of federal procedures, appeals would be exhausted before imprisonment in a larger percentage of cases than in state crimes. Hence, the number of habeas filings that occur after imprisonment would be proportionately lower than in state courts, where appeals at the federal level remain possible after appeals in state courts have failed. Third, federal prisons tend to be smaller and therefore presumably less prone to excessive inmate and staff violence and other abuses than are state prisons. This, presumably, would reduce the problems that impel prisoners to litigate. Fourth, the recruitment criteria for federal prison officers and administrators tend to be higher than in state prisons. Hence, there may be less turnover among staff, better training, especially for guards, and thus more professionalism, all of which contribute to improved inmate management. Staff, because of better training and stricter standards of accountability, would presumably be less inclined to abuse power, although this may not always be true, as suits filed by prisoners from Marion federal prison have suggested.[2] Fifth, both the average sentence length and the actual time served is dramatically less for federal than for state prisoners.[3] Finally, unlike lawyers representing state prisoners, federal law prohibits lawyers from collecting attorney fees when the United States is a defendant. This could dramatically reduce the motivation of lawyers to assist prisoners.[4]

Civilian and Federal Prisoner U. S. Filings

If it is true that the United States is a litigious society (Lieberman, 1981), then prisoner litigation may simply reflect a broader social trend. Comparing the proportion of prisoner to civilian suits provides a useful indicator of this relationship. If the proportion of filings between each group remains fairly stable over time, it would suggest that there may be similar factors effecting the filings of both. As Table 3b shows, the proportion of federal prisoner to civilian filings has varied considerably since 1966. Civilian litigation has increased 347 percent between 1960 and 1986, compared to 240 percent for federal prisoners. The proportion of federal prisoner to civilian filings, an indicator of the relative litigiousness of each group, peaked in 1974 at about 18 percent of all U. S. filings, and dropped to 5 percent in 1986. This curvilinear relationship suggests that federal prisoners, as a group, are becoming less litigious than the general population, and that federal prisoner filings are not a function of civilian filings. These data do not support the contention, for federal prisoners at least, that suits are "exploding" at

Table 3a Breakdown of federal prisoner litigation by filing
category, 1960–86

Year	Parole	Vacate Sentence	Habeas Corpus	Civil Rights	Mandamus & Other	Totals
1960	(a)	(a)	886	(a)	419	1,305
1961	161	560	868	(a)	(b)	1,589
1962	84	546	866	(a)	(b)	1,496
1963	50	595	862	(a)	123	1,630
1964	58	972	882	(a)	186	2,098
1965	82	1,244	974	(a)	259	2,559
1966	64	863	1,017	15	333	2,292
1967	104	958	1,045	58	474	2,639
1968	131	1,099	1,045	60	516	2,851
1969	150	1,444	1,373	81	564	3,612
1970	232	1,729	1,600	136	488	4,185
1971	202	1,335	1,671	214	699	4,121
1972	268	1,591	1,368	252	700	4,179
1973	466	1,722	1,294	414	639	4,535
1974	371	1,822	1,718	445	631	4,987
1975	662	1,690	1,682	478	535	5,047
1976	538	1,693	1,421	502	626	4,780
1977	237	1,921	1,508	483	542	4,691
1978	121	1,924	1,730	636	544	4,955
1979	(c)	1,907	1,577	588	427	4,499
1980	(c)	1,322	1,413	603	375	3,713
1981	(c)	1,248	1,629	834	393	4,104
1982	(c)	1,186	1,927	834	381	4,328
1983	(c)	1,311	1,914	790	339	4,354
1984	(c)	1,427	1,905	822	372	4,526
1985	(c)	1,527	3,405	957	373	6,262
1986	(c)	1,556	1,679	770	427	4,432

Source: Annual Report of the Director of the Administrative Office of the U.S. Courts, Table 3c.

(a) Petitions included in category of "other."
(b) Petitions included with Habeas Corpus filings.
(c) Parole petitions not classified separately after 1978.

Table 3b   Civilian and federal U.S. prisoner filings, 1960–86

Year	Total U.S. All*	Total Civilian	Total U.S. Prisoner	Prisoner As % of All U.S. Lit.
1960	20,840	19,535	1,305	06
1961	19,843	18,254	1,589	08
1962	20,298	18,802	1,496	07
1963	21,385	19,755	1,630	08
1964	22,268	20,170	2,098	09
1965	21,651	19,092	2,559	12
1966	23,181	20,889	2,292	10
1967	21,593	18,954	2,639	12
1968	19,666	16,815	2,851	14
1969	22,295	18,683	3,612	16
1970	24,965	20,780	4,185	17
1971	25,086	20,965	4,121	16
1972	26,729	22,550	4,179	16
1973	27,484	22,949	4,535	17
1974	24,585	22,598	4,987	18
1975	31,779	26,732	5,047	16
1976	39,864	34,084	4,780	12
1977	40,210	35,519	4,691	12
1978	46,811	41,856	4,955	11
1979	55,840	51,341	4,499	08
1980	63,628	59,915	3,713	06
1981	61,845	57,741	4,104	07
1982	75,773	71,445	4,328	06
1983	95,803	91,449	4,354	05
1984	111,867	107,341	4,526	04
1985	117,488	111,226	6,262	05
1986	91,830	87,398	4,432	05

Source: Annual Report of the Director of the Administrative Office of the U.S. Courts, Table 3c.

*In some years, civilian and prisoner categories do not match "total filings" because of exclusion of "others" from federal classification.

Table 3c   Breakdown of state prisoner litigation by filing
           category, 1960-86

Year	Habeas Corpus	Civil Rights	Other	Totals
1960	871	(a)	1	872
1961	1,020	(a)	(a)	1,020
1962	1,408	(b)	44	1,452
1963	2,106	(b)	518	2,624
1964	3,694	(b)	448	4,142
1965	4,845	(b)	484	5,329
1966	5,339	218	691	6,248
1967	6,201	878	725	7,804
1968	6,488	1,072	741	8,301
1969	7,359	1,269	684	9,312
1970	9,063	2,030	719	11,812
1971	8,372	2,915	858	12,145
1972	7,949	3,348	791	12,088
1973	7,784	4,174	725	12,683
1974	7,626	5,236	561	13,423
1975	7,843	6,128	289	14,260
1976	7,833	6,958	238	15,029
1977	6,866	7,752	228	14,846
1978	7,033	9,730	206	16,969
1979	7,123	11,195	184	18,502
1980	7,031	12,397	146	19,574
1981	7,790	15,639	178	23,607
1982	8,059	16,741	175	24,975
1983	8,532	17,687	202	26,421
1984	8,349	18,034	198	26,581
1985	8,534	18,491	181	27,206
1986	9,045	20,072	216	29,333

Source: Annual Report of the Director of the Administrative Office of the
          U.S. Courts, Table 3c.

(a) Included with Habeas Corpus petitions.
(b) Included with "other" prisoner petitions.

Table 3d   Civilian and state prisoner private filings, 1960-86

Year	Total Private	Total Civilian	Total Prisoner	Prisoner As % of All Filings
1960	38,444	37,572	872	2
1961	38,450	37,430	1,020	3
1962	41,538	40,086	1,452	3
1963	42,245	39,621	2,624	6
1964	44,662	40,520	4,142	9
1965	46,027	40,698	5,329	12
1966	47,725	41,477	6,248	13
1967	49,368	41,564	7,804	16
1968	51,783	43,482	8,301	16
1969	54,898	45,586	9,312	17
1970	62,356	50,544	11,812	19
1971	68,310	56,165	12,145	18
1972	69,444	57,356	12,088	17
1973	71,076	58,393	12,683	18
1974	75,945	62,522	13,423	18
1975	85,541	71,281	14,260	17
1976	90,733	75,704	15,029	17
1977	90,357	75,511	14,846	16
1978	91,958	74,989	16,969	18
1979	98,826	80,324	18,502	19
1980	105,161	85,587	19,574	19
1981	118,731	95,124	23,607	20
1982	130,420	105,445	24,975	19
1983	146,039	119,618	26,421	18
1984	149,618	123,037	26,581	18
1985	156,182	128,976	27,206	17
1986	162,998	133,665	29,333	18

Source: Annual Report of the Director of the Administrative Office of the U.S. Courts, Table 3c.

Table 3e Annual percent change in U.S. and private civilian, state, and federal prisoner filings in federal district courts, 1960–86

Year	U.S. Civilian	U.S. Prisoner	Private Civilian	Private Prisoner
1961	−07	22	−N*	17
1962	03	−06	07	42
1963	05	09	−01	81
1964	02	29	02	75
1965	−05	22	+N*	29
1966	09	−10	02	17
1967	−09	15	+N*	25
1968	−11	08	05	06
1969	11	27	05	12
1970	11	16	11	27
1971	01	−02	11	03
1972	08	01	02	−N*
1973	02	09	02	05
1974	−02	10	07	06
1975	18	01	14	06
1976	31	−05	06	05
1977	01	−02	−N*	−01
1978	18	06	−N*	14
1979	23	−09	07	09
1980	17	−17	07	06
1981	−04	11	11	21
1982	24	05	11	06
1983	28	01	13	06
1984	17	04	03	01
1985	04	38	05	02
1986	−21	−29	04	08

(N* indicates negligible change, less than 0.5 percent, plus or minus.)

Table 3f   Increase of state and federal prisoner populations*
           and filings,** 1960–86

| Year | Federal | | State | |
	Prisoners	Suits	Prisoners	Suits
1960	23218	1305	189735	872
1964	21709	2098	192627	4142
% CHANGE				
1960–64:	-6.5	60.8	1.5	375.0
1965	21040	2559	189855	5329
1969	19623	3612	176384	9312
% CHANGE				
1964–69:	-6.7	41.1	-7.1	74.7
1970	20038	4185	176391	11812
1974	22361	4987	196105	13423
% CHANGE				
1970–74:	11.6	19.2	11.2	13.6
1975	24131	5047	216462	14260
1979	26371	4499	287635	18502
% CHANGE				
1975–79:	9.3	-10.9	32.9	29.7
1980	24363	3713	305458	19574
1986	44330	4432	484615	29333
% CHANGE				
1980–86:	82.0	19.4	58.7	49.9
% CHANGE				
1960–69:	-15.5	176.8	-7.0	967.9
% CHANGE				
1970–86:	121.2	5.9	174.7	148.3

*Source: U.S. Department of Justice, 1986.
**Source: Administrative Office of the U.S. Courts.

Table 3g Rate of prisoner filings (federal, state, and all
          prisoners) per 100 prisoners, 1960–86

Year	Federal Prisoners	State Prisoners	All Prisoners
1960	5.62	.46	1.02
1961	6.71	.52	1.19
1962	6.25	.75	1.35
1963	7.05	1.35	1.96
1964	9.66	2.15	2.91
1965	12.16	2.81	3.74
1966	11.91	3.46	4.28
1967	13.48	4.45	5.36
1968	14.47	4.93	5.93
1969	18.41	5.28	6.59
1970	20.89	6.70	8.14
1971	19.67	6.86	8.21
1972	19.25	6.93	8.30
1973	19.88	6.99	8.43
1974	22.30	6.84	8.43
1975	20.92	6.59	8.02
1976	16.42	6.37	7.48
1977	14.62	5.54	6.51
1978	16.63	6.12	7.13
1979	17.06	6.43	7.33
1980	15.24	6.41	7.06
1981	14.59	7.08	7.67
1982	14.59	6.64	7.22
1983	13.64	6.52	7.04
1984	13.21	6.19	6.71
1985	15.57	5.87	7.10
1986	10.00	6.05	6.38

an abnormal rate or that federal prisoners are squeezing out civilian suits with a plethora of complaints.

State Prisoner Filings

In contrast to federal prisoners, state prisoners have generally filed under two categories—habeas corpus petitions and civil rights complaints. Together, these two categories have historically constituted nearly all private prisoner litigation (about 99 percent after 1976), as Table 3c indicates. By limiting analysis to total filings, which have increased 34–fold since 1960, it is tempting to accept critics' contentions that an epidemic of litigation is spreading from prisons. Even between 1981 and 1986, state prisoner filings have increased by 50 percent. But such simplisitic analysis conceals some important trends. Petitions for writs of habeas corpus, the most numerous of state prisoner suits from the 1960s through the mid–1970s, have declined dramatically in recent years, while civil rights complaints, especially since 1967, have increased. The issues these data raise will be discussed more fully in Chapters 4 and 5, but two significant trends emerge from Table 3c. First, the decrease in habeas challenges to confinement indicates that state prisoners, unlike their federal counterparts, are not using federal courts simply as a "key to the front door." Second, the increase in civil rights suits, which challenge prison conditions and policies, suggests that most prisoners have accepted their confinement status and are more interested in making their environment more habitable than in overturning their original conviction.

Civilian and State Prisoner Filings

The relationship between state prisoner and civilian filings differs markedly from federal prisoner patterns. In the early 1960s, state prisoner filings as a percentage of all private filings sharply increased, from 2 percent in 1960 to 13 percent in 1966. This was largely the result of favorable federal court decisions that provided motivation for state prisoners to take their grievances to court, and in part the result of increasing public attention to the problems of prison conditions. In Table 3d we see the stability of the percentage of federal prisoner to all filings. This proportion did increase dramatically between 1960 and 1965, but since 1967, the proportion of prisoner to civilian suits has remained reasonably constant, ranging between 16 and 20 percent. By 1986 private civilian filings also increased, but not as dramatically (only half the rate of prisoners' increase since 1966). Explanations for this are unclear, but a preliminary interpretation suggests that state prisoners may import into the institution with them the same litigious attitudes possessed by persons in the general population (Thomas, 1987).

Annual Change in Prisoner and Civilian Filings

The explosion metaphor implies a constant and dramatic increase in prisoner filings, one differing from the filing patterns of civilians. One way to examine prisoner filings, then, is to compare the annual changes in civilians' and prisoners' suits. This provides a means of assessing the changes in relative litigiousness between each group. As Table 3e indicates, the filing pace of neither state nor federal prisoners has matched that of civilians. In the mid–1960s, federal prisoners were proportionally more active than civilians, as were state prisoners in the early 1960s. Since the mid–1970s, however, the rate of increase in prisoner filings has slowed, despite increased sensitivity to the conditions of the nation's prisons and the quantum increase in state prison populations in recent years. By contrast, Table 3e shows that, despite periodic fluctuations, U.S. civilian litigation has been increasing inexorably on an average of about 11 percent annually since 1966. While federal prisoner filings have, in the aggregate, increased comparably since 1966, the bulk of the increase occurred prior to 1971. Because there were relatively few prisoner suits filed in the early 1960s, a modest change in the number of petitions would create a significant change in the percentage of filings over previous years, making comparisons with the early 1960s misleading.

On the whole, the annual increase of federal prisoner filings has in recent years been dramatically less than that of civilians. The number of U.S.-classified civilian suits increased by 321 percent between 1970 and 1986, while the number of similar federal prisoner suits climbed by only 6 percent during the same period. In only three years since 1971 have federal prisoner suits risen at a greater rate than those of civilians. Further, since 1971, in only one year (1981) did federal prisoner filings increase by more than 10 percent (with the exception of 1985, the year of anomalous filings by Cubans). In short, both the frequency and magnitude of federal prisoner filings has been less than those of civilians.

State prisoners, too, have exhibited a lower annual increase than their civilian counterparts in private litigation, although the difference is not as dramatic. Between 1960 and 1970, the annual increase by state prisoners ranged from 6 percent in 1968 to 81 percent in 1963, while civilian filings changed relatively little during the same period. This trend reversed in the next decade. Between 1970 and 1986, private civilian filings had increased by 164 percent, and state prisoner suits increased slightly less, 148 percent. Between 1981 and 1986, by contrast, civilian suits have increased far more rapidly, 41 percent, to only 24 percent for prisoners. Since 1971, the annual increase in private prisoner filings exceeded civilian suits only five times, and in only two of those years (1978 and 1981) did filings increase by more than ten percent over the previous year. While the data do indicate a steady but slow increase, they provide no evidence for the continued use of the "explosion" metaphor.

Litigation and Prison Population

If prisoner filings are primarily the result of an expanding prisoner population, it follows that when there are more prisoners, there would be more suits. As Table 3f indicates, this has not been the case. Both the state and federal prisoner population decreased between 1960 and 1969, but their litigation increased. The number of federal prisoners dropped by nearly 16 percent, but their filings nearly tripled. Since 1970, a different trend has emerged. Between 1970 and 1974, federal prisoners increased by about 12 percent, and their filings increased by 19 percent. Between 1975 and 1979, however, the number of filings decreased by 11 percent despite the 9 percent increase in population. In the 1980s, however, the trend has again reversed, and federal prisoner filings have dramatically outpaced the increase in population.

State prisoners' filings reflect a similar pattern during the 1960s. A slight population increase of 1.5 percent between 1960 and 1964 was greatly outdistanced by a 475 percent filing increase. A 7 percent decrease in population in the next five years did not reduce litigation, which increased by 75 percent. Table 3f shows, however, that after 1970, the increase in state prisoners was roughly comparable to the increase in filings. Between 1970 and 1979, state prisoner filings rose about proportionately to the increase of prisoners, but this trend has shifted slightly since 1980. This countercyclical trend for federal prisoners suggests that the genesis of their litigation reflects something more than a rising tide of prisoners. It does appear, however, that especially since the 1970s, state prisoner filings may be in part a function of a rapidly expanding population.

One final way to assess the relationship between prison population and number of filings is by examining the number of suits per prisoner. This provides an indicator of the alleged "increased contentiousness" of prisoners. If prisoners are becoming more attuned to the utility of suits in hassling captors or in seeking release, then there should be an increased proportion of suits per prisoner. Table 3g suggests that this is not the case. Granted, from 1960 through 1974, the combined number of suits for federal and state prisoners increased rapidly, from about 1 suit per 100 prisoners in 1960 to over 8 from 1970 through 1975. After 1975, however, the number of filings per prisoner decreased slightly, declining to the 1986 ratio of about 6.4 suits per 100 prisoners.

More significantly, *Table 3g* indicates that federal prisoners are proportionately far more litigious than are state prisoners. Between 1970 and

1975, federal prisoners filed about 20 suits per 100 inmates, compared to about 8 per 100 for state prisoners. Since 1975, this proportion has declined for both groups, but federal prisoners still out-filed their state counterparts by about a 2 to 1 ratio.

In 1960, state prisoners filed about 1 suit for every 200 prisoners. By 1964, the year after the Monroe decision, this had quadrupled to over two suits per 100 prisoners. This ratio reached its highest level in 1981, when 7 suits per 100 prisoners were filed, but despite this one-year proportion, the trend since the mid–1970s has been one of decline. By 1986, slightly more than one prisoner in 20 litigated, the lowest rate since 1969.

However one interprets these data, it is clear that prisoner litigation has increased. This increase, however, has not matched the increase in the prison population, and since the initial expansion of prisoners' rights in the 1960s, prisoner litigation has not kept pace with civilian filings. The data also cast doubt on the hyperlexis thesis by revealing that prisoner suits have ebbed and waned, but after the initial filing surge of the 1960s, have stablized. This suggests that deeper factors may generate litigation. The past twenty five years has been a time of dramatic social change, and these changes have included the manner in which rights are defined and wrongs corrected. Crucial to these changes were the growth of self-help movements and social protests, expanding rights of blacks, women, gays, and inmates of prisons and mental hospitals. Social protest permeated virtually all levels of social life, and made itself felt in prisons. Prison protest was originally led by black Muslims and later by jailhouse lawyers who first challenged their lack of access to law, and once access was won, activists turned their energies on prison conditions. The courts have become increasingly utilized as a means for dispute resolution: lacking internal forums, prisoners have turned to external agencies for relief.

The issues of prisoner litigation are complex, and the impact of prisoner filings on legislation, fiscal resources, judicial workloads, and institutional policy has been profound (Jacobs, 1982). Such litigation has also contributed to increasing public attention to prison conditions and policy (Ackerhalt, 1972; Dick, 1977; Jacobs, 1982; Natale and Rosenberg, 1974; Thomas, 1984a), and in fiscal allocations (Harriman and Straussman, 1983). Despite the visibility of litigation and its impact, a number of misconceptions surround prisoner litigation, and to these we now turn.

CONCEPTS AND ISSUES

There are a number of issues, some legitimate, others based on misconceptions, that currently guide discussions of prisoner litigation. Many tend to be unsubstantiated notions, elevated to the status of "facts" that serve to organize perceptions and suggest corresponding policies. Some of the most salient issues and problems include the following.

First, there is a belief that prisoners abuse the courts through litigation, as "proved" by its "explosion" in the past two decades (see Bator, 1963 and Reed, 1980). This trend is often interpreted as reflecting the contentious nature of social offenders or the abuse of courts by prisoners seeking release or striking out against their keepers, and some critics argue that federal legislation should be enacted to curtail prisoners' use of federal courts in resolving grievances (Smith, cited in "Curb of Convicts," 1984: 6; "New Rules," 1984: 3). In this view, the rapid increase in prisoner suits by convicted felons is alone sufficient evidence to warrant the judgment of court abuse. But neither the relationship of prisoner to civilian litigation nor the fairly stable prisoner filing patterns support the "explosion" thesis. Further, filing rates vary, the legal theories underlying litigation shift, and federal prisoner filing patterns and rates differ from those of state prisoners. This suggests that whatever value this position holds, it is alone insufficient to explain the alleged hyperlexis.

A second conception holds that prisoners tend to file frivolous suits, and that most cases "ought be dismissed, even under the most liberal definition of frivolity" (Federal Judicial Center, 1980: 9). Chief Justice Warren Burger, for example, has deplored the conditions of the nation's prisons while simultaneously cavilling at prisoners' attempts to peacefully change those conditions through the legal system:

> Federal judges should not be dealing with prisoner complaints which, although important to a prisoner, are so minor that any well-run institution should be able to resolve them fairly without resorting to federal judges (Burger, 1976: 190).

No reliable figures exist to allow determination of how many filings lack either legal or substantive merit. The problem is further compounded by the very meaning of the term. For lawyers, frivolity is a *legal* term used to describe suits lacking *Constitutional merit*. For prisoners and civil rights advocates, the term refers to suits lacking *substantive* merit. Thus, whether a suit is frivolous or not seems to depend as much upon one's perspective as upon the content of a specific suit.

The legal meaning of frivolousness connotes a value orientation implying worthlessness, even if there is a substantive grievance to be remedied. Media dramatizations of frivolity tend to emphasize the extreme cases, such as a female prisoner seeking a sex change operation or complaints of prison commissary deodorant (Possley, 1980: 20), cold toilet seats, failure to provide outside television antennas (Locin, 1981: 6), or the Illinois case of a prisoner who filed an injuction to stay prison officials from reading his thoughts. Other suits may be dramatized to make them seem trivial, even though there is a legitimate underlying grievance. For example, a suit over a protracted kiss between a prisoner and his wife or seminude pictures of a girlfriend, while portrayed by the media as trivial, in fact represented grievances of harassment of a prisoner's family by guards during visits. As the Supreme Court observed in 1973:

> The relationship of state prisoners and the state officers who supervise their confinement is far more intimate than that of a State and a private citizen. For state prisoners, eating, sleeping, dressing, washing, working, and playing are all done under the watchful eye of the State, and so the possibilities for litigation under the Fourteenth Amendment are boundless. What for a private citizen would be a dispute with his landlord, with his employer, with his tailor, with his neighbor, or with his banker becomes, for the prisoner, a dispute with the state (*Preiser v. Rodriguez*, 411 U. S. 475, 1973: 492).

Third, many observers argue that prisoner litigation reflects attempts by prisoners to retry their cases once they have been lost (Bator, 1963; Burt, 1985; Friendly, 1970; Reed, 1980). As early as 1948, Justice Jackson argued that liberalization of the writ of habeas corpus "put into the hands of the convict population of the country new and unprecedented opportunities to retry their cases" *Price v. Johnson* (334 U.S. 266, 1948). Most prisoner suits in recent years, however, have been civil rights-related suits, indicating that the bulk of litigation is not intended to secure release, but to challenge prison policies and conditions. Further, many habeas issues do not challenge the original case, but allege police brutality, challenge disciplinary practices that extend prison sentences or allege inaccurate record keeping, which has prolonged release date. Hence, it is critically important that we distinguish between the nature of prisoners' complaints as well as the particular legal theories on which complaints are based. Without such a distinction, the misconception that prisoners sue primarily for release is perpetuated, thus supporting the claim that suits are seen as "keys to the front door." It is useful to remember, however, that even if every single suit challenged the original conviction or sought release, there is nothing improper in efforts to appeal one's incarceration.

Fourth, prisoner litigation is perceived to undermine the criminal justice system by reducing respect for the law through delaying finality of punishment and making "certain punishment" for crimes uncertain (Bator, 1963). According to this argument, litigation may in fact promote crime by conveying to prisoners that even if they are convicted and sentenced, they may soon be released by finding a technicality in their criminal proceedings. This, it is argued, reduces the punitive principles of celerity and certainty by opening the possibility that even the most heinous acts often go unpunished. This latter argument, however, is unrelated to prisoner litigation and shifts attention from the broader issue of crime in the United States to prisoner behavior.

The "subversion" argument is based on several false assumptions. First, it assumes that the majority of suits are intended to seek a prisoner's release. Second, it assumes that litigants simply do not accept their legal defeats, file repeatedly if they lose, and will continue to pester the courts indefinitely unless litigation is curtailed. This will be shown in Chapter 5 to be false. Third, this view assumes the existence of a "prisoner attitude" that is bent upon defying authority for its own sake. This attitude has the further consequence of encouraging criminality, so the argument runs, by subverting respect for law. It has already been shown that most prisoner filings are challenging conditions more than they are seeking release. Evidence also suggests that only a relatively small percentage of prisoners challenge their original conviction, and these tend to be "one-shot" rather than "repeat" "players" (Galanter, 1975). Finally, although there is evidence that courts have some impact on clarifying prison policies or rectifying administrative errors in calculating a release date, there is no evidence that a significant number of prisoners are released on technicalities arising from original case proceedings. Releases are often publicized because of their dramatic or "landmark" nature, but such releases are "miniscule" (Burt, 1985: 372; Justice, 1973: 708). Illinois data suggest that prisoner litigation may actually increase prisoners' respect for law rather than reduce it (see Chapter 8).

Fifth, there is some feeling that the proliferation, especially of frivolous habeas suits, may result in the worthy cases being overlooked in the deluge of unworthy ones. Supreme Court Justice Robert Jackson has written:

> It must prejudice the occasional meritorious application to be buried in a flood of worthless ones. He who must search a haystack for a needle is likely to end up with the attitude that the needle is not worth the search (*Brown v. Allen*, 344 U.S. 443, 1953: 537).

This view is shared by both liberal and conservative observers, and even by most jailhouse lawyers. It adopts a "Gresham's law" theory of judicial decision-making, in which groundless cases are seen as debasing the value of meritorious ones, both increasing the work and decreasing the credibility of those active in prisoner rights. Even advocates of prisoners' rights are sensitive to the need to assure that legitimate complaints not be jeopardized because of possibly less meritorious complaints (Friendly, 1970). Although jailhouse lawyers themselves seem as critical of "garbage suits" as opponents of prisoner rights, many prisoners circumvent prisoner law clerks and file on their own. Further, judges do seem to evaluate prisoner petitions primarily on merit (Suchner et. al. 1986), suggesting that the wheat in fact remains when the chaff is separated. Judges quickly dismiss "garbage suits," and as one judge indicated, prisoner suits are, on the whole, conceptually simple, and it rarely takes more than a few minutes in reading a case to ascertain whether an adjudicable issue exists. This criticism is based on a cynical view of judicial decision-making that implies that judges become more jaundiced against prisoners' petitions the more they review them, and existing evidence does not support it (Suchner et al. 1986).

A sixth issue suggests that federal intervention in state correctional affairs exaccerbates tensions between state and federal governments (Bator, 1963). This argument, grounded in the opposition between federalism and states' rights, makes a causal leap by assuming that both a political and structural breach between federal and state governmental levels is necessarily precipitated by prisoner challenges.

Much of the current controversy over civil rights litigation has its roots in post-Fourteenth Amendment decisions in which the federal government effectively expanded its power over state judicial decisions, thus giving this conflict view some credence. This argument has been rekindled especially in recent years due to the interpretation of the "Reagan mandate," which has been perceived by some as grounds for limiting the scope of federal intervention in state affairs (Meese, 1986). There may be some merit in this view in that federal intervention has placed fiscal and administrative strains on states (Harriman and Straussman, 1983; Trubek et al. 1983). Federal court orders have required changes in prison conditions and policies, many of which have rankled both administrators and legislators. On the other hand, there is also some evidence that state politicians and prison administrators occasionally welcome certain types of law suits as politically expedient; they appear to be forced to comply with decisions that result in prison reforms that would have otherwise been politically unpalatable (Thomas, 1984a). Court-imposed demands to upgrade prison facilities also provide a rationale by which prison administrators can justify increased operating budgets (Harriman and Straussman, 1983; Lane, 1986a; Thomas, 1984a). This is a complex issue, and prisoner litigation cannot so easily be dismissed by claiming states' rights perogatives.

A seventh issue centers on the relationship of legislative to judicial branches of government in shaping prison policy. Chief Justice Burger, among others, has suggested that federal legislation should be implemented to make prisoner access to federal courts more difficult, thereby curtailing habeas filings. In his view, the judiciary has usurped legislative power, and "judge-made law" should be curtailed by the intervention of congressional action that provides more narrow guidelines for federal litigation, especially by state prisoners. By promoting the imagery of jurisdictional abuse, proponents of this view have played on a public mood of hostility toward encroaching government. In so doing, they are seeking to manipulate this mood by inciting at the ideological level a hostility toward civil liberties that has not yet been possible at the judicial level (Thomas, Doherty et al. 1987).

Eighth, it is perceived that the costs of prisoner litigation may place considerable drain on prison resources and state budgets. There have been no detailed studies of the costs of litigation, largely because of the difficulties in defining what constitutes a "cost," and partly because of the reticence of correctional systems to reveal prison settlements. Costs include labor of court personnel, allocation of prison and court resources for processing, punitive and compensatory payments to plaintiffs and implementation costs when prison policies (or even entire prison systems) must be modified.[5]

Ninth, the conventional view of prisoner litigation portrayed by the media, politicians, and critics pejoratively conveys the image of hordes of jailhouse lawyers who have nothing better to do with their time than "hassle" administrators. Yet, prisoner litigation means different things to different people. Prisoners view it as a legitimate means to peacefully and lawfully redress grievances. Influenced by media presentations, the public views it as an aberration of justice. Some pschologically oriented interpretations view litigation as a form of transference in which hostile impulses are merely shifted from targets outside the walls to the courts or prison personnel. Does litigation reflect poor prison conditions or violations of constitutionally protected rights in criminal proceedings? Does it reflect a growing awareness on the part of prisoners of the power of courts, or is it simply a consequence of an expanding prison population? Is prisoner litigation the tail end of the civil rights struggles of the 1960s? Are prisoners, because of their social label as deviants, simply acting out their alleged antisocial attitudes? This issue has not been fully explored and remains complex and not easily reduced to any single simplistic answer.[6]

A tenth issue challenges the philosophical issue of the appropriateness of allowing those convicted of social wrongdoing to participate as equals in the judicial process. Why, so one argument runs, should prisoners be allowed access to the courts? Prisons are supposed to be dreadful places; they are houses of punishment. Hence, we should keep prison conditions minimal. Others ask: is litigation really needed? Is is justifiable, especially when so many private citizens often cannot afford legal counsel? Is it effective in resolving procedural or administrative problems? Is it the most efficient and cost-beneficial means of resolving problems? These are essentially ideological questions, and thus not particularly amenable to an empirical answer. Given the state of the nation's prisons, however, and judging by the policies that have changed because of litigation, the courts arguably have provided at least some salvation from the more dramatic prison abuses.

A final issue portrays judicial review as inappropriate for redressing prisoner complaints. This issue is not limited to prisoner litigation; but because of its highly emotional, political, and ideological nature, prisoner litigation dramatizes the scope of court intervention in matters normally considered beyond its ken, and far beyond the mandate provided by the Constitution. At stake in this issue is nothing less than the relationship between state and federal law and society, and between the Constitution and judicial activism. Opponents of court review of prisoner grievances argue that judicial review was never intended to include convicted felons, and that courts have gone too far in expanding the legal rights of prisoners. Prisoners' rights advocates counter that prisoners retain many Constitutional rights, and it remains the responsibility of courts to protect them. This is not particularly amenable to empirical analysis, because it is based on one's view of the role of the Constitution and the federal judiciary in protecting and expanding rights. In the absence of empirical evidence, opponents of prisoner litigation tend to allude to broader abuses of judicial power, and ground their argument in historical allusions to "original intents."

These are important issues, but many of the conclusions are either tenuous or unfounded. Others may be partially true, or even quite accurate but lacking empirical support. The implications of these views for policy and for prison administration are shaped by lack of information and tend to be grounded in popular conceptions shaped by media or political expediency. The next step in examining these issues requires distinguishing between habeas corpus and civil rights filings. This not only helps identify filing trends in the past twenty five years, but allows examination of the hyperlexis theory of a litigation apocalypse.

NOTES

1. These suits are based on different legal theories, but they both have the same function, namely, that of securing release.
2. In 1983, about one-third (147 of 463) of the suits filed in Illinois' Central District originated from the federal penitentiary in Marion.
3. In 1984, the average sentence for state prisoners was about 92 months, and the average length of stay was about 26 months. For federal prisoners, the sentence length was about 48 months, and the time actually served about 16 months (Camp and Camp, 1985b: 10–12). As a consequence, there is less motivation to litigate, and less time to become proficient in litigation.
4. This possibility has been suggested by attorneys on both sides of prisoner

litigation. However, it seems an unlikely explanation, because the overwhelming majority of prisoners' suits are prisoner-initiated, and lawyers tend to be appointed after a case is filed.

5. In addition, fees awarded to lawyers successful in representing prisoners are usually far larger than their clients' awards. Prisoner awards tend to be small, typically under $100. Lawyers fees, by contrast, are awarded on a flat hourly basis in the range of $100 an hour. In one dramatic example of a successful class action suit, the complainants received no monetary award, and the lawyers' fee in the nearly decade-long battle exceeded $400,000 (*Duran v. Elrod*, 74–C–2949, N.D. Ill., 1974). Such costs are difficult to obtain, however, and are often hidden in state budgets. Further, it becomes difficult to calculate the indirect costs of personnel time lost in taking depositions, administrative processing of subpoenas, maintaining prison law libraries, processing documents and conducting bench and especially jury trials.

6. This issue has been addressed further in Thomas, Harris and Keeler, 1987.

4

Habeas Corpus and Civil Rights: Some Historical Distinctions

We disagree . . . that there is some sort of 'one man, one cell' principle
lurking in the Due Process Clause of the First Amendment (Justice William
Rehnquist, *Bell v. Wolfish*, 441 U.S. 520, 1979.

IN OUR CONTEMPORARY SYSTEM, civil and criminal law are procedurally
intertwined. This conflation tempts us to erroneously view all types of
prisoner litigation as of a single kind. Just as civil and criminal law have
different histories, however, so too does prisoner litigation. Therefore,
it becomes necessary to distinguish between the separate development
of the legal theories of habeas corpus and civil rights.

Rights are located in the social context that generates and nurtures
them, and prisoners' rights are no exception. This chapter traces the
separate histories of habeas and civil rights litigation. The intent is not
to provide a detailed legal history; these have been provided elsewhere.[1]
Instead, a general sketch of how each has emerged and the genesis of
several of the most important themes will help display the differences in
their development and use. The historical patterns underlying the
development of prisoner litigation helps understand it as a process
deeply rooted in the history both of law and societal change, rather than
a recent development bursting onto the contemporary scene.

THE EMERGENCE OF HABEAS CORPUS

The history the writ of habeas corpus lies not only in the development
of jurisprudence, but in the political conflicts through which it evolved.
In our own day, the writ reflects changing views of social justice as well
as the proper remedy for social injustice:

> The Great Writ highlights with special clarity many irreconcilable conflicts
> between society interests of considerable practical and symbolic importance.
> Its unique position in American law is at the root of the debate. Support
> for broad federal habeas review stems from our devotion to individual

74

justice, the symbolic value of the writ as the hallmark of democracy under law, the safety-valve effect of providing an additional forum for testing constitutional claims, as well as a belief that the federal judiciary is often in the best position to further these interests (Allen et al. 1982: 682).

The Meaning of Habeas Corpus

Habeas corpus translates from Latin as "you have the body," and enables an inmate to "challenge a criminal conviction, an administrative procedure, a prison regulation, or a condition of confinement that violates his rights under the Constitution" (Hoffman, 1981: 15). A habeas writ usually originates with a written appeal that challenges confinement by a prisoner or authorized representative to a judge. The judge reviews the petition, and if there is sufficient reason to doubt the legality of confinement, a hearing is granted at which the judge reviews the complaint and the circumstances. If confinement is deemed lawful, the petition is denied and the prisoner remains imprisoned. If, however, the petitioner is successful, the judge issues a ruling occasionally resulting in unconditional release, but more often, in a new trial. This was not always so.

The English Roots

The roots of Habeas corpus date back to the Magna Carta:

No free man shall be taken or imprisoned or dispossessed, or outlawed, or banished, or in any way destroyed, nor will we go upon him, nor send upon him, except by the legal judgment of his peers or by the law of the land (Magna Carta, 1215: Chapter 39).

The writ was originally used as a device for compelling appearance before the king's judiciary. As such, it was actually a coercive rather than an emancipatory instrument in that it functioned to establish court jurisdiction rather than protect the rights of an individual. It was in the nature of the developing view of the individual in society rather than in the nature of the writ itself that an otherwise repressive instrument (i.e., one *compelling* appearance) was transformed into one that safeguarded individual freedom (Duker, 1980: 62).

The writ became routinely used as early as 1567 by imprisoned political opponents of the king to obtain release, but it was not until the seventeenth century that it was expanded as an explicit right for all subjects imprisoned for other crimes as well. Nonetheless, it remained a class-bound legal weapon generally unavailable to those lacking some wealth or social status. By late 1620s, the sociopolitical conflicts that had been emerging for a generation between the legislative and executive branches of parliament promoted further evolution of the legal theory underlying the writ. Legal reform during this period was not intended

to alleviate the abuses of judicial practices so much as to protect opponents of the king from misusing royal authority to arrest. The crown
attempted to weaken its political opposition by imprisoning its leaders,
and the cases of the "Five Knights," John Lilburn, William Prynne, Dr.
Leighton, Francis Jenckes, and William Penn typify the manner in which
the seventeenth-century writ was used to free those who resisted or
spoke against royal policy. A series of seventeenth-century acts, including the Petition of Right (1628) and the Habeas Corpus Act (1689),
gradually but unequivocally defined and established the use and scope
of the writ as a safeguard of individual liberty, and by the end of the
century it was increasingly extended to all English subjects. The principles—if not the acts themselves—provided the foundation of law in the
American colonies.

The Transformation of Habeas Corpus
in the United States

The writers of the United States Constitution perceived that the writ
of habeas corpus was among the greatest securities to "liberty and
republicanism" contained in the document:

> The privilege of the Writ of Habeas Corpus shall not be suspended, unless
> when in Cases of Rebellion or Invasion the public Safety may require it
> (U.S. Constitution, Article I, Section 9).

The Constitution explicitly provided for the power of the writ, and
The Federalist Papers provided the initial logic and intents by which it was
to be used. The Judiciary Act of 1789 further held that the federal
government could issue the writ in cases of unlawful commitment, but
its scope was narrow and vague:

> Traditionally [habeas corpus] was used only for challenging the unlawful
> detention of a prisoner by executive officials—as when military authorities
> arrest and hold civilians when civil courts are in operation or law enforce-
> ment officials hold a captive without pressing charges or proceeding to a
> trial. Technically in its use involving state prisoners, a federal *habeas corpus*
> action is a proceeding ordering the jailer to bring the prisoner to court and
> to indicate the basis for detention. Its effect, however, is to allow a federal
> district judge to review state court proceedings to make sure that federal
> Constitutional norms have been followed (Goldman and Jahnige, 1985: 17).

The early nineteenth-century Supreme Court tended to follow the
common law principle that the writ was not available to those convicted
of a crime by a court of competent jurisdiction (Bator, 1963: 466), and
in one of the earliest federal prisoner habeas cases (*ex parte Taws*, Fed.
Case No. 13,768, 2 Wash. C.C. 353, 1809), the Court explicitly articulated its "hands-off" philosophy:

> We do not think it right to interfere with the jailer in the exercise of the

discretion vested in him, as to the security of prisoners; unless it appeared that he misused it for purposes of oppression, of which there is no evidence in this case.

Nineteenth-Century Evolution

Since the early nineteenth century, the debate over whether the Constitution was intended to provide the federal government with powers to review custody of state prisoners, or whether it was intended to grant relief to federal prisoners held by states, remained unresolved. The Court ruled in *ex parte Kearney* (20 U.S. (7 Wheat.), 1822) that, while it had the authority to issue the writ to any other court of the United States, it nonetheless possessed no appellate jurisdiction in criminal cases, and therefore a writ of habeas could not be considered a proper remedy by which to seek release from a conviction by a court of competent jurisdiction. The Court strengthened its "hands-off" position in *ex parte Watkins*, (28 U.S. (3 Pet.), 1830: 193), by ruling that a substantive error by a lower court is not sufficient to justify appellate review. The Court concluded that if no federal law were violated, it possessed neither Constitutional nor Congressional power to issue the writ:

> We have no power to examine the proceedings on a writ of error, and it would be strange, if, under color of a writ to liberate an individual from an unlawful imprisonment, the court could substantially reverse a judgment which the law has placed beyond its control; an imprisonment under a judgment cannot be unlawful, unless that judgment be an absolute nullity; and it is not a nullity, if the court has general jurisdiction of the subject, although it should be erroneous (*ex parte Watkins*, 28 U.S. (3 Pet.), 1830: 193).

Following the Civil War, the scope of federal jurisdiction began to expand. The Habeas Corpus Act of 1867 empowered the federal courts and judges acting within their respective jurisdictions to grant writs for persons restrained of liberty in violation of the Constitution or of law. The Act expanded the scope of the writ for federal prisoners, and also allowed lower federal courts to proceed in review of state prisoner petitions without the aid of the Supreme Court, and post-Civil War decisions indicated an increased willingness of federal review of state decisions. Although some observers have argued that these decisions did not necessarily reflect a softening and expansion of the concept of jurisdiction (c.f. Bator, 1963: 471), they nonetheless opened the door to prisoner challenges to both sentence and confinement.[2]

Despite the implied scope of federal powers in granting the writ, the Supreme Court did not review a state prisoner case under the Habeas Corpus Act until 1886 (*ex parte Royall*, 117 U.S. 241, 1885). Federal courts had long recognized their power to review state cases in advance of or during a state trial, but Royall challenged the constitutionality of a Virginia statute for a prisoner awaiting trial. The Court ruled that, lacking exceptional circumstances, it would be improper to assume jurisdiction until after state trial courts ruled on the issues. Thus was created the doctrine of "exhaustion of state remedies" requiring state prisoners to first pursue all state channels prior to appealing in federal courts. This doctrine continues to guide habeas and some civil rights litigation.

The exhaustion doctrine came to be applied with increasing rigidity, and the notion of federal court discretion to review habeas cases actually meant discretion of the Supreme Court, because lower court discretion in issuing habeas corpus writs tended to be reversed (Duker, 1980: 200), partly because of the changing role of the federal government:

> By gradually extending federal habeas to state prisoners Congress restruc-
> tured the concept of federalism. After the Reconstruction period, however,
> affections for strong federal government, symbolized by the Civil War,
> began to moderate. The issuance of habeas by lower federal courts to
> release state prisoners became a source of discontent. Congress, therefore,
> restored the Supreme Court's jurisdiction under the 1867 Habeas Act with
> the mandate that federal courts should respect state judicial systems.
> Accordingly, the Supreme Court responded with the exhaustion doctrine
> (Duker, 1980: 308.)

It should also be remembered, as Bator (1963: 473) reminds us, that throughout most of the nineteenth-century, federal criminal convictions were generally not appealable, thus reducing motivation and grounds for litigation. Some scholars have suggested that this produced a sense of uneasiness among some jurists in that it gave unreviewable power to a single trial judge. This may have contributed to the gradual "softening" of the concept of jurisdiction and to the expansion of the writ in the twentieth century.

Twentieth-Century Expansion

By 1915, federal courts generally held that any decision in a criminal case rendered by a court of competent jurisdiction was final, subject only to appeal, and not to redetermination on a writ of habeas corpus. Despite some exceptions (See *Powell v. Alabama,* 287 U.S. 45, 1932), this interpretation of federal habeas law did not change substantially until 1953, the beginning of the Warren Court. In a landmark case, *Brown v. Allen* (344 U.S. 443, 1953), the Court reviewed exclusion of blacks on juries, and expanded the scope of federal habeas review by deciding that federal courts may redetermine a Constitutional issue in state proceedings on case merits.

In 1963, three additional Supreme Court cases dramatically expanded the scope of the writ, firmly entrenching the right of state prisoners to pursue federal relief in complaints of unlawful detention. The first, *Fay v. Noia* (372 U.S. 391, 1963), granted prisoners the right to pursue in federal courts issues that were not previously raised in state courts, narrowed the requirements of the "exhaustion" doctrine, and laid firm claim to the power of federal courts to review state decisions. In writing for the majority, Justice Brennan observed:

> Although in form the Great Writ is simply a mode of procedure, its history is inextricably intertwined with the growth of fundamental rights of personal liberty. For its function has been to provide a prompt and efficacious remedy for whatever society deems to be intolerable restraints. Its root principle is that in a civilized society, government must always be accountable to the judiciary for a man's imprisonment: if the imprisonment cannot be shown to conform with the fundamental requirements of law, the individual is entitled to his immediate release. Thus there is nothing novel in the fact that today habeas corpus in the federal courts provides a mode of redress of denials of due process of law. Vindication of due process is precisely its historic office (Fay v. Noia, 372 U.S. 403, 1963: 829).

Brennan's rationale is noteworthy for several reasons. First, it explicitly recognized the common law nature of the writ as a substantive principle rather than simply a formal procedure to be decided by the letter of case law or federal legislation. This represented a shift from formal to substantive justice, in which the spirit of common law justified judicial intervention. Second, it explicitly defined the mandate of federal courts as a proper forum for redressing fundamental rights. The federal courts, especially the Supreme Court, became accepted as a legitimate arbiter between keepers and those who could provide strong rationale of unlawfully being kept. Finally, it created an explicit legal rationale for review of subsequent habeas complaints and an implicit legal rationale for other types of cases by expanding the types of cases properly brought before the Court.

This "softening" of the writ continued in two cases immediately following. In *Townsend v. Sain* (372 U.S. 293, 1963), the Court reviewed the admissibility of confessions, and ruled that in some situations, federal courts may conduct de novo evidentiary hearings in reviewing the constitutionality of a conviction. This provided a basis for reviewing fact-finding proceedings in state trials that were judged to be inadequate.[3] It was now clear that the writ could be used to challenge convictions even if the trial court acted properly, creating a new category of grounds for habeas litigation.

The final case in this trilogy was *Sanders v. U.S.* (373 U.S. 1, 1963), in which the court further expanded habeas review when it specified the basic rules allowing a prisoner to relitigate issues that were previously raised. This increased the opportunity for prisoners to challenge their convictions by making more liberal the criteria used in reviewing successive claims on the same conviction. This, too, created a new category of grounds on which habeas petitions could be filed.

Perhaps the most important prisoner habeas decision of this period was *Gideon v. Wainwright* (372 U.S. 335, 1963). Gideon, the plaintiff, was serving a sentence in Florida for breaking and entering into a pool room. Writing from his prison cell, he filed for a writ of habeas corpus, claiming that he was not represented by counsel at his state trial. This, he argued, violated Constitutional guarantees to representation by counsel. For 30 years, the nation's courts had operated on a principle established in *Betts v. Brady* (316 U.S. 455, 1942) that the concept of due process did not necessarily entitle state defendants to counsel in every noncapital case. The *Gideon* decision overturned *Betts* and established the right to counsel as fundamental and essential to fair trials, and must be protected. This decision was far-reaching because it provided both a model and the motivation for other state prisoners to petition for writs of habeas corpus in federal courts if they could identify violations of constitutionally protected rights.

By the end of 1963, the right of prisoners to pursue claims of wrongful confinement in federal courts was firmly established.[4] It was expected that an avalanche of petitions would follow in the coming decades and courts would be overwhelmed, but as we shall see in Chapter 5, these fears were exaggerated.

Concluding Observations

Contemporary habeas law in the United States has been shaped by a combination of factors, including the historical development of common law, Constitutional case law, and—what tends to be forgotten—by federal statutes defining the scope and domain of judicial action. The jurisdiction of current habeas actions is generally provided in 28 U.S.C. 2254, and federal courts have neither greatly expanded nor reduced these criteria in recent years.[5] Prisoners currently may challenge convictions when 1) the merits of the factual dispute are not resolved in a state court hearing, 2) the fact-finding procedures employed by state courts are not adequate to provide a fair hearing, 3) material facts are not adequately developed, 4) the state court lacks proper jurisdiction, 5) procedures are clearly unfair or improper, 6) the defendant has been not properly represented by counsel, 7) general due process was denied and 8) case facts are not fairly supported by the record. Further, habeas challenges may be brought to federal court only if state remedies have been exhausted, and only if explicit Constitutional issues are clearly identified that might have had a bearing on the original trial outcome.

Federal decisions in the last decade have generally held that even if errors occurred in the original trial, this is not a sufficient basis to grant a writ if it had no obvious bearing on the case's outcome. Further, prisoners cannot raise new issues in a federal habeas claim that they had opportunity to raise in the original trial, or that were raised and correctly resolved. Nor can prisoners raise noncourt errors or other technicalities that, even if obvious, are unrelated to the trial proceedings. Above all, prisoners cannot—contrary to the rhetoric of critics—relitigate a case simply because they did not like the outcome.

Some prisoners may abuse the filing privilege, but in general, courts quickly dismiss such cases, and they do not proceed into the system. There is no evidence that prisoners are particularly successful in obtaining release, and as Allen et al. (1982: 683) noted in a study of multiple jurisdictions, federal courts grant total or partial relief to only about 3 percent of the petitioners, of which outright release is rare. Relief, however, is a legal term, and can result even if previously objectionable practices are curtailed, whether by court order or not. Hence, even if one concedes that the "liberalization" of habeas review has led to an initial increase in the number of filings, it certainly has not opened the prison doors.

This section has argued that the history of the Great Writ has been one of a fluid process of transformation. To dismiss its use by prisoners on the grounds that "it was never intended to get crooks out of jail" is to ignore this history. The principle of habeas corpus—that no one shall be confined without good reason—has become stronger over the centuries, and prisoners have contributed by challenging procedures or policies that lead to or prolong imprisonment. Rather than impose an ideological predilection for a given interpretation of habeas law that may fit the public mood at a particular moment of history, it makes more sense to understand the emergence of the application of the writ as a long process that has functioned to protect one fundamental cornerstone of liberty.

THE EMERGENCE OF PRISONER CIVIL RIGHTS

Once rights are defined, they become translated into two abstract components, the first ethical, the second legal. As an *ethical* concept, rights refer to those inalienable liberties we are perceived to possess solely by nature of our humanity, and to which we are entitled regardless of law, political constraints, or even social norms. These have traditionally meant the rights of life, liberty, and the pursuit of happiness, all based on the ideal of fairness. As a legal concept, "civil rights" are whatever the law says they are, or whatever a plaintiff can convince a court they should be.

Obviously, these two components do not always coincide. Rights recognized by courts may not keep pace with public norms or values. Conversely, courts may go beyond conventional expectations by granting to prisoners more rights than seem necessary, as occurs when prisoners are released *en masse* because of overcrowding, inadequate conditions, or technicalities in criminal proceedings. The concept of human and civil rights has been expanded to protect a variety of previously unprotected categories, or what Meyers (1984) has cogently argued are more appropriately termed "oppressed groups." Convicted prisoners are one such group.

Prisoner Rights in Transition

Most reasonable persons agree that abhorrent treatment of prisoners is unacceptable. As Thomas Paine long ago observed:

> The law ought to impose no other penalties but such as are absolutely and evidently necessary: and no one ought to be punished, but in virtue of a law promulgated before the offense and legally applied (Paine, *Rights of Man*, 1974: 314).

But "abhorrent treatment" is contingent upon historically changing values, and what is accepted at one time may be considered reasonable at another. The contemporary conscience would be shocked by the treatment of prisoners in the mid-nineteenth-century:

> Perhaps the most incredible torture instrument of the period was the "water crib," in use at the Kansas prison. The inmate was placed in a coffin-like box, six and one-half feet long, thirty inches wide, and three feet deep, his face down and his hands handcuffed behind his back. A water hose was then turn on, slowly filling the crib. The effect was of slow drowning, with the inmate struggling to keep his head up above the rising water line. As one keeper boasted to an investigatory committee, the crib was marvelously efficient (Rothman, 1980: 20).

Such practices continued until recent years, as, for example, in Arkansas' Tucker facility:

> Physical brutality, gross medical neglect, the silence rules, racial discrimination, kangaroo courts for disciplinary matters, incredible tortures such as the Tucker telephone (a device used at the Tucker Reformatory in Arkansas where telephone wires were attached to the prisoners' genitals and an electric current was cranked through), hot boxes and dark cells (segregation cells with a solid door and no light), chain gangs, bread and water diets and worse, economic exploitation by the convict lease system and otherwise, rigid censorship of mail and reading matter, narrowly restricted visitation rights, along with meaningless and brutally hard work (Bronstein, 1979: 20).

Other recent policies judged flagrantly abusive have included the use of prisoners to physically control other prisoners (Marquart and Crouch, 1984; Marquart, 1986b), discretionary guard violence, deleterious conditions, and medical neglect. But consistent judicial judgment of such treatment as inhumane has come only in the past 20 years, and only after a long process of evolution beginning in the nineteenth-century.

Nineteenth-Century Roots

Prior to the middle of the twentieth-century, prisoners possessed few legal rights, and state prisoners rarely filed in federal courts. Between 1820 and 1866, the *Decentennial Digest* lists only seven prisoner cases addressing civil rights issues, which is not surprising considering that the concept had not yet emerged as a legal theory. The few nonprisoner civil rights cases that were filed before the civil war and those filed in the decades immediately following were generally challenges to racial restrictions, particularly in public accomodations and transportation. It was not until the legislation and amendments enacted immediately after the Civil War, especially 42 U.S.C. 1983, that civil rights became recognized as a general legal concept providing the basis for litigation.

Section 1983

Section 1983 was not originally intended to protect prisoner rights. It was originally enacted after the Civil War to protect freed slaves from potential civil rights abuses, and became known as the Klu Klux Klan Act. Although modified and renewed several times between 1866 and 1877, the relevant language of the Act today remains essentially unchanged:

> Every person who, under color of any statute, ordinance, regulation, custom, or usage, of any State or Territory, subjects, or causes to be subjected, any citizen of the United States or other person within the jurisdiction thereof to the deprivation of any rights, privileges, or immunities secured by the Constitution and laws, shall be liable to the party injured in an action at law, suit in equity, or other proper proceeding for redress.

Despite the post-Civil War legislation, prisoners rarely used state or federal courts to challenge their conditions of confinement. From the Civil War to the turn of the century, scarcely 20 prison-related civil rights suits were filed in federal courts, and about half of these involved use of jails to house prisoners, staff issues, and other complaints not directly related to prisoners' treatment. These suits were routinely dismissed on their merits or on jurisdictional grounds.

The Hands-Off Doctrine

As Alpert and Huff (1981: 309–10) have argued, the "hands-off doctrine" of judicial nonintervention in prison matters is attributable to the system of separation of state and federal powers, lack of judicial expertise and fear of undermining the authority of corrections' officials. The hands-off philosophy was articulated especially in the Virginia decision of *Ruffin v. Commonwealth* (21 (Gratt.) 790, 1871), which reinforced the legal theory that effectively stripped offenders of virtually all Constitutional protections. Woody Ruffin, convicted of murder, was tried and sentenced within the judicial jurisdiction of the prison, rather than where the offense occurred. Sentenced to death, he appealed his conviction, arguing that he was constitutionally guaranteed trial within the jurisdiction of the offense. The court ruled that convicts forfeit not only liberty, but all personal rights except those that the law "in its humanity accords them." The court rejected Ruffin's claim, ruling that "he is for the time being the slave of the state," suffering "civil death," and "his estate, if he has any, is administered like that of a dead man," which he soon became.

This decision is significant for two reasons. First, the ruling explicitly circumscribed the legal status of the prisoner as a legal subject, holding that prisoners had no rights. Second, and more importantly, the court explicitly accepted jurisdiction of the case, implying that superior courts possessed the *right* to hear prisoner petitions without necessarily granting rights to the petitioner. This decision clearly defined the subject status of prisoners, and was not significantly altered until the twentieth-century.

Twentieth-Century Development

After 1900, prisoner suits gradually increased, albeit slowly. Between 1930 and 1939, for example, more rights-related prisoner suits (27) were filed than in the entire nineteenth-century. Most of these (20) were for sentence reduction or review of goodtime policies. Nonetheless, Section 1983 was virtually forgotten by the turn of the 20th century, and prior to the civil rights movement of the 1960s, federal and state courts continued the *hands-off* policy. Although the Supreme Court recognized as early as 1910 that notions of "cruel and unusual punishment" are not rigid, but change as "public opinion becomes enlightened by humane justice" (*Weems v. U.S.*, 217 U.S. 349, 1910), courts rarely intervened in prisons' administration of punishment in the early decades.[6]

The Tide Turns (1930–1960)

The liberalism of the New Deal and the changing social and political attitudes helped to chip away some of the traditional unwillingness of judges to intervene on behalf of prisoners. By 1941, the Supreme Court recognized that some Constitutional protections followed prisoners into prison (*ex parte Hull*, 312 U. S. 546, 1941), a position more fully expanded in the 1960s and 1970s. The philosophy that the federal courts were the appropriate forum for the protection of rights was also occasionally acknowledged in nonprisoner opinions and contributed to the gradual erosion of the hands-off doctrine:

> We yet like to believe that wherever the Federal courts sit, human rights under the Federal Constitution are always a proper subject for adjudication, and that we have not the right to decline the exercise of that jurisdiction simply because the rights asserted may be adjudicated in some other forum (*Stapleton v. Mitchell*, 60 F.Supp 51: 55, 1945).

A variety of civil rights concepts, such as deprivation of rights "under color of law" and "cruel and unusual punishment," were periodically tested in nonprisoner cases, which gradually formed the later justification upon which prisoner cases were built.[7] These decisons did not guarantee protection, however. The Supreme Court, in *Tenney v. Brandove* (341 U.S. 367, 1951), weakened the scope of Section 1983 by offering limited immunity of state legislators and judges, and the "good faith" doctrine established in the early twentieth-century continued to protect state officials from responsibility for Constitutional violations.[8]

Other suits also continued to protect the discretion of prison administrators. Through 1951, most federal judges agreed with the decision in *Stroud v. Swope* (187 F.2d 820, 9th Cir., 1951), which explicitly rejected federal review of the discipline and treatment of prisoners. In 1953, a federal district court in Illinois ruled against a prisoner who alleged racially motivated policies in restricting free speech (*ex rel Morris v. Radio Station WENR*, 209 F.2d 105, 1953). The suit alleged that prison administrators systematically denied freedom of religious expression to incarcerated Black Muslims. Because the warden was not a *federal* official, the petition was judged not relevant, and the court concluded that prisoners cannot fight in court rules and policies to which they object. As late as 1964, a federal district court ruled that arbitrary isolation and deprivation of food and comfort were not unconstitutional, because prison administrators could do whatever they felt appropriate in running an institution (*Knight v. Ragen*, 337 F.2d 425, 1964). Even whipping as a form of disciplinary punishment was considered Constitutional as late as 1963 (*State v. Cannon*, 55 Del. 587, 1963), and corporal punishment was not rejected as "brutal and medieval" until 1968 (*Jackson v. Bishop*, 404 F.2d 571, 8th Cir., 1968). As recently as the early 1970s, some states still retained the "civil death" doctrine established in the nineteenth-century *Ruffin* case, until a federal court once and for all abolished the doctrine (*Delorme v. Pierce Freightlines*, 353 F.Supp 258, D. Or., 1973).

The official judicial policy remained "hands-off" until Eisenhower's Warren court (1953) demonstrated an explicit willingness to become an "engine of social reform" (Howard, 1980: 7). For nearly two decades, the activism of the Warren court redefined racial inequality and social conflict by enforcing the "one person one vote" principle, reshaped civil rights liability, and dramatically expanded the rights of criminal defendants. With the advent of civil rights struggles in the 1950s, both the state and federal judiciary become more attuned to the rights of minorities, and since the late 1960s, federal courts have more actively intervened on behalf of prisoners seeking relief from alleged Constitutional violations of prison policies and practices.

Post–1960s Decisions: A Watershed

The 1960s were remarkable for the expansion of prisoners' rights. Many of the changes stemmed from court decisions, but other social forces contributed as well (Alpert and Huff, 1981: 318–319).

Creeping Federalism

First was the growth of the federal government in providing its citizens with safeguards against abuses of power by government officials. The "New Frontier" and subsequent "Great Society" programs of the early 1960s reflected a shift toward the belief that the federal government, with sufficient will and resources, could resolve fundamental social problems. The subsequent "encroaching federalism" changed the relationship of the federal government to the states by weakening the jurisdiction of state courts and expanded the domain of the federal judiciary. This has led to increased intervention by the federal judiciary into state procedures in courts and corrections.

Legal Changes

Second, a series of federal court decisions have made prisoners more aware of their rights, given them motivation to pursue litigation and a method of redressing grievances and have removed many obstacles previously curtailing litigation. Since 1960, such precedent-setting cases as *Monroe v. Pape* 365 U. S. 167 (1961); *Cooper v. Pate* 382 F.2d 518 (1967); *Johnson v. Avery* 393 U.S. 483 (1969); *Wolff v. McDonnell* 418 U.S. 539 (1974); *Holt v. Sarver* 300 F.Supp 896 (D. N.J. 1976); *Bounds v. Smith* 430 U.S. 817 (1977); and *Ruiz v. Estelle* 650 F.2d 555 (5th Cir. (1981) recognized the status of prisoners as legal subjects, strengthened access to legal services, and brought policies and actions of prison staff under the purview of the federal courts. These typified the decisions that have reaffirmed and protected the rights of prisoners, thus ushering in the era of prisoner litigation.

The *Monroe* case was not actually a prisoner case, but arose out of a claim of police misconduct. *Monroe* resurrected Section 1983 when the Court characterized police conduct as a misuse of state power made possible only because the wrongdoer was clothed with the authority of state law. In ruling against Monroe, an Illinois federal court had earlier concluded that the officers' acts, although illegal, were not done "under color of law." The Illinois court argued that adequate state statutes existed under which to prosecute state violators, making federal litigation unnecessary. This decision, a vestige of the federalist-derived theory that state courts were relatively autonomous, was inconsistent with more recent nonprisoner decisions increasing the power and autonomy of federal courts, and Monroe successfully appealed to the Supreme Court. Writing the majority opinion, Justice Douglas identified three justifications for Section 1983: 1) to override discriminatory state laws, 2) to provide a federal remedy when existing state law was inadequate and 3) to provide a federal remedy where the state remedy was adequate but unavailable.

Cooper is usually perceived as the first actual prisoner suit (Irwin, 1980: 102; Jacobs, 1983: 36), and expanded both prisoners' access to courts and court willingness to review civil rights complaints. This decision involved a series of suits and appeals over nearly a decade challenging the right of prison administrators to deny religious expression to incarcerated Muslims. The Supreme Court explicitly affirmed the right of freedom of religion in prison, but more broadly, also reaffirmed the principles of judicial review of civil rights complaints. The decision explicitly expanded prisoners' legal status by affirming the right of freedom of religion in prison; but more broadly, it especially affirmed the principle of judicial review of prisoner rights and prison policy. This was a substantial prisoner victory, for it combined issues of racial discrimination with religious freedom and administrative discretion, providing several avenues by which prisoners could proceed with their complaints into federal courts. This and other cases, such as *Wright v. McMann* (387 F.2d 519 2d Cir., 1967), established federal courts as a forum for prisoner grievances over prison conditions by recognizing federal district court jurisdictions in Section 1983 prisoner cases.

In one of the most significant decisions of the 1970s, the Supreme Court held in *Bounds v. Smith* (430 U.S. 817, 1977) that a state must provide prisoners with "adequate" access to courts and legal facilities. Nonetheless, despite a series of decisions ostensibly making prisoner access to courts easier (see, e.g., Bronstein and Hirschkop, 1979, Jacobs, 1982; Palmer, 1985), such obstacles as repressive administrative policy, prisoner indigence, lack of legal resources, and lack of access to lawyers have made filing cases difficult.

Social Activism
A third factor contributing to the development of prisoner civil rights was the social activism of the 1960s and 1970s. In a period in which many groups were struggling to have their rights constitutionally protected, the concept of "civil rights" was expanded, and the logic by which the concept was applied extended to other groups. This contributed to the development of prisoner law in several ways.

First, it expanded social welfare programs, established, in principle, minimal acceptable standards of health and living conditions, and contributed to recognition that prisoners, too, should have basic needs met. The issue of "racisim," especially after passage of 1960s civil rights legislation, provided legal grounds on which to challenge discriminatory prison policies. As Jacobs (1983: 36–37) and Irwin (1980: 102–3) have argued, Black Muslims in New York and Illinois became a powerful force in expanding prisoner rights in the early 1960s.

Second, in 1971, expansion of civilian rights provided federal prisoners with a weapon for litigation in *Bivens v. Six Unknown Named Agents of the Federal Bureau of Narcotics* (403 U.S. 388, 1971). The Supreme Court ruled that even in the absence of statutory authorization, federal courts could review private actions brought against federal agents. This allowed federal prisoners, who do not have Section 1983 protections, a method to bring civil rights complaints against federal prison staff into court.

Student protests also contributed to the expansion of prisoners' rights. In one significant case, *Scheuer v. Rhodes* (416 U.S. 232, 1974), the Supreme Court altered the method by which states had previously dismissed cases challenging abuses "under color of law." The case resulted from civil rights suits filed after the Ohio National Guard fatally shot four students at Kent State University. States had previously been able to dismiss most civil rights suits against state officials on the basis of "good faith immunity." State defendants were previously able to avoid trials by claiming that as long as state officials acted in "good faith," the plaintiff was not entitled to relief. In *Scheuer,* however, the Supreme Court argued that "good faith" is a question of fact, and facts are to be decided by trial. One veteran Illinois state's attorney judged this decision to be the most crucial of all civil rights decisions, because it expanded prisoners' legal arsenal by weakening the state's ability to dismiss claims and liberalized the grounds for trials:

> So what they basically did is say that these cases have to start going to trial if good faith is going to be the defense. So after that, it became the law, and federal courts starting saying, "Hey, we're not going to grant you a motion to dismiss. Under Scheuer it says, "If it's a bench trial, the judge will do it, if it's a jury trial, the jury will decide." They will determine whether in addition to whether the guy is liable, or whether he's injured and this other stuff, they will determine whether you acted in good faith or not, because the Supreme Court now tells us this is a question of fact. Well, when that happened, the flood gates just opened up. We were being sued in bushel baskets, the suits were coming in. That, coupled with a couple of distinct elements of history in prison cases, the prison cases started coming in, and the courts, the liberal courts we'll call them, the Douglas court, the Warren Court was basically a liberal court, and letting a lot of things go. So consequently the federal court docket started opening up. . . . They put

real meaning to the—remember the old saying—why are you making a federal case out it? That came to be because federal courts only took significant and important cases. But when this trend in the sixties and seventies came, everything started going to them. I mean literally everything. Consequently, prisoners, as well, would look at the social ends of this spectrum, with nothing on their hands but time, they don't want to be where they're at to start with, so they're disgruntled in their setting, and what they see and read in the papers, "Wait, these federal courts are protecting our rights." So it's become a right to everything. A right to this, a right to that, so all this litigation starts coming into federal courts. Now we can't knock it out on motions any more, so we got all these cases going to trial[9] (State's attorney, interview, 1986).

Prison Changes
A fourth factor contributing to the expansion of prisoners' rights, and one that has received little attention, is the transformation of correctional models. The "big house" model of prisons lasting into the 1950s (Irwin, 1980) was replaced by other ideologically based models, but staff policies and prison structures lagged behind these changes. This contributed to litigation intended to bring the past in line with the present. The 1970s, especially, were a period of dramatic change in criminal justice practices and procedures. The actions of police, courts and prisons came under increasing public scrutiny. One response to this visibility was to alter the organizational goals and how various agencies defined their mandates and their "clients." Prisons moved to an organizational model based on "human management" and tighter bureaucratic operation (See Jacobs, 1977; Stastny and Tyrnauer, 1983), many of which could be challenged in court when violated. Suits challenged states' failure to implement these changes in such areas as rehabilitation, self-help and treatment programs, classification, transfer procedures, and health care. Further, changes in policies or management procedures often created new problems for which resolutions were slow in coming. For example, one irony of deemphasizing custodial control and increasing prisoner freedom was an escalation of violence, for which prisoners then petitioned the courts for relief (Jacobs, 1977; Marquart and Crouch, 1985; Ekland-Olson, 1986).

Prison Composition
Fifth, prisoners themselves have become more savvy in recognizing their rights and in their ability to protect them. Jailhouse lawyers particularly have helped their peers challenge, or have themselves challenged, a variety of prison conditions perceived as substandard. Typical prisoner cases in the late 1960s and early 1970s alleged violations of freedom of speech, religion, or access to law (Bronstein and Hirschkop, 1979; Palmer, 1985; Practising Law Institute, 1972). Challenges ranged from class actions against entire prison systems to suits against specific

policies and abusive officials.[10] Using available legal resources and encouraged by some successes, prisoners have become unwilling to passively accept what they perceive to be violations against their dignity.
Prisoners became better educated, more aware of rights and the resources available to protect themselves, and generally more savvy to the
political and bureaucratic procedures by which prison reform might
occur.

Legal Changes

Finally, the 1960s marked the beginning of considerable civil rights
legislation. In the past 20 years, antidiscrimination laws provided a
means to resist unfair practices in housing, employment, education, and
transportation. In 1980, the "Civil Rights of Institutionalized Persons
Act" was passed authorizing the Attorney General to intervene when
state practices were judged to violate "any rights, privileges, or immunities secured or protected by the Constitution or laws of the United
States" (42 U.S.C. 1997). Since the late 1970s, many states revised their
criminal codes, including provisions guiding correctional policies, to
reflect the general ethos of civil rights that had emerged since the 1960s.
Although the letter of the legislation fares better than its implementation, these laws nonetheless reflected an attempt to establish basic
institutional guidelines, and provided the basis for evaluating the merits
of prisoner complaints.

These are but a few of the forces that have contributed to the
emergence of civil rights legislation. Others include the more liberal
interpretation of rights and their method of protection by the courts,
the emergence of outside prisoner support groups and reform agencies,
the growth of prison law libraries and other legal resources, and societal
recognition that prisoners will ultimately return to society angrier and
more "debilitated" than when they entered unless conditions are at least
minimally habitable. All of this suggests that prisoners' civil rights are
not simply the consequence of "soft on crime" attitudes, permissiveness,
or what Ronald Reagan has labelled "sociology majors on the bench"
(Reagan, cited in Curry, 1986: 2), but a phase in broader societal
changes that both affect and are affected by prisoners' struggle for
rights.

Some Observations on Civil Rights

Will the rights of prisoners continue to expand, or has retrenchment
set in? Attorney General Edwin Meese (1986) typifies the federal assault
against civil rights, and his contention that Supreme Court decisions
may not be the "law of the land" to be obeyed by state officials indicates
that rights may be lost as well as won. In addition, several cases in the
past few years appear to have curtailed prisoners' rights. Unsuccessful

prisoner challenges to substandard conditions, for example, have provided prison systems with considerable discretion and a capacity to resist reform (See *Hutto v. Finney,* 437 U.S. 678, 1978; *Bell v. Wollfish,* 441 U.S. 520, 1979; *Rhodes v. Chapman,* 452 U.S. 337, 1981; *Madyun v. Thompson,* 657 F.2d 868, 1981; *Parratt v. Taylor,* 451 U.S. 527, 1981; *Davidson v. Cannon,* 752 F.2d 817, 1984). Nonetheless, despite setbacks, prisoners' rights seem irrevocably ensconced, and the courts have imposed no substantial new limitations on the substantive and procedural Constitutional claims that prisoners may bring (DeWolfe, 1986: 1093). The number has not decreased, and judges do not seem less willing to review petitions, especially those addressing abuse of power or prison violence (Suchner et al. 1986). On the other hand, rights have been eroded in more subtle ways. Prison staff also retain considerable discretion to simply ignore the law, or to obey the letter while violating the spirit (Thomas, Aylward, Mika, and Blakemore, 1985). For example, consent decrees, the process by which suits are settled with an agreement by prisoners to modify conditions, may be more easily modified because of easing of the conditions (DeWolfe, 1986), thus allowing prison administrators to delay or avoid reform. Further, a "hands-off" doctine may have emerged under a new guise:

> Courts do not deny jurisdiction or claim that the Constitution does not apply to prisoners, they simply accept conclusions, allegations, and predictions made by prison officials as better evidence than any amount of facts, law, expert testimony, or common sense mustered by prisoners (Irwin, 1980: 104–5).

Whether Section 1983 will continue to provide prisoners with a powerful legal weapon to challenge prison conditions remains uncertain. Some have argued that the statute has been eroded in recent years, or, at best, has been only marginally effective (Caracappa, 1976; Irwin, 1970; Jacobs, 1983; Mandel, 1986). Others remain more optimistic (Dick, 1977; Mika and Thomas, 1987; Thomas, 1984a). This uncertainty of the future of prisoners' civil rights rests mainly on which of two competing visions of Section 1983 will prevail.[11] The first is *historical,* and would limit its application to race relations as specified by the original nineteenth-century legislation. The second is *functional,* and would expand it to a civil mechanism for vindicating all Constitutional rights (Eisenberg, 1982: 483). Both views have some merit: adherents of the historical view correctly cite the statute's original intent and limited language, while adherents of the functional view cite the ambiguity of the statute's wording and its implied intent as a means of preserving the spirit of Constitutional protections.

Whatever the future direction of court response to prisoners' complaints, two conclusions are certain. First, prisoners will continue to resist conditions against which they object, as evidenced by the continued increase in civil rights litigation. Second, because law is a process, changes in the use of current legal theories or statutes do not necessarily reflect losses for civil rights advocates. Prison conditions have been improved, public sensitivities have been challenged and the structure of corrections has been modified. Civil rights and habeas corpus law have been partially responsible. But it must also be recognized that as the goals and philosophies of corrections change, the nature of prisons and prisoners change as well, and these changes create new problems requiring attention. Hence, reforms over the short run may not be appropriate for these new conditions, and it is easy to interpret new prison problems and staff responses to these problems as proof that "law doesn't work."

SUMMARY

Whatever the contributions of any set of factors in expanding rights, it is clear that this expansion cannot be explained simply by the increased number of enlightened individuals thinking nice thoughts (moral idealism), or by some immutable evolutionary development of a progressive society bringing social practices into line with social ideals (philosophical idealism). Rights have emerged steadily and gradually, sometimes the result of ironic legal struggles, such as the role of corporations in expanding Fourteenth Amendment rights, other times the consequence of direct action by oppressed groups.

The liberalization of the right to request a habeas writ began in the nineteenth century and gradually increased. Judicial willingness to review habeas claims ebbed and waned, was shaped by social and political influences, and generally has corresponded to changes in broader social views of legal rights, especially the rights of accused persons. The growth of prisoners' civil rights, grounded in post-Civil War legislation, emerged far more slowly, but expanded dramatically in the 1960s, impelled largely by social attitudes toward rights in general and the efforts of prisoners to translate these attitudes into legal action. Despite the confluence of the liberalization of both legal theories in the past twenty five years, their divergent roots and their different uses have led to different filing trends. To these trends we next turn.

NOTES

1. For useful histories of habeas corpus, see especially Allen et al. (1982); Bator (1963); Bator et al. (1973); Barrett and Cohen (1985); Duker (1980); Reed (1980); Shapiro (1980); and Sharpe (1976). For an overview of issues

in civil rights case law, see particularly Antieau, 1980; Bronstein (1979); Eisenberg (1982); Eisenberg and Yeazell, 1980; Palmer (1985); Robbins (1980, 1986); and Turner (1979).

2. For example, *ex parte Lange* (85 U.S. (18 Wall.) 163, 1873) was the first significant use of the writ to reexamine a lower-court sentencing decision.

3. Ironically, the lawyer actively pursuing prisoners' rights in the *Townsend* case was later appointed to the federal bench and has been considered a leading opponent of prisoners' rights by inmates, especially in habeas cases. His record in reviewing prisoner cases confirms this reputation.

4. For a discussion of the impact of habeas decisions in the 1970s, see especially Reed (1980).

5. Federal prisoners have two alternatives in requesting federal review of their detention. The first is 28 U.S.C. 2241, and is the contemporary codification of the 1789 Judiciary Act. 28 U.S.C. 2255 is the federal equivalent of 28 U.S.C. 2254 for state prisoners.

6. Perhaps the first landmark case mandating federal review of "cruel and unusual punishment" was *Logan v. U.S.* (144 U.S. 263, 1892), in which the Supreme Court held that federal prisoners must be afforded protection against lawless violence.

7. Some notable examples include *Screws v. U.S.* (325 U.S. 91, 1945), in which Justice Douglas, writing for the majority, elaborated the concept of "willful intent" in determining whether a state official deprived a citizen of rights. *Trop v. Dulles* (356 U.S. 86, 1958) clarified the changing concept of "cruel and unusual punishment" in ruling that a native-born citizen cannot be stripped of U.S. citizenship as punishment. *U.S. v. Price* (383 U.S. 787, 1966), further strengthened the "under color of law" concept by ruling that it is inappropriate for a sheriff to murder civil rights workers. Although dramatic, these cases typify how various concepts gradually expanded in the decades following World War II.

8. See, in particular, *Moyer v. Peabody* (212 U.S. 78, 1909) and *ex parte Young* (209 U.S. 123, 1908). For an excellent discussion of the problems *Tenney* created for Section 1983, see Eisenberg (1982).

9. Litigation did *not* increase abnormally after the Scheuer decision nationally or in Illinois. In Illinois, in fact, civil rights filings dipped from 268 in 1974 to 193 in 1975. Civil rights litigation by federal prisons did continue to increase after the *Scheuer* decision, but this increase began in 1970. Nonprisoner civil rights cases, however, increased (from 620 in 1972 to 883 in 1973 and 1,139 in 1974). Hence, the decision did not generate "bushel baskets" of prisoner suits, and illustrates how hyperbole becomes accepted as "official fact"

10. Examples of cases challenging entire prison systems include *Pugh v. Locke* (406 F.Supp 318, M.D. Ala, 1976) and *Ruiz v. Estelle* (650 F.2d 555, 5th Cir., 1981). Challenges to specific prisons include *Holt v. Sarver* (309 F.Supp 362, E.D. Ark., 1970) and *Duran v. Elrod* (No. 74–C–2949, N.D. Ill., 1974). For an example of staff resistance to litigation and abuse of power, see *Lamar V. Steele* (693 F.2d 559, 5th Cir., 1982).

11. For an excellent discussion of the nature and legal logic underlying this debate, see Eisenberg (1982).

5

Habeas Corpus and Civil Rights: Some Filing Distinctions

Prisoners suits are prisoner suits, clear and simple! (Conference critic)

JUST AS HABEAS CORPUS AND CIVIL RIGHTS SUITS have different histories, so too do each exhibit different filing patterns. One way to clarify the meaning of prisoner litigation is to identify the separate filing patterns of the two basic legal theories under which they are filed. These patterns, however, must be examined at both the national level and within individual states. Aggregating filing trends at the national level tells us little about the variations among states, some of which have significantly increased, some have greatly declined, and still others have remained stable.

Failure to separate habeas and civil rights filings contributes to inaccurate generalizations about the extent and nature of each type.[1] Cavalier use and uncritical acceptance of "common-sense" perceptions distorts and inflates the picture of prisoner filings. By comparing federal prisoner filings with those of state prisoners, and by distinguishing between the filing patterns of civil rights and habeas suits, the diversity of prisoners' litigation becomes clearer.

This chapter compares shifts in the filing trends of federal and state prisoner habeas and civil rights filings to display the variations between federal and state jurisdictions, and then examines prisoner suits filed in Illinois to identify the nature of complaints.[2] Despite the numeric overload encountered here, we must nonetheless pause long enough to bring filing differences into sharper focus.

TRENDS IN HABEAS CORPUS LITIGATION

The differences between state and federal prisoners and between state prisoners in individual states reveal a complex pattern that defies simple explanation.[3] But first, we must separate the filings of federal from state prisoners.

Federal Prisoner Filings

The pattern of federal prisoners' habeas filings differs considerably from those of state prisoners. Using three basic indicators of number of filings, rate of filings per prisoner, and percentage of habeas to nonhabeas filings, several patterns emerge from Table 5a.

First, there was no spate of federal prisoner habeas filings immediately following the 1963 Supreme Court trilogy; filings remained fairly stable from 1960 through 1968, increasing by only 18 percent. By 1969, the number of federal habeas filings began to increase more rapidly, and by 1985 exceeded 3,400. However, the rise in 1985, an apparent quantum leap over previous years, is misleading. Filings in Georgia's Northern District increased from 19 in 1984 to 1,811 in 1985 because of habeas petitions by incarcerated Cuban refugees.[4]

Second, despite modest fluctuations of annual filings since 1970, the general trend has been one of stability, averaging about 1,626 (excluding Georgia's Northern District in 1985), and the volume of habeas suits has consistently reflected periodic cycles rising and falling around this average. This suggests relative stasis in the number of habeas suits filed, and further indicates that there has been no rush of federal prisoners to the courts to seek release.

Third, and more significant than the relative stability of the number of habeas filings, is the decrease in the rate of habeas filings per federal prisoner. As Table 5a shows, between 1960 and 1971, the filings-to-prisoner proportion doubled from roughly 4 per 100 prisoners to about 8 between 1970 and 1971. This proportion began decreasing in 1972, and despite modest fluctuations, the decline continues. When the anomalous filings from Georgia's Northern District are excluded for 1985, filings dipped to 4.3 per 100 prisoners, and in 1986, further decreased to 3.8, the lowest proportion since 1963. It is clear, then, that habeas filings have not kept pace with the increase in the federal prison population. The federal prisoner population increased by 82 percent between 1980 and 1986, while the number of habeas filings increased by only 18 percent. This indicates that the relative frequency of federal prisoners using the writ to secure release is declining, and that habeas has not increasingly become viewed as a "front door key."

Another indicator of the prevalence of habeas filings is their proportion to all federal prisoner filings. This provides a picture of the general grievances that prisoners feel are sufficiently troublesome to attack in federal court. Despite fluctuations, this proportion, too, has remained fairly stable. Between 1960 and 1963, habeas filings annually constituted over half of all federal prisoner filings. Since 1964, however, they have ranged between 29 and 45 percent. If prisoners were responding to the "judicial liberalism" perceived to dominate post–1960s decisions, then this proportion should show a consistent increase rather than sporadic fluctuations. However, it has not, suggesting that so-called "liberalism in the courts" has not prompted federal prisoners to turn to the federal bench for release.

State Prisoner Habeas Filings

Habeas filings by state prisoners differ dramatically from those by federal prisoners.[5] This occurs in part because the confinement situations are dissimilar and also because filing procedures vary. State prisoners have more flexibility in the grounds that may be used in applying for a writ of habeas corpus. For example, motions to vacate sentence, challenges to parole denial, or requests for recalculation of goodtime credit or sentence length are categorized separately for federal prisoners, but are often brought as habeas actions by state inmates. Alleged staff misconduct that precipitated discipline resulting in goodtime loss may also be filed as a request for a writ of habeas corpus. Further, state prisoners on occasion incorrectly file on habeas grounds petitions more properly brought under civil rights action. Although these are quickly dismissed, they are nonetheless counted as, and thus inflate, the category of "habeas filings." This flexibility does not offer state prisoners greater advantage (or disadvantange); it is merely a different process of litigation.

It is often believed that most state prisoner suits reflect nothing more than attempts to seek release, and, as a consequence, most suits must necessarily be habeas-related. If this is true, we would expect most prisoner filings to be habeas filings. Such is not the case. The general pattern of the number of state prisoner habeas filings reflects three broad trends. First, the 1960s were marked by a dramatic increase. Following the 1963 Supreme Court trilogy, filings increased dramatically, by 75 percent in 1964 and 31 percent in 1965. By 1970, filings had increased nearly four-fold over 1963. It is tempting to interpret this as a consequence of the trilogy's liberalization of habeas law, but the trend actually had begun several years earlier, suggesting that the trilogy contributed to, rather than "caused," increased filings.

The second trend, characterizing the 1970s, was one of stability tending toward decline. Annual filings averaged about 7,500 over that decade, ranging from a high of 8,372 in 1971 to a low of 6,866 in 1977, and between 1971 and 1980, filings actually decreased by 16 percent. The trend of the 1980s, by contrast, appears to be one of slow increase, but has averaged less than 3 percent each year from 1981 to 1986.

Despite the shifting trends in the number of filings, the trend in the proportion of habeas to civil rights suits has been one of consistent decline. Table 5b shows that since 1965, when habeas complaints comprised 91 percent of all state prisoner suits, the proportion has steadily

Table 5a   Habeas-only cases filed by federal prisoners,
           1960-86 (number, as percent of all federal prisoner
           filings, and as percent of all U.S. filings)

Year	Habeas-only	Filings/100 Prisoners	As % of All Federal Prisoner Filings
1960	886	3.82	67.89
1961	868	3.66	54.63
1962	866	3.62	57.89
1963	862	3.73	52.88
1964	882	4.06	42.04
1965	974	4.63	38.06
1966	1017	5.28	44.37
1967	1045	5.34	39.60
1968	1045	5.30	36.65
1969	1373	7.00	38.01
1970	1600	7.98	38.23
1971	1671	7.98	40.55
1972	1368	6.30	32.74
1973	1294	5.67	28.53
1974	1718	7.68	34.45
1975	1682	6.97	33.33
1976	1421	4.88	29.73
1977	1508	4.70	32.15
1978	1730	5.80	34.91
1979	1577	5.98	35.05
1980	1413	5.80	38.06
1981	1629	5.79	39.69
1982	1927	6.49	44.52
1983	1914	6.00	43.96
1984	1905	5.56	42.09
1985(a)	3405	9.04	54.38
1985(b)	1619	4.30	36.00
1986	1673	3.77	37.70

Source: Administrative Office of the U.S. Courts.

(a) Includes Georgia's Northern District
(b) Excludes Georgia's Northern District

dropped, and since 1981, habeas suits have constituted less than one third of prisoners' court activity.

Although the *number* of state prisoner habeas filings exhibits a generally increasing trend, the *proportion* of state prisoners filing such suits does not. Only in the 1960s did the increase in the proportion of suits to prisoners roughly match the increase in the number of filings, but both the number of habeas filings and the proportion of prisoners filing them peaked in 1970. Since 1971, fewer prisoners have been filing habeas claims, declining from about 5 suits for 100 prisoners in 1970 to less than 2 since 1984. Hence, the increase in the number of filings may reflect little more than the increase in the prison population. This suggests that most prisoners—contrary to the claims of critics—accept the finality of their confinement, because very few prisoners challenge their conviction after incarceration.

State Variations

One major problem with conventional discussions of prisoner litigation is the tendency to focus on national trends and ignore differences between various states.[6] For example, the heavily abnormal 1985 federal prisoner filings from Georgia's Northern District, which generated more than half of all habeas suits that year, illustrate how federal prisoner filings in a single jurisdiction can dramatically distort images of the litigation landscape when viewed from a nationally aggregated perspective. Some explanations of prisoner litigation, such as the hyperlexis view, do not take into consideration these often dramatic filing variations between states. This failure ignores the problems specific to particular prison or court systems by assuming a constancy in filing patterns between states that does not exist. Some states may have special problems in processing criminals, which inflate the national average. Others may have a lower prison population, and hence, fewer suits. Breaking down filings by individual states also provides a convenient way to take individual state prison population into account, because states with high prison populations have a disproportionately greater number of prisoners litigating.

Number of Filings

The average number of habeas filings for the 50 states and District of Columbia in 1970, 1975, 1980, and 1986 was 177, 154, 140, and 181 respectively. These averages are misleading, however, because of the filing disparity between states. In 1970, for example, the six most litigious states accounted for over half (52 percent) of all habeas filings. By 1986, state variations had decreased, and the six most litigious states accounted for only 35 percent of the nation's habeas filings (see Appendix 1 for individual state variations). In 1970, a dozen states, invariably

Table 5b   Habeas filings by state prisoners, 1960–86

Year	State Habeas Filings	As % of All Prisoners'	Filings/100 Prisoners
1960	871	99.89	.46
1961	1020	100.00	.52
1962	1408	96.97	.72
1963	2106	80.26	1.08
1964	3694	89.18	1.92
1965	4845	90.92	2.55
1966	5339	85.45	2.96
1967	6201	79.46	3.54
1968	6488	78.16	3.86
1969	7359	79.03	4.17
1970	9063	76.73	5.14
1971	8372	68.93	4.73
1972	7949	65.76	4.56
1973	7784	61.37	4.29
1974	7626	56.81	3.89
1975	7843	55.00	3.62
1976	7833	52.12	3.32
1977	6866	46.25	2.56
1978	7033	41.45	2.53
1979	7123	38.50	2.48
1980	7031	35.92	2.30
1981	7790	33.00	2.34
1982	8059	32.27	2.14
1983	8532	32.29	2.10
1984	8349	31.41	1.94
1985	8534	31.37	1.76
1986	9045	30.80	1.87

Source: Administrative Office of the U.S. Courts.

those with small prisoner populations, filed fewer than 25 suits each. By contrast, California prisoners in 1970 filed more habeas petitions than the lowest 30 states combined. By 1986, however, habeas filings in heavily litigious states had decreased dramatically over the previous fifteen years, and in states with fewer prisoners, filings tended to rise, but not dramatically. The general interstate pattern, then, has been one of decline in the number of habeas filings in litigious states and an increase in litigiousness in previously quiescent ones, and the extremes between the states have gradually lessened.

Prisoner and Civilian Litigation

Appendix 1 also shows that in nearly all states, habeas filings have also declined as a percentage of all federal filings. In 1970, state habeas filings accounted for 14.5 percent of all private litigation, declining to 9.2 percent in 1975, 6.9 percent in 1980, and 5.5 percent by 1986. Here, too, there has been considerable state variation, but the trend is gravitating toward the national mean. In Washington D.C. and Minnesota, habeas filings in 1970 constituted less than 3 percent of each state's U.S. filings. By contrast, prisoners accounted for 31.3 percent of California's U.S. filings, but dropped dramatically over the next two decades. By 1986, California's proportion (4.9 percent) was among the lowest in the country.

In only ten states did the proportion of prisoner habeas to all filings either increase between 1970 and 1986 (Alaska, Delaware, Hawaii, Idaho, Louisiana, New Hampshire, North Dakota) or remain about the same (Alabama, Indiana, Washington). Even in states evidencing an increase, the change was not dramatic, and with the exception of Indiana, those states with increased habeas filings had among the fewest prisoners (and prisoner filings), and a slight change in the numbers thus created a misleading shift in the percentage. By 1986, in only three states did prisoner habeas filings exceed 10 percent of all federal filings (Alabama, Arizona, North Carolina), compared with 19 states in 1975 and 35 in 1970. This suggests that not only have prisoner habeas filings stabilized in proportion to all litigation, but also that in no states do prisoners currently crowd out civilian cases with increasing attempts to seek release.

Civil Rights and Habeas Suits

Another useful indicator of the shifts in filing patterns is the proportion of habeas to all prisoner filings. In most states, habeas suits have decreased dramatically relative to other types of prisoner complaints. In 1970, habeas petitions comprised about 77 percent of all state prisoner actions in federal courts. This dropped to 55 percent in 1975, 38 percent in 1980, and 31 percent in 1986. In 1970, state habeas filings comprised over half of all prisoner filings in all but five states (and two of those,

Hawaii and North Dakota had no habeas filings). Habeas filings comprised over 75 percent of prisoner suits in 33 states, and over 90 percent in 11 states. By 1975, habeas litigation still comprised over half of all prisoner litigation in 34 states. In California, habeas suits accounted for three-quarters of all prisoner petitions, and in 10 states, habeas filings constituted over two-thirds of all prisoner petitions.

By 1980, the shift was clearly discernable, and in only 10 states did habeas cases exceed 50 percent of all prisoner filings. By 1986, most states approximated the national mean of about 32 percent, and in only one state (North Dakota) did filings exceed 50 percent of all prisoner filings. In only seven other states did it constitute 40 percent or more. (Alaska, California, Hawaii, Maine, Montana, New Hampshire, and South Carolina). These states, excepting California, also had among the lowest prisoner population and fewest number of habeas filings. This tells us that, nationwide, "let me out" pleas continue to decrease relative to other complaints.

Proportion of Prisoners Filing

Because states with large prison populations obviously have more prisoners litigating, one way of examining state differences is by comparing prisoner litigation as a proportion of the prison population. This displays filing trends as a function of the increase in size of prison population, rather than as an abstract figure unaffected by other social factors. Per prisoner ratios should be interpreted with some caution, however, since not all suits classified as "prisoner petitions" are filed by persons in prison. Further, some prisoners may file numerous suits, thus providing a somewhat misleading picture of how many prisoners actually sue. Nonetheless, despite the possibility of multiple filings by prisoners, per prisoner filing rates indicate at least the "worst case" limit (or ceiling) of how many prisoners actually sue, since, obviously, the number of prisoners litigating cannot exceed the number of suits filed.

Appendix 1 reveals that, between 1970 and 1986, in only ten states did litigation increase (Hawaii, Idaho, Iowa, North Dakota) or remain the same (Delaware, Indiana, Minnesota, Mississippi, Nebraska, Washington). Further, in 1970, only 9 states had filing ratios as low as 2 filings per 100 prisoners, and 21 had filing ratios of over 5 suits per 100 prisoners. By 1975, this shrank to 16 and 11, and by 1980 to 23 and 3 respectively. In 1986, 27 states had habeas filing rates below 2 per 100 prisoners, while only four states (Montana, New Hampshire, Tennessee, and West Virginia) had rates in excess of four filings per 100 prisoners.

The trend is obvious: In nearly all states, fewer prisoners are using the writ of habeas corpus as a means of release, and the percentage of prisoners filing habeas petitions has decreased quite remarkably: If less than two prisoners per 100 seek relief through the courts, then over 98 prisoners per 100 do not. Thus the claim that habeas litigation has impelled prisoners to avoid the finality of their conviction is simply wrong: most prisoners do not sue.

Preliminary Interpretations

What can we infer from this discussion of state variations? First, despite the ebb and flow of habeas filings, state prisoners' habeas suits are declining when compared with other key indicators. It also appears that federal and state prisoners may file for quite different reasons, with federal prisoners petitioning for release at a considerably greater rate than state prisoners. It may be that, because federal prisoners generally spend considerably less time incarcerated than state prisoners (16 and 26 months respectively, Camp and Camp, 1985b: 10–11), they lack the motivation required for a long-term challenge to prison conditions, focusing instead upon release. The judicial factors of knowledge and homogeneity may also have played a role in reducing federal prisoner habeas suits: Federal judges are more likely than their state siblings to know and follow Constitutional procedures, and the procedural rule-following in federal courts is likely to be more uniform than between the numerous state jurisdictions.

Second, however one interprets the actual number of filings, it is clear that there has been no "flood" of requests for habeas writs by state prisoners in the past fifteen years. Despite the increase in the number of prisoners, the number of habeas petitions has diminished. The trend suggests that proportionally fewer prisoners are filing fewer habeas suits. It would appear, then, that expanding litigation does not reflect a "disrespect for law" by cynically petitioning for release, but rather a respect for law by recognizing its potential in nonviolent grievance resolution, an issue addressed in Chapter 9.

Third, despite a strong leveling trend, there remain significant filing variations between states. This suggests that caution be exercised when interpreting "prisoner litigation" as if it encompassed a single population or identical causes and motivations for filing. The differences among practices of criminal procedures and prison administrators must also be taken into account in assessing prisoner's use of courts to resolve problems.

Prisoner Habeas Corpus Litigation in Illinois

To examine the habeas filings more fully, Illinois' Northern District has been chosen to illustrate the specific complaints that impel prisoners to sue. The data show that prisoners do tend to complain of original-case errors more than other problems, but that there are a variety of grievances unrelated to the original case for which relief is sought.

In many ways, the Illinois prison system typifies many of the nation's prisons, and therefore provides a useful exemplar; it has a rapidly expanding prison population, increasing annually by over 10 percent; its maximum security prisons are old, three of which date to the 19th century, and one from the early 1920s; the ethnic composition of prisoners is a mix of black (about 61 percent), white (32 percent), and Hispanic (7 percent), but these figures are misleading in that they are not representative of any single prison.[7] Illinois prisoners are also among the most litigious in the country, and the state annually ranks among the top 10 in both civil rights and habeas filings.[8]

Twenty-nine percent of both civil rights and habeas petitions listed multiple complaints, but only the primary complaint is used in this analysis.[9]

There is a general belief among critics of prisoner litigation that identification of a prisoner's specific grievance is difficult, because they tend to be poorly written, logically confused, and rambling. It is true that few petitions will win a Pulitzer for style (if not for fiction), but it is categorically untrue that complaints are difficult to ascertain. A prisoner may complain of being denied adequate counsel because "my attorney is a bigoted racist misanthrope." Despite such hyperbole, the complaint is clearly one of incompetent counsel, and is so classified. The primary problem in classifying petitions is not one of deciphering the prisoner's complaint, but rather determining the analytic purpose of classification and constructing useful categories. Further, the utility of legal defini-tions and social definitions may not coincide; it may be that the legal theory justifying adjudication of a suit is unclear, but when prisoners feel they should be released because of capricious parole-board deci-sions, for example, the substantive issue is obvious. A case in which an inmate sued his mother for improperly rearing him, so that he became a criminal, would be classified as a "private civil suit," even though it is obviously frivolous. More common are complaints of unfair sentencing, parole revocation without hearing, or incompetent counsel. These are quickly and easily classified without ambiguity.

Despite a myriad of substantive complaints, petitions can generally be reduced to several basic categories.

The first is *violence,* which alleges physical assault by police, prison officials, or other prisoners. This category is generally a civil rights complaint, and only two habeas petitions (both immediately dismissed) were filed between 1980 and 1986.

A second major category is *internal prison policies.* Complaints in this category challenge policies or practices over which a particular prison's staff has direct control. Examples include unconstitutional disciplinary procedures that may result in loss of good time, or allegedly inaccurate staff reports to the parole-board that may result in denial of parole.

Third are complaints of *external policies* over which a prison has no control. Examples include legislative revisions of the criminal codes, which exclude some categories of prisoners from receiving possible release benefits of sentence recalculation, departmental policies employed for calculating goodtime, or state parole revocation procedures.

Fourth are complaints about *prison conditions.* These are generally civil rights actions, and are rarely appropriate for habeas litigation.

The fifth category, *Bill of Rights,* typically raises explicit Fourth or Eighth Amendment issues, such as privacy, cruel and unusual punishment, or Fourteenth Amendment claims of violation of due process in deprivation of liberty or property. This category differs from "original case" complaints in that suits challenge the constitutionality of an entire class of practices (such as exclusion of blacks from juries) rather than discrete practices affecting a single prisoner.

Sixth, complaints arising from alleged procedural violations in the original case, typically challenge conviction proceedings or sentencing. These are *original case* challenges, and are of the kind generally criticized when claiming that prisoners are unhappy with a trial's outcome and seek to retry the case.

A final category, and one not examined here, is *civil suits,* in which inmates seek relief unrelated to their status as prisoners. Typical defendants in this category include former wives, landlords, or employers.

Table 5c shows that the most common grounds on which prisoners seek habeas relief are original case proceedings, and from 1980 to 1986, these cases accounted for 64 percent of all habeas cases filed, ranging from a low of 56 percent in 1982 to a high of 73 percent in 1983. Typical trial complaints included evidentiary procedures and illegal search and seizure, constituting 42 percent of all habeas filings in the District, and 64.7 percent of this category. Less-common complaints included sentencing and arrest procedures.

The second most common complaint arising from the original case is legal malpractice—incompetence of counsel—which accounts for about 9 percent of all habeas claims. Challenges to sentence length or sentencing procedure constitutes the next highest "original case" suit (4 percent), followed by bond issues (2.9 percent), and arrest complaints (2.7 percent). Despite claims by conservatives that landmark decisions such as Miranda are responsible for "turning crooks loose," only 13 prisoners challenged their cases on the basis of Miranda (and all were immediately dismissed). Although most Miranda-based actions arise prior to conviction, these data do indicate that once convicted, such decisions—in this District, at least—have virtually no impact on release.

The next, most common grounds for habeas writs are those challenging external policies that function to prolong one's prison stay (24 percent). Denial of parole is the most common issue in this category, comprising 14.5 percent of all habeas filings, and roughly 60 percent of

Table 5c Grounds of Habeas Corpus complaints filed in
　　　　　Illinois' Northern District, August 1980 through 1986

Grounds of Filing	Frequency	Percent
Original Case Issues		
General trial procedures	628	41.5
Legal malpractice	137	9.0
Sentencing	61	4.0
Bond	44	2.9
Arrest policies/procedures	41	2.7
Administrative processing of case	13	.9
Habeas-related	13	.9
Postconviction complaint	13	.9
Miranda	13	.9
No access to legal records	8	.5
Subtotal	971	64.1
External Policies		
Parole granting	219	14.5
Parole revocation	52	3.4
Extradition	40	2.6
Calculation of sentence	27	1.8
Release date	20	1.3
Transfer	3	.2
IDOC Prison policies	2	.1
Subtotal	363	24.0
Internal Prison Policies		
Disciplinary procedures	68	4.5
Goodtime loss	43	2.8
Denied privileges	5	.3
Excessive discipline	4	.3
Work or prerelease	3	.2
Forced medication	3	.2
General due process	2	.1
Unfair regulations/practices	1	.1
Censorial	1	.1
Cell assignment	1	.1
Job assignment	1	.1
Subtotal	132	8.7

all external policy challenges. Since 1980, federal court decisions have
created considerable ambiguity about the procedures and criteria that
may be used in parole review. Some decisions have specified that parole
boards must provide the prisoner with reasons for parole denial and
that the seriousness of the offense may not be taken into consideration
in parole review. Under current Illinois law, parole may be denied if it
would "deprecate the seriousness of the offense." In 1982, a federal

Table 5c (Cont'd.)		
Other		
Bill of Rights issues (prison)	22	1.5
Prison conditions	7	.5
Prison violence	3	.2
Private suit	3	.2
Police harassment/original case	2	.1
Juvenile age issue	2	.1
None identifiable	1	.1
Police brutality/original case	1	.1
Unknown	8	.5
Subtotal	49	3.2
Total	1515	100.0

appellate court ruled that retroactive application of this criterion should be disallowed when reviewing prisoners for parole (*Welsh v. Mizell*, 668 F.2d 328, 7th Cir., 1982). Encouraged by the 1982 decision, Illinois prisoners filed 88 petitions in the Northern District, accounting for 30 percent of all petitions that year, and 79 percent of all external policy complaints. In *Heirens v. Mizell* (729 F.2d 449, 1984), the court overruled the order of a district magistrate to release a murderer who had served over 35 years in prison for murdering, then carving up, his victim(s). Following this decision overturning *Welsh*, prisoner parole complaints accounted for 19 in 1984 and 22 in 1986. This general decline in parole challenges, however, may also result from the declining number of prisons eligible for parole, since Illinois Criminal Code revisions in 1977 abolished indeterminate sentencing (e.g., Goodstein and Hepburn, 1986).

Complaints of internal (or prison) policies are the third most common reason cited in seeking habeas relief, but account for only 9 percent of all habeas requests. Nearly all of these suits complain of good time loss or prison disciplinary procedures entailing loss of good time. Together, these two issues comprise 84 percent of this category and about 7 percent of all habeas writs. The remaining categories are more common for civil rights filings, and the complaints are rarely found in habeas petitions.[10]

Several conclusions may be drawn. First, Illinois habeas filings, as are national filings, decreasing steadily.[11] Despite 290 filings in 1982, the general trend continues to be one of steady decline, and the 171 filings in 1986 represent a decrease of about 31 percent over 1980. Second, most habeas petitions challenge the proceedings of the original conviction or sentencing. However, few of these petitions claim innocence.

Nearly all cite ambiguous laws or policies that resulted in what is perceived to be an excessive sentence, incorrect charges, or reneging on plea-bargaining agreements. Most suits are not so much attempts to retry the original case, but are rather attempts to seek relief from procedures that are perceived to have led to conviction of the wrong charge or to sentences disproportionate to the crime. More simply, these suits attack continued incarceration rather than conviction.[12]

Are these cases frivolous? That depends. Interviews with criminal justice practioners indicate they so judge them, and federal judges also believe that the bulk of prisoners' habeas petitions lack sufficient *legal* merit to be adjudicable. Even prisoner rights advocates concede that many habeas corpus complaints lack sufficient legal justification to warrant relief. But this does not necessarily mean that habeas suits are *substantively* frivolous. As one judge said, "Yeh, they're screwed, but there's no Constitutional redress." When, for whatever reasons, justice is flawed, courts err, prosecutor malice reigns, and power is abused, prisoners—even while acknowledging guilt—appeal for at least limited relief. And in Illinois, at least, justice may miscarry, court personnel may abuse power, and corruption is not uncommon. Most prisoners (about two-thirds) come from the Chicago area, are black, and do not have resources to retain skilled counsel. Hence, there is a perceived economic and racial bias built into the judicial system.

The distinction between legal merit and substantive merit is often fuzzy. The general attitude among prisoners is "I've been screwed, and I'm gonna sue." A prisoner who receives ten years for an offense for which his "rappee" (partner in crime) received a lesser sentence in a separate trial perceives injustice. This, in turn, may trigger a litigation response. There may be no Constitutional basis for the response, but in the prisoner's eyes, this is irrelevant. Prisoners reason that their punishment should be decided according the "rules of the game." Further, some Illinois judges have instituted a "pay-out, stay-out (of jail)" system of justice, in which pay-offs to judges, attorneys and others has become a common practice. For example, "Operation Greylord," an ongoing FBI investigation into corruption among Cook County (Chicago) judges and attorneys, continues to disclose numerous violations of judicial abuse.

The issue of racism may also trigger habeas suits. Blacks are often systematically excluded from juries, which may result in reduced credibility of nonwhite witnesses by all white juries. There was also an instance of an "arson expert" who was valued by insurance companies for his ability to find evidence of arson when other investigators could not. In a twist of conscience, he revealed that his "expert" credentials were fraudulant, and that he had sent innocent men to prison (*Chicago Tribune*, June 1, 1980, p. 1). When examples of flagrant judicial abuse occur, even prisoners who freely acknowledge "guilt" are motivated to challenge their convictions in hope they may benefit from perceived injustices in original trial proceedings or sentencing.

Challenges to the nature of the charges may also promote litigation. One state's attorney in Champaign, Illinois, has in the past few years succeeded in charging shoplifters (misdemeanants) with burglary, a felony ("Prosecutor gets Burglary Charge for Shoplifting," 1986). Whether legally permissible or not, such lattitude is perceived as unfair both by defendants and defense lawyers, and has resulted in at least one broad legal challenge. Hence, the practice of justice may not match the constitutionally protected ideals of justice, and prisoners litigate as a means of securing these protections.

Some Observations on Habeas Filings

For state prisoners, attempts to seek release through the Great Writ have given way to an emphasis on civil rights complaints, suggesting that filing trends may reflect specific problems against which prisoners resist, rather than generally indiscriminate use of courts primarily for the sake of suing: Prisoners simply may be responding to specific grievances rather than maliciously attempting to overturn their convictions. Haas (1981: 554), however, has argued that a series of Supreme Court decisions by the Burger Court may have narrowed the situations in which lower federal courts can review state convictions under the federal habeas corpus statutes, thus contributing to the habeas filing decline. Further, few habeas petitions result in release (Justice, 1973; Shapiro, 1973), thus discouraging many prisoners from pursuing original case complaints at the federal level.

The current decrease in habeas suits reflects several other factors. First, the different filing patterns between states suggest that there may be specific social factors occuring in particular states that impel prisoners to seek relief through the courts. Hence, when we speak of litigation, we should be aware that not all states experience litigation similarly, and that prisoners' problems may vary between states. Further, some states may be taking heed of prior decisions protecting the rights of suspects, thus eliminating one common cause of action. Second, since the mid–1970s, many states have revised their criminal codes in attempts to reduce ambiguities, eliminate obvious discrepancies, and bring state laws up to federal standards, especially in capital offenses.[13] This indicates that habeas litigation is not "opening the gates" to freedom for prisoners. Finally, it appears that the filings of federal prisoners are highly associated with such nonprison variables as civilian suits and federal prison population.[14]

The lesson of this section is easily summarized: from the Illinois example, we must conclude that prisoners do in general accept the finality of their conviction, but may not accede to the full—and allegedly unconstitutional—consequences of it. Whether habeas filings reflect— or reduce—respect for law is a question for attitude questionnaires, but there is certainly no basis for this claim in these data. And even conceding the existence of frivolous cases, an occasionally frivolous claim seems a small price to pay for maintaining the oldest protection of liberty in our judicial system.

TRENDS IN STATE PRISONER CIVIL RIGHTS FILINGS

Critics of prisoners' civil rights litigation have observed that civil rights suits have increased by over 9,100 percent between 1966 and 1986. Further, state prisoners have tended to turn to the courts to redress civil rights conflicts proportionately more than their civilian counterparts.[15] Hence, the contention that civil rights complaints have increased astronomically has some merit, but is misleading when examined out of the context of the annual trends. By examining the national trends of civil rights filings and comparing these with variations among the individual states, a more detailed picture of litigation patterns emerges.

Table 5d shows a dominant national filing trend of steady increase, but the rate of this increase has slowed in recent years. Between 1971 and 1980, complaints rose by 325 percent, or by about one-third annually. Between 1981 and 1986, by contrast, filings increased by only 28 percent, or about 6 percent annually. This clearly indicates that civil rights petitions are not increasing at an abnormal rate, and that only slight increases have occurred in recent years.

The proportion of filings per prisoner also reflects a substantial increase since 1967. By 1970, the rate of filings was about 1 prisoner per 100, increasing steadily to almost five per 100 by 1981. Since 1982, however, this proportion has generally decreased, and in 1986, about 4 prisoners per 100 litigated. Therefore, the increase in civil rights filings are partially attributable to the increase in the proportion of prisoners filings, and as we shall see, to the increase in the nation's prison population, which provides a larger at-risk population likely to litigate.[16]

The contention that prisoners are using the courts to reverse unfavorable trial outcomes or to seek release has been a favorite complaint of litigation's critics. Table 5d illustrates that in the initial years of prisoner litigation, this may have been the case, but the tide has steadily shifted. In the previous section, we saw that the ratio of civil rights to habeas filings has shifted dramatically in the past two decades. Since the late 1960s, when civil rights complaints constituted less than 20 percent of all annual filings, the proportion has steadily increased, and by 1986, they accounted for over two-thirds of all state prisoner suits. Nationally, then, prisoners have become far more concerned with the conditions of confinement than with ending it.

State Variations

Civil rights between states vary far more dramatically than habeas filings in that there has been no leveling trend among states. The average number of filings in 1970, 1975, 1980, and 1986 was about 54, 120, 240, and 393 respectively. Appendix B shows that in 1970 individual state filings ranged from no filings (Alaska, North and South Dakota) or two

Table 5d Civil Rights cases filed by state prisoners, 1966–86, rate per 100 prisoners, and as percent of all state prisoner filings

Year	Civil Rights Filings	Rate/100 Prisoner	As % of All Federal Prisoner Filings
1966	218	.12	3.49
1967	878	.50	11.25
1968	1072	.64	12.91
1969	1269	.72	13.63
1970	2030	1.15	17.19
1971	2915	1.65	24.00
1972	3348	1.92	27.70
1973	4174	2.30	32.91
1974	5236	2.67	39.01
1975	6128	2.83	42.97
1976	6958	2.95	46.30
1977	7752	2.89	52.22
1978	9730	3.51	57.34
1979	11195	3.89	60.51
1980	12397	4.06	63.33
1981	15639	4.69	66.25
1982	16741	4.45	67.03
1983	17687	4.36	66.94
1984	18034	4.20	67.85
1985	18491	3.82	67.97
1986	20072	4.14	68.42

Source: Administrative Office of the U.S. District Courts (Data for 1960–65 not maintained separately).

or less (Delaware, Hawaii, Idaho, Montana, New Hampshire, Nevada, Rhode Island, and Wyoming) to 464 (California). The five most litigious states (California, Pennsylvania, New York, Virginia, and Illinois) accounted for about 78 percent of all civil rights suit in 1970. In all states, the number of filings dramatically increased between 1970 and 1986, and by 1986, the gap had widened: five states had 40 filings or less (Alaska, Hawaii, North Dakota, Rhode Island, and Vermont), and 15 states had in excess of 500. By 1986, the five most litigious states (California, New York, Pennsylvania, Texas, and Washington) accounted for only 29 percent of state prisoner habeas litigation. Not surprisingly, the states with among the most of civil rights suits were those with among the largest prison populations.

The tendency to turn to the courts to resolve prison problems affected virtually all states, but some felt the impact more than others. In Nevada, for example, suits surged from one in 1970 to 270 in 1986, an increase of 26,900 percent. In Iowa complaints jumped from 2 in 1970 to 338 in 1986, an increase of about 16,800 percent. Other states with dramatic increases between 1970 and 1986 included Alabama (2,672 percent), Arizona (6,209 percent), Arkansas (3,673 percent), Louisiana (3,917 percent), Mississippi (3,225 percent), New Mexico (2,367 percent), Oregon (2,860 percent), Ohio (3,691 percent), Texas (1,767 percent), and Washington (1,825 percent). None of these states were among those with the lowest prison populations, but all were among those with particularly endemic prison problems, especially the southern states. The disparity in the number of filings among states and the consistent increase in specific states suggests that prisoners may be responding to specific problems, rather than randomly filing simply because they have increased court access.

Filings per Prisoner

The rate of prisoner filings per 100 prisoners, displayed in Appendix 2, reveals that in all jurisdictions the proportion of prisoners filing has increased in the period 1970–86. This general increase, however, has significantly varied between states. In many of the most litigious states (California, Illinois, New York, Pennsylvania), the increase has been either sporadic or gradual. In other states, particularly in the south and southwest, the increase has been dramatic (Alabama, Arizona, Louisiana, Texas, Tennessee). In 1970, the national filing rate was about 1.2 per 100 prisoners; in only 11 states did more than two prisoners per 100 file, and only two states evidenced filing rates of higher than 5 suits per 100 prisoners (Washington, D.C., 7.1; Pennsylvania, 5.8). In 30 states, the filing rate was less than 1 per prisoner. By 1975, the national rate had more than doubled to 2.8, but much of this increase occurred in jurisdictions in the south and southwest, inflating the national average.

By 1980, the per prisoner rate decreased in 14 states, despite the 43 percent increase in the national per prisoner filing rate between 1975 and 1980, from 2.8 to 4.1. The national per prisoner filing rate of 4.1 in 1986 also conceals the individual state changes. Seven states still had rates under 2 per 100, but three states possessed rates over 10 per 100, and another eight over 7 per 100. In the main, then, the national decrease in 1986 glosses over the *number* of states in which more prisoners were filing while in some of the highly litigious states, the filing rate was stable or decreased slightly. Hence, it appears civil rights remain a significant issue in all states, but both filing volume and rates have fluctuated significantly between them.

Proportion of Prisoners' to Civilians' Filings

Critics have argued that prisoners' complaints tend to overwhelm courts and push out civilian claims through sheer bulk of numbers. In some states, this claim has merit, but in most others, it does not. Prisoners' civil rights suits, it is true, have increased in proportion to all private suits, but in only 11 states did 1986 filings represent more than 20 percent of all private filings, while in 22 others, prisoners' civil rights claims constituted 10 percent or less of all private filings. However, in 1970, this proportion exceeded 10 percent in only one state (Virginia), and in 1975, in only 12 states was the proportion 10 percent or more. In some states, the increase from 1970 to 1986 was dramatic (e.g., Alabama, 2.2 to 23; Arizona, 2.3 to 38.2; Delaware, 0.7 to 27.5; Iowa, 0.6 to 27; Nevada, 0.6 to 21.2; North Carolina, 9.3 to 34.6; Virginia, 11.6 to 25.4; Washington, 2.3 to 16.2). In only one state (California) did this proportion decrease (9.9 to 7.3). This suggests that the civil rights suits are not overwhelming civilian suits, despite the increase in the numbers of filings, for the reason that civilian litigation has also increased.

Civil Rights to all Prisoner Filings

If prisoners are filing proportionately fewer habeas suits, this obviously means that they are filing more civil rights complaints. Appendix 2 shows that in no state did the proportion of civil rights suits decrease between 1970 and 1986. In 1970, civil rights complaints accounted for 25 percent or less of all prisoner suits in 37 jurisdictions, and over 50 percent in only one (Washington, D.C., 53.7 percent). By 1975, civil rights filings comprised less than 25 percent of all prisoner suits in only four states, and the number of states in which they exceeded 50 percent or more increased to 20. The trend has continued, and by 1980, civil rights suits constituted over half of all filings in 44 states. By 1986, only one state (North Dakota) reflected a civil rights proportion less than 50 percent. In most jurisdictions (31), civil rights filings comprised two-thirds or more of all suits, and in ten of these, they represented over three-quarters of all prisoner suits. In short, prisoners have become far more active in seeking to improve the conditions of their confinement than in obtaining release, and this trend continues.

Prisoner Civil Rights Litigation in Illinois

In Illinois, civil rights filings have approximated national filing patterns, increasing both in numbers and in relation to habeas suits. In the Northern District, however, civil rights filings have remained relatively stable between 1978 and 1986, ranging from between 275 and 424 annually.[17]. Further, as with habeas suits, conceptual precision of civil rights calculations are hampered by the number of claims from persons who are not incarcerated in state prisons (21 percent). Nearly all of the suits (98 percent) originated in Illinois, although prisoners from 17 others states also filed claims. Most of these were either by federal prisoners, by state prisoners challenging extradition to other states or by nonresidents bringing complaints while previously incarcerated in Illinois.

Not surprisingly, the grounds of civil rights complaints differ dramatically from those of habeas corpus. Using the same classification system employed in the previous section, civil rights complaints are distributed unequally among seven broad categories.

Internal Policies

Table 5e shows that challenges to prison policies or practices are the single most contentious area, constituting about 28 percent of all court actions. Of these, 11 percent complain of unconstitutional disciplinary proceedings, adducing *Wolff v. McDonnell* (418 U.S. 539, 1974) protections of limited due process in disciplinary hearings[18]. Other challenges to prison policies or staff practices include those of staff misconduct, typically involving verbal harassment, staff precipitated property loss complaints, or interinstitutional transfers. Less common complaints allege implementation of rules (job assignments, revocation of good time, cell assignments) or general complaints of inadequately implementing existing rules (e.g., censorial complaints,[19] deprivation of resources or privileges, and improper or inaccurate keeping of prisoner records.

Original Case Issues

Some critics have suggested that one reason for the decrease in habeas complaints is simply that inmates have discovered that section 1983 can be used as a functional equivalent for habeas petitions, and so file in the belief that the probability of a favorable review is higher. Table 5e indicates that a fairly large proportion of civil rights cases does in fact raise questions related to the original offense (18.6 percent). Of these, complaints of due process violations in the original pretrial or trial proceedings (e.g., illegal evidence, purjury of witnesses, "conspiracy" of judge and defense or prosecuting attorneys) are the most common (8.4 percent). Allegations of improper arrest procedures or violations of Fourth Amendment protections of search and seizure constitute the second most common in this category (4.2 percent). Other less common complaints include incompetence of counsel (2.4 percent) and failure to provide adequate access to legal records during trial or for postconviction appeals.

The volume of these complaints would seem to give some credence to the claim that some prisoners are using civil rights as a backdoor mechanism to secure release. But it should be remembered that the intent is often not so much one of overturning a conviction, but seeking a "more just" sentence, obtaining material for appeal, or attempting to right a wrong not directly related to release (e.g., excessive bond).

Critics, however, do raise one legitimate concern. Prisoners are allowed to file habeas and civil rights suits simultaneously, and many of the "original case" complaints have also been filed as habeas claims, and the additional civil rights filing is perceived by some prisoners to be a hedge against a loss in one arena by hoping to convince those in a second forum of the legitimacy of a claim. In a study of 831 prisons filing over an 18 month period between 1983 and 1984, Thomas et al. (1985: 95–96) found that only 68 prisoners (8.2 percent) filed both types of suits. Of these, 30 filed but one of each type, and only 23 prisoners filed more than two of each type. Hence, the number of double-dippers is relatively small, and most filers are not experienced or repetitious litigators. This further suggests prisoners do not indiscriminately flood the courts with both types of petitions. If one counts civil rights claims challenging original case issues as a means of assessing the degree to which prisoners seek to challenge their confinement, we must then deduct complaints unrelated to habeas corpus from the habeas category. When this is calculated for all Northern District habeas and civil rights filings for 1980 to 1985, we find 475 civil rights cases addressing conviction proceedings (19.6 percent). By contrast, 544 habeas suits (35.9 percent) address issues other than the original case proceedings. In other words, habeas corpus is *more likely* to challenge prison policies and conditions than are civil rights filings to challenge conviction, indicating that prisoners are not increasingly turning to civil rights law as an alternative to habeas corpus. Therefore, the "substitution thesis" has no merit.

It is clear that, in the past decade, Illinois prisoners have not *increased* their reliance on Section 1983 as an alternative to habeas litigation, because the percentage of original case complaints between 1977 and 1986 has not risen, but instead fluctuated between 14 and 26 percent. These fluctuations were sporadic and evidenced no linear trend toward increase, indicating that there was no tendency to increasingly replace habeas with civil rights as a mechanism for release.

Violence

The third most common category of complaints, violence, accounted for about 18 percent of prisoner suits, distributed mostly between "official assault," in which prisoners alleged actual or explicitly threatened violence by prison staff, usually correctional officers, and "failure to protect." "Failure to protect" complaints did not claim direct guard assault, but rather alleged guard complicity—usually with street gangs (40 percent of all cases alleging violence)—in leaving prisoners vulnerable to assaults. This occurred either through direct incitement of prisoner-on-prisoner violence, or through deliberately ignoring imminent assaults.[20] Perhaps predictably, the overwhelming majority of violence-related suits originates from the Illinois' four maximum security prisons and from Cook County Jail (totalling 89 percent), suggesting that violence may be an endemic problem in these institutions.[21]

Prison Conditions

Although most civil rights complaints challenge some aspect of prison conditions, a separate category has been created to identify those suits that focus specifically on the state of the facilities, the existing resources or the general environment. Complaints of prison conditions comprised the fourth most common category of suits (16 percent). However, the single issue of inadequate health and medical care was cited in 11 percent of all cases, the most frequent grievance of all suits. Health problems may be common in other systems as well, as suggested by Eisenberg (1982: 555) and Turner (1979: 661), who each found medical problems the most common complaint cited (also 11 percent) in their intrajurisdictional studies. It may be that litigation has had some impact on improving health care, because the trend in recent years has been one of considerable decline, suggesting prisoners have fewer complaints.[22]

Other complaints impelling litigation, although far less frequent, include poor physical facilities or dangerous conditions, such as faulty wiring or loose rails on staircases. Surprisingly, among the fewest complaints were those charging that conditions were not conducive to the legislatively mandated correctional goal of rehabilitation. Only two suits challenged rehabilitation in general, and only four attacked lack of educational and vocational programs.[23]

This relatively low rate of challenges to prison conditions is surprising, because those prisons generating the most suits, maximum security prisons, are old, poorly maintained, and prisoners tend to be double-celled. In fact, only 14 suits challenged overcrowding, despite the initial success in Illinois' Central District of a consolidated attack on overcrowding.[24] Further, despite the unsavory reputation of prison food, only 17 complaints attacked this issue, and most of these were allegations of lack of special diets for health or religious needs. Surprisingly, there were no damage claims from Dwight prison following successive outbreaks of food poisoning in the early 1980 (Aylward and Thomas, 1984). From this, it seems clear that—with the exception of health issues—Illinois prisoners are not sufficiently dissatisfied with prison physical facilities to pursue their complaints in court. This relative quiescence may be due to the American Correctional Association's accredition program to upgrade prisons, which Illinois administrators take quite seriously. By late 1986, all Illinois prisoners were accredited.

Bill of Rights Issues

The first ten amendments of the Bill of Rights guarantees religious liberty, access to law, and protections aganst cruel and unusual punishment, but few suits raised an explicit Bill of Rights claim (8 percent). Of these, complaints of thwarted access to law and violations of mail privileges were the most common (about 2 percent each). Complaints of denial of religious freedom were relatively infrequent (1.1 percent), and the bulk of these involved either inadequate facilities for Muslim practices or "cults" (often street gangs) seeking recognition as a religion in order to obtain more freedom of movement and congregation. General grievances over Eighth Amendment protection against cruel and unusual punishment were rare (0.4 percent), and typically constituted unspecific claims that were quickly dismissed.

External Policies

The least common prison-related category of suits—external polices—constituted only 6 percent of all claims. Among these, parole granting procedures were the most common, followed by administrative miscalculation of sentence and challenges to perceived unjust intersystem transfers. Other complaints of IDOC policies totalled less than 2 percent of all suits.

Other Suits

About 6 percent of all prisoner suits were unrelated either to prison or department policies or original case proceedings. The bulk of these listed police brutality, alleging physical ill-treatment by officers prior to or during arrest. Most of the remaining suits in this category were private suits against landlords, former employers, or mail-order firms. Prisoners generally seek resolution for personal problems with private individuals in state, rather than federal, courts.

Litigation in Women's Prisons

Discussions of prisoner litigation tend to exclude the experiences of incarcerated women. This reflects, in part, the gender bias of criminal

Table 5e Grounds of Civil Rights complaints filed in Illinois'
Northern District, August 1977 through 1986

Grounds	Frequency	Percent
Internal Policies		
Disciplinary procedures	347	10.7
Staff misconduct	103	3.2
Loss of property	87	2.7
Unfair regulations or policies	50	1.5
Transfer	40	1.2
Excessive discipline	39	1.2
Deprivation of resources, property	34	1.1
Visiting	33	1.0
Goodtime loss	32	1.0
Job assignment	30	.9
Work or prerelease	19	.6
Censorial	17	.5
Denied privileges	16	.5
Improper record keeping	14	.4
Grievance procedures	7	.2
Search complaints	7	.2
Cell assignment	5	.2
No access to nonlegal records	5	.2
Objects to female guards	5	.2
Lockdown	4	.1
General due process	3	.1
No female guards	2	.1
Parental rights	1	.0
Conjugal	1	.0
No child care	1	.0
Subtotal	902	27.9
Original Case Issues		
General trial procedures	272	8.4
Arrest policies/procedures	137	4.2
Legal malpractice	79	2.4
No access to legal records	50	1.5
Bond	21	.6
Habeas related	17	.5
Sentencing	14	.4
Street files	6	.2
Post conviction complaint	4	.1
Miranda	1	.0
Subtotal	601	18.6

Table 5e   (Cont'd.)

Grounds	Frequency	Percent
Violence		
Official assault	233	7.2
Failure to protect from assault	230	7.1
Prisoner assault	65	2.0
Sexual assault	18	.6
General violence	15	.5
Life threatened	13	.4
Excessive staff force	7	.2
Gang-Related Violence	4	.1
Subtotal	585	18.1
Conditions		
Lack of health care	350	10.8
General conditions	49	1.5
Poor facilities	44	1.4
Dangerous conditions	41	1.3
Food	17	.5
Overcrowding	14	.4
Lack of heat	8	.2
Lack of educational programs	2	.1
Lack of rehabilitation programs	2	.1
No vocational programs	2	.1
Subtotal	529	16.4
Bill of Rights Issues		
Inadequate access to law	78	2.4
Mail	68	2.1
Religion	37	1.1
Forced medication	20	.6
Eighth Amendment	10	.3
Literature, reading material	10	.3
Racism	9	.3
Civil rights, general	5	.2
Privacy	4	.1
Equal protection	4	.1
Speech	1	.0
Subtotal	246	7.6

Table 5e   (Cont'd.)

Grounds	Frequency	Percent
External Policies		
Parole granting	103	3.2
Parole revocation	28	.9
Release date	28	.9
IDOC prison policies	14	.4
Extradition	9	.3
Hiring discrimination	2	.1
Calculation of Sentence	1	.0
Subtotal	185	5.7
Other		
Police brutality/original case	97	3.0
Private suit	72	2.2
None identifiable	5	.2
Many listed	4	.1
Police harassment, original case	3	.1
Unknown	3	.1
Subtotal	184	2.7
Total	3,232	100.0

justice researchers, but is also due to the paucity of women litigating.[25] In Illinois, women constitute about 3 percent of the state's prison population, but file only 0.6 percent of the state's prisoner suits. Not only do women not litigate with the frequency of their male counterparts, but they have not participated equally in the fruits of men's litigation (Leonard, 1983). Between 1977 and 1986, only 18 civil rights and 6 habeas suits have been filed in the Northern District by women, all originating in the state's only prison for women.[26] Of these, only one—a child care complaint—has addressed a problem related to sex or gender.[27] One-third complained of prison policies and another 25 percent of generally poor conditions. The rest were evenly distributed among the other categories.

Most litigation emerging from Illinois' women prisoners tends to be state actions addressing problems of divorce, other family matters, and state trial proceedings.[28] Reasons for this relative quiescence have been suggested by others (Alpert, 1982, 1978a; Alpert and Wiorkowski, 1977; Aylward and Thomas, 1984; Kates, 1984; Leonard, 1983), and seem tied to gender socialization rather than environmental satisfaction. One female law clerk, a law school graduate, explained that the sanctioning system of the prison discouraged, even penalized, women from litigating, a view for which there is some evidence (Aylward and Thomas, 1984).

Some Observations on Civil Rights Filings

Preliminary Inferences

Four conclusions may be drawn from the national filing trends. First, the number of civil rights filings by state prisoners has been steadily increasing in all states, but the rate of increase has begun to slow. Second, unlike habeas cases, the proportion of civil rights cases to incarcerated state prisoners has been steadily increasing through the early 1980s, but this proportion seems to have stabilized in recent years. Third, civil rights complaints are increasingly replacing habeas corpus petitions, indicating that state prisoners are, in general, more concerned with correcting perceived wrongs than in seeking to overturn their sentences. Finally, there are dramatic differences between states in the numbers, proportion, and rates of cases filed. This suggests that either the sources of prisoner complaints inherently vary, or, more likely, some prison systems have devised strategies—either through cooling out complaints or by restricting access to courts—to reduce litigation, while others have not.

From the Illinois data, several additional inferences may be drawn. First, prisoners have not turned to Section 1983 to replace the writ of habeas corpus; only a relatively small percentage of civil rights suits challenge substantive original case issues. Second, the most common complaints, those of inadequate health care, violence, and unjust disciplinary proceedings, indicate that many prisoners share common problems throughout the state's institutions. These three categories alone account for 40 percent of all civil rights filings. Equally telling is the silence of prisoner complaints of racism, overcrowding, rehabilitation programs, lockdowns, and segregation. Prisoners, in general, seem most concerned with those problems that address fundamental conditions of confinement, rather than with issues that raise broader political or social issues. This casts doubt on one view of prisoners, common especially among radicals of the early 1970s, that prisoners are on the cutting edge of political struggle. Third, as with prisoners nationwide, the increase in Illinois litigation is highly associated with a combination of demographic and civilian litigation factors, particularly prison population and civilian—especially civil rights—litigation. Fourth, it is not possible to determine whether a suit is legally frivolous by identifying only the grounds of filing, but the overwhelming majority of complaints are able to identify an explicit substantive grievance by which to justify the filing. Further, the general pattern of these complaints clusters around problems commonly perceived by prisoners to plague them all (i.e., violence). Further, as we shall see in Chapter 7, the high proportion of prisoner suits receiving some relief (about half) suggests that there are far fewer frivolous cases filed than commonly assumed. Fifth, certain types of prisons are more likely to generate certain categories of complaints than others. Complaints of violence, for example, are more likely to originate in maximum security prisons, while complaints of improper disciplinary practices are distributed among all prisons. Sixth, women are simply not litigating. The paucity of Illinois' women challenging the conditions of their existence suggests either that the women's prison has few serious problems, which is unlikely (Aylward and Thomas, 1984), or that other factors operate to curtail women's use of law. Seventh, as Table 5f illustrates, filing patterns across substantive grounds vary from year to year, suggesting that some problems erupt periodically, while others diminish. It also suggests that—with the exception of health care— prison officials have not systematically addressed those problems which impel prisoners to turn to the courts, since they keep recurring.

Institutional Variations

Institutional variations provide useful insights into the filing differences between civil rights and habeas suits. In Illinois, filings are consistent with Turner's (1979) thesis that most civil rights suits originate from maximum security institutions. Illinois' maximum security population has decreased from about 60 percent of the state's total in 1977 to about 40 percent in 1986. Yet, as Table 5g shows, 69 percent of all civil rights and 64.1 percent of all habeas filings originate from these institutions. Table 5g also also reveals that nonprisoners constitute over 20 percent of both categories, with about 15 percent of all civil rights filings coming from persons challenging jail conditions. This strongly supports the

Table 5f Annual distribution of Civil Rights suits filed in Illinois' Northern Federal District, 1977-86 (N=3,232)

Year	Violence	Internal Policies	External Policies	Conditions	Original Case	Bill of Rights
1977	17.1	30.1	7.5	15.8	17.1	8.9
1978	15.9	25.9	4.3	26.1	13.9	9.1
1979	14.6	33.5	2.4	16.2	17.1	10.1
1980	16.9	24.6	8.0	23.4	18.0	5.6
1981	20.0	29.8	6.2	13.5	17.5	6.9
1982	21.5	23.3	8.8	14.8	19.4	6.1
1983	17.6	27.4	4.6	11.9	25.8	7.3
1984	18.9	31.1	4.3	11.9	21.0	7.9
1985	20.8	27.2	6.1	14.5	17.4	7.1
1986	17.5	28.3	6.1	14.9	18.4	7.8

view that prisoners in "hard time" institutions are more likely to experience the problems that encourage litigation.

Who Litigates?

How many prisoners actually litigate? In Illinois, 4.9 suits per 100 prisoners were filed in 1980 and 4.7 in 1986. But, this is somewhat misleading, because many prisoners are "repeat players" (Galanter, 1974) who file multiple suits. Between 1977 and 1984, about 66 percent of all litigators filed two or more claims (Thomas et al. 1985: 95). Of those who filed multiple suits, 13 percent filed two, and 19 percent filed between three and six. During this period, 15 prisoners filed more than 10 suits, five of whom filed 25 or more. Two of these heavy litigators filed 52 and 57 suits respectively.[29]

The most active 1 percent of civil rights litigators accounted for 17 percent of all civil rights filings, and the most active 5 percent accounted for 28 percent. Of 2,256 civil rights suits, 1,309 prisoners filed, or about 1.7 suits for each litigating prisoner. This would indicate that in a state with a suit-per-prisoner proportion of 5 per 100, the number of prisoners actually litigating would be closer to 3.4 per 100, rather than 5 per 100. Hence, there are significantly fewer prisoners litigating than presumed, and the "suits per prisoner" statistic provides only the maximum number of litigants.

Habeas petitioners, by contrast, are more likely to be "one-shotters,"

Table 5g   Institutions of origin of Civil Rights and Habeas Corpus suits from Illinois' Northern District, August 1977-86 (in percent)

Institution	Civil Rights	Habeas Corpus
State Prisons	79.0	74.7
Maximum security	69.0	64.1
Medium security	6.9	7.7
Minimum security	1.1	1.3
Unknown	2.0	1.6
Jails	15.0	5.8
Federal prisons	4.2	14.1
Other/unknown	1.8	5.4
Total	100.0 (N=3,232)	100.1 (N=1,515)

filing only a single suit. Thomas et al. (1985: 95) have found that 57 percent of habeas prisoners are one-shotters, and 19 percent file only two claims. Five prisoners accounted for 6.1 percent of these suits (Thomas et al. 1985). Only three prisoners filed more than two habeas suits over the 18 month period studied, and none over five. Since habeas claims are more likely than civil rights suits to be returned and then refiled, many of these multiple litigators are essentially filing the same suit the second time, thus inflating the filing data. Hence, the proportion of suits per 100 prisoners is far more likely to reflect the actual number of prisoners filing (only a ten percent inflation) than civil rights suits.

One final statistic bears note. Some evidence suggests that states retaining the death penalty are significantly more likely to experience disproportionately greater rates of both civil rights and habeas corpus litigation than states that have not (Thomas, 1987). One explanation for this may be found in Durkheim's distinction between restitutive and punitive law. If we view the death penalty as the ultimate form of punitive sanction, then it may be that those states that have adopted it administratively proceed from a "repressive" model of social control, and are, therefore, more likely to be less concerned with changing conceptions of rights than are other states. Conversely, those states that have abolished this sanction may be both more willing to administer institutions less repressively, and—when complaints arise—be more likely to enact strategies of mediation and response, thus circumventing the need to appeal to higher authorities. This tentative hypothesis has not been explored here, but suggests one possible contributing factor to litigation.

SUMMARY

The legal enterprise entails not only the processes by which law is accomplished, but also the social perceptions of what is accomplished. The perception that all prisoner litigation is of a single kind obscures the complexity of and problems for which prisoners litigate. The differences in filing patterns between habeas and civil rights suits clearly demonstrate the need to examine each legal theory separately in order to understand the motives, sources, trends and problems underlying litigation. For example, many habeas suits do not properly fall within the domain, and many civil rights suits are not limited to prison conditions.

Prisoners' complaints are varied, and whatever the credibility of any individual complaint, such problems as violence, health care, and discipline have long been recognized as endemic in the nation's institutions. The shift from habeas to civil rights litigation also underscores the changing direction that jailhouse lawyers are taking in their use of law to change their environment.

It is no longer acceptable to speak simply of "prisoner litigation" as a generic category, any more than we can speak of civil and criminal law as isomorphic. We must not only distinguish between civil rights and habeas suits, but must also examine the different subcategories of prisoner civil rights suits as a means of ferreting out the problems that prisoners face and the strategies they choose to solve them. How these problems are viewed by those who process them is the next stop in our tour of the prisoner's world of litigation.

NOTES

1. As a typical example, in criticizing the "excessive" use of the habeas writ by prisoners, Reed (1980) uses the base year 1953, in which only 541 habeas petitions were filed, to dramatize the "swelling" of prisoner habeas petitions. She also commits the common error of assuming that all prisoner litigation is habeas litigation, using the total 1979 filings (18,502) rather than state-only habeas filings (7,123). Burt (1985) also engages in intellectual aerobics when, after identifying a 1969 filing figure of "7,359," she notes that filings "had swelled to 6,648 in 1979, 6,599 in 1980, and 7,302 in 1981." Her figures are inaccurate, and the stability of filings over the decade, especially given the increase in prisoners, hardly indicate a further "swelling."

2. For stylistic convenience, the terms "state" and "jurisdiction" are used interchangeably, even though Washington D.C. is not a state.

3. Some readers have suggested a section describing how state and federal litigation trends are mutually interactive and affective. Pearson product-moment correlations indicate a strong relationship between state and federal prisoner filings. However, when relevant variables are regressed to measure the strength of interactive influence, the relationship is less conclusive. This will be further examined elsewhere (Thomas, 1987).

4. In 1983 and 1984, there were 22 and 19 habeas filings respectively in Georgia's Northern District. Filings soared to 1,811 in 1985, nearly all of which were filed by incarcerated Cubans in Atlanta's Federal Penitentiary. When a federal court ruled that Cuban refugees did not possess the same legal protections as U.S. prisoners, and thus were not entitled to the same habeas rights, petitions dropped dramatically. Despite the 1,800 Cuban prisoners still incarcerated in Atlanta's federal penitentiary in 1986, only 141 habeas petitions were filed in that year.

5. These data exclude habeas-related issues brought under civil rights actions, but include all petitions classified as "*mandamus* and other." *Mandamus* suits were included for several reasons. First, there are very few cases classified as "other" (about 2 percent), and although their loss would not skew analysis significantly, it is useful to have as complete a picture of state filings as possible. Second, some clerks and attorneys estimate that most (if not "nearly all") petitions classified after 1971 as "other" are habeas-related. Because this discussion focuses on U.S. prisoners, territorial jurisdictions

(e.g., Guam, Virgin Islands) have been excluded. The figures used here will thus be slightly below the national totals provided by federal agencies.

6. This distinction is inappropriate for federal prisoners, since few states have federal prisons, and some states have several. Further, the state in which a federal prison is located may not be the state in which the alleged complaint occurred. Therefore, state variations in federal prisoner filings are meaningless.

7. In Illinois, whites tend to go to "easy-time" lower security instititutions, and minorities are concentrated in maximum security institutions, from which most litigation originates (Thomas et al. 1981). By late 1986, the state's maximum security prisons housed about 37 percent of the state's male inmates, although this figure dropped substantially since the late 1970s, when they housed up to two-thirds of the population (Lane, 1987: 1). In Pontiac and Stateville, the population hoovers around 90 percent non-Anglo; in Menard, located in the southern tip of the state, the non-Anglo population is about 63 percent, and in Joliet, reserved for "vulnerable" offenders, the non-Anglo population is about 66 percent (Lane, 1986b: 96).

8. The Northern Federal District in 1986 reviewed over half (52 percent) of all prisoner cases filed in the Illinois. In earlier years, however, the proportion was much higher. The data here were compiled from court records maintained on all prisoner filings by the District's law clerks. The Northern District's Office of Prisoner Correspondence receives all petitions filed by state and federal prisoners, and classifies them as either "habeas corpus" or "civil rights" suits, but include both attorney-assisted suits and requests to proceed *in forma pauperis.* Hence, these data reflect all prisoner habeas filings for the Northern District.

9. Multiple complaints may be substantially lower in this District than in others. Allen et al. (1982: 759), for example, found that more than one ground was offered in 78.2 percent of all habeas petitions, and 51.6 contained three or more. Secondary complaints were excluded here for several reasons. First, the primary complaint is considered to be the strongest legal grounds on which to file, and thus the most important. Second, in most cases (about two-thirds), the secondary complaint was directly related to the first. For example, a prisoner might complain that an "incompetent public defender conspired with the prosecutor to withhold evidence." "Incompetency of counsel" is the primary complaint, and coded as such. The allegation of "withholding of evidence," ostensibly a complaint about trial procedures, was considered as the "proof" of counsel's incompetence, and not the primary filing category. Hence, little would be gained by examining "tack-on" complaints. Third, about a quarter of those suits listing multiple complaints tended to present a shopping list of general grievances that tended not to relate to the primary complaint. For example, a prisoner who complained of an "unfair trial" might also complain of police brutality, "innocence," and lack of prison medical care. These are considered "tack-on" issues, used especially by inexperienced prisoners who erroneously believe it will strenthen their original complaint.

10. For a comparison of habeas complaints in Illinois' Northern District with other jurisdictions, see especially Allen et al. (1982).

11. As nationally, habeas petitions in Illinois' Northern District have dropped considerably from the early 1970s:

Year	Number of filings	Percent Change over Previous Year
1970	242	—
1980	247	2.1
1981	226	−8.5
1982	290	8.3
1983	228	−21.4
1984	194	−14.9
1986	171	−11.9

12. Some observers have wondered if death row prisoners might not file a disproportionate number of suits in federal court. Illinois courts have sent 131 mean to death row between 1977 and 1986. They have filed only four habeas corpus petitions and 21 civil rights complaints in the Northern District. Hence, death row inmates account for relatively few suits. On the other hand, their suits-per prisoner ratio is considerably above average (about 19 per 100). Most of the civil rights suits complain of conditions on death row.

13. In Illinois, for example, the 1977 criminal code revision created new categories of offenses and corresponding penalties, and changed formulas by which prisoners would be allotted good time, and in general, attempted to create legal order from archaic chaos (Goodstein and Hepburn, 1986). This left prisoners sentenced under the old law in a state of confusion, and in early 1986, about 8 percent of the state's prison population remained with release dates to be determined under the pre–1977 law. Most habeas suits in this District, especially those challenging parole, parole revocation, good time loss, or sentencing, are seeking retroactive relief by applying new case law to prior convictions. Even those suits challenging the procedures of the original case tend to raise postconviction issues decided under new case law.

14. The relationship between civilian filings and prison population is not as strong for federal prisoners as for state prisoners (see note 16). Nonetheless, zero-order partial correlation coefficients ($p > .001$) between private civilian filings (.64), state prisoner filings (.62), and federal prisoner population (.45), indicate a common link between the litigiousness both of prisoners and civilians.

15. In 1972, the first year in which systematic federal records were kept on all civil rights filings, civilians filed 5,482 civil rights complaints. This had increased to 17,872 by 1986, an increase of 226 percent. During the same period, prisoners' complaints increased twice as rapidly, from 3,348 to 20,072, or about 500 percent.

16. For those preferring statistical descriptions, the number of prisoner civil rights filings is highly associated with a combination of increasing prisoner population and civilian litigation. Zero order partial correlation coefficients ($p > .001$) of selected key variables with the number of individual state's prisoner civil rights complaints between 1970 and 1986 produces the following: Private civilian suits (.99), civilian civil rights suits (.97), state's prison population (.96) and habeas petitions (.62). It would seem that prisoner civil rights actions are more closely associated with trends in civilian litigation and with increase in the prison population than are habeas filings. Although partial correlations are of themselves insufficient as a form of data analysis, they nonetheless provide a powerful heuristic indicator of the relationship between prisoner litigiousness and broader social factors. For a more detailed discussion, see Thomas (1987).

17. Year	Number of filings	Percent Change over Previous Year
1978	352	—
1979	328	−6.8
1980	340	3.7
1981	275	−19.1
1982	331	20.4
1983	329	0.6
1984	328	0.3
1985	379	15.5
1986	424	11.9

The increase in Illinois between 1978 and 1986 was about 20 percent, well below the national average, which doubled. More significant is the dramatic variance between years, indicating sporadic filing activity.

18. For discussion of how Constitutional protections are subverted in disciplinary proceedings, see especially Thomas, Aylward, Mika, and Blakemore, 1985.

19. Following Carroll (1977a), a "censorial challenge" refers to a complaint in which a prisoner sues to enforce staff compliance with established prison rules or laws.

20. In Table 5e, "failure to protect" is substantively similar to "prisoner assaults." Legally, however, they raise different issues. The former charges staff negligence, and the latter challenges conditions of confinement.

21. Prisoners often fail to recognize the distinction between recklessness and negligence when filing violence complaints. Federal courts have consistently ruled that, in general, individual negligence does not constitute a violation of civil rights. Recklessness, or gross miscarriage of duties, does. A recent class-action suit has charged Illinois Department of Corrections with reckless disregard of prisoner welfare in creating a state-wide situation that generates violence (*Calvin R. v. Lane*, 82–C–1955, N.D. Ill., 1982). The suit alleges cruel and unusual punishment through "failure to protect" inmate safety, and by deliberately administering Stateville so as to permit and encourage repeated acts of violence, including beatings, extortion, intimidation and sexual assaults. The danger of guard-on-inmate assault was dramatized by the recent conviction of three Stateville guards for beating inmates (Possley, 1981).

22. Health-related filings between 1977 and 1986 ranged from 7 (1983) to 17 (1980) percent, but they have decreased somewhat in recent years. Health-related complaints, unlike other types, tend to decrease because demonstrating a violation of health standards usually requires demonstration of actual harm. When harm can be shown, damage awards are more easily determined, and thus more often awarded. As a consequence, it becomes fiscally expedient to improve health standards that, in the long run, save the state money in damage claims. In other types of suits, it is more difficult to demonstrate or assess actual damages, and there is less financial incentive to reduce problems that generate complaints. Courts are also more likely to grant relief to medical claims than many other types of suits, increasing the likelihood of a judgment against prison officials, thus adding to the incentive to reduce health-related problems.

23. Federal courts have ruled that prisoners have no Constitutional right to rehabilitation, but cases raising this claim are filed on the grounds that

prison practices violate state statutes that explicitly mandate rehabilitation, and deprivation thus represents a Fourteenth Amendment claim.

24. In *Smith v. Fairman* (690 F.2d 122, 7th Cir., 1982), an Illinois Central District judge ruled that overcrowding in Pontiac prison constituted cruel and unusual punishment. The decision was reversed on appeal when the IDOC successfully demonstrated the costs of implementing single celling.

25. Some cases filed by women, however, have had a dramatic prison impact, such as *Glover v. Johnson* (4 F.Sup 1079, 1979), which required prison administrator to establish parity between men's and women's institutions.

26. Five of the 18 civil right suits were filed by a single prisoner. Two suits originated from an out-of-state federal prison for women, and one habeas and two civil rights suits were jointly filed by a male and female.

27. However, two class action suits requesting parity with men's prisons were filed in the Northern District. (e.g., *High et al. v. Thompson*, 85–C–5484, C.D., Ill., 1985).

28. For a comprehensive summary of the nature of women's legal problems, see especially Kates (1984), *Legal Issues* (1982) and Fuller et al. (1987).

29. Neither was considered competent by their peers, and nearly all (about 90 percent) were dismissed on a preliminary screening of the request to proceed *in forma pauperis*. Experienced jailhouse lawyers are highly critical of such filings in the belief that it creates "bad vibes" for others, as we shall see in Chapter 9.

6

Prisoner Cases as Narrative

[T]he prisoner will sit down and type out . . . what he believes to be a very common layman's explanation of what happened to him. Some of them are more sophisticated than others, but nonetheless, they tell their story (Federal judge, interview, 1986).

Whenever a story is told, there is a possibility that it will take on a life of its own, a life beyond the intentions—and perhaps beyond the understanding and control—of the writer, a life so compelling that the auditor, whatever his wishes, cannot shake it off (White, 1985: 249).

As AN YOUNG APPRENTICE RIVERBOAT PILOT, Mark Twain once suddenly changed course to avoid running aground on what he perceived to be a bluff reef. The captain assured him that there was no reef, and commanded Twain to run over it. To Twain's surprise, the boat "slid over it like oil," for it was only a harmless apparition created by the wind. "How am I ever going to tell them apart?" wondered the nonplussed Twain. The captain replied: "I can't tell you. It is an instinct. By and by you will just naturally know one from the other, but you never will be able to explain why or how you know them apart." Twain wrote:

> It turned out to be true. The face of the water, in time, became a wonderful book—a book that was a dead language to the uneducated passenger, but which told its mind to me without reserve, delivering its most cherished secrets as clearly as if it uttered them with a voice. And it was not a book to be read once and thrown aside, for it had a new story to tell every day. Throughout the long twelve hundred miles there was never a page that was void of interest, never one that you could leave unread without loss, never one that you would want to skip, thinking you could find higher enjoyment in some other thing (Mark Twain, cited in White, 1985: 8).

Like the experienced riverboat pilot, the astute reader of prisoner cases soon recognizes that some suits are mere chimeras, but others, like bluff reefs, require skillful attention to avoid potentially disastrous misinterpretation. The prison case is a story narrated by one person to another, describing a violation and pleading for assistance. It provides the text that "reduces to permanence a process that is otherwise ephemeral and renders public, through the multiplication of readings, what is in the first instance essentially private" (White, 1984: 280). The story possesses a structure and contextual pattern shaped by many factors, then set down on paper, thus becoming frozen in a narrative document to be

> employed among those who are simultaneously required to interact and yet remain social strangers. Typically interaction in the frozen style occurs among those between whom an irremovable barrier exists (Lyman and Scott, 1968: 56).

Here, we leave the vapid world of historical patterns, legalistic argument, and filing patterns and enter the culture of those who actually perform the litigation rituals. This shift is required in order to more fully appreciate the interactional and structural dimension of filings. Law, as a type of drama, is enacted through the interplay of numerous persons acting out their assigned role. Roles may shift, conflict may be poorly done, or well done, or may be rewritten when opportunity allows. Prisoner litigation typifies this drama. This chapter describes the beginning of prisoner litigation, prisoners' stories, and illustrates their diversity by showing how each story portrays different meanings, intents, concerns, and configurations otherwise indiscernible when viewed from the vantage point of abstract filing trends.

Prisoners' stories generate organizational and individual action by providing the primary cues that guide interpretation and meaning. Insignificant tales quickly fade; more worthy ones take on a life of their own as the retellings ripple through the judicial arena and demand attention from readers. The story is thus the single most important element in prisoner litigation, because it "is an everyday form of communication that enables a diverse cast of courtroom characters to follow the development of a case and reason about the issues in it" (Bennett and Feldman, 1981: 4). It describes the plot, characters, incidents and motives of an incident, arranges themes, offers value judgments, demarcates in Manichean fashion "good" against "evil," and centers attention upon wrongs to be righted.

Despite a permeating appearance of mundane commonality, prisoner stories, like Twain's river reefs, possess nuances of meaning reflecting properties, some inherent, but others brought to it by the reader. Among the most important of these properties are case facts (What happened?), legal relevance (Is there a Constitutional issue?), organizational implications (What levels of jurisdictions are involved?), practical implications (What should be done and how?) and "truth" content (Is the story credible?). The telling of the story thus becomes patterned by two occasionally incompatible goals: satisfying structural requisites and persuading an audience of an injustice.

THE NATURE OF STORIES AND AUDIENCES

Prisoners' stories are *situated structural accounts* of "what happened" couched in appropriate linguistic and conceptual forms of discourse, and told to a "speech community" of lawyers, judges and defendants. Stories are situated because the nature of their telling depends upon and becomes patterned by the discrete circumstances of the tale being told and the audience toward whom the telling is directed. They possess a structural meaning in that narrations are contained within delimiting and specific spatio-temporal boundaries of unique social or organizational relevance. They are accounts because they offer an explanation of a state of affairs that needs "attending to" (Lyman and Scott, 1968). Stories attempt to elicit new ways of perceiving that, if successful, will compel audience reaction. The story recreates through the medium of language and shared symbols of right and wrong the relationship of organizational unity between narrators and multiple audiences (cf. White, 1984).

All prisoner stories begin with a dispute: someone did the prisoner wrong, and that someone is invariably a state official or one acting on the state's behalf. Some disputes are both legally and substantively minor; e.g., a prison physician keeps a prisoner waiting for several hours before administering a prescribed pain killer. Other disputes are quite serious; for instance, a prisoner is unfairly disciplined and loses good-time as a consequence, or the staff brutally beats a prisoner in the showers. The alleged improper conduct of state officials becomes the specific cause of action on which the prisoner keys the claim.

Storytellers *key* their accounts to specific events and to the meaning these events are perceived to have within the prison's organizational setting. The manner in which stories are keyed shapes not only the probability of a favorable decision (for the teller), but defines as well the style of narration. Readers, by contrast, *frame* their interpretations using a cognitive device that might be called a *master frame* (Manning, 1986). Frames and keys arise from a dual context, the first structural, and the second rhetorical.

Frames: The Structural Context

Few readers have reason to read prisoner stories unless required to do so as a requirement of their organizational duties. Lacking such a requirement, most stories would seem rather meaningless, and a frame renders meaningful a story that would otherwise be of no immedediate relevance (Goffman, 1974: 21). A master frame refers to the primary set of rules or "de-coding devices" that provide the symbolic indicators by which meanings are inferred and actions taken (Manning, 1986; Goffman, 1974). As Manning (1986) has argued, the frame is a structural property of legal settings in that it provides the essential interpretive rules and defines appropriate fields of action.

In keying stories to their audience, prisoners often presume that their audiences share similar values, norms, or expectations. This presumption is the fundamental working strategy upon which narrative persuasion builds. Readers do not share identical organizational mandates or goals, and as a consequence, they do not share identical frames. Courts and corrections are a community of uneasy neighbors. Each has different organizational goals and rhetorical styles, neither is well integrated with the other, and their goals and operative styles often conflict. Prisoner stories force these neighbors to interact, but they often cannot agree on what the stories say or how to react to them.

Even when frames are shared, readers on occasion may misframe and thus misinterpret the stories in ways that shift their meanings. For example, a prisoner complaining of cold toilet seats, a favorite media example of a frivolous case, might be decoded by one reader as a "bad faith" complaint lacking merit. This suit occurred in the Illinois Northern District only once, but has been cited at least since 1980 as an example of frivolity (e.g., Possley, 1980). The story is retold because the state's Attorney General's office repeatedly cites it, and the claim assumes the character of false iterative in that constant telling elevates a single past event to the status of an oft-repeated occurrence. In this manner, stories are easily reframed by cynical readers with the consequence that both originally intended and legal meanings are replaced with new ones connoting frivolousness. One law clerk complained that lay readers especially tend to reframe the legal meaning of frivolity into its more common meaning that implies worthlessness. This produces both a public frame, one intended for mass consumption, and a private frame, one employed by "official" readers. Strategic frame-shifting, in turn, easily mystifies the prisoner litigation process as well as the nature of the court system, when the public interpretations are embedded in the demagogic and self-serving ideological rhetoric of public officials.

Sense-making is complicated when readers' readings become influenced by institutional frames external to the master frame. Clerks read cases framed by federal and district rules; forms, motions, and orders must be filed according to established protocol; hearings and trials are conducted in a ritualized and predictable fashion; and judicial sense-making ostensibly derives from Constitutional interpretation and the logic of case law. Defendants frame the narrative as a means of establishing subsequent exonerative stories of their own or as a means of devising strategies to disassociate themselves from the "facts," whether true or not. They do not so much read the story as selectively exerpt and respond to those passages that can be manipulated to absolve them from culpability or liability. Because courts are information processing systems, participants create a social reality by manipulating, interpreting, or creating information in ways guided by their needs of their own domain. Hence, in addition to formal rules, judicial readings may be mediated by fiscal requisites, political expediency, or personal biases based on predilections for the genre.

Frames furnish the primary working symbols that define the cognitive contours upon and around which other readers create a meaning-laden context, or a "message about how a message is to be heard" (Manning, 1986: 287). To be successful, the storyteller must key the contextual significance of the narrative to the fit the context of the audiences' readings.

Keying: The Rhetorical Context

Successful stories must contain a sufficiently convincing plot and denouement to persuade the audience that a violation of a constitutionally protected right has occurred. But compelling stories require more than detailed accounts. Some stories are brief, told in a few succinct sentences. Others are epic narratives running sixty pages or more. The prisoner attempts to communicate a true proposition in a manner that can be understood by multiple audiences. The goal is to persuade the audience of both the validity of fact and the meaning of those facts within the broader context of Constitutional law. Persuasion, however, is an ambiguous and problematic enterprise, for not all readers possess identical frames. Facts may be misinterpreted or rituals unrecognized or ignored. Prisoners and court personnel might not understand in the same way the phrase "I'm being punished in prison." The lexicon is clear and the individual words are relatively uncomplex. Translating this phrase into something substantively or legally meaningful requires either further explication of meaning on the part of the prisoner, or a sophisticated understanding of the story's contextual transformative rules by the reader in order to reconstruct the meaning intended by the author.

The prisoner story resembles a narrative dictionary by which prisoners key their lexicon to the audience by taking a set of facts, as they perceive them, and retranslating these to correspond to the frame by which they believe the audience might be persuaded to act. Disciplining a prisoner for possession of illicit alcohol seems a perfectly reasonable response when read from the staff master frame of "maintaining social order," and the ostensible meaning of the staff action possesses obvious meaning. If, however, the prisoner rekeys the events to indicate that a guard provided the alcohol in return for a favor and then disciplined the prisoner when the favor was not fully delivered, the events take on a quite different meaning. The storyteller must, therefore, properly rekey the events by anticipating the frame by which the reader will infer the preferred interpretation as one of staff impropriety and "deprivation of liberty or property."

The coherence of a story centers around the rhetorical goal of persuasion, and the keying of the story becomes structured for an intended audience. A key refers to:

> the set of conventions by which a given activity, one already meaningful in terms of some primary framework, is transformed into something patterned on this activity but seen by the participants to be something quite else (Goffman, 1974: 43–44).

Through their keyed story telling, those who are powerless hope to change their status or conditions by appealing to those who are not. By reciting incidents and defining concepts, it conveys the meaning of the properties of behavior similar to a *correlational code,* or sets of expressions and contents evoking meaning and significance of other expressions and contents (cf. Eco, 1984: 165). The symbols in the case correspond to broader legal symbols that illustrate the Consitutional relevance of the story. For prisoners, the story says "Help me! I've been screwed." For court personnel, the story must display a Constitutional violation. For defendants, there are no good stories, only nuisance exercises that are studied to identify plot flaws, inaccuracies, and lack of logical denouement. The public and the media often do not understand the story at all, doubting that it ever need have been told. As a consequence, the case must not only be compelling, but must also convince a variety of audiences that it is a story worth telling. The rhetorical power of the story thus requires a sophisticated understanding of the multiple frames and readings employed by divers audiences. As a mechanism for unlocking access to courts, stories are embedded in and patterned by a vocabulary and preferred discursive style, link facts to legal relevance and suggest what organizational action should occur. This shapes the narrative style.

NARRATIVE STYLES

Prisoner stories are not alike; they differ in how they are told and what they want done. The strategies by which prisoners key their story to an audience provides the narrative style. Stories take the style they do for two reasons. First, prisoners make assumptions about how the audience interprets their narrative, and second, as a structurally and societally powerless group, they attempt to portray their plight as convincingly as possible to generate sympathy and relief.

Each story possesses a particular style of rhetoric, or "ingratiation strategy," attempting "to gain favor by the hypnotic or suggestive process of saying the right thing'" (Burke, 1984: 50). The narrative style reveals the motive of the suit. Motivation, as used here, does not imply an understanding of the psychological urge or the incitement of will that impelled any given prisoner to sue. It refers instead to the motif and underlying rhetoric that powers the story itself. The motive provides the organizing theme and reveals the action requested.

Narrative styles may be distinguished by how they are keyed. In some, the intent of the petition is *discrete* and in others, *universalistic*. Both types attempt to convey the urgency of a wrong that needs righting, but each contains a different mode of telling, a different style of rhetoric, and different keying mechanisms. Discrete tales are keyed to an isolated incident as experienced by a single litigant, and universalistic stories are keyed to broader issues and shared experiences. Discrete stories are keyed to personal problems, and say "Help me." Universalistic tales are keyed to a shared plight and say "Help us."

Discrete Narratives

The discrete narrative pleads for individual justice. Similar in some ways to dramatic Greek tragedy, it describes the travails endured by the victim resulting from unjust powerful external forces. In the cosmology of the discrete narrative, capricious and vindictive gods determine social existence and the Furies rule the prisons. Like a mortal appealing for divine intervention from the Olympians, a powerless prisoner, the victim in a discrete story, appeals for deliverance from an evil in order to restore justice. Because of his or her fundamental powerlessness, the prisoner cannot gain deliverance without the intervention of the appeals process.

The discrete narrative in many ways resembles the impressionistic tale of ethnographers in that a prisoner attempts to reconstruct in dramatic form events and behaviors that are notable. In this style:

> Events are recounted in the rough order they are said to have occurred and carry with them all the odds and ends that are associated with the remembered events. The idea is to draw an audience into an unfamiliar story world and allow them, insofar as possible, to see and hear what the fieldworker saw, heard what they felt (Van Maanen, 1988).

Unlike more sophisticated tales, however, the discrete story tends to "stand alone," often failing to adequately connect the specific details with the broader conceptual or legal issues.

Many habeas cases are discrete, because they allege a personal injustice that either results in or prolongs the suffering of continued incarceration.[1] About two-thirds of civil rights cases are discrete, and fall into two broad categories, harassment and copycat.

Harassment Narratives

Harassment stories are a type of weapon wielded in retaliation for a specific wrong suffered by the prisoner, usually from a particular employee. The act of filing symbolizes the prisoner's helplessness and frustration, and the act itself, rather than the decision, provides a reward of sorts. Harassment suits serve both an instrumental and a cathartic function. They are cathartic because they provide a pressure valve for prisoners who feel wronged and have no internal remedy. They are instrumental because, win or lose, they ultimately may reduce suffering by preventing further undesirable actions.[2] A harassment petition may arise when a prisoner feels a guard unjustifiably "has it in for me!," and responds by filing suits against that guard when an opportunity occurs. Harassment suits "make waves" within the institution. While making waves might seem frivolous, this response increases the costs of undesired behavior by alerting the staff that perceived improper behaviors are susceptible to nonviolent prisoner resistance and possible external sanctions. Even if the case is dismissed during IFP review or on a preliminary motion, defendants may still be required to respond with depositions (written statements), or interrogatories (questions and answers) that serve a nuisance function by requiring the time and resources of staff. Harassment suits also make visible staff abuses or inadequate conditions, which may prove embarrassing to prison administrators. In discussing his early litigation career, one nationally recognized jailhouse lawyer described the motivation and consequences of a harassment suit:

> I was really antagonistic. I got down on [guards]. I said, "Who the hell are they to boss me around, and to do this and that, and blah, blah, blah, and if you fuck up one instance, I'm going to sue you. Because if I fuck up for one instant, you're definitely throwing me in the hole, and you're taking my life away more." So, you know, we got a real battle going here. I ain't going to lay down, you know? . . . Guys lined up outside of my room. I had a typewriter in my room, and I would take them through the administrative remedies. "What beef you got with the joint?" For ten months straight I did this. I told myself, "I got a mark to make. I'm going to file a suit against this joint everyday for at least a month or two straight." And I filed for 60 days, a suit every day for somebody in that joint. For guys who just didn't know what the fuck to do. Guys would always come to me then, and I did get to serve interrogatories on [one exceptionally abusive guard], and asked him a lot of questions, a whole lot of embarrassing ones. He was forced by the court to do it. But even though I didn't win the suit, a lot of times you can lose the battle and win the war. And that's what it was a lot of times. It was the principle, and it was, "Hey, wait a minute, you're just not going to get away with doing this and never answer for it." So I didn't win no money,

but that ain't no big thing. I wasn't after the money. I just wanted them not to do that again. Who the hell is he to tell a guard to fuck with me every chance that he gets? (Jailhouse lawyer, interview, 1983).

"Winning" a harassment suit, then, need not be a court victory. Even if summarily dismissed by the court, harassment cases may nonetheless fulfill their retaliatory function. It is not the content of the story so much as that the story is told at all:

> I got in an argument the other day with a lady who said that one of our famous jailhouse lawyers, [R. S.], lost one of his cases, and I said to her, "Lady, he ain't lost nothing." And she said, "I read what the judge said. It sure looked like he lost." I said, "Lady, that was just the first step. Next we go to the Seventh Circuit, and after that, maybe even to the Supreme Court, but we ain't lost nothing, because just doin' it means we win." We win from the outset, before we even go to court. Just the doin' of it wears them down, maybe make them more careful about their petty harassment and policies in the future. Just filing the grievances is part of the system [of struggle] (Jailhouse lawyer, interview, 1983).

Harassment cases, however, are the weakest of all prisoner stories. They are easily fabricated because they tend to pit the account of a prisoner against the account of an employee. They also tend to challenge legally and substantively minor issues, of great significance to those who file them, but usually of little Constitutional consequence. Hence, harassment stories are often immediately dismissed.

Frivolous harassment stories are also easily discernible by what is left unsaid in that they often omit crucial facts of the context of an alleged infraction while greatly detailing the infraction itself. A harassment case that alleges guard assault, for example, may describe in detail the method of attack, the extent of injuries, and considerable irrelevant detail, such as time of day, weather conditions or unrelated legal cases that proscribe guard violence. What is omitted may be the motive of the assault (the prisoner first attacked the guard and was forcibly subdued), the context (a guard accidentally brushed against the prisoner, who then slipped on the stairs), or a logical consistency in the chronology or denouement. This does not mean that all harassment suits are fabricated, but because this type of suit tends to be filed more often by inexperienced and angry litigants, there may be inappropriate and disproportionate embellishment in these stories compared to others. Whether frivolous or not, harassment cases represent a *peaceful* forum, often one of last resort, by which a prisoner can attempt to resolve a grievance:

> I don't know whether [this prisoner] wrote this [story] or not—it was probably written by a guardhouse lawyer. But whoever wrote it, it's one of

the few times in his life that he has tried to communicate with someone and persuade someone without using a gun (Federal judge, interview, 1986).

Copycat Narratives

A second type of discrete narrative occurs in the *copycat* case. Like Hollywood sequels and spin-off imitations, these are "me too" stories by which some litigants attempt to exploit an earlier tale. News of settlements and monetary awards spreads quickly through a prison, and, hoping for similar success, other prisoners file similar suits on the theory that "if it worked for him, it will work for me." Such stories, then, take their form partly because of the inability of a prisoner to construct an original narrative, and partly because of an attempt to exploit the successes of others, even if lacking an identical experience. Despite their occasional nuisance value, copycat cases reflect a measure of powerlessness by which novice litigants attempt to tip the odds of success a bit more in their favor.

One characteristic of the copycat suit is the recirculated motif. Sometimes copycat narratives derive from broader tales that circulate through the prison. When these tales are blatantly plagiarized, or the facts do not fit the law, the stories are easily identified and rejected. The story that originally impelled subsequent suits need not have been successful, especially if it captures the imagination and enthusiasm of subsequent storytellers. Recurring copycat stories resemble such urban folk tales as "the disappearing hitch-hiker" or "spider eggs in bubble gum" in that the origins are obscure, appear contemporaneous, stretch credibility, are believed to be true but easily disconfirmed, yet are repeated and sometimes embellished (Brunvand, 1981: 3–6). In Illinois prisons, for example, several less astute litigants have filed habeas petitions based on the belief that convictions in Cook County District Court are illegal, because they explain, the court, in fact, has no jurisdiction in criminal cases. The basis of the complaints derive from the name of the court, "Cook County *District Court*," which was interpreted by litigants to mean that the court was an independent county court, rather than a state circuit court, and thus not mandated to pass judgment upon state crimes. This, according to state law and "home rule unit" theory, would presumably make convictions illegal, because the county would not have jurisdiction to incarcerate independent from the state. Attempts to convince litigants that their stories contained a flaw based on terminological misunderstanding fails to dissuade hopeful litigants who believe "it's a technicality in the law that doesn't give the courts jurisdiction to put us in jail!"

A second characteristic of the copycat story is its tendency to be filed immediately after an earlier case. For example, when an Illinois court ruled that heinous circumstances of a crime could not be used in determining parole eligibility, suits challenging parole increased significantly until the ruling was overturned (*Welsh v. Mizell,* 668 F.2d 328, 7th Cir., 1982). In 1981, only 23 combined habeas and civil rights suits related to granting parole were filed, compared with 111 in 1982. This was reduced by half in 1983 (54), and by half again in 1984–86 (27, 31, and 27 filings in each year). Hence, when parole-related suits were successful, others followed, but when success appeared less certain, they declined.

A third characteristic of the copycat case is the "canned-memo" format that repeats the text of a previous case. Court personnel describe this as "legal Cliff Notes," in which prisoners key the names and facts of law to fit their own situation. Because narrators key their tellings to the case being copied rather than to the audience, such narratives are easily recognizable, occasionally absurd, and do not help the storyteller. The canned brief often produces incoherent stories that, like student term papers recycled from term to term, are quickly identified and dismissed:

> What you'll find is the same complaint that might have been drafted by an attorney popping up in every single individual case. So I think if a case has been notorious, there will sometimes be a filing of that type of case for several months or a year or two after that (Department of Corrections staff attorney, interview, 1986).

The particularistic storyteller relates the facts of a personal event and attempts to convince the reader that the event requires attention as a matter of law. Sometimes, however, the story is keyed to the events rather than to the audience, and the legal frame by which relevance becomes interpreted requires dismissal of the story. Because discrete narratives tend to be told by inexperienced tellers, the probability of dismissal is high, the chances of legal relief slight and the future utility of the story curtailed. The failure to recognize the master frame of law and the strategies by which the story must be appropriately keyed jeopardizes both readings and action.

Universalistic Narratives

Some prisoners, typically jailhouse lawyers, have developed considerable rhetorical mastery, and tend to narrate a different kind of tale. These *universalistic* narratives address issues that affect other inmates, rather than just a single litigant. Universalistic tales are keyed to reform, and they illustrate conditions or behaviors that can be framed within context of systemic or institutional, rather than individual, relief. There are two kinds, censorial and class action. These suits are not so much an expression of individual powerlessness, but a calculated resistance to prison existence. Universalistic narratives resemble parables in that they contain an implied doctrine and make the duty of the audience clear.

Censorial Narratives

Censorial challenges (Carroll, 1977a) demand enforcement of or compliance with existing federal or state law, state policies, or institutional regulations. State statutes, case law, or prior decisions all provide the stuff of the telling, and the stories arise when prison officials do not follow the rules. Although usually filed individually, it is not uncommon for several prisoners to file simultaneously in order to dramatize the impact of the grievance. The most common censorial suits in the Illinois system seek disciplinary committee compliance with federally mandated due process rules, which are consistently violated in Illinois. Disciplinary punishment may include extending the time actually served in prison by reducing the goodtime deducted from a sentence. Prisoners argue that failure to follow established disciplinary procedures deprives them of Fourteenth Amendment protections against loss of liberty when established rules of evidentiary proceedings, punishment or rule invocation are violated. These filings simply request that the institution follow mandated rules, and are generally not attempts to avoid punishment or rule-following by prisoners.

Censorial narratives proceed from the basic syllogism that "all state officials must obey the law, and corrections' staff are state officals. Therefore, they must obey the law." The story's structure, therefore, takes on a simple form. First, appropriate statute or case law is identified. Second, staff violations are documented. Finally, legal relief—remedial actions and usually punitive damages—is requested. When properly keyed and documented, the censorial narrative becomes a powerful weapon in the hands of a skilled litigator, and the logic and legal precedents cited lead the reader to an inescapable conclusion.[3] Although rarely creating new law, the well-told story reverses the hierarchy of staff-prisoner power, and the courts become a helpful ally against staff abuse.

Class-Action Narratives

The second type of universalistic narrative, the *class-action* suit, generally attempts to establish case law that would have a far-reaching impact on prison administration and conditions. Unlike censorial challenges, which attempt to *enforce law*, universalistic narratives are keyed to *make law* by establishing precedents that raise the standards of prison policies and conditions.[4]

Rather than attack discrete polices, as do censorial suits, the class action narrative describes fundamental problems endemic in a given prison or—more often—in an entire prison system. Chronic overcrowding, failure of staff to protect against inmate violence, or inadequate medical care typify the complaints class-action suits address, and their resolution often requires drastic reformulation of policy, increased prison construction, or significant fiscal expenditures. One Illinois suit, for example, has challenged administrators' inability to curtail prisoner-on-prisoner violence by charging the Department of Corrections with reckless violation of the Eighth Amendment by directly and indirectly perpetuating violent conditions (*Calvin R. v. Lane*, 82–C–1955, N.D. Ill., 1982). If the plaintiffs win, the impact on disciplinary tactics, classification policy, and celling practices would require considerable reevaluation and modification.

Class-action narratives share several features. First, they appeal to explicit principles of Constitutional philosophy. Rather than identify a single staff member or complain of a single instance in which one prisoner was abused, such stories describe endemic problems and seek broad prison reform. Second, these stories challenge the fundamental policies of prison administration and, when successful, result in drastic revision of policy, or—as in the case of overcrowding complaints—dramatic expansion of facilities and allocation of resources. Third, these stories tend to be exceptionally well written, often because the issue is sufficiently important to attract outside assistance, or because the issue stimulates the interest and energies of several jailhouse lawyers who devote their time to researching and writing the best narrative possible. Because of the seriousness of the issues raised, the potential impact on prisons, and the usually dramatic nature of the claims, readers tend to take these suits more seriously than particularistic or censorial challenges. Defendants marshall more resources, judges pay closer attention to issues and are more willing to appoint counsel, and the media tend to follow the proceedings, which rarely occurs in other types of cases. Fourth, class action suits tend to be two-stage inductive processes in which, first, existing prison conditions are inferred to violate Constitional protections, and second, these violations are generalized to a broad category of victims. The general logic runs as follows: "If the Constitution prohibits a set of conditions A, and if existing conditions correspond to conditions A, than existing conditions are unconstitutional." All members of the affected class thus become those on behalf of whom the suit is filed. Fifth, because both types of reformist suits challenge policies, they rarely cite a single defendant. They instead tend to cite classes of defendants and couch issues in broad terms, taking mundane events and grounding their meaning in explicit Constitutional related issues. Finally, the narrators tend to be experienced litigators, and their stories skillfully draw from a wide range of other stories, integrating bits and pieces of both case law and other prisoner petitions to weave the tale and capture the reader's attention.

To assume that all prisoner stories are alike creates a distorted picture of the nature of filings. The allegation that prisoner suits are "frivolous" often reflects the narrative's structure or style rather than its substance.

Not all stories are keyed in the same way; without proper keying, the probability that the master frame by which and audience interpretively reconstructs the story "out of frame" increases. By categorizing stories, it becomes possible to distinguish the motifs and motivations by which stories are keyed, and by which they are subsequently read. Identifying the nature of a story, however, tells us little about the quality of the story.

READING CASES:
GOOD STORIES, BAD STORIES

As a *legal case*, the story requires transformation into a document, or an organizational processing device. But, something may be lost in the translation, creating an insurmountable abyss between meaning and interpretation. As a consequence the probability of failing to tell a convincing story increases, because the details and accounts may not be consistent with the situated ways in which participants read and react to the reading (e.g., Atkinson and Drew, 1979). Whether this occurs largely depends on the readers' frame, because readers are not interested so much in how a story was produced, but why it should be told at all. Hence, the quality of "frivolousness," the standard by which stories are judged, is shaped by the frame in which they are read. What constitutes a good or bad story differs between audiences, and court personnel, prisoners, and others have dramatically different views on what counts as a "good case."

A strict legal reading of prisoner stories asks a single question: What is the Constitutional issue? A more skilled and flexible reader discovers additional layers of meaning, some obvious, others hidden. The lexicon, rhetoric, and descriptions of a story display the social deprivation of prison existence, the problems of controlling and being controlled, hostile encounters between prisoners and staff, pathetic individual biographies, and human despair.

To assess a story by focusing only on precise legal merits limits one's vision of its immensely rich and variegated tapestry. A prisoner who successfully sued his captors for unjust punishment when caught "having sex with a dog" provides a comic example of frivolous suits for critics of prisoner litigation (*Russell v. Franzen*, 79–C–3774, N.D. Ill., 1974). A deeper reading, however, reveals the deprivations of prison life, the arbitrary nature of prison discipline and the power of captors to publically define prisoners' social reality. A story challenging apparent petty harassment of a prisoner by a guard, perhaps not a Constitutional violation, may depict prisoners' helplessness when both they and staff become victims of staff tension, burnout, alcoholism, and frustration.

Prisoner Readings

For prisoners, a good case means more than a winning one: it tells a story that exposes what they perceive to be inhumane and unjust treatment. Prisoner litigants, especially those not experienced in case filing, tend to emphasize the incident, and the narrative speaks to the grievance rather than to the relationship between that grievance and its derivation from prison policy. The discrete case claims "a guard hit me;" the universalistic case claims "the prison generally does not enforce restrictions on guard brutality." The inexperienced storyteller often remains at the level of impressionistic description, neglecting the crucial analytic discourse that provides the reasons that the story relates to law. These are "bad cases" even if they are "good resistance," because they do not transcend individualism.

If the quality of prisoner stories could be placed on a continuum, the best stories would be class action narratives told by experienced jailhouse lawyers. Because of the multiple grievances of such stories, they invariably have substantial basis in fact, and the ability of talented narrators enhances the telling. The worst type of stories would be habeas corpus petitions, especially those challenging a technicality of the original case. Despite their occasional dramatic creativity, courts give no credence to such claims as "I couldn't have molested that boy because I only like sex with girls," "I am in prison; that proves my counsel was incompetent," or "the judge and prosecutor conspired against me." These examples must not be construed to mean that all habeas petitions lack serious foundation. Many, probably most, have some substantive merit, and the instances of miscarried justice in Chicago criminal courts are numerous. Nonetheless, the ease by which some prisoners justify habeas filings was illustrated by one jailhouse lawyer (considered incompetent and a "bad example") who argued with considerable passion, if not logic: "Everybody could get out of prison [on habeas petitions] if they knew how, because there are so many loopholes in the law." His continued incarceration despite his own appeals, and the fact that prisoners are rarely released on habeas petitions did not dissuade him.

Some jailhouse lawyers admit to having filed "bad" (or frivolous) cases, usually early in their careers, but none of the more experienced litigants condone it because of its personal and legal costs:

> [Filing frivolous cases] depends on your ethics, too. I'm not saying I never filed anything frivolous. There's been times when I've stretched out a little too far, and really got pissed, and filed something vindictively because it was vindictive against me first. And I went out of the bounds a couple of times there, but you lose that real quick. You can't keep doing that. It happens, and somebody realizes that on the other end real quick, and says "frivolous," boom, and if you keep doing that, you ain't getting nowhere.

You get sick of that real quick. It's better when you've got them really neat, and you go all the way truthful through the thing, because then you know you've really got them, and if you lose, you know they're wrong. And you can fight a better case that way,'cause you come right from the heart. You don't have to start thinking of fabrication for any testimony, because it's right there. It's really there (Jailhouse lawyer, interview, 1986).

Narrative power, or the ability to convincingly and compelling select and manipulate symbols for sharing with others, provides a resource unequally distributed among narrators. As a consequence, power in prisons not only exists in relationships between and among staff and inmates, but inheres as well in the access even to symbolic resources. Less adroit litigants, especially "one-shotters," are not as apt as experienced litigants to craft a careful story. They believe that to simply tell the story suffices to demonstrate the credibility of their claim. Most prisoners, however, agree that "bullshit" cases, those that are fabricated or exaggerated, should be avoided:

Once in a while you run into a jailhouse lawyer who will [file "bullshit" suits] to be a real bastard, but it gets old. Even to them guys, it gets old. You keep filing stuff like that, and you're just wasting your time. There's enough real stuff around to do it, to really fight the system on real issues where they're really doing wrong to people (Jailhouse lawyer, interview, 1986).

For prisoners, then, a good story describes the deprivations of prison life or the abuse of power and alerts the courts to improper conduct of the criminal justice system. This does not mean, however, that the good case is necessarily humanitarian or altruistic. A suit challenging restrictions to religious freedom, ostensibly a worthy cause, may in fact be an attempt by street gangs to establish their legitimacy and increase their freedom to convene meetings.[5] This case is considered "good" not because prisoners support gangs—which most do not, despite their possible affiliation—but because it challenges the alleged capriciousness of policies regulating group assembly.

Further, although the motives of self-serving suits may be challenged, the motif of the story invariably reflects prison problems that provide the vehicle by which questionable interests may be expressed. This suggests that even the most trivial or malicious suits cannot be examined independently from the context in which they are filed. One easily identified frivolous suit requested a court injunction to force prison staff to cease using sophisticated equipment to read the prisoner's thoughts. Some critics might see the inmate's story as an example of the dangers of liberalizing prisoners' access to courts. If read diagnostically, however, the suit reveals insights into classifying and assigning prisoners: what, one might ask, is such a prisoner doing in a state prison, and what type of treatment is he receiving?

Court Readings

The readings done by judges and their clerks are crucial, because the meanings they impute to a story determine not only whether there will be further readings, but what types of subsequent readings will be allowed. Court personnel ostensibly read stories to answer a single question: is there a meritorious and adjudicable issue that deserves further inquiry? Not all court personnel employ the same frames when reading stories. Some adopt a narrow perspective, others one more broad. Further, sometimes multiple frames coexist, as when a reader uses a story to implement a personal agenda, one that enhances or obstructs the probability of reform. This occurs especially when judicial or social ideology intrudes into the reading. In practice, then, how one reads a story may be shaped by a variety of factors.

It occasionally happens that prisoners identify sound legal claims, but tell their story to the wrong audience. This occurs especially in complaints of lost or damaged property, many negligence claims, and many habeas requests that have not exhausted state remedies. Federal courts have recently held that property claims usually have a state remedy available through small claims actions, and negligence claims are resolvable through tort actions. Such claims are consequently dismissed as legally frivolous, adding credence to critics views that most prisoner stories lack substance. In fact, however, these stories contain legally relevant complaints, and the reader's task then becomes one of determining proper jurisdictional audience.

Readings are further keyed by readers' Constitutional philosophy. Some court readers use statute or case law as a literal code to which the case must conform. If the story lacks unequivocal correspondence to this strict legal code, it is a bad story and is rejected accordingly. Other readers may be guided by flexible transformative rules and actively engage in sense-making, using the case as a dictionary by which to infer adjudicable meanings.

Some judges assume primary responsibilty for interpreting the narrative, some pass the responsibility on the law clerks, and some request a quick précis—a predigested summary—from a designated reader.

Judicial Readings

For judges, two stylistic elements generally constitute a good story: it must communicate, and it must state a cognizable claim:

> So the first thing [prisoners] are doing is trying to communicate to me. And that's the first mark of a good *pro se* lawsuit. Do they write in a fashion that I can understand? (Federal judge, interview, 1986).

Each litigant competes with all other litigants for judicial time and attention, and judges faced with heavy case loads require stories that

"grab" attention with style and merit.[6] Some judges favorably respond
to legibility and style:

> What makes a good case? Well, the first thing that makes a good case is
> good spelling, good typing, good grammar. You don't see a lot of that in
> prisoner cases, but that's the first thing that makes a good case. . . . Now,
> that's number one. Can I read it? If I can read it, I take the time to read it.
> If it's illegible, I don't take the time to translate it. I just can't. I don't have
> the time (Federal judge, interview, 1986).

Like any compelling story, the good prisoner narrative should flow
smoothly, concisely, and compellingly as a means of assuring the attention of the reader. When inexperienced prisoners are unable to relate
their story to law, there may be a tendency to expand the narrative:

> [O]casionally, every now and then, you'll get a complaint that the guy has
> probably been working on for a couple of years. It goes on, and on, and
> on. He recalls and documents every little grievance that has befallen him in
> the joint. Those guys have some problems, because I have almost this
> compulsion to read, and I run out of time. So I've got to do something else,
> and I'll put it aside, and I'll read it again another time. Finally, I'll wade my
> way through it, I'm not talking five pages single spaced, I'm talking fifty,
> sixty pages single-spaced (Federal judge, interview, 1986).

It is useful when narrators tailor their story to the audience, but this
can create a problem when a narrator does not fluently speak the
audience's language. Stories then become hampered by unsuccessful
attempts to write in the language of and intended audience—the legal
community—rather than simply narrate events as they occurred:

> And, of course, they try to work in the jargon of the lawyers, and what-not.
> Instead of just telling their story, they try to sound like lawyers, and they
> get all screwed up with the syntax (Federal judge, interview, 1986).

Good story-telling must make sense in a way that communicates
meaning to those who review cases. These meanings must justify federal
intervention by clearly identifying an adjudicable issue. The threshold
of meaning may differ among decision-makers, but in general, all are
able to describe a "bad case" by example, if not by precise definition.

Past case law defining or clarifying prisoner rights and staff obligations
also may provide a partial code for assessing the quality of a story.

> If a correction's officer realized that you, the inmate, have no medical need,
> and I deliberately ignore you, causing pain and suffering deliberately, that
> might be a violation of the Eighth Amendment. Now, this is a common
> case. A prisoner sends a complaint in: "I have a skin rash, and I've been to
> the clinic 52 times, and the doctor hasn't done anything to cure me, and
> they give me something to put on it, and it's still not cured, and they've
> subjected me to cruel and unusual punishment." Well, that's a frivolous

case. There's no deliberate indifference or neglect that I can see. The guy's been to see a doctor, literally, I'm not exaggerating, 23 times, and he doesn't like what the doctor's doing. He's got a malpractice claim, but that's not a Constitutional violation. That's a frivolous claim under Section 1983. There's no civil rights issue there. You can go to the state court and get the doctor for malpractice, but not civil rights (Federal judge, interview, 1986).

Recent federal decisions distinguishing between staff negligence and recklessness also have shaped how one reads a prisoner's narrative:

A not-uncommon prisoner case is the claim that a prisoner was injured in the prison. . . . Now, the Supreme Court of the United States has said in those kinds of cases that a prisoner cannot recover if all he is able to demonstrate is negligence on behalf of the administration of the prison, quite unlike what would happen to you if you were negligently injured by someone else in prison. There you would have a claim, but here, you would have to demonstrate that the guards that were there, or the administration itself, was acting recklessly toward you, not just negligently. In that kind of a situation, the kinds of things that I perceive make a good case is where I get the idea after reading pleadings or depositions that the prisoner has a *meaningful* sort of an injury, i.e., a broken arm, a concussion; something that seems significant. And, two, if there is some indication that the people at the jail simply knew about the problem that he might be beaten up inmates, or a particular guard, for example, had it in for him. . . . knew about that situation and just ignored it. Now you're beginning to talk about what I perceive as a meritorious claim (Federal judge, interview, 1985).

One judge, considered a judicial moderate, typifies a philosophy judges generally share on the definition of a meritorious civil rights claim:

I've dealt with three or four in two years where a prisoner was pretty badly hurt because of his fellow inmates, or because of a guard. They are significant things, and by God, in a sense, I guess I have sort of a feeling that sure, these people are locked up, but the federal courts cannot ignore reckless conduct by prison officials which endangers the health and safety of the inmates. So to the extent that they meet the standards set down by the Supreme Court, they should have a right to, and do, file cases that I think are *not* just junk, but are meaningful cases.

Court personnel seem to find most prisoner stories tedious reading, but exceptions can be exciting:

You know, the most intriguing case to me that ever was filed by a prisoner was *Gideon v. Wainright,* which you gotta know about, where an age-old practice that nobody had challenged—well, it had been challenged from time to time—but the right to a lawyer at your trial was left to the state, except in exceptional circumstances. If you couldn't speak the language, or were mentally defective, or whatever. And Gideon files this case out of a Florida prison, and by God, the Supreme Court of the United States listens to it, appoints a great lawyer to represent, and changes the whole rule. And that's why prisoner cases in one sense are kind of fun, because, yes, a lot of cases lack merit, and every once in a while you find one that's sort of a pearl that you look at and say, "You know, he's put his finger on what I perceive to be a real problem" (Federal judge, interview, 1985).

Although judicial criteria and thresholds of tolerance may vary in assessing prisoners' stories, Constitutional relevance remains the prime requisite of the denouement:

I think a working definition [of a good case] is that if a prisoner is complaining about something that has no substance, they have to rise to the level of Constitutional deprivation. It isn't every incidence of unhappiness that gives the prisoner the right to file a law suit. After all, [Section] 1983 is for violations of privileges, rights, immunities protected by the Constitution. It isn't every hassle with a guard or warden that gives the prisoner the right to file a law suit. That statute is a very important statute, and we shouldn't let a prisoner misuse it. To the extent that a prisoner is allowed to misuse it, to that extent, those that have a case won't be heard. See, because if I'm busy, if I have a whole bunch of, uh, frivolous matters, or matters. . . . I'll give you an example. Supposing what the prisoners complain about is that the statute allows him three showers a week. And they're only giving him two. And he wants the third shower. Now, you know very well if you heard that case, the people at the penitentiary may explain why they couldn't let him have three showers—the place was clogged up, or the pipe was frozen, or something like that. Now, are you going to give a person a trial on something like that, because he doesn't have a third shower every week? He has two, and he doesn't say that he's suffering from a skin disease. He doesn't say that, you see. I wouldn't let him file that law suit. And other examples can be found. I had one over here involving a prisoner at Metropolitan Correctional Center. He's complained that [he's in segregation] and they have not inspected him as the regulations require, every 60 days. Well, let's assume that's true. What harm comes to a prisoner because he's not inspected every 60 days? They're inspected, say, instead of 60 days, every seven weeks or so. . . . Now, it would be different if from lack of inspection he had suffered this, or suffered that, or didn't have food, or didn't have medicine, or didn't have medical care, that would be very different, wouldn't it? But, because those inspections are intended to detect conditions of incarceration of administrative segregation that are injurious to the prisoner. If he's suffering no injury, of what importance is the right to have an inspection precisely as the rules [specify]. . . . They don't say they haven't inspected them, they only complain that they haven't inspected them every 60 days as the rule requires (Federal judge, interview, 1985).

Law Clerk Readings

The delegation by judges of the authority to read and interpret stories to law clerks introduces a new layer of readers who may possess and use frames other than the master legal frame. Unlike judges, law clerks may be more willing to engage in an interactive reading by digging below the surface for concealed meanings. Perhaps clerks retain an enthusiastic idealism for law, or perhaps they are less bound by the accountability and responsibility faced by judges, but clerks seem more willing than judges to participate in sense-making. One clerk provided the example of a prisoner suit demanding a Sears catalogue. The suit survived the IFP review, despite the possibility that it could be interpreted by the casual reader as frivolous:

> But [frivolousness] has different implications. It's not just the Sears catalogue. I mean, if it's really frivolous, it's not going to get past the *in forma pauperis* review. I mean, it's not even going to be filed as a lawsuit. So the cases that do get by have, for one reason or another, they have some merit. It may not be the merit that the plaitiff intended when he or she filed the law suit. We might see something in it that they might not see. The Sears catalogue—he may just want the catalogue, and he may want to win, and that's all. But we might go back to a different viewpoint, you know, First Amendment or due process or whatever.

Although law clerks rarely employ a precise definition of a good story, sometimes the dramatic injustice of a story makes readings easy:

> [A good case] is hard to define. You can define it by example. One of our litigants has two cases against the Cook County jail, and one of them, he had a tattoo, and was being hassled. . . . [A street gang] kept telling [J.P.] "get rid of that tattoo, or we'll get rid of it for you." Now, they did. The gang members eventually burned the tattoo off. Now, by itself, that wouldn't be a Constitutional violation for which you could sue the jail. But this guy wrote letters, he told the guards, he told the warden, he said, "Look. I've got this tattoo, and they're going to burn it off. They've been threatening me, they're going to burn it off, you know from their track record, they will burn off my tattoo." And they ignored it. They didn't put him in segregation, they didn't do anything to try to help him. . . . [case number] 86–C–1867, and there's another one, he has a second case which is very similar, 86–C–2718. . . . It's against the same parties. Basically, it was a prisoner who was on death row, or was supposed to be in segregation because he'd been sentenced to death, and he wasn't. He was in the general population. The guy is crazy, and he picks on [J.P.] and says "I'm going to beat you up, I'm going to beat you up." And [J.P.] writes letters saying, "Help, help, he's going to beat me up, and you know he's going to do it." And they didn't do anything, and lo and behold, they beat the snot out of him. So he's got a second law suit for that. I mean, this guy has got a streak of bad luck. But that's the kind of thing, if he hadn't done anything, if the guy had just beaten him up, that isn't a Constitutional violation for which you can sue the jail. What you're getting them on, essentially, is gross negligence, willful misconduct. You know, you knew this guy was going to be assaulted, they were warned, they knew the people he's complaining

about were likely to assault him, and they didn't do anything (Federal law clerk, interview, 1986).

Some clerks, in fact, frame their readings in the context of advocacy and aggressively search for adjudicable meaning, even if the story does not provide an immediately obvious correlative code by which to do so:

> Clerk: That's our job. Just take their facts, and figure out if there's some way that they have a claim. That's what we do, and I don't think it's necessarily up to them at the stage at which they file their initial complaint to say, it's a First Amendment violation because of this case and this case and this case." That's not the purpose of the complaint. The purpose is to set out the facts that give you the claim. It might be our job to sit down and say, "Yeh, there's a case there, and that says this is a First Amendment violation." You know, so you get to proceed *in forma pauperis*.
>
> JT: How would that differ from their appointed lawyer? Wouldn't that be part of their job?
>
> Clerk: Um, yeh. Sure. This is when you get in trouble (N.D. law clerk, interview, 1986).

Other Readings

For some readers, a "good story" is a contradiction in terms. One judge has publicly labelled prisoner litigants as "psychopaths," and read their stories accordingly (McGarr, cited in Warren et al. 1984: 8). The media tend to sensationalize the most trivial prisoner suits and tend to publicize litigation's critics (e.g., Harger, 1981; Possley, 1980; *Sixty Minutes,* 1982; Warren et al. 1986). Media readings, in fact, tend to be inaccurate, highly distorted and biased, reflecting as they do the "official" position of prison administrators.

Other readers, especially defendants, have similar disdain for the prisoner narrative genre. Department of Corrections' staff and attorneys are unanimous in their hostility toward prisoner stories and feel they serve little purpose other than to harass employees, and should be curtailed. Illinois state's attorneys—those who actually defend against litigation—are somewhat more sympathetic than corrections' officials, but equally prone to criticize the stories. The former participants key stories with one predominant question in mind: "Where are the flaws in the story?" Corrections' officials are most concerned with the impact of a suit on policy, so stories are keyed in the context of potential organizational changes required if the case is lost. Hence, suits that appear exceptionally meritorious and contain explicit documentation by the prison may be fought if correctional staff read into the suit a danger of massive policy change. State's attorneys are guided by their task of saving the state money, and are willing to concede issues if it will in turn permit a face-saving settlement or, barring that, ultimately reduce official liability. For prison reformers, cases provide an index of the problems faced by prisoners, and they frame their readings in a way that elicits from diverse tales common problems of prison existence. And, of course, researchers read stories—not only for the insights they provide into prison life—but as a window into the broader social world of law, society, or language.

THE IRONY OF STORIES AND JUSTICE

Justice, the presumed ideal of judicial decisions based on universalistic rules, fair play, and truth, ostensibly guides all litigation. The irony of narration arises from the replacement of the contextually bound judicial frames with others when translating a narrative into decision-making activity.

Irony connotes a double meaning. The first implies an unanticipated outcome of originally intended actions when they result in something quite other than planned. The second implies a discursive trope in which an audience translates intended meanings into something "more real" or "superior" to the meanings originally suggested (e.g., Manning, 1979, 661–62; Burke, 1969, 511–19). Prisoner narratives, like other legal stories, reflect both types in several ways. One involves the consequences by which an apparently unsuccessful legal outcome, one lost by the prisoner, may reverberate back into the prison organization and create changes. A staff member may be exonerated of an accusation, but the context in which the incident occurred may result either in temporary relief for prisoners, in sanctions imposed against staff because of the revelations made, or in raising the visibility of prison conditions for outsiders.[7]

A second irony arises from the framing behavior of audiences when the legal master-frame of due process and Constitutional relevance becomes replaced by subframes patterned on nonlegal mandates, organizational expediency or personal self-interst. Although the goal of the adversary process requires rekeying and framing of stories in a manner that challenges the original account, such challenges nonetheless tend to shift the focus of attention from "what happened" to "who did it happen to." The result is often an ideological, rather than factual, battle in which the moral character of prisoners is raised in order to discredit the narrative or to justify the offending action, and the factual account may become secondary.[8] The stigma of prisoner immorality may become the criteria by which to assess the justice of a claim. In addition, court personnel may recode events and frame them within the "more real" context of Constitutional law, with the result that even the most flagrant abuses of power may be overlooked because narrative keying fails to unlock access to the appropriate frame.[9]

A third irony results from the organizational nature of legal rituals and their relationship to stories. This, in turn, may subvert the primary goal of justice, that of truth. As Manning has noted, the intended truth function of law becomes subverted by ritualistic story-telling. Ritual depresses factual truth and sanctions lies. In situations of high uncertainty and under conditions of low fact consensus, ritual sacralises truth and elevates it to mythological status (Manning, 1987).

All stories are ostensibly equal before the court, but not all storytellers possess equal narrative ability. Prisoners do not have equal access to the symbolic or material resources by which to build their case, and as a consequence, the power of their narrative does not lie so much in its truth but in an ability to counter the accounts and ploys of the opponent.

The irony of ritualistic legal narratives, then, lies in the manner by which they must be patterned to fit a predefined organizational process, and in the manner in which this process is enacted by other participants in ways that transform "doing justice" into "doing bureaucracy." Like all ironies, the tensions, contradictions and conflicts that emerge cannot be resolved *a priori*, but must be worked through in practice, and ironic stories often engender ironic practices.

SUMMARY

Prisoners become narrators by retelling what to them is an important event; judges become poets through their attempts to produce an opinion or judgment that communicates a more perfect legal life; defendants become critics by unravelling a narrative and providing an alternate interpretation or description. How a prisoner narrates the story depends as much on how the story is keyed to an audience as on how the audience reads the narrative patterned by the frame that provides intepretive rules. Keying shapes the narrative style by selectively generating specific meanings, and these meanings, in turn, pattern reading by constraining the framing options available to readers. The well-keyed story allows little slippage for alternative meanings so that it is almost impossible to assume alternative interpretations that may make the story unacceptable or legally weak. Thus, the intent of the well-keyed story becomes impossible to avoid. Conceptualizing prisoner suits as stories rather than simply as legal documents shifts the emphasis to the diversity of cases, the different styles of telling, and the diverse roles of readers. This, in turn, provides a better way of illustrating how different readers use different vocabularies, standards, and goals in their readings.

The storyteller finds meaning in representations of events as they occur in time and in imagined experience. The audience interprets these representations within a framework relevant to their own experience. Unfortunately, there may be not only an incompatibility of discourse, but a conflict between competing agendas. The force of the prisoner narrative depends on an ability to overcome discursive and substantive obstacles persuasively. If these cannot be surmounted, the story will not survive for a retelling. If the story is sufficiently compelling, it will enter into the more public realm of judicial processing. Here, it will be retold and subjected to more thorough scrutiny. It will be broken down and reconstituted according to the interpretive rules of successive members of the litigation community.

If it is true that liberty and equality are simultaneously affirmed in the act of writing (White, 1984: 283), then the prisoner narrative represents a crucial safeguard in promoting justice. Obviously, not all prisoners achieve the goal of their telling, some prisoners may tell false stories, and some dramatic stories may be told to the wrong or inappropriate audiences. Further, prisoners do not share equal power with their audiences, and the audiences possess far more opportunity and resources to provide alternative accounts of their own. Nonetheless, the stories are told, they are read, they are acted upon. How our readings are acted upon is our next tale.

NOTES

1. Notable exceptions include habeas challenges to endemic practices of criminal procedures, such as *Gideon v. Wainwright* (372 U.S. 335, 1963), *Mapp v. Ohio* (367 U.S. 643, 1961), or *Miranda v. Arizona* (384 U.S. 436, 1966). Although most habeas cases adduce broad legal principles, few expand or address new issues, as do many civil rights claims.
2. Typical of such a case is the prisoner who sued a guard for failing to deliver marijuana when paid to do so. The prisoner requested either that the "contract" be fulfilled or his money returned. The case was immediately dismissed, but the filing makes public the illicit economic order of prisons and the staff who participate in it in a way that could not be done through normal procedures without the risk of being labelled a "stoolie."
3. The classic example is *Monroe v. Pate* (365 U.S. 167, 1961). The plaintiffs precisely identified existing statutes and case law, keyed the argument to such concepts as "civil rights," "under color of law," and "due process," and successfully connected case facts to legal arguments such that the legal conclusion was, upon appeal, accepted.
4. *Duran v. Elrod* (74–C–2949, N.D. Ill., 1974), an Illinois suit challenging conditions at Cook County Jail, illustrates how consent decrees can shape corrections' policy. This case—despite continued intransigence by jail officials—modestly improved conditions, especially overcrowding.
5. In one recently unsuccessful case, a number of prisoners filed individual suits which were consolidated into a single class action challenge to the prison's failure to recognize an alleged religious group (*Faheem-El v. Franzen*, 79–C–2273, C.D. Ill, 1979). Although the judge ruled that the organization was a street gang rather than a religion, the suit nonetheless raised First

Amendment issues of religious liberty, and a decision favorable to the plaintiffs would have had a profound impact on how prison officials respond to perceived "street gang" organization.

6. In 1984, the unweighted number of filings per judge in Illinois' Northern District was 721, compared with 580 nationwide (*Judicial Business of the United States Courts of the Seventh Circuit,* 1984: 32).

7. One example of an ironic outcome occurred in the landmark *Wolff v. McDonnell* (418 U.S. 539, 1974), in which a prisoner lost most of his issues, but nonetheless succeeded in establishing criteria for prison disciplinary procedures for all state prisons. Less dramatic examples include allegedly improper disciplinary proceedings that—even when rejected by the courts— may result in substantial policy modification or staff training, because the costs of eliminating the cause of litigation may often be more cost-effective than continual court defense.

8. For a discussion of the "moral stigmatization" of prisoners in the due process game, see especially Goffman (1961) and Thomas, Aylward, Mika, and Blakemore (1985).

9. Jailhouse lawyers all relate similar tales to illustrate this irony. The most common involve unskilled prisoners who file their own cases, only to have them dismissed. They then turn to jailhouse lawyers who take the same story, reorganize the tale's structure, make it "more real," and successfully petition on the prisoner's behalf. The tale remains unchanged, the issues remain the same, but the tale was told "properly," carrying through the gatekeepers of law. All that changed in the narrative was the keying, which illustrates the importance to prisoners of mastering an understanding of the connection between keys and frames.

7

Doing Litigation:
Players and Processes

[Organizations] transform diverse information into culturally patterned and constrained messages by means of technology, preestablished codes, a structure of rules, and interpretative activities. One aspect of the work of organizations . . . is to encode and decode messages and thus create social realities in quite specific and differentiated fashion (Manning, 1986: 284).

M OST STUDIES OF JUDICIAL ACTIVITY tend to focus on the context of decision-making, not on the context of "social reality" from which they emerge. The general image promoted of processing prisoner litigation by media accounts and implied by critics entails a two-stage process: the prisoner writes the story, and then sends it to the judge who decides the case. This image promotes only a two-stop tour, the first offering a cursory glimpse of the prisoner's story-document, and the second paying brief homage before the shrine of the judicial decision. The organizational processing, however, is far more complex. Even prior to a decision, the story passes through numerous hands and multiple phases, and is read, screened, reread and acted upon by numerous players in the judicial system.

This chapter traces these phases of the litigation process step-by-step from initial filing through termination, and displays the dilemmas generated by asymmetrical power, diverse and often contradictory goals and agendas, participants' repertoire of strategies and interorganizational tensions that make up the litigation game. We shall visit the significant members of the judicial and corrections culture to learn how they process prisoner stories.

The term "judicial system" connotes an image of a reasonably integrated, self-contained agency acting as a cohesive whole. Yet, despite formal rules and the pervading philosophy that law is at least partially a "deductive science," the procedures and outcomes of litigation are often surprisingly ad hoc and unpredictable. Prisoners, especially, tend to view the judicial process as a monolithic entity, pitting "them," the power of the state, against "us," the victims of injustice. In the initial stages, however, the litigation process does not occur through a well integrated series of bureaucratic routines characterized by information control, systematic communication loops, or explicitly defined task performance. Court procedures may be arbitrary, episodic, highly discretionary and inconsistent, or mediated by various networks of individual and collective organized activity. As a consequence, prisoner suits are not so much adjudicated as bureaucratically processed (Turner, 1979: 625).

Unlike other types of litigation, in which private parties vie against one another, prisoner litigation brings into play a variety of official agencies, including courts, corrections, and attorneys general. This contributes to the loosely coupled organizational activities in which not all participants are in agreement, and in which vertical and horizontal linkages exist that create competing goals, strategies, and processing techniques (Thomas, 1983). As a consequence, litigation may be viewed as a *social process* in which players act out their roles upon the stage provided by formal organizational structures (e.g., prisons, courts) and legal rules (e.g., legislation, case law, court policies). But players do not share an identical script. The meanings of the litigation drama differ, and the individual goals and agendas vary: prisoners request relief or compensation, prison staff pursue exoneration, state's attorneys attempt to cut the state's losses, corrections' attorneys subvert prisoner claims, and court personnel desire procedural harmony and legal consistency. Within this context, the drama unfolds. The longer the play runs, the more characters enter and exit. Hence, the story of the *process* of prisoner litigation requires detailing how the various players enact their respective parts.

THE FILING PROCESS

Contrary to some views, prisoner suits are not driven by "legal carpet-baggers" or other "outside agitators" who promote litigation for their own ends.[1] Prisoners nearly always litigate for themselves *(pro se)* as indigents *(in forma pauperis)*. To file a *pro se* and *in forma pauperis* petition, a prisoner obtains the appropriate filing form for either habeas corpus or civil rights actions. The forms consist of several pages and require general information describing the prisoner's prior attempts to redress the grievance, the prisoner's past legal activity, the nature of the complaint, the names and addresses of the defendants, and the nature of relief sought. The description of the complaint may be completed on the form itself, but experienced litigants often attach a separate sheet detailing the incident and documenting case law to justify the filing. The current fees of $60 for civil rights and $5 for habeas filings are established by federal statute. If prisoners intend to proceed without paying the filing fee, they must also file a separate IFP form that requires information detailing the prisoner's finances and a statement by the institution describing the inmate's prison trust fund. Forms and filing instructions are usually available from an institution, but if not, plaintiffs can request them directly from the federal court.

When the forms are completed, the prisoner next submits them to the appropriate court of jurisdiction. Usually, the jurisdiction is that of the court where the defendants reside or have their primary offices. When defendants have several offices, prisoners often choose the jurisdiction that is perceived as most likely to favorably review the complaint. Judges, either on their own volition or at the request of defendants, may transfer cases to another jurisdiction if the chosen one is inappropriate.

Petitions are either mailed or hand-carried to the court. Because of the heavy volume of prisoner suits, many federal jurisdictions have created a special office with designated personnel who function solely to process prisoner cases. Upon receipt in the Illinois Northern District, prisoner cases are delivered directly to an intake clerk responsible solely for prisoner litigation, the Office of Prisoner Correspondence. Here, the clerks begin the processing.

Federal legislation under 28 U.S.C. 1915, the "federal pauper's statute," defines the filing procedures for prisoners and civilians who file as "poor people." Nearly all prisoners file as *pro se* paupers, although civil rights cases are more likely than habeas petitions to be filed IFP (98 percent and 75 percent respectively), a ratio perhaps slightly higher than other states.[2] Section 1915 also defines court authority, sets filing and processing costs, delineates permissible discretion, specifies rules of processing, and authorizes the court to dismiss any complaint that is judged to be irreparably frivolous or malicious. But the criteria for this judgment are intentionally broad, leaving judges and clerks with considerable discretion. The precise processing details may vary between or within federal jurisdictions, but the basic format does not. The process in Illinois' Northern District is typical.[3]

The Office of Prisoner Correspondence

In Illinois' Northern District, two law clerks, both lawyers, share the processing tasks equally. The clerks first review cases to assure that they contain sufficient copies, that documents are in order and signed, that IFP affidavits are enclosed and that other basic filing procedures have been followed. If documents are not in order, they are returned to the prisoner with an explanation of the corrections required. If prisoners have not stated a cognizable claim, for example, the clerks may write the prisoner a letter saying, "Nobody can act on this complaint; send us an amended complaint that tells us the specifics." If the papers are in order, the clerks send the plaintiff notification of receipt and prepare a civil cover sheet and submit the case to the docket clerk.

Court docketing is the administrative procedure of taking all court orders and pleadings and placing them on the "docket sheet." The docket sheet chronicles the various court orders and subsequent motions and actions. The case first receives an identifying docket number. Next, docket clerks randomly assign cases to a judge.[4] By local court rule, if a prisoner has filed a previous habeas suit, the new case is assigned to the previous judge. Civil rights cases are assigned randomly. However, other jurisdictions, even in the same state, may follow different procedures. In Illinois' Central District, for example, prisoners may begin the filing process simply with a letter of complaint rather than by submitting the forms, and the clerks directly assist in the subsequent filing process:

> What the clerks do [upon receiving a complaint in a letter] is pull out all the stuff he needs and send it back to him, and tell him: "We have a standard letter, and your letter's been received, your mailing has been received, but it's inadequate." and we would check things. "If you want to file a suit, here's the complaint form." The guy would fill out the complaint form, fill out the summons sheet, [then] send it back in. Then the clerks will look and say: "Here's the things he needs to do in order to file a suit. Does he have everything he needs?" If he does, then they put it all into the files, and the case is opened (Federal law clerk, interview, 1986).

Under the provisions of Section 1915, intake clerks are authorized to summarily dismiss a claim if it lacks merit. In some districts, the *pro se* clerks often possess considerable discretion to weed out frivolous cases, but in the Northern District, the intake clerks refer their recommendation to judges.[5]

IFP REVIEW AND DECISION MAKING

After docketing, intake clerks review the substance of the claims and recommend a decision. The case and recommendation then proceed to the assigned judge for further review. The judicial IFP review is the first and most important gate-keeping hurdle a prisoner suit faces, because once past this initial review, the probability of some form of "victory" is quite high. At this stage, prisoners are particularly vulnerable to discretionary actions of a myriad of court personnel, including extreme thresholds of tolerance for prisoner claims, different methods of reading stories, ease of penetration of extralegal decision-making influences, and inconsistent practices and polices of processing. However, as Turner (1979: 619) has observed, decision-making in this phase is invisible, and there often is little direct involvement by judges.

At the IFP stage of the review process, several decisions may occur. In some jurisdictions, the review is limited solely to the prisoner's claim of indigence, and the decision is confined to the request for filing fee exemption. In other districts, including Illinois' Northern District, the IFP review also includes a preliminary judgment of the case's Constitutional merits. Courts generally have employed a broad threshold of tolerance in reviewing case merits,[6] and the Supreme Court has ruled:

> Whatever may be the limits on the scope of inquiry of courts into the internal administration of prisons, allegations such as those asserted by petitioner, however inartfully pleaded, are sufficient to call for the opportunity to offer supporting evidence. We cannot say with assurance that under the allegations of the *pro se* complaint, which we hold to less stringent standards than formal pleadings drafted by lawyers, it appears "beyond reasonable doubt that the plaitiff can prove no set of facts in support of his claim which would entitle him to relief" *Haines v. Kerner*, 404 U. S. 519 (1972): 520–21.

Even an Illinois judge who dismisses more prisoner cases than any other defends liberal interpretations of IFP petitions:

> [There is] the general doctrine that the court should always be open. You know, access to the court is a Constitutional right, so consistent with that maxim, we *liberally* review the complaint to see if it states a claim. We are required to bear in mind that the complaint is a form complaint, prepared by an untutored layman, and we are to construe it most favorably to the pleader, and if it can be said that the claim states a basis for relief, we allow the person to proceed *in forma pauperis* (Federal judge, interview, 1985).

Filing Fees

Federal rules require all persons to prepay a modest filing fee, but under 28 U.S.C. 1915, any U.S. court may waive prepayment of filing fees for indigent plaintiffs. This lies within the "reasonable discretion" of the judges or their designated officers, and the criteria of indigence vary. In the Illinois' Northern District, permission to proceed IFP provides a "free ride" in that the prisoner pays no fees. In other districts, however, an IFP decision may require that prisoners pay a percentage of the fee prior to filing (Willging, 1985). In Illinois' Central District, for example, prisoners must pay half of their average trust fund balance for the previous six months before permission to file is granted. This has been interpreted by some prisoners as a form of harassment that limits access to courts, but Central District court personnel disagree:

> It isn't to curtail [law suits], but it's to make them be serious about the law suit and pay at least a *pro rata* share of what any other litigant would have to pay. You don't have a free ride just because you're in the penitentiary. And if you're able to pay something, you should pay something. In fact, that's true of all *in forma pauperis cases*. . . . You find that some have [an

average of] $235, and we'll tell them that they can pay. The filing fee is $60. Inasmuch as the inmate has no food, shelter, or clothing costs, that stuff in the trust account, that goes for commissary, to buy cigarettes, things of that sort. So we took to doing this a couple of years ago, because there's such an avalanche of suits that we thought we would make them serious about it. And we waive it [when necessary], and some go straight IFP; they don't have anything in the trust account, and they allege a meritorious case, so they're allowed to proceed as a poor person (Federal judge, interview, 1986).

Because the fee must be paid prior to any assessment of the merits of the case, it often happens (in about one-third of the cases) that a prisoner pays the fee only to have the case immediately dismissed for lack of judicial merit. Prisoners have complained of the apparent injustice in such cases, and are currently challenging the legality of the policy.

The attempt to use prepayment fees as a form of docket control to reduce the number of filings does not seem to have been successful. Willging (1985:20) has argued that enforced partial payment of filing fees appears to have had little significant impact on the number of civil rights filings, and this is true in Illinois' Central District. In 1983, the year prior to the partial prepayment rule, the Central District's civil rights filings totaled 237. They declined to 231 in the year of the rule, and in following year, declined to 210. Although this represents an 11 percent decrease, filings remain substantially higher than in the first three years of the 1980s, when filings averaged about 150 annually. In Illinois Northern District, which does not require partial payment, filings increased by only 4 percent between 1983 and 1985, suggesting that the number of filings in both districts have been relatively stable and not strongly related to whether prisoners bear partial costs of filing fees.

In districts where judges limit IFP review only to determining whether a prisoner is indigent and thus eligible to proceed as a poor person, the sole criterion is the difference between the prisoner's trust fund balance and the court's figure that defines eligibility. But in those courts where IFP review also includes a judgment of case merits, the criteria for decision making expand.

These criteria, ostensibly based on Constitutional issues, may not hold in practice. If judges consistently used legal criteria in decision-making, one would expect that, over time, there would be consistency between judges in the percentage of cases dismissed. But Northern District judges differ dramatically in their willingness to allow prisoner complaints to go forward into the review process, and dismissal rates among judges vary between 17 percent and 67 percent with an average of 38 percent (Suchner et al. 1986). This suggests that decisions may be influenced by factors unrelated to case law. These factors may include ideological views of law, views toward punishment and social control, predilections toward particular issues perceived as more important than others, matters of organizational or procedural expediency, or attitudes toward particular legal theories. Hence, the assumption that judicial decisions are made strictly on merit may be inaccurate, since extralegal criteria penetrate in various ways.[7]

One extralegal factor may be the degree to which judges involve law clerks in the review process. Judges typically submit IFP cases to their law clerks prior to making a decision. Although some judges rely more heavily on their clerks' recommendations than other judges, all judges ostensibly make the final decision:

> [The clerk] won't dismiss a case unless he brings it to me and says, "Here's what he tries to plead. I don't think it states a cause of action." I look at what he's filed, and I'll say, "Oh, it's all right," or "No it isn't, it's terrible," so we'll dismiss it (Federal judge, interview, 1986).

Law clerks have no *de jure* authority to decide cases, but their influence nonetheless may be substantial:

> We have no power. The judge is the only one who has the power. But the judge has 400 and some pending cases. The judge can't work on everything by himself, besides be in court all day. He has to have people who work on part of this stuff for him. . . . "I want your draft on this question, and I want somebody else to work on this question on the same case." But the judge will take what we have worked on, and sometimes he's reading it verbatim, a paragraph here or a paragraph there, and then writes his own in between, and comes up with his order and stuff (Federal law clerk, interview, 1986).

If there is a disagreement between the judge and clerks, the decision may be negotiated:

> [T]here have been times when we have granted it, and [the judge] has come back and said, "No, you shouldn't have," but we usually straighten him out after one of these brilliant minute orders that said he improvidently granted leave to proceed *in forma pauperis* (Federal law clerk, interview, 1986).

Clerks may devote more time to reviewing and writing recommendations than do judges. Although most cases can be disposed of quickly, other cases may take much longer:

> But something where [prisoners] have five or six different claims, it's apparent that not all of them are meritorious, and it may take longer [for clerks] to sit down and research it, to find out exactly why it's not, to type up an order as to why it's not meritorious. To deny leave may take up to an hour or a day. It depends on what it is. I had one that came in just this last week that had six different counts, six different claims. And two of them stated a claim, and the rest of them didn't. So I had to sit down and write

up a denial on the ones that didn't, and grant leave on the other two. . . . I can do one in about 15 minutes, but an hour if you actually have to read a case to see if the guy actually states a claim. If it states a claim, that's easy. The presumption in favor of finding they state a claim is so easy, in addition to being a good thing to do, to give them leave to proceed *in forma pauperis*, that's no problem. I mean, an hour at the outside (Federal law clerk, interview, 1986).

Ironically, cases that are most frivolous may require the most attention by clerks:

When it doesn't state a claim, that takes more [time]. The time you spend may be proportional to the reason why it doesn't state a claim. If somebody is suing to recover personal property, that can be handled fairly easily, because there's Supreme Court precedents that you can't sue just for recovery of lost property (Federal law clerk, interview, 1986).

Reviewing Habeas Petitions

Judicial processing of petitions for a writ of habeas corpus may require more effort than civil rights petitions. This occurs for several reasons. First, because habeas cases usually challenge proceedings of a prisoner's conviction, judges must read the original case before making a decision, which can be time consuming.[8] In civil rights cases, by contrast, IFP decisions are made primarily on the basis of the issues raised in the petition, requiring a reading only of the plaintiff's suit.

Second, if the judge grants a habeas petition, the next step is a hearing, because there are no trials in federal habeas review of state cases. In most cases, however, the original trial transcripts provide sufficient basis for a decision, and a hearing is unnecessary. One judge described how an issue may be decided from transcript review:

[If the prisoner claims], "My lawyer was incompetent, and it made a difference in the outcome of the case," and [state's attorneys] file a motion to dismiss, which says, "Even if this is true, he can't get any relief," and I deny that, saying, "No, that's wrong, if in fact he was incompetent, and in fact it made a difference in the outcome of the case," he has the right to proceed. Then they get through with all the discovery, and [defendants] file a motion for summary judgment, which says, "Here are all the uncontested facts." Well, it may be that there are contested facts. Suppose, for example, that the petitioner in prison says, "My lawyer told me that he wasn't going to bother to interview any of my witnesses, in fact he told me he didn't even talk to them, and he didn't call any witnesses for me. Therefore, that's not fair representation." The lawyer, on the other hand, files an affidavit, who represented him in trial, that says: "Oh yes, I did talk to the other witnesses, yes I did talk to the prisoner about it, and I didn't call any witnesses, because I perceived that their testimony would not be helpful to our case." Now I've got a clear conflict in "What are the facts?" I don't know. I know the prisoner says one thing, and the lawyer says another.

I can't resolve that by looking at the pieces of paper. I have to hear the witnesses. So I have to order a hearing at which the inmate will testify, and the lawyer will testify, and I'll have to make a finding as to who is the truth teller and who is not [in order] to resolve the issue of whether or not there was an appropriate dealing with the prisoner's potential witnesses. That would take a hearing. Thus, the third possibility after those two are exhausted is, I actually have a hearing at which I determine what the facts are, much as you do in a trial. That's all a trial is, is the determination of the facts. Then you apply the law to what the facts are as you have now determined them, and come out with a result. So that's the last possible step. . . . And I figure out, "What are the facts? Did you really talk to these witnesses?" And any other evidence they want to bring in, like, "I told this lawyer about witness *A*, and they bring in witness *A*." And then witness *A* say "They didn't talk to me. And if he talked to me I would have told him this." And those kinds of things (Federal judge, interview, 1985).

In making the habeas rulings, judges attempt to identify specific cues that signal improprieties that may have prejudiced the outcome. If, in the judge's view, the cited behavior had no discernible consequence, the case is invariably dismissed. Judges typically examine several interrelated issues:

Take the situation where a petitioner says, "I have a writ of habeas corpus because of ineffective assistance of counsel." Not uncommon. Well, in order to deal with that issue, you have to make two determinations. One, was his representation by a lawyer at this earlier trial ineffective or below the level that should be expected from a person in this community as a lawyer, and two, did it make a difference? Did it prejudice the outcome? Because even if a lawyer may have fallen below the standards you'd expect from this mythical competent trial lawyer in the criminal field, it may not have made a difference. The evidence may have been so overwhelming that even Clarence Darrow couldn't have won the case. So you make this double analysis. One, was there ineffective assistance? Was the lawyer not doing his job well? To figure that out, there may be all sorts of things at issue. One, he didn't prepare the witnesses. Two, he didn't cross-examine somebody at the trial. Three, he didn't file a motion to suppress that he should have. Four, his closing argument was ridiculous. To figure out whether that's true, you have to read all that material, perhaps read his closing argument, deal with affidavits and so forth, and in short, it takes quite a bit of time to figure out if he was up to this level that he should have. Then, two, you have to turn around and say: "What was all the other evidence? Would it have made a difference if he had a good lawyer as opposed to this cluck?" That takes an analysis of the whole record of the case to say, as I did, "Could anybody have gotten him off? Could any competent lawyer have made a difference in the outcome of this trial?" If there's only one eyewitness to it, maybe. If there's five eyewitnesses in the bank who all say "I stood two feet away from him, and this is the guy who held a gun on the teller," you say, "Well, even though his closing argument wasn't very good, and even though you say he didn't interview witnesses, it's hard for the court to perceive how, if he had done those two things right, it would have made any difference at all" (Federal judge, interview, 1985).

Judges' own predilections or interest in particular substantive issues or legal theories may motivate them to put more effort into some habeas cases than others. One judge's interest in the history of the writ of habeas corpus typifies such an influence:

> The first case, the first writ I had up here—I can't remember the facts anymore—but I read it, and got concerned about it, studied it, and I spend in actual working time about 20 hours on it. Myself. And then I spend probably another 10 hours just thinking, you know, thinking at home, unable to go to sleep thinking about it, waking up in the middle of the night thinking about it because I always keep a little pad by my bed. I even went down and talked to another judge who was senior to me about it. . . . That's what I miss so much in this job, because in a law firm you can bounce ideas off your partners. "What do you think about this? I'm planning to do this?" The people I have to bounce things off, although extremely talented, are very young people, and sometimes on these things I like to get the thinking of someone who's done this job for a long time, so I kicked it around with that person, always recognizing that I have to make the decision, but I'm just interested in what that person perceived. Well, anyway, I granted that writ and ordered the guy retried, or released if he wasn't retried, and I thought about it a long, long time. So sometimes those habeas corpus cases are significant and very important, and I don't perceive that we should do *anything* to limit the right of the state court prisoner to ask a federal court to take another look at what's happened to him in the state court (Federal judge, interview, 1985).

Civil rights IFP decisions are usually made within three to five days of filing, but habeas cases may take substantially longer, because it is usually necessary to first obtain state trial records. Habeas cases are often held in abeyance (a decision is postponed or delayed) for a few weeks or a year or more. Sometimes a habeas petition may be rejected for procedural inadequacies (rather than for substance), and the prisoner must make corrections and refile. This process may take several years. Because of the time involved in hearings and appeals, which range between several months and five years or more, it is not uncommon for prisoners to complete their sentence while pursuing their claims. In a typical example, one prisoner's documents indicate that a case filed in 1979 was variously delayed, returned to state court, and delayed again. Barring bad fortune, the prisoner will be released prior to a final hearing, making his case moot.

Time constraints, in fact, may be an important factor in processing the habeas review. Some prisoners recognize that the time elapsed between their trial and subsequent hearing or retrial works to their advantage:

> If they ever do grant me a new trial, they're in trouble, first of all, because it's eight years ago. Yeh, go ahead and find the witnesses now. Now that I'm out, lurking around, who's going to testify against me? I mean, when I was in there, I ain't shitting you now, once I went in there, they were in droves going, "Yeh I'll testify," and I wasn't known to be a nice guy on the streets. One thing I hated was a guy that was a traitor like that. . . . But still, now seven years [after conviction], where they gonna get their evidence? The guy that got shot, he might be dead now, who knows? He was an older guy. He was like 55 years old. A black guy. So he's got to be what, 63? So, who knows. Maybe he moved. Who knows? Let them try me again. I want a new trial (Jailhouse lawyer, interview, 1986).

Judges are aware of this attitude and therefore may be more reticent in granting a habeas petition if an excessive time has elapsed since the original trial:

> [Y]ou've got to recognize that the state, after the time has gone by, when you consider how much time has gone by, if he's pursued his remedies in appellate court, and in the Supreme Court, and the writ over here, there may be four or five years gone by, and so it may be that the state is unable to retry. So I always recognize that (Federal judge, interview, 1985).

Habeas challenges to a criminal conviction rarely result in any form of relief to the prisoner, and outright release by a habeas challenge is rare (Justice, 1973; Shapiro, 1973). Relief is somewhat more common in noncriminal cases that challenge administrative errors of record-keeping (e.g., credit for jail time served, calculation of good time), because such cases often can be resolved prior to trial by simply correcting the error.

Reviewing Civil Rights Petitions

Because they are grounded in disparate legal theories and social issues, judges may not read civil rights complaints as they do habeas petitions. Several factors shape how judges review civil rights cases. First, as with habeas, judges ostensibly assess the legal basis of a case (legal merit, adjudicability, identifiable defendants), but standards differ. Civil rights complaints are diverse, raise relatively new issues of law, are constantly changing and are far "looser," thus providing additional layers of discretion.

Second, changing federal case law, especially Supreme Court decisions, variously expands or limits the acceptable criteria to be used in reviewing prisoner cases. Complaints of staff complicity in prisoner-on-prisoner assaults, for example, have been in recent years the easiest type of case on which to receive a favorable IFP review (86 percent). Decisions in the early 1980s, however, changed definitions of responsibility, making it more difficult for prisoners to successfully pursue claims of staff responsibility in inmate assaults:

> In a case where you're hurt by another inmate, the state of the law is, under the Supreme Court decisions, that these are mostly actions for money, not for release from prison. The standard is that the prison officials are not liable if [the prisoner is] hurt by another prisoner unless they were reckless and indifferent to the prisoner. Simple carelessness is not enough. If you're hurt out on the street by a car, all you have to show is that the person was careless. In prison, that's not good enough. The prisoner must show not carelessness, but *recklessness*, that is, a *gross* disregard for the prisoner's safety.

Third, changing social attitudes may transform how courts interpret civil rights concepts. Prison violence raises issues of cruel and unusual punishment, the role of prisons in creating a habitable and rehabilitative social environment and problems of control, discipline, or prison management, among many others. Changing social conceptions of "adequate health care," "access to law," and even "civil rights" provide further examples of how broader social attitudes can contribute to successful prisoner challenges to unresponsive prison administration. One moderate conservative judge provided an example of his attempt to balance changing concepts of prisoner well being and "common decency" with judicial principle and personal predilections when reviewing civil rights cases:

> I'll give you one very interesting one I had. The FLAN [violent political organization]. Ever heard of them? The FLAN had four people, a woman and three men, seized by the FBI and charged with conspiracy to break into the Leavenworth prison in Kansas to free other FLAN members, and as part of this, they seized explosives in their safe house and all that. And these people were regarded by the [Federal Bureau of Prisons] as extremely dangerous, and when they were incarcerated, this is pretrial, they were not convicted of anything, they were put over in the [Metropolitan Correctional Center] kitty-corner from here. . . . So the lawyers representing the FLAN came over before me, I happened to be the emergency judge, and said they were being deprived of equal treatment over there, because as pretrial detainees, there's a place for those folks, where they're convicted of nothing, and there's the general prison population over there, which means you have sort of the run of the floor instead of being locked in a cell for 23 hours each day. I heard the case, and decided on the basis of what information the prison bureau had from the FBI that they were justified in keeping them in this condition. And I noted in the opinion that, in any case, it's not going to last more than 90 days, because the speedy trial act requires that they go to trial. They had a motion to supress, in front of, I think it was in front of Judge L. Judge L. suppressed part of the evidence against them, and an appeal started. As a result, these people were held over nine months in that same condition. Those lawyers came back in

before me with another petition to take them out of solitary, and after listening to evidence about what that does to a person, and even though I was aware of the fact that there was a risk that their friends on the outside might try a prison break, I decided it was unfair, cruel and unusual to keep them locked in that kind of condition for almost a year, and ordered them put back in the general prison population. So I actually changed on that, not that I really changed my view about the law or them, but the time that went on and on and on, I finally decided that enough is enough over there. You can't keep people under these kinds of conditions convicted of nothing, indefinitely (Federal judge, interview, 1985).

Finally, despite willingness to review cases and offer modest individual relief, judges remain hesitant to intervene directly in prisoner administration by providing a legal relief.[9]

[I] don't think the court, except in exceptional circumstances, should be telling the prison how to run its own operation and how to sort out good time and how to sort out when you have to discipline, and so forth. We're not there, we don't know the problems that they face, and unless there's some pretty compelling reason, generally I don't do much with those. But there are always exceptional cases (Federal judge, interview, 1985).

Dismissing Cases

About 62 percent of all civil rights complaints and 43 percent of habeas petitions survive the initial IFP review. Table 7a indicates that civil rights complaints have a higher probality of surviving IFP screening in the Northern District than do habeas petitions. However, 29 percent of habeas petitions ultimately are paid, thus circumventing the IFP review. Further, the meaning of a "granted" IFP petition differs somewhat for each theory. A "granted" habeas petition means only that the judge agrees to place it on the court docket to review it, and most "granted" habeas petitions are ultimately rejected at a later stage. When a civil rights complaint is granted, defendants are required to answer, and more court action is generally required. Hence, the 43 percent rate of habeas petitions granted considerably inflates the apparent disposition and "success rate" compared to civil rights suits, perhaps by 50 to 75 percent.

Habeas petitions are dismissed at the IFP review about equally for two reasons: failure to state an adjudicable claim and failure to first exhaust all state remedies prior to federal filing. Civil rights cases are dismissed about equally for failing to articulate an adjudicable grievance, for failing to state an adjudicable remedy or for failing to adequately name specific persons responsible for the complaint:

It's not simply enough to say "guards," for example. You have to name people. "You haven't told us what right you think you had that was taken way from you." For example, you get a prisoner come in and say in a

Table 7a   Judicial decisions for application to proceed _in forma pauperis_ (initial screening) in Illinois' Northern District for civil rights (1977-86) and habeas (1980-86)*

	Civil Rights	Habeas
IFP granted:	1,580	443
percent:	60.1	43.1
IFP denied:	931	145
percent:	35.4	14.1
Failure to exhaust state remedies:	1	133
percent:	--	13.0
Court costs paid:	70	297
percent:	2.7	28.9
Case transferred to another district:	46	0
percent:	1.8	0.9
Total	2,628	1,018

*Excludes decisions that are unknown.

complaint: "I was required to work in the laundry." Well, the law is such that they can assign you or not assign you to whatever they like. You have to show something more, like, "I was black," or, "I was not allowed to work in the laundry because they thought I was a troublemaker" and there's no grounds for that (Federal judge, interview, 1985).

If the case is dismissed, the prisoner can either refile by rectifying errors, revise and file a new case, or drop the grievance:

Dismissal, however, doesn't mean he's barred from bringing the claim again, but only that this _case_ is dismissed without prejudice, and to start all over again. But he's now advised by the minute order I've signed that, "You've failed on two occasions now, to state who, for example, you are complaining about" (Federal judge, interview, 1985).

In contrast to civil rights complaints, the prisoner has the additional option of appealing a dismissed habeas petition in federal appellate court. IFP appeals are not permitted, however, if a lower court rules that the original case was not filed in "good faith."[10]

Several inferences can be drawn from the initial gate-keeping review of prisoner petitions. First, the relative invisibility of the process allows for considerable discretion and diverse extralegal factors to mediate the role of law as the primary criterion in determining which cases survive or perish. Personal predilections, varying interpretations of the relationship between courts and prisons, or pragmatic influences may trigger discretion and thus mediate decision-making. Second, even at this initial phase of the litigation process, the variety of participants involved adds multiple layers of discretionary judgments that determine whether a case proceeds or not. Judges or clerks who tend to support prisoner rights tend to use their discretion to allow "the day in court," and clerks especially may read merit into IFP petitions when prisoners themselves are unable to articulate an issue. Those opposing prisoners' rights tend to invoke literal Constitutional readings limiting discretion, thus narrowing the grounds on which to grant IFP petitions. Hence, the law often becomes a motive to justify a decision at least as much as it determines the decision. Despite the apparently tightly coupled connection between law and decision-making, substantive rationality rather than rigid rules reigns and continues into the next phase, that of the appointment of counsel.

APPOINTMENT OF COUNSEL

If prisoners survive the IFP review, they must next decide whether to request that counsel be appointed to assist in the legal proceedings, but there is no evidence that routine cases fare better when represented by an attorney than without one (Eisenberg and Schwab, 1986). Judges usually guide unrepresented defendants through the trial, and because most civil rights suits ultimately hinge on matters of fact rather than law, the role of attorneys tends to be minor. Nonetheless, appointment of counsel plays a symbolic role to the extent that prisoners perceive inherent injustice when they are not formally represented.

By both federal statute and case law, prisoners who are unable to employ counsel in pursuing their case may have attorneys appointed in criminal cases, but courts are not required to appoint counsel in civil cases. Nonetheless, district courts do possess the authority and discretion to appoint counsel for *pro se* defendants, and in the Northern District, do so routinely. In cases that promise a potential monetary award to the plaintiff, or in cases that are exceptionally dramatic, private attorneys may volunteer. In most cases, however, counsel are randomly drawn from a *pro bono* ("for the public good") panel. The decision is based on the merits of the claim, judiciability of the case, the prisoner's ability to investigate the facts, the nature of the evidence, the capability of the prisoner to present his or her own case, and above all, the complexity of the legal issues:

The complexity of the legal issues is the big one. Most cases that get to trial are not complex, because it's "the guard hit me." Fine. "Did he assault you, or was he protecting himself?" Who do we believe? The inmate can tell his side of the story, the guard can tell his side of the story, you don't much need counsel for that. "Motion for appointment of counsel denied." But the El Rukn case. [The El Rukns, a powerful Chicago street gang, unsuccessfully argued that they were a religion, and as such, had First Amendment protections granted to other religions—JT]. That raises a colorable issue. It's not unreasonable to believe that the El Rukns were a religious group and were entitled to religious rights just like the Christians and Jews and everybody else there. And that's really complex, and that's hard enough to deal with it. You don't want somebody who doesn't know anything about the law having to deal with it, so appointing counsel in that type of case would be appropriate. But where they really stumble is the complexity question, because most of the cases that we get that go to trial just aren't that complex. And to top it off, the court will generally guide the inmate on what he needs to do. The court doesn't do it until he's there, but the court will tell him: "Now's the time for you to tell the jury what you're going to show in this trial. Take a few minutes to tell them." And he'll sit in his chair and tell them. "And the defense attorney will now tell the jury what he thinks the trial will show." And they will do that, and then the court will come back and say: "Now you can present your case. Who do you want to call as a witness?" And they'll bring him up like that, and the court will say: "Do you have any further questions for this witness? Who's your next witness?" And like that. Kind of help him. That's all you can do for him, but like I said, those kinds of cases are not complex. The jury can see that the guy said [the guard] beat him up, and the inmate says: "This is what happened on this date," and the guard says the opposite, or: "That never happened." Or: "Yes, I hit him, but I stumbled on the step, [while] we were mopping" (Federal law clerk, interview, 1986).

Most judges, however, generally prefer that prisoners not represent themselves in jury trials:

[An unrepresented prisoner] removes me from my role. It brings me down to where I have to help the prisoner understand, and explain to the jury that the prisoner is representing himself. That's the lawyers job. I have to tell the prisoner what's going to happen next, what he's supposed to answer next, help him phrase a question, you know, it doesn't in any way indicate that I in any way have an opinion as to what the proper outcome of the case should be, but it removes the judge from the appearance of impartiality and objectivity. And the prisoner might have a claim, if only he knew how to present it. Marshalling evidence requires some skill. It requires a lawyer (Federal judge, interview, 1986).

Sometimes, however, a judge may invoke rules in a way that adds unintended comic relief and an element of absurdity to trials. Court personnel relate a standing story about a late Northern District judge who made an exceptionally litigious *pro se* defendant explain his version of events by stepping down from the witness stand to address the empty chair, then climb back into the chair to answer the question. Stepping down and returning, as Woody Allen did in the court scene in the film *Bananas,* the game was repeated until his testimony was completed.

Appointing counsel may not solve the problem of representation, however. Prisoners may oppose their court-appointed attorney and request they be dismissed, thus remaining unrepresented:

[A leading local attorney] was appointed, and since he was with [a top Chicago law firm], he brought into the case three other lawyers, and they were working like beavers for these indigent prisoners, except the prisoners then wanted them removed. And I did. You see, the prisoners get very smart! And they get smarter than their self-interests! So I allowed [a top Chicago law firm] to withdraw. I have a personal policy that if I appoint a lawyer for an indigent plaintiff, or an indigent defender, and for some reason he can't get along with that lawyer, I don't appoint another lawyer for them. That's because I happen to know from experience that if he don't get along with *this* lawyer, he most likely won't get along with that lawyer either (Federal judge, interview, 1985).

There is a strong feeling among jailhouse lawyers that appointed counsel are not particularly committed to prisoner cases, and some of the better litigants prefer to argue their own case at trials. Further, some prisoners take pride in their ability to litigate on their own behalf. One of Illinois' best jailhouse lawyers wrote:

I am inviting you to a live show-down entitled [case name]. I will be acting as my own lawyer before the [federal court] on [date] at the first floor courtroom. I will be representing myself in my first jury trial. *Don't miss this show—it will be something you'll never forget in your life* (Jailhouse lawyer, personal communication, 1986; italics in original).

Despite the infrequent ambivalence of some prisoners toward appointed counsel, it serves several important functions. First is the instrumental value for prisoners in complex cases. Lawyers from a high quality law firm experienced in prisoner litigation are likely to present a stronger case than an inexperienced junior member of a mediocre one. Because many prisoners are not competent to represent their own interests, their success may hinge on the luck of the draw. Second, counsel may be as helpful for judges as for prisoners to the extent that knowledgeable pleadings facilitate court proceedings and allow judges to preserve the appearance of impartiality. Third, appointment of counsel possesses the symbolic value of promoting in the eye of the prisoner the appearance of justice by granting a perceived "right." But appointing counsel can be costly if the prisoner wins, because under federal rules, the unsuccessful defendant must pay attorney fees in civil rights cases. Hence, appointment of counsel can potentially escalate the costs of litigation to the state. Finally, appointment of counsel makes cases more visible by drawing more players into the process, further rendering public matters that would remain private.

THE PRETRIAL PROCESS

One myth of our legal system portrays trials as the focal point of legal activity. In fact, few civil or criminal cases go to trial in federal courts.[11] Most cases are either dismissed or settled prior to trial, depending on the success of the attorney's efforts in pretrial negotiations, in the discovery process or in motion-filing. The pretrial battleground becomes the arena in which the credibility, relevance, and persuasiveness of the prisoner's account provide the stuff toward which the various organizational responses are mustered.

Pretrial Conferences

Pretrial activities bring the various participants together into the judicial arena for the first time. Court procedures require a preliminary pretrial conference, normally scheduled within 120 days of filing. Here, the presiding judges meets with attorneys for both sides in the first attempt to identify the legal and substantive issues, discuss questions raised by the pleadings, jurisdiction, venue, pending, or contemplated motions, probable time needed for discovery and the possibility of settling the case without trial. Northern District policy explicitly encourages settlement, but if no agreement is possible, the case is placed on the court's trial calendar. Settlements rarely occur in the preliminary stages, and most cases that survive the IFP gate-keeping hurdle require further examination of the issues before settlements are reached. This begins the *discovery process.*

Discovery

Discovery is the process of fact-finding. The object of discovery is to compile a body of information that can be strategically used by either side to support a preferred account. Witnesses are selected who can substantiate or subvert a story, including eye witnesses, experts, and others who become secondary storytellers. Judges now assume full case responsibility, defendants plot strategies, opposing counsel confer, motions are filed, witnesses identified, depositions (testimony through interviews) taken, interrogatories (reciprocal written questioning of witnesses and experts) occur, and evidence submitted.

In civil rights cases, state employees are the defendants, and except in extreme cases, the state provides the legal resources for staff accused of violations.[12] In Illinois, notification forms are sent by the state employee defendants to IDOC legal staff assigned only to prisoner suits. This department includes six attorneys, two half-time law clerks, and a support staff of at least three secretaries.[13] IDOC attorneys then review the case and consult with the attorney general to devise strategies for responding to the suit:

> When the institutional employees are served with a suit, they would send me [IDOC staff attorney] the law suit. [We] would review it, send it to the appropriate division of the attorney general's office, and if it was a suit that [we] felt impacted on policy or procedure, or if the inmate were represented by counsel, or if there was an issue that [we] thought was particularly significant, then [we] would assign one of *this* staff to work with the attorney general on that case. Likewise, if [we] think, for instance, that there is a trend of numerous suits being filed on the same issue, [we] would generally look into whether there might be some merit to the case. If there's a particular problem, perhaps send someone out to the institution to give a training session, or whatever option [we] might think to be advisable to do at that time (IDOC staff attorney, interview, 1986).

Although coordinating suits remains the primary task of Corrections' attorneys, they also perceive their role, in part, as "trouble-shooters," and may use suits diagnostically to identify prison problems:

> What we did in response to [one disciplinary case], while not addressing an individual case, and certainly not admitting any liability or anything, we sent out our lawyers to every single institution, and did training once a month with the adjustment committees, we would look at what they had done for the previous month, and we would train extensively. We had training in our training academy in Springfield. We simply went around the state *vigorously*, and trained everyone we could find, and we set up a program, which we had had going before-we had always had training on that issue—but we decided that if there were a problem, we were going to get the better of it, and if this were indicative of a problem, we would try to get to the bottom of it and train the people more extensively. And so we did. . . . I think it's the expectation of the Director that if there's a problem, any employee that sees it should bring it either to the attention of somebody who could do something about it, or should try to solve it. He certainly is all for problem-solving to be done quickly and effectively.

After review by IDOC attorneys, the case is next submitted to the attorney general:

> Generally, what happens is that the Department of Corrections has instituted a form that somebody who is served will file, will fill out and file, and send to their legal counsel, [PB's] division, who will then log it in as having received it, so they're aware of what's in [the suit], and send it to us for a request to represent it. Thereafter, we take over, and the rest of it is between us and the defendants. We look at [the suits], we assign them to an attorney right away [JT: By lot?]. Usually by expertise. . . . You like to have all a prisoner's, say all Johnny [Jones's] cases, all done by the same group.

That way, Johnny [Jones] isn't playing one assistant off against another assistant. Settlements become a lot easier. If you wind up settling it, you don't have to bring eight other people in. So we try and keep them by subject area assigned to certain attorneys that are maybe experts in discipinary proceedings. Because they've done a lot of those cases, and they know that law. Maybe there's other attorneys that are more knowledgeable in the medical end of it, so we take that into account. We also take into account what we perceive to be the difficulty of the case. A case that would be very difficult, we're not going to give it to a rookie lawyer, but to a little bit more experienced lawyer. Some cases come in right away with attorney's on them, big class action type things, and we'll say right off the bat, "Shit, we'd better give this to some of the more senior guys, 'cause we've got Jenner and Block on the other side, we've got Winston and Strong, or whoever it would be." And we handle it that way (State's attorney, interview, 1986).

Another reason for appointing the same lawyers to the same litigants' suits is the probability that fabricated narratives become easier to detect:

Once in a while, this is one of the reasons we like to assign the same guys. There are certain guys in the prison system who are very litigious. I mean, they file 30 or 40 cases, and like all unsophisticated people, some of them are very sophisticated, but legally unsophistcated, they're going to trip themselves up. They're going to say something in one case that's exactly the opposite of what they said in another case. And we'll try to do, if the same lawyer is dealing with all the Johnny Smiths, or all the Paul Jones, or whoever they are; . . . we're able, by being consistent, to show the court, "Listen. This guy's lying. He's lying here or he's lying there." So that's basically where we're at (State's attorney, interview, 1986).

Once the decision to fight the suit has been made, next come the strategies of resistance, initially in the form of motions intended to dismiss the suit.

Motions

Prior to or during discovery, either side may file a motion requesting the judge to decide the case prior to trial. While gathering or contesting facts, a lengthy and often costly process, the state normally files one or more motions in an attempt to dismiss the case. This is done by either a *motion to dismiss* or a *motion for summary judgment.*

In a motion to dismiss, defendants concede that a complaint is true (only for the sake of the motion, not as an admission of guilt), but that even if all facts are true, the facts are either insufficient or there is no legal basis to justify redress or recovery. For example, a prisoner may claim to have been transferred from a minimum to a maximum security institution without a hearing. The defendants may agree that this occurred, but that such a policy is lawful; hence, there is no legal basis for the suit, and the claim should be dismissed.

In a summary judgment, the defendants also do not contest the facts, but rather than ask for dismissal, they request a summary judgment on the basis of those uncontested facts. A summary judgment is a shorthand way of saying that there are no factual controversies, everybody agrees what happened, and the question is, "Does the law provide a remedy for it":

> To give you a perfect example, we had a case where an inmate claimed that a dentist had pulled the wrong tooth. We went in and submitted affidavits and X-rays, and said, "No indeed, we pulled the right tooth." This is the X-ray before and after." And because of that, there was no issue of material fact. The inmate either simply made a mistake, or he lied. And there was unequivocal evidence that could not be refuted (IDOC staff attorney, interview, 1986).

Both motions attack the suit, and if granted, both do away with the need for a trial. The motion to dismiss does it solely on the basis of what is pled, and assumes all facts are true. The motion for a summary judgment does it by assuming that *some* facts are uncontested, and the legal result must necessarily follow from those uncontested facts.

The choice of motions becomes a crucial part of the defense strategy:

> We look at each case, and if the case we believe is susceptible to a motion to dismiss, in other words, see, the federal courts, when you do a motion to dismiss, you have to write a brief in support of it, and the other side writes a brief, and [the judge] spends time writing an opinion, denying it or granting it. It's very time consuming, both for the court and for our office. So what we do a lot of times is just answer the complaint. Deny, admit, deny, deny; file an answer. And then shortly thereafter use another mechanism called "a motion for summary judgment," which means that, "Look at it. What this guy said and what we answer doesn't rise to a Constitutional problem, in that without trial we should win." And the judge will say yes or say no, or may say yes in part: "Counts 3 and 4 of the guys complaint are gone, we'll try this one issue." If that's the case, then we'll try the issue. They'll put us on a discovery schedule, and when we're done with the schedule, we'll go down to a trial (State's attorney, interview, 1986).

When defendants file a motion, plaintiffs in turn respond with arguments opposing the motion. Because either side may file motions, final termination of a case can be delayed by up to a year or more if one side or the other files numerous motions or requests an extension of time to respond. If the defendants are unsuccessful in their preliminary attempts to dismiss the suit, only two options remain. The case is either settled prior to trial, or it advances to a jury or bench trial.

SETTLEMENTS

A case settlement refers to a situation in which both sides arrive at a mutually agreeable resolution, thus avoiding the necessity of a trial. The underlying logic derives from game theory and implies a cost-benefit analysis in which both plaintiffs and defendants calculate rewards and risks. Some analysts have suggested that prisoner cases are not amenable to settlements because "meaningful negotiations between prisoners acting *pro se* and state's attorneys are practically impossible" (Turner, 1979: 637). However, this view underestimates the role of prisoners' counsel, judicial patience, and defendant and prisoner recognition of mutual self-interest.

Most cases surviving IFP screening are settled prior to trial. No hard data exist, and settlement stipulations have increasingly barred revelation of settlement details. There is no consensus between or among prisoners or court and corrections personnel on settlement rates of petitions surviving IFP review, and estimates range from "very few" to "nearly all." Those affiliated with corrections tend to opt for the lowest settlement figure, but court staff and prisoners generally claim "no less than half are settled." Experienced jailhouse lawyers believe strongly that the IFP decision is the most crucial barrier they face, for once past that, the chances of some form of relief range from "highly probable" to "excellent." Some corrections' officials concede that they prefer to maintain an appearance of "minimal settlements," and the cases settled may, in reality, be quite high. Table 7b suggests that perhaps as many as 82 percent of all cases advancing beyond IFP review are ultimately settled, comprising over half (53.2 percent) of all cases filed.[14]

Hence, the perception that prisoners "rarely win" should be read with considerable caution.

The variety of relief available to a prisoner complicates identifying and assessing settlements. Because of diverse stakes, and because the term "settlement" has an ambiguous social—although not legal—meaning, it may appear when looking at court files that few cases are actually settled. Prisoners rarely win substantial monetary awards, and when they do, the awards are low.[15] The most common settlements involve negotiating monetary awards and attorneys' fees. Both the state and IDOC attempt to resolve all suits as inexpensively and painlessly as possible, and IDOC settlement strategies are guided by an adage one pundit described as: "Be reasonable: Offer nothing!" Prisoners, on the other hand, may be happy to settle for far less than their initial requests.[16]

Administrative relief is another settlement stake, but it is neither dramatic nor highly visible. Many cases can be readily resolved through minor changes in policy, restoration of lost or damaged property, rectifying administrative errors, or conceding token awards that allow mutual face-saving. Such relief is common, but because it is relatively

Table 7b Estimated disposition of civil rights cases
          processed in Illinois' Northern Federal
          District (August 1977-86)*

Disposition	Number	As Percent of all filed
IDOC Decisions**	2900	100.0
IFP denied	1093	37.7
IFP granted	1807	62.3
Settled	1048	34.7
Dismissed	759	25.2
Trial	130	4.0
Won	65	2.2
Lost	65	2.2
Total "wins" (settled + trial)	1113	34.4***

*Because of nonavailability of data, figures are intended to estimate
 broad parameters rather than precise outcomes. See note 14 for method
 of calculation.
**Figures exclude suits from jails, federal prisons, and private
 litigants, as well as decisions on which outcomes were unknown.
***Figure represents a "victory" in 61.6 percent of all cases surviving
 IFP review.

invisible, it tends to be de-emphasized when examining prisoners' "victories."

Settlements may be motivated and decided by a variety of reasons. First, rather than lose the entire game, players may opt for a tie, or at least for an outcome in which they can claim partial victory. Neither side may be totally confident that a judge or a jury would award a "better deal" than one offered by negotiation. The opportunity for even the most legitimate or absurd claim to be reformatted by trial lawyers in a manner that changes the context, meaning, or significance of events and accounts makes trials risky for both sides. Because trials tend to be forms of storytelling, the best storyteller usually wins. Hence, the outcome of trials contains a high element of unpredictability, and court personnel estimate that the outcome of prisoner cases in trials compares statistically to a flip of the coin.

A second reason for settlements arises when the presiding judge "strongly encourages" the parties to settle. A grievance might be substantively minor, but nonetheless legitimate and so blatantly in violation of rules that a judge might say, "There's no way I'm gonna try this case and have this on the books. You [the state] are going to lose, so you take it out and settle it." Some judges take an active role, feeling that their role in processing settlements jeopardizes their image of impartiality. Others aggressively pursue settlements, perceiving their role to include that of mediation:

> We don't have the facilities, we don't have the money, but you try to get them settled, though, like you do in any other case. You bring the lawyers together before you try the case, and you talk about settlement. I regard my principle responsibility from the standpoint of disposing of cases that are not disposed of on motions to dismiss, are not disposed of by summary judgment, and are not disposed of by the lawyers trying to settle the case. Lawyers try to settle cases. Every now and then you get a case where the lawyers haven't tried to settle, but that's very unusual. My feeling is that when all of those thing have failed, the principle responsibility is to try the case. If I become too involved in the settlement process, and I don't get the case settled, don't get the case settled because one side says "no" to my suggestion, OK? Cases that aren't settled, somebody has said no. Now, if the side that says no, then loses the case, there is a great risk that that side will feel, "We lost the case because we refused to settle." People rationalize their defeats. . . . People lose cases because the facts are against them. So, I am really not an aggressive settler. Now, if the case comes down to, we're sitting there talking, and there's a lawyer there, and a lawyer there, and I'm here, and the lawyer for the plaintiff says, "Well, judge, I tried very hard to settle the case, and we haven't been able to do it." And I say to them, "OK, tell me where you are." And the plaintiff's lawyer says, "Well, judge, my demand is $15,000, and the offer is $12,500." I say, "This case has just been settled for $13,500." I'm not going to try a $2,500 law suit. I'm just not going to do it. And they can't afford to try a law suit for $2,500. And that's what it's come down to. Now, the difference between them is $2,500, and it started out that the difference was a million. Now it's down to $2,500. Now. The state pays nominal [settlement] amounts, but they do not pay substantial amounts. And sometimes, they won't even pay nominal amounts. . . . So I understand when the state says, "Judge, as a matter of policy, we can't settle." I say, "OK." But, now we get back to the attorneys' fees. Most of the lawyers that I have appointed, and some of them I appoint selectively—I know a lawyer, and I say, "This is a good case for that lawyer," but over half of them are just selected off the list that the clerk maintains. Most of the lawyers who are appointed to these civil rights cases are willing to settle a case, their client is willing to settle the case. You know, two grand is a lot of money in the joint. They're willing to settle the case for $500, $600, a

thousand, $2,000, and no attorney's fees. The lawyers are willing to write off their time. The state says, "No. As a matter of policy, we can't settle the case." And at this point, I will say to the state, "All right. I understand, and I'm not going to quarrel with your policy. But I want you to understand something. This is a very, very reasonable settlement offer. You gotta recognize that in the big scheme of things. To offer to settle a case for $500 or $1,000 is giving it away." This is a case now, keep in mind, Jim, that a motion to dismiss either has not been made, or if it's been made has been denied. A motion for summary judgment either has not been made, or if it's been made it's been denied. This is a case that's going to go to trial. Which means that there's a dispute of fact as to what happened. And I know from my experience, that when that takes place in the courtroom, the plaintiffs win half of the time, and the defense wins half of the time. Those are the statistics on the trial cases. . . . And the plaintiff's lawyer is a good trial lawyer, a very able guy. He says, "Judge, we'll take $1,500 and no attorney's fees." The state says "Judge, as a matter of policy, we can't do it." At this point, I say, "*OK*, I understand your policy, and I'm not going to quarrel with it, but I want you to know that if the case is tried, and if the plaintiff wins, regardless of the amount of the recovery, I'm going to give Mr. Flynn his regularly hourly rate as fees for the plaintiff. Because you're forcing him to trial. I appointed him, he's done a good job, he's willing to waive his fees and settle the case for a nominal amount, and you say as a matter of policy you're turning him down. But that's the price that you pay." So Mr. Flynn tried that case, got a $2,500 verdict, and a $25,000 fee (Federal judge, interview, 1986).

Some inmates feel that judges occasionally intimidate prisoners into settling cases that could easily be won at trial:

The judge will say, "You aren't going to win. We aren't going to let you win this. You'd better settle for $500 or $1,000." And it works. It works! It works! There's a guy's case I've got here. He got stabbed in the head. Here, stabbed here by another resident. I tell this guy, "Come on, we've got a good case. We've got an excellent case." He's not a gang-banger [gang member]. The other guy was a gang-banger. This guy. . . . they scared the hell out of him. The judge scared him. Judge [B]. He's known for that. Ask [LB] over there [points to another clerk]. Just like [Judge L.]. I don't know what they told him, but they scared him to death (Jailhouse lawyer, interview, 1986).

Because settlement decisions often entail different bureaucratic goals and competing definitions of roles, they can create a tension between the attorney general's office and the Department of Corrections. This, in turn, may lead to disagreement over strategies for handling a particular case. The attorney general's office defines its primary obligation as "saving the state some money," even though personnel are senstive to the administrative requirements of prison officials. IDOC lawyers, by contrast, first assess the impact on prison policy. As a consequence, the intraorganizational criteria for settling a case may be quite different.

The conflicting goals between the Department of Corrections and state's attorneys are grounded largely in organizational tensions that prevent defending state's attorneys from fulfilling their task of expedient litigation and fiscal responsibility. In theory, the attorney general's office assumes this responsibility, but in practice, it lies with IDOC. The consequence is not always harmonious, but fiscal restraints often present an insurmountable obstacle:

> Well, we have a policy that we've worked out with the Department of Corrections. Theoretically, the attorney general's office is the only spokesman for the state in a court. Theoretically, we have the ability to go in and say, "Judge, this case is settled." No matter what our defendants think about it, no matter what the Department of Corrections thinks about it. As a practical matter, we don't do that, and we don't push that, although someday there may be a case that we'll do that, where we'll want to settle, and Corrections won't. Basically, we've had some disagreements on cases, but we basically work them out. One of the reasons we're compelled to work them out is because the money comes from them, but the authority to settle comes from us. So it doesn't do us much good to go to court and say, "Judge, we'll settle" if corrections won't come up with the cash to pay the settlement. So consequently, we have to do this jointly. Now, some cases you can buy off for 100 bucks because of the principle involved, where the precedential effect for letting the inmate sue for this type of wrong, whatever it would be, would wreak havoc on the administration of prisons, that in that case the principle won't let us settle (State's attorney representative, interview, 1986).

One state's attorney explained how fiscal constraints and competing goals affect the determination to settle:

> One of the big downsides to us is that we have very little money available to us to settle cases for nuisance value. You'll see in the insurance industry, if we use personal injury as an example, automobile accidents and whatnot, insurance companies have found it economical, even when they think their insured is not wrong, to throw out a settlement for nuisance value, because it will save in the long run the court costs of depositions and all this other stuff. We don't have that available to us. There is no way in state government right now that we can go get a check for 300 bucks or 400 bucks and settle a law suit. We have to go through this massive bureaucratic thing. So what happens is that we wind up, because of the very mechanisms we have available, or don't have available, we let a lot of cases that should be settled actually go to trial. We should pay this guy 200 bucks to get him off our backs, not because he's right, but simply because it's not worth the time, the effort, the inconvenience to the department, or our office, or the courts, to try it. There's an example of a case I can give you that was out of the prison system, where an inmate was moved. Periodically, they'll go in and move an

inmate out of the cell and search the place for weapons and other things. In the course of one of these shakedowns, a prisoner's trial transcript was lost, *OK?* He had been in there, and he was doing his own appeals on his criminal conviction, and he had the transcripts from his criminal trial. They got lost. He sued under civil rights statute. Now, the easiest thing would have been to go buy him, give him $1,000, let's say he paid $1,000 for the transcript. Give him $1,000, and let him buy another one. Another copy of it. We had no mechanism to do it, it went to trial, and we lost; the judgments against the state in that case, with attorneys' fees, ranged to about $30,000–35,000. And that's not counting the expense of trial, appeal, and everything else. The point of the matter is that it's like the Fram Oil commercial. "Get me now, or get me later." If I had $1,000 now, I could have got rid of this whole thing. There's cases that are even worse. There's cases were you can settle for $100, $200, and sometimes we can do it, if the guy is willing to wait for his money for a while, and stuff, we can do it (anonymous state's attorney, interview, 1986).

Lacking authority to settle can greatly escalate the costs of litigation:

If we can pay $100 now, or $200, and not run the risk of losing either a judgment for a greater amount, plus attorneys' fees, plus the expense of trial, I mean, the expense of trial, even if we win, is way more than $100. It's thousands more, depending on the type of law suit, who has to come up from where. Maybe the witnesses to do this $100 case are guards in Menard. So if it's up here in the Federal District Court, we have to fly guys up and pay them to testify, get replacements for them while they're down there, to try this case. And that's a tremendous amount of expense. For $100, we could get rid of it, get it off our back, get it off the court docket. We're more likely to settle a suit if the prisoner who has brought the suit is not in the institution anymore. If he's, say, been released, we're more likely settle it than if he's back there, because the one thing you don't want happening in the prison setting is a guy going back saying, "Yeh, they took my toothbrush," or whatever the thing might have been, "and I sued them, and I got $100, or $200." And all that stuff. So you want to avoid that type of precedential effect in cases within the prison, because it makes administration so difficult (anonymous state official, interview, 1986).

State's attorneys also must confront a pragmatic problem: refusing settlements that are suggested by the presiding judge may jeopardize future nonprisoner litigation in which the attorneys are a party. The lack of real authority to settle is perceived by judges to be partially the fault of the attorneys, who are visible and actively participating, rather than of IDOC staff, who are not:

Consequently, we get a lot of judges who are hot at us. I mean, they'll sit there in a pretrial, and he's trying to settle the case, and you get the guy down to 300 bucks, and, "Yeh, but we can't get the money. There's no way for me to go get a check for $300." So one thing that we have to work on in years to come is to provide our office, and corrections, but more our office, since we do more than just corrections work. We do state police, civil rights claims, and everything else. To provide our office, through state government somehow, with a pot of money that is readily accessible in order to buy-off some of these cases. . . . The biggest difference between our office and the Department of Corrections. . . . we'll go to them and say, "Geez, you know, we've got to settle this case. $200, and the judge is pushing us," is that we're the ones sitting there in court getting dumped on by the judges, not [the chief IDOC attorney]. She can say, or her staff, that "we're not going to settle this." They don't have to go to court and listen to the judge, and they don't have to practice in front of them next week on another case that's serious, and the judge remembers that you were the unreasonable person that wouldn't settle last week. Now, it's like a referee in a basketball game. If you're constantly yelling at them and not cooperating with them, then the odds, the psychological odds of getting the break on a call are not going to be there (State's attorney, interview, 1986).

Haggling over settlements can occasionally delay the termination of a case when parties cannot agree or when IDOC is particularly intransigent. One experienced jailhouse lawyer drew from his experiences to explain why a lingering guard brutality case was taking so long to be resolved:

What they're doing is haggling over the settlement they can offer her. The judge has done indicated that, "Hey, you can't win on trial," or "you can't win on the pending motion." That is, the motion to dismiss or the motion to summary judgment, and he's giving them all this information, you [the state] can't win there, so "what is the best thing for us to do?" Now, that's what he's talking to the lawyers about. What's the best thing for us to do in this case. "I don't want to carry this junk to trial. This is garbage. We don't want this kind of case law on the books. This is garbage here, this will set a precedent" (Jailhouse lawyer, interview, 1984).

Experienced prisoners' attorneys invariably relate "horror stories" about IDOC intransigence to settle even the most hopeless cases. This, they argue, leads to ostensibly irrational actions, as illustrated by a seasoned Chicago civil rights attorney's experiences:

It doesn't matter, I don't think, how many statistics you give them, [settlements are] not what they care about. Maxine's case, you know, Maxine's case we offered to settle before we went to trial, after we went to trial, at every point along the way [The Maxine Smith case, (Smith v. Rowe, 77–C–1029, C.D. Ill., 1977), resulted in a six figure settlement against IDOC for disciplinary and prison employment violations—JT]. And we wrote a letter calculating out what this case was going to end up costing the department before the appeal. The attorney general who did the trial and who recommended that the AG [attorney general] and the DOC settle, that attorney general, who handled the trial, they fired him because he blew it on the trial, hired a private lawyer at even greater hourly rates, they recommended that we settle, and the DOC said, you know, "Screw you, we're going to fight this one to the hilt." We wrote a letter laying out exactly what it was going to cost. Now. We got a $100,000 verdict for Maxine. Our fees for the injunction and the damages trial and all that, right? That was a healthy chunk of money for the state. And instead of settling in a very clean trial, since the AG stipulated to most of this stuff so it wasn't going to be contested on appeal, you know, we told him, "You're looking at a $250,000 bill projected, including our work on the appeal." And they could have settled for far less than that. You know? Forget it. Now, ever since the appellate decision came down in April, we have been fighting. . . . I've been on the phone with them almost every single day fighting to collect that money, all right? They are paying 9.59 interest on the judgment, and 9.98 percent interest on the fee, and they aren't paying! They tell us we'll get it by the end of this month, and we don't have the money yet. And it's gotten, you know, on her judgment, let me think, what is it? Our fee award is $48,000 for the damages trial. They're going to have to pay us [$57,000] including the interest. They're not interested in cutting their losses. We have another case. Charles Williams was beaten up. A black 72–year-old blind prisoner, beaten up by Captain [JH] on the farm at Stateville. Case in front of Judge B. He said, "Settle for [$24,000] before trial." And he told the DOC, it was the AG representing DOC. "If they believe this plaintiff, you're going to go down in a big way." So go to trial, because they know I want to settle, I get a $42,000 verdict, and a $30,000 fee award, and afterwards the judge says, "Settle for 55," and we said we'd take a little bit more than that, for the whole, fees and judgment together, and they said "No. No!" The other AG who's handling it is recommending that we settle because we're about to launch off and want 10 or 15 thousand dollars more, so that their projected liability on a case that the judge said settle for 24 is now three-quarters of a hundred thousand, that'd be 75, three times what they could have settled for initially.

The Department of Corrections' response to such experiences, however, suggests that factors other than monetary awards shape their behaviors. Such apparent "irrational" behavior may serve several functions. First, the apparent stalling may buy additional time to decide whether to appeal, how to implement subsequent policies once the case is finally terminated or may simply be required to obtain the funds. Second, refusing to settle establishes the policy that no suit, regardless how strong, can be assured of settlement. Settlement intransigence serves a prophylactic technique of sorts, by which the message is sent to inmates that they simply will not win without a protracted battle. This, so the argument runs, symbolizes "toughness" and indicates to plaintiffs that "they'd better know know what they're getting into." Third, avoiding settlements may be a face-saving strategy by which the Department both refuses to acknowledge wrongdoing, and, even when in error, symbolizes support of employees by reaffirming their policies and actions. Fourth, pursuing a case that will probably be lost in a district court may, in fact, be fiscally expedient over the long term. Remedial actions related to the suit may be in progress, and such actions might be strategically used as "good faith" indicators that the previous problem no longer exists, as might occur when prisoners complain of inadequate physical facilities. Fifth, corrections' officials might fight a losing challenge at the district level, reasonably confident that, either because of previous appellate decisions or recent extrajurisdictional case law, they might win on appeal.

The factors shaping the decision to settle are essentially pragmatic, and have little to do with attaining justice for inmates. At root, such organizational goals as fiscal restraints, control of prisoners, stable prison administration, and face-saving denial of culpability dominate the state's strategy of settling cases. Because of the diversity of settlement stakes, suits often may be settled quickly without expending scarce resources or changing policies. At times, however, neither side will concede, and the case then goes to trial.

TRIALS

Trials function as fact-finding rituals, and prisoner trials proceed as do any other. Both sides tell their story, marshall evidence, attempt to discredit the opponent, and bring to bear the usual rhetorical and legal resources to influence the outcome.

Compared with all private federal cases, especially nonprisoner civil rights complaints, relatively few prisoner suits are tried. Between 1975 and 1985, about 7 percent of all private cases reached the trial stage nationally. By contrast, about 15 percent of civilians' and 5 percent of prisoners' civil rights cases went to court (Annual Report, Office of U.S. Courts, 1985). Most prisoner cases, in fact, are terminated before pretrial (72 percent in 1984), although this figure has been declining in recent years. By contrast, only about a third of civilian civil rights suits have been dismissed before pretrial since 1975. Hence, the trial process constitutes only a small proportion of the processing of prisoner litigation, and prisoner suits reach trials less often than most other types of suits.

Despite claims of critics that prisoners prefer jury trials, neither side seems to have an innate preference, and the decision is generally a strategic one. In the past two decades, about three quarters of all prisoner trials were nonjury trials (Annual Report, Office of U.S. Courts, 1985).

When a case raises complex legal issues, defense attorneys express a preference for bench trials on the grounds that juries might become easily confused:

I think the prisoner often asks for a jury trial, but I think that the attorney generals certainly use the strategy. . . . It's like any case. If you feel that a jury is going to be confused. . . . a typical case might be where, you know, if anything happened, it was merely negligence, but is a jury going to really be able to understand the difference between deliberate indifference and negligence? So I think one of the factors you look at is the probability of juror confusion, you know, a juror, maybe there's nothing that anybody did wrong, but an injury resulted. Would the jury be sympathetic to the injury? And even though nobody did anything wrong, give a sympathy vote to a particular individual (IDOC staff attorney, interview, 1986).

In addition to the complexity of a case, jury decisions may be influenced by such external factors as attitudes toward prisoners or racial biases, which may on occasion favor some plaintiffs. One law clerk's account of how apparent jury racism against black prison officials might favor white prisoners typifies the unpredictability of juries:

The inmate was white, looked about 50, pretty much looked like an old hood, and came across on the stand like a nontrustworthy old hood, and he sued only the warden of the prison, who was black, on six different counts of racial discrimination, violating his First Amendment rights of mailing and job opportunity. It was a big thing. And every one of them, somewhere along the line, the warden was involved with. But the warden usually doesn't make any decisions like that, he gives them to somebody else, but somewhere along the line, he has to review them. Now, [the warden] is real clean cut, and from what I've seen of him, he could probably mingle with any kind of crowd and not look out of place. He comes across on the stand very believable, and the jury found for the inmate on five out of six counts and awarded him $50,000. And you wouldn't have given that guy $100 to dismiss that case! It was a six woman jury, and I sat there the whole day, it was six white women. The court of appeals reversed them, and said there was no evidence of any racial discrimination claim, so he ended up with nothing. But I wouldn't have given that guy $100 to start (Federal law clerk, interview, 1986).

Jailhouse lawyers, too, make strategic choices, and agree that neither a bench nor jury trial has any inherent advantage:

It all depends on the circumstances of the jury system. . . . For example, I wouldn't take a jury trial in Springfield, because those people are against prisoners. Now, if I was in the Northern District with that, here in Chicago, I would probably take a jury trial (Jailhouse lawyer, interview, 1986).

Despite the idealized "impartiality of law" and "official rhetoric" to the contrary, prisoners suffer several disadvantages in a jury trial. First, because of their limited mobility as prisoners, they have a more difficult time mustering evidence. Their witnesses may have been released, intimidated, or bribed by staff against testifying, or simply be unreliable. This obviously works to the advantage of the state by reducing the testimonial resources prisoners possess. Second, prisoners suffer a double stigma: their status as social deviants undermines their credibility, and their past criminal history may be used to discredit both their case and their testimony. For example, a prisoner who was actually beaten by guards may find his account damaged when defense attorneys discredit his character by revealing that he was sentenced for violent crimes:

> I suppose that one important question when you're trying a civil rights case is, "Do I want to tell the jury why my client's in jail? Do I want to tell them where he is, or why he's doing time?" And necessarily, if he's going to testify, some of those details might come out. I mean, this guy happened to be an armed robber. He also had some other case that dealt with a machine gun. I don't know if the machine gun ever came out in court, but those are things that might be a disadvantage before a jury (Federal law clerk, interview, 1986).

Third, prisoners are generally not able to retain specialized counsel, and must rely on appointed attorneys who may or may not have experience in prisoner litigation. This problem is more pronounced in jurisdictions where prisoner trials are rare and where there may be a small pool of attorneys from which to choose. Fourth, many prisoners simply do not make credible storytellers, especially before juries. Most prisoner litigants are black, poorly educated, and unfamiliar with court decorum and public speaking. White jurors especially may find such litigants less credible for reasons of both class and race. In Illinois prisons, the functional illiteracy rate has been estimated at no less than 50 percent, and a review of prisoner petitions and trial documents indicate that most stories are told by persons unskilled in the rules of "conventional" communication. Fifth, public adherence to the view of "tough prisons" subverts prisoner claims of unjust treatment or poor conditions, and media accounts of frivolous litigation and "country club prisons" are difficult obstacles to overcome when pursuing related claims. Finally, despite the expansion of prisoners' civil rights, judges remain hesitant to intervene in correctional matters. Although willing to correct occasional abuses of individual or organizational power, the nation-wide tendency to "let prisons be prisons" also persists in Illinois' Northern District. Hence, it is usually only the more serious or outrageous cases that ultimately come to trial and require judicial intervention.

COSTS OF LITIGATION

Litigants play for high stakes. Whatever the impact of prison law on prison reform, there can be no denying the fiscal costs. Playing the game requires considerable resources, borne primarily by state and federal agencies. Among the heaviest costs include processing staff (judges, clerks, special correctional employees), support staff (secretaries, court reporters), operating resources (offices, official machines, xerox, and mail costs), maintaining prison law libraries, personnel costs of guarding prisons in court, housing guards when travelling to and from court, attorneys fees, paying juries, and numerous other indirect expenses. The processing costs of U.S. and private prisoner litigation in Illinois alone in 1984 has been conservatively estimated at about $3.1 million (Hardesty and Thomas, 1986). This comes to about $2,749.77 for each case filed in Illinois Federal District Courts. This figure probably approximates litigation costs elsewhere, since the bulk of the costs are "fixed" by market factors (e.g., salaries, federal expenditures), which means that litigation annually drains no less than $85.5 million from various national treasuries.

Minimizing the direct and indirect costs of litigation, especially during periods of fiscal retrenchment, provide a sub-frame by which readers read and respond to prisoner stories and, in part, pattern how responses are keyed. A thorough study of these costs should include not only awards, fees, salaries, and other operating costs, but should include as well such remedial costs as court-ordered reforms and the costs of implementing consent decrees. If jailhouse lawyers and many private attorneys are correct in contending that considerable litigation could be reduced by such cost-effective strategies as better staff training, modest reform of conditions and more sensitivity to such basic needs as prisoners' health and physical protection, substantial savings should follow. Fiscal input-output models, however, shall be left for others to pursue.

SUMMARY

This chapter began by conceptualizing litigation as a social process performed by diverse actors with different agendas, strategies, and goals. Rather than view prisoner litigation as a bipolar Manichean conflict between prisoners and the state, it was instead presented as a more complex event possessing organizational tensions, gaming strategies, conflicting mandates, and reactive behavior by many different groups. Cases are acted upon by clerks, judges, a variety of state officials and others, each setting separate agendas and pursuing different ends. Further, the various steps of processing provide considerable opportunity for diverse social actors to influence and act upon litigation, thus requiring that litigation be recognized as a multivectored outcome of disparate forces. Prisoner rights, then, have been expanded not by a "permissive judiciary," but by a process of interaction among a variety of actors who bring a repertoire of goals, strategies, and claims into the legal forum to address an alleged Constitutional injustice.

The flexibility and discretion available to litigation participants creates a loosely coupled system that detaches the formal rules of "ideal justice" and replaces them with the substantive goals of the particular agency that a given player represents. The actual work of acting on cases occurs not so much through rule-following as through enacting various contexts of action that justify how a particular group can attain its own ends rather than the ends of "justice." These contexts vary between actors and are conducted as much by what Mills (1940) has called a "vocabulary of motive" as by rules of law. Hence, as Rawls (1986) has observed in a related context, the court becomes an institution that frames and constrains possible story meanings and ways to act upon them rather than creates a forum to resolve injustice. This is what Turner meant when arguing that prisoner litigation is not so much "justice by trial" as "justice by bureaucracy."

NOTES

1. In cogently describing the emergence of litigation as a sociopolitical movement, Berkman (1979) has emphasized the role of broader political issues and the support of outsiders as one crucial contributing factor. This may, however, be overstated. To date, there has been no careful empirical study of the role of "outsiders" in the emergence of prisoner litigation. The trend in the past 15 years has been one of prisoners themselves initiating suits, and outsiders then participating after the suit has been filed. In Illinois, lawyers rarely file civil rights cases on behalf of prisoners, and this appears to be consistent with other jurisdictions (e.g., Eisenberg and Schwab, 1986: 87). Perhaps this has always been the case, but obscured by those occasional dramatic suits in which outside participation was visible from the beginning.
2. In a study of five federal jurisdictions, Turner (1979: 617) found that IFP civil rights filings ranged between 85 and 95 percent. According to experienced jailhouse lawyers, two factors explain why a higher proportion of habeas cases are prepaid. First, habeas filing fees ($5) are substantially less than civil rights fees ($60). Second, habeas cases tend to be denied at IFP review, which motivates some prisoners to circumvent this phase by retaining private counsel.
3. For discussions of procedures in other jurisdictions, see Haft and Hermann (1972), Hermann and Haft (1973), Shapiro (1973), Turner (1979) and Willging (1985).
4. Assignment cards that have been printed and sealed in a packet by a private contractor contain all judges' names an equal number of times. Cards are randomly distributed in each packet, and no card can be pulled out of sequential order. As each case, whether criminal or civil, comes into the docketing office, the next card is pulled, and on the back of it is a number and the judge's name. Some judges may review an inordinate number of prisoner cases in one month because of the luck of the draw, but over the course of time, distribution of cases evens out. For a detailed description of procedures used in filing new cases, see U.S. District Court, Northern District, Rule 2.20–2.23.
5. In some federal districts, magistrates may either function as clerks or assume

the duties of federal judges in reviewing cases. In the Northern District, judges assume responsibility for all prisoner cases. There was no evidence of magistrates' decision-making involvement in any of the civil rights cases filed between 1977 and 1986 or habeas cases from 1980 and 1986.

6. Examples of cases that reaffirm liberal interpretations of prisoner access to courts include: *Anders v. California*, 386 U.S. 738, 1967; *Haines v. Kerner*, 505 U.S. 519, 1972; *Morgan v. LaVallee*, 526 F.2d 221 (2d Cir. 1975).

7. For a summary of extralegal factors affecting judicial decision-making on prisoner suits, see especially Carp and Rowland (1983) and Suchner et al. (1986).

8. For whatever reasons, judges do not always read this material. Court transcripts and other documents indicate that some judges in some cases are not familiar with the issues to be decided, and rely on testimony of plaintiffs and defendants to "wing it."

9. Legal *relief* refers to any court-ordered redress a prisoner is able to obtain from a suit. Relief can come at any point during the proceedings. A legal *remedy*, by contrast, occurs only after an injury has been fully proven to a court and the relief is granted as a matter of law.

10. A civil rights case denied IFP status may, however, be appealed if the full filings fees are prepaid.

11. In 1986, only 6.4 percent of all private civil cases reached the trial stage. Only 4.4 percent of private prisoner civil rights suits were tried, compared to 12.8 percent of nonprisoner civil rights suits (Administrative Office of U.S. Courts, 1986, Table C4).

12. If a state employee has acted in a blatantly illegal or reckless manner, state defense will not be provided. For example, if a prison guard was drinking on duty and savagely beat a prisoner for no apparent reason, the officer would be deprived of state representation.

13. In addition to advising correctional employees on legal matters, this office also delivers legal training to prison staff, handles a variety of contracts with the private sector (food and medical services), and coordinates the civil rights litigation of the Department of Corrections.

14. Because of nonavailability of data, Table 7b is intended to estimate broad parameters rather than precise outcomes. The figures refer only to cases within IDOC jurisdiction, and thus exclude jails, federal prisons, and nonprisons. Also excluded are 926 cases on which no decision was made or on which the decision was unknown. Data furnished by the Illinois Department of Corrections and Northern District Court were used to calculate estimates of number of prisoners and cases receiving monetary settlement awards. Excluded from IDOC figures were settlements in which no monetary awards were given, such as cases that were resolved through administrative corrections (e.g., record-keeping or expunging a disciplinary infraction from a prisoner's institution records). Their figures also exclude cases that may have been dismissed on pleading, but substantively "won" in that the prisoner gained what was originally requested (such as rectification of record errors). The proportion of suits in which the prisoner received at least partial relief would, therefore, be substantially higher than the figures indicated. State officials providing the data did so with the caveat that, because no formal records are kept, their own calculations are "unofficial." Nonetheless, if used with caution, Table 7b provides broad indicators of the disposition of civil rights cases.

15. In a study of monetary awards to prisoners between 1982 and 1984, The

Contact Center (1985) correctly suggests that, nationwide, prisoners win little. However, the methodological, conceptual, and empirical flaws in the study render the data of minimal value, providing, at best, the lowest estimate of payments. In 1984, Illinois' fiscal records indicate that a total of *no less than* $160,200 was paid out to 339 claimants. Of this, about three-quarters ($117,600) went to 17 prisoners in separate cases. Of the remainder, most settlements were under $20, many a token $1 in nominal damages. These figures are unofficial, however, and should be interpreted with caution. Most suits (96.2) are filed by single defendants, and in larger class action suits, defendants "virtually never" win monetary awards beyond a token (usually $1) sum. Hence, the compensation for victory rarely lies in monetary gain, and critics are simply wrong when they say that prisoners litigate because they can "win a fortune."

16. Prisoners routinely request six and seven figure punitive awards. Jailhouse lawyers acknowledge this as strategic: high requests, they feel, add credibility to the claim and provide a working figure from which to bargain. They also feel that unless substantial awards are requested, they ultimately will receive nothing.

8

The Making of a Jailhouse Lawyer

Who are these guys, and what do they want, anyway? (Criminology conference critic).

[A jailhouse lawyer] would be one who enjoys championing the cause of fellow prisoners. He has to enjoy that, because it's too painful for him not to enjoy it (Jailhouse lawyer, 1984).

I don't consider myself as a jailhouse lawyer. I just help these people with their legal problems. It's just like Jesus did. Jesus helped the people who couldn't walk. Jesus was a lawyer. Jesus was a doctor. When you were sick, he healed you. When you got in trouble, he would be a lawyer. All right? And this is the same thing I do (Jailhouse lawyer, 1986).

R<small>AJ</small>, A SUCCESSFUL JAILHOUSE LAWYER, was typing at his desk in the law library of a maximum security prison. His staff supervisor gave him a clerical assignment and an order: "Now, don't let anybody else use that typewriter!" A few moments later, a guard came over and demanded that Raj relinquish the typewriter, one of the few functioning, to another inmate. Raj explained that to do so would violate his supervisor's directive, which could result in a disciplinary infraction. The guard interpreted this response as a challenge to his authority, and issued a disciplinary ticket for "failure to obey a direct order," "inciting a riot," "possession of stolen property," and "violation of rules." Raj was immediately taken to segregation. The disciplinary report confirmed Raj's account, but a disciplinary committee nonetheless found him guilty and issued sanctions, including disciplinary segregation, loss of goodtime, and loss of privileges. The time in segregation—prior to the disciplinary hearing—disrupted Raj's exceptionally heavy case load (in excess of 150), delayed his filings for other prisoners, and caused him to miss at least one legal deadline: "It sure fucked up my day!"

Such apparently capricious disruptions are common in the life of jailhouse lawyers (JHLs), and they typify both the nature of prison life and the problems that litigants face. Staff are hostile, resources are scarce, and reputations as "troublemakers" are easily won, rarely lost.

191

Rather than say, "Just another day in the joint!," a common prisoner expression of resignation, Raj sued the staff, asking for $1 million in punitive and compensatory damages. The suit was dismissed on pleading, but he successfully overturned his ticket, restored his goodtime, and was temporarily left in relative peace.[1]

The frontstage performances of JHLs—their cases and subsequent decisions—are the most visible, and therefore provide the basis of public conceptions and interpretations of the meaning of prisoners' litigation. However, the backstage of prison performances, rarely accessible to public view, contain considerable information about the complexity of the enterprise. Jailhouse lawyers do what they do and present what they do within an organizational and interactional framework out of which emerges their career orientation, emergent definitions, and rules of litigation. A peek behind the curtain reveals how the substance and processes of JHL activity is patterned by structural rules and organizational limitations, by interactions with other prisoners, by the deprivations and degradations of prison life, and by existential choices. A description of the context in which jailhouse lawyers practice their craft helps illuminate the connection between the prison experience and their law.

On this tour stop, we return to the beginnings of our journey, jailhouse law, and listen as jailhouse lawyers tell their story by describing their careers, identifying their problems, and displaying their view of practising law in prison.[2] Their accounts depict a complex culture with its own recruitment and reward system, often conflicting norms and goals, and problems unique to their particular enterprise.[3]

WHAT IS A JAILHOUSE LAWYER?

The term "jailhouse lawyer" is broad and often erroneously used to describe any minimally skilled prisoner who has filed a law suit. But not everyone who files a suit is considered a jailhouse lawyer, and becoming a JHL requires more than hanging out in the law library. In practice, a JHL is any prisoner who has developed legal skills that are recognized by others as a resource in filing suits:

> A jailhouse lawyer is somebody who knows about the law and . . . a guy whose job is to help others with their lawsuits, but doesn't define himself as a lawyer. It's somebody who will do something for you if you don't have the money. It's somebody who is active in litigation.

Used here, the term "jailhouse lawyer" refers only to those prisoners who are recognized and sought out by others because of their competency, and who themselves have filed five or more federal suits, either for themselves or for others. This operating definition excludes both the "would-bes" and those who have attained some proficiency, but are not yet recognized as fully competent.

Types of Jailhouse Lawyers

Not all jailhouse lawyers are alike, although in Illinois, they tend to be older, and a disproportionate number are black.[4] JHLs can be classified by their legal proficiency, their motivations, the fees they command, or, like civilian lawyers, by the nature of their practice (public/private), the type of law (criminal/civil) or their legal speciality (corporate, civil rights). However, one useful distinction that helps us understand how law is practiced, for whom and why, is the position the JHL holds within the prison structure. These two positions are law clerks and freelancers.

Law Clerks

Law clerks are assigned to their litigating tasks by the institution. Because theirs is a formal work assignment, law clerks tend to have reasonable access both to legal resources and to their clients, thus giving them somewhat more institutional mobility than other prisoners. They are also paid directly by the institution. The pay is relatively low (in 1987 beginning at about $45 a month), but competent practitioners are able to creatively supplement their resources. Law clerks, however, have little control over their case load or clients, and they do not enjoy the degree of personal autonomy that freelance JHLs possess. They are also highly vulnerable to institutional repercussions, and may be removed from their position or transferred should staff perceive excessive enthusiasm for or success in addressing complaints. In fact, one occupational hazard of a law clerk assignment seems to be the danger of termination, either through transfer or through reassignment if they are perceived as excessively "disruptive to the institution." In some institutions, continual turnover of clerks has created the problem of insufficient staffing by untrained personnel to meet inmate needs.

Freelancers

The second type of JHL, the *freelancer,* more closely fits the popular public conception of an active litigant. Freelancers are prisoners who rarely have an institutional work assignment, and who work on their own time studying law and filing cases, both for themselves and on behalf of others. Freelancers tend to be older, more experienced in prison life and law and more savvy and capable than most law clerks, since they themselves usually began as law clerks. They tend to assume the role of mentor to newer litigants, which adds to their institutional status. Non-participation in formal organizational tasks also provides freelancers greater freedom to control their clients, negotiate for greater resources, select preferable clients, and adopt legal specialities. They also have greater freedom to pursue opportunities for compensation, since they may more freely select their clients, but they do not enjoy the same access to resources as clerks because they are not assigned to the library on a daily basis. Unlike law clerks, who are assigned their position, freelancers earn their status through force of reputation and, on occasion, the market value their skills command.

These categories are not mutually exclusive, and some clerks may also freelance. They do, however, help distinguish between the paths open to litigants, which in turn helps understand the manner in which law is done in prison. The position of law clerk might be analagous to that of a government researcher whose tasks, productivity levels, and advancement criteria are reasonably well defined. The position of the freelancer, by contrast, resembles that of conventional academics in that careers are built on networking, personal initiative, and the development of a reward structure external to the university setting. Despite these differences, however, both types share the same entry experiences, learning problems, and career development.

What does a Jailhouse Lawyer do?

Prisoners, both because of their status as social offenders and because of the problems this status may generate, confront a myriad of legal snarls (Alpert, 1978a; Fuller et al. 1987). Prisoners face numerous legal problems beyond these relating to their conviction or to their prison environment. Their vulnerability to inequitable divorce proceedings, deprivation of child visitation, problems with inheritance, taxes, name changes, compensation claims, or property leins are but a few of their legal entanglements. For assistance, they often turn to jailhouse lawyers.

The popular image of JHLs scurrying around the institution digging up problems, then locating appropriate case law to justify a suit, is belied by the reality of their work. Obviously, litigating is their job, or they would not be called "jailhouse lawyers." But JHLs are not simply litigators. They also function as counsellors, therapists, mediators and, of course, legal advisors. A skilled jailhouse lawyer must be a jack-of-all trades and master of a few as well:

> Mainly in the library . . . we deal with legal problems, we deal with problems with the administration, we write complaints, we write letters, we deal with problems between a resident and his private attorney, his attorney's going around in circles, we try to go through those changes with him.

Some tasks are officially defined by the institution or created by case-filing procedures. Other tasks are informal, unanticipated, time consuming, and frustrating. Official tasks, those defined or implied by the rules or the specific legal task, range from providing basic assistance in locating resources to conducting all phases of a suit to its conclusion[5]:

> The best that we can do is address a person's legal problems on a reasonable

level, in the courts, and we've run the whole gamut here. We go from the smallest local court to the U. S. Supreme court. We do it all. We're not lawyers. But we take the function of lawyers, because there's no one here to address those problems.

The informal tasks that JHLs perform are rarely recognized by outsiders. These include providing emotional support, mediating— rather than litigating—conflict, solving personal problems or simply serving as sympathetic listeners. On occasion, experienced jailhouse lawyers even assist staff with legal problems for future "good will."

Emotional Support

The successful jailhouse lawyer becomes therapist, diplomat, counselor, sibling and confessor, and the initial interactions between JHLs and to their clients often entail a period of negotiation during which hidden agendas that inhibit assistance are identified and discarded. Even before listening to a case, it may be necessary to first act therapeutically in order to put the potential litigant in a proper mind-set:

NJ: You have to be therapeutic. You know, a guy don't just bring you his legal problems. He brings his family problems and all that. You got to see all that, I mean, when you get a guy's case, you're adopting a family.

JT: Is that an emotional or psychological drain for you guys?

CR: Yeh!!!

NJ: It can be. It's real painful. The guys that brings you the problems are not conscious of the fact that you have problems also.

CR: [A client] not only lays the legal problems on you, but all that ego stuff, about all the holes they had, the Cadillacs they were driving, all the fine clothes, the good wine [Chorus: "Yeh!" "Right!"]. You have to put up with all that. You have to cut through all that, but you have to cut through without hurting anybody's feelings and making them mad. So that makes the situation even more compounded.

NJ: What you find yourself doing is really trying to put a guy back on track. A lot of guys are misdirected, like he says, the wine, the cars, the highheel boots. What you have to do is try to establish or reconstruct a guy's standards of values. His principles. His principles are all screwed up when he comes back here.

JT: How would you do that?

CR: Just by talking and explaining to him the reality of the situation. Like, "I'm here to help you with your legal problems, and that ego-tripping, put that in your pocket."

JT: Does it work?

CR: For some it does, but not for all of them. For some, we got some who's awfully strong. Strong psychologically, but also strong physically, and with the groups [street gangs]. It's a delicate situation. A fellow gets to ego-tripping, you have to say, "Let's get to this." You have to keep bringing him back. After a while he can get to where, "Let's deal with this, and I'll deal with my ego with somebody else." In most cases, that is a problem. A big problem. But we cut through it. We cut through that.

NJ: In many of the cases, the professionalism that's conveyed by the guy working with him on cases sometimes rubs off. Just like [CR] said, eventually all this tomfoolery is put to the side, and they guy comes into the law library everyday. It takes therapy. It takes time. Over four or five months.

Mediators

There is some evidence that prisoner litigation functions as a means of reducing prison violence (Alpert and Huff, 1981, a finding corroborated by Illinois' JHLs). JHLs recognize that both their position within the institution and their generally high status affords a unique opportunity to discover and resolve potentially volatile situations. This occurs through mediation, or the active intervention by which negotiation, rather than a less pleasant alternative, is sought:

> We can sit on top of it . . . when we see that problems are getting ready to arise in the penitentiary, we do have a little influence. We can sit with groups of brothers and talk to them, say, "Hey, let's put the problem on the table and deal with it." We're able to do that. We have done that.

All JHLs can identify at least one instance in which they personally intervened to defuse potential violence. Sometimes mediation spared a guard from being "hit" [intentionally attacked], and sometimes it prevented a prisoner-on-prisoner assault. An example of dispute resolution might occur when a gang member has been having problems with a guard:

> We have some officers here who harass certain individuals, and individuals who associate with other individuals. They belong to organizations [street gangs], you know? So if an officer is constantly harassing this guy, he might get an attitude, he might see himself as a man, and he don't mess with nobody, just trying to do his time, so maybe he want to kill him. He say, "Hey, I'm tired of this shit, I want to bust his head." And we'll talk to this man and say, "Now, if you do that, they'll lock the joint up, and a lot of repressive action will come down. . . . Let's try to solve this problem some other way." So he'll come over here and we'll all sit down together and begin to rap about it.

Sometimes JHLs' influence results in the transfer of a troublesome guard, but the replacement may be no better. When this occurs, prisoners have few options, but choose them carefully, striving to maintain harmony:

> [The former guard] is gone now. That guy's gone now. But he's got another one who's basically the same.

JT: How can you change that?

I [sarcastically] suggested that we start killing some. That was my suggestion.

JT: Would that be effective?

Of course it would!!! [laughs]

JT: Wouldn't that create problems?

We wouldn't have no problems. We wouldn't have no problems, we could eliminate them. Now, that was one answer. The other answer is that we sit down as brothers and talk about our interests here, because this environment has to be conducive to our needs, and it's not!

Problem Solving

Sometimes inmates may be confronted with simple nonlegal problems, such as not being able to contact a counsellor, being unable to resolve a bookkeeping error in their commissary account, or not being able to add a name to the visitors list. When this happens, they may seek the assistance of JHLs, which adds another layer of tasks:

XL: And guys are forever coming down, saying, "I need help," and a lot of times, the counsellors are powerless to help them, and the clerks [try to resolve] the minor problems that counsellors should resolve but are passed over to clerks, like questions over goodtime, whether jail time can be credited. Every little thing, they come to the library, as though we all had a little magic wand in our pockets, and we wave it, and [it's solved]. There's a lot of things, I think too, a lot of the counsellors [are asked to do too much]. A lot of the things they're asked to do, the guys could do themselves. They'll ask a counsellor to put so and so on my visiting list, and they could send it up front themselves and do it, and I think because of that, counsellors have an attitude towards them, because they look at the inmates as being just a bunch of helpless people. You depend on [the administration] for everything. A lot of times, they'll have a grievance or something, "See the law clerk. He'll solve the problem for you." [sarcastically] We've got all the answers down here!!

M: But if we don't do it, nobody else will do it.

JHLs, then, perform numerous tasks, many of which are unrelated to law, but most of which entail skilled conflict resolution and management skills. Many of these tasks reduce frustration, curtail potential violence, and provide an often unrecognized control function that serves the interests of the administration by "keeping the lid on" the normally occurring tensions and less productive forms of release. As a consequence, JHLs' activities, often seen as counter to institutional goals, actually help promote a more secure and humane environment, and their interests often correspond with those of their keepers.

"You Got what it Takes, Brother??!!": A Profile

Becoming a competent jailhouse lawyer requires several critically important attributes. Obviously, JHLs must be literate, but even this does not deter a motivated prisoner willing to develop literacy skills, either by private tutoring or enrolling in prison educational programs. Other criteria, however, many of them intangible, may deter some from pursuing the career. The potential JHL must be articulate, bright, and "possess the character to fight." Among the most essential requirements are love of law, persistence, empathy, and aggressiveness.

Love of Law

The love of law refers to a commitment both to the principles and the processes of litigation and justice. The erotic metaphor has a deeper connotation, for some JHLs suggest that their attachment and faithfulness to their enterprise helps assuage the lack of other basic human needs. As with any human attachment, without sufficient love, the energy and willingness to work through the many problems would drive many to seek alternative outlets. Experienced jailhouse lawyers reject critics' contentions that they have no respect for law, arguing that a love of law is the primary characterisitic required for a successful career[6]:

> Like I said originally, you have to develop a love. . . . It's a love-hate relationship with the law. You have to develop a love in working with the law, and in developing that love, people come to you, and recognize that, and a relationship will be established between you and them, and you will begin to work with *their* case, and it begins to develop from there. Like I've got tied up in it in the past eight years, and I can't get up out of it, as hard as I've tried, I can't get away from it.

Empathy

Empathy, the ability to identify and sympathize with the problems of other prisoners and place one's self in the position of another to better understand and respond to that other, helps JHLs perform legal duties and manage their clients. Law clerks, because they are not as able to choose their clients, must possess a special willingness to want to solve cases and help others, regardless of who the clients are:

> [W]e try to carry everybody as if he was a brother. We don't discriminate, we don't pass judgment. If you got a thousand rapes, and if you sit down before me and tell me you've got a problem, I must address *that* problem, and not the psychological problem.

Empathic rapport does not necessarily mean that JHLs perform their tasks out of altruism, for empathy and avarice are not mutually exclusive categories. But most JHLs perceive themselves to be more "caring" than their civilian counterparts, because they themselves share the experiences, frustrations, and problems of their clients. Hence, empathy is perceived to enhance litigation by improving the ability to identify and narrate relevant facts, create motivation, and establish a common bond with the client. Without it, a litigant becomes less able to identify the deeper sources that justify a legal response, and thus is not able to construct as strong a legal story.

Aggressiveness

I have yet to meet a passive jailhouse lawyer; perhaps none exist. Passive combatants do not long survive in any competitive field, and without a strong aggressive personality, one that exhibits initiative, drive, assertiveness, and the will to succeed, a novice would soon become discouraged and quit.

> It's something you pickup. That's what I say about the profile of the jailhouse lawyer. You've got to come in aggressive. You've got to come in trying to get down for yourself, and we recognize those people when they come into the library. They come in asking questions. "Show me what's in this book. My lawyer cited this case, where do I find this at?" And one thing leads to another. The aggressiveness of a person when he comes in is detected not only by the other prisoners, but detected by the administration. When he comes into this library and says, "Brother, can you show me where I can find this case here?" He has no idea where he can find it. All this is Greek. All these law books here is Greek to him, and he's got to attack this big monster, this monstrosity, and just looking at all these books [waves hand and laughs] is enough to scare you to death.

Persistence

The capacity to continue litigation even when obstacles seem insurmountable, and to recognize that legal struggle is a long-term enterprise, requires considerable persistence:

> Persistence! I'd say you gotta be relentless, you know what I mean? Otherwise you're going to get discouraged, because the system doesn't work your way a lot of times. But you gotta keep searching for that little loophole, or whatever, because in a lot of cases there is [one]. And when you win one, it kind of builds your ego up to keep going on and say, "Hey, maybe it was worth it."

Persistence, is not in itself a sufficient trait to guarantee the successful development of a novice learner. It can, however, earn one the respect of others who, in turn, then become more willing to provide assistance:

> I liked the guy for one reason, because he was persistent, and he kept trying, and he wasn't an educated guy at all. You could tell he never went through any schooling, and he just learned like MZ did. And somebody like that is eventually going to get better anyway, by persistence.

A deficiency in a single attribute increases the probability that a novice will not survive the trek toward becoming a jailhouse lawyer. Some of these traits may be developed, but such development itself requires a diligence of character and will of purpose. As a consequence, many JHLs see their vocation as character building, and thus a strong rehabilitative exercise that critics ought recognize.[7]

THE CAREER OF THE JAILHOUSE LAWYER

In most ways that count, the process of becoming a jailhouse lawyer resembles that of any conventional *career*. As Becker (1963: 24) has argued, careers involve a "sequence of movements from one positon to another in an occupational system made by any individual who works in that system." Luckenbill and Best (1981) have expanded the escalator metaphor to describe paths in "deviant" careers, identifying five basic levels, and members ride from one floor to the next:

> First, the organizational structure through which individuals move contains a set of formally defined positions. Written rules articulate the qualifications, responsibilities, benefits, and privileges associated with specific positions. . . . Second, individuals move from one position to another along established pathways. Members cannot move wherever or whenever they choose. Rather, organizational rules prescribe the sequences of positions through which members must move, so that an individual usually cannot reach one position without having served in certain other positions. Third, the expected career path involves upward movement through the organization's ranks. Progress depends on acquiring certain competencies or serving a specified period of time at a particular rank; members who fail to meet the standards for upward mobility may be forced out of the organization. . . . Fourth, as members move upward, they receive greater rewards, including more money and fringe benefits. . . . Finally, the organizational career is a central involvement in the individuals life. Simultaneous involvment in another occupation (moonlighting) may be discouraged; the individual should view other, part-time jobs as less important than the organizational career (Luckenbill and Best, 1981: 198).

These levels correspond to entry and learning, career stages, mobility, compensation and commitment.[8]

Entry and Learning

Very few suit-filing prisoners ultimately become jailhouse lawyers, probably only 3 to 5 percent.[9] Like members of other professions, prisoners usually drift into law, then become sufficiently socialized to the life style and dependant upon the rewards that progression into the career escalates. Some prisoners simply do not "have the right stuff" to continue the arduous study and manage the problems that come from pursuing the career. Others, interested only in addressing a single, one-shot issue, drop out. Most litigants do not file their own cases, but rely on jailhouse lawyers to do the work. Hence, the entry process weeds out "them's that is, and them's that ain't!"

There are two aspects of the entry phase. The first is the initial motivation that channels prisoners to the law. Second is the decision to remain. Both of these may vary.

Motivations

One motivating factor driving prisoners to the law is the desire to solve their problems, or *self-help*. The primal emotions of desperation, anger, and resistance are the three basic reasons both experienced and novice JHLs cite in explaining their initial entry. Each is a form of self-help in which those for whom law is not readily available may attempt to secure relief in unconventional ways (e.g., Black, 1983). For most, treatment prior to or during trial provoked the need to respond, and law became the means of response. For others, the continuous degradation by staff prompted a strong desire for vengeance. Some attempted to overcome feelings of powerlessness and alienation by developing such skills as literacy or analytic thinking in order to improve their situation.

When JHLs narrate the story of their entry, one dominant motif emerges: a perceived injustice occurred somewhere in the conviction proceedings, and no one seemed to care. As a consequence, prisoners turned to law in a final attempt to overcome the powerlessness they felt. Inequitable indictments, excessive charges, plea-bargaining betrayals, weak defense by public defenders, and unjust sentences are the most common reasons driving potential litigants to self-help. One JHL's explanation for his entry was simple:

> I got convicted. Got convicted!! I got into it because I was trying to fight my conviction. One thing led to another. I wasn't illiterate; I was educated, and these things started piling up. I started by writing letters to the warden, then filing grievances, and pretty soon I found myself litigating in court.

Desperation may also drive prisoners to the law. JHLs are unequivocally hostile to the legal profession, and all express in various ways the maxim that "when you have to depend on a lawyer, you're up shit's creek." As a consequence, frustration with lawyers has motivated some to pursue their own case. For example:

> Now, I started out as a jailhouse lawyer. I went to the joint, and was just totally fed up with all the lawyers who represented me, you know, and I got convicted, you know, not that [my crimes] didn't rightfully happen in certain instances. A whole lot of shit that [my lawyers] should have done [to mitigate the sentence], they didn't do, you know what I mean? And they're treating me like, "Hey, you've got nothing to say about this." And I'm paying them serious dollars. All right. I run out of money, and they want more, and I ain't got it, so I finally say, "Hey, I got all this time, to hell with it. I'm going to do my own shit."

Desperation produces the feeling that there is no where else to turn other than to self-litigation, and sometimes the inability of a prisoner to find affordable legal assistance creates sufficient motivating anger to learn the necessary skills:

> I got into law, when I first came here, I didn't know anything about no law. When I came to the law library, all this was foreign. . . . Let me tell ya how I got into law. I came to this law library—I was railroaded on my original conviction. I came to this law library seeking help on my case. I went from one clerk to the next clerk, and the next clerk sent me to the next clerk, and the last clerk, he was going to charge me $50. It was B.L. This was in '79 . . . I would give cash, money voucher, whatever's available. Even commissary. So I told him, "Shit, I'm not paying no $50."

Third, anger at the social or legal system, at one's defense counsel or the trial judge can be a powerful motivator. Most JHLs would not have embarked on their career without a strong sense of victimization requiring a response. Without such an intitial motivation, it would seem that there would be fewer litigants and lawsuits. One prisoner's dramatic behavior during his trial and his observation of the treatment of others similarly situated, stimulated his interest in law:

> Oh, yeh, when I first came in, I was angry, and I came through the Cook County system, and because I knew a little something about the law, I tried to represent myself. . . . I was before Judge B. [who tried the FALN], and he's got them in the bullpen [where they were placed for disrupting their trial] with a loudspeaker, and he almost did me the same way. He didn't do the loudspeaker with me, though, he just had me drug out of the court, and appointed two attorneys to represent me, and said if there's any communcation, you have to get it through them. Because I called them a bunch of racists and told him he was a nut, he come off the bench. But what he's doing to those [FALN] people is saying, in essence, by hook or crook, it don't make no damn difference, any way we can get you in there, you're going to jail and we don't care if you go in five years from now and get it reversed and we come back, and we'll do it all over again until you keep coming back. I was just talking to one of my clients today, and four times he's had a reversal from the Seventh Circuit, and he's been locked up seven years, got a murder case, and he's been back to court four times and they had hung juries and everything, but they keep on trying him, and the state's attorney say, "It don't make no damn difference, we're gonna keep on trying you, because we're gonna run you through that mill until you get tired and quit." They have the resources! They have the resources, and they got the law on their side. . . . So I was forced into it. It's overwhelming. It'll burn you up. And it burns up some of the best lawyers. I've been forced to fight [because] I've been pushed into a corner.

A fourth reason impelling prisoners to turn to law, *resistance*, is also a form of self-help. Resistance involves attempts to take responsibility for altering one's current conditions of existence, rather than rectify an alleged error of the past. A typical example might be a disciplinary infraction that was allegedly unfair, but which was nonetheless upheld by the disciplinary committee. Subsequent grievances may meet with a "standard rejection" lacking cogent justification, and the prisoner has one of two options: Passive acceptance or response. When the latter alternative is chosen, law may become the weapon:

> One time an officer gave me a dumb ticket, and they gave me a reprimand, and I wanted it dismissed. I come through here [the law library] and said, "Can you help me with this ticket?" And this guy said, "Man, [law] is a weapon," and I wanted to attack the officer for his nonsense, and he took me, and put me in his [law] classes, and now here I am [doing law], you know, just because of a minor ticket that was so small.

Recognizing the potential benefits of litigating provides a fifth motivation for entering the JHL career. For a few, entry comes from observing the privileges that jailhouse lawyers seemed to have that other prisoners did not, and, on occasion, the simplest of artifacts may be perceived as a means of improving one's conditions, and convinced one prisoner to enter the career:

> I ran into a guy, the first jailhouse lawyer I ever ran into was [E.F.], who was in county jail. . . . The guards, they gave him a lot of play, and he had a little rapport with the guards, and this and that, and he was the only guy who could have a typewriter, and I said, "How do I get one?" And they said, "Well, you know, it's hard to get one, and blah, blah, blah," and I seen him, and I kind of said, "Hey, this is neat. I should have one." And I was writing out my classes, and he's sitting next to me, and he's typing away, and you know, that what his only thing. He said, "This typewriter's my life, the only thing that gets me through the time."

Sixth, most prisoners do not consider themselves "bad guys," but just errant travellers who "fucked up a few times." Once the realization of their predicament settles in, perhaps after listening to the prosecution's or judge's characterization of them, a revelation of sorts may occur that leads to law. Prisoners may then decide to reconstitute their life by engaging in what Irwin (1980: 16) has termed *gleaning,* or using institutional resources for self-improvement. Unlike self-help, which is an attempt to address past or current problems, gleaning refers to a possible future enhanced by self-development:

> About 1978 when I went in [long pause] For the first three or four months, I screwed off, like anybody else. I was smoking reefer everday, you know, a friend of mine smuggled in a big ounce of reefer, and everybody got high on the floor. I wasn't making money, I didn't really realize where I was. I thought it was a big joke, you know? I said, "Hey, yeh, yeh, yeh, right, 22 years, ha ha, I'll be out in two years," you know what I mean? Well, I didn't

realize. Finally, after a couple of calendars [months], you snap, and it's serious: I'm not getting out for a long time. Judge M. said I was the most vicious and antisocial person who ever came before him when he sentenced me. He revoked my bond. And, uh, I'm thinking to myself, "What the hell? Geez, you know, is this really me he's talking to?" I ain't that bad, you know what I mean? I'm gonna show him, so I start taking all the sociology courses I can find. So that's what I did, all kinds of sociology, psychology, English, and then I get into the law library.

All jailhouse lawyers interviewed have agreed that their activities have sharpened their skills, changed their attitudes toward law and society, and given them an education not otherwise attainable:

I'm guilty of committing the crime that I committed, but that doesn't stop me from trying to better myself. I recognize my wrong. But when I come here, I try to get a better education, I learn something about the law, I'm trying to help people, I'm associating with people on the streets with organizational things, and we're exchanging ideas. I'm trying to become a better person, to get ahold of myself. I'm saying that instead of 75 percent of the residents going out and coming straight back, 75 percent of them, if you would allow themselves to develop themselves in that manner, [they'd] go out and stay out.

Finally, once one has begun litigating, overt results, usually in the form of some type of "victory," produce a powerful incentive to continue. For many people, successful completion of a task produces a reward of its own, which provides both a sense of satisfaction and accomplishment as well as encouragement to continue. Prisoners are no different. The following dialogue between several JHLs affirms the importance of the first success:

WJ: Oh, yeh. I remember your first win. That was your first one. I remember, you kept bugging me about questions, but you actually learned. But anyhow, that's how you start. Once you start off, these guys start the same way. [The plaintiff] couldn't find anybody to help him, and GM did. And he's been filing litigation every since. Once he started off, he [learned it] the same way.

GM: I was *excited!!* You know, see. . . .

WJ: That give you incentive to go. . . . [GM] filed his first major case, and it was accepted, and he's walking around the cellhouse happy!! It's great. He's learning, though, he's learning a lot. He's improved a lot. I've read some of his work, and he's improving.

Observing institutional changes or even being "hassled" by staff can also generate incentive:

Like, when I first got a petition granted, everybody come around, when somebody gets a favorable decision or order back from the court, everybody goes around and shows everybody, and everybody get a copy of it, and then they commend you on it, and that makes you feel good. And that's what pepped me up. Everybody saying, "That dude, that dude, he panned them up." And the officers kept telling me, "You're a pain in the ass." And that actually motivated me. When I knew that it was causing them a reaction, that it was actually affecting them negatively, and I learned, and I got better and better and better.

Entering and remaining in law, then, derive from a multiplicity of motives, but the common thread uniting each is a feeling of "self-help" to right a wrong. This overarching ethos of law as a weapon is consistent with the type of litigation most JHLs prefer—challenging convictions or conditions. Motivation, however, is only the first step. Once "turned on" to law, novices next must learn it.

Learning the Law

Following the recognition of law as an enterprise, learning it begins. A JHL learns the skill in prison, slowly, gradually and often painfully.[10] In many ways, entry into the career of jailhouse law parallels that of conventional law schools in that newcomers with potential are identifed, encouraged, and screened to avoid wasting time on "bozos."

Despite the popular conception, JHLs do not learn the law in isolation, for it is initially too mysterious. Even when novice litigants embark alone, they soon realize that learning requires assistance:

And I went down [to the law library], and it was like shooting in the dark. I mean, I know I had an attempted murder case, so I'd pick out the book. "Attempt." And I'd start just writing. "Ah, here's a case here." And I'd write, boom, boom, boom. And I'd write pages and pages full of stuff. . . . I never even used the stuff I was researching. I didn't know what I was doing. Finally, you start narrowing it down to where you're really at. "Hey, this issue is really pertaining to my case." But at that stage, I wasn't a jailhouse lawyer, I just came in, I was green, I'd never been in the joint before. Shakespeare, I think said, or one of them guys, "By indirection we find direction."

Learning the law occurs in four basic ways: mentors, training either formally or informally, competition with others and collegial interaction.

Mentors

First attempts at learning the law are much like trying to piece together a jigsaw puzzle with no guiding image of the picture. When institutions lack formal or informal training programs, mentors—wise counsellors willing to share their expertise—help flesh out the puzzle's picture. Mentors possess a charisma that excites and motivates, but above all, they are willing to help novices. As one prisoner describes his first mentor:

He said, "I'll tell you what. I can't help you with [your case], but I'll teach you how to do it." The next thing I know, he was giving me tutoring classes [at that] little desk back there, and every day, I'd come down here, I'd get a call-pass every day. So I got fucked over by the criminal justice system. But he told me, he said, "I'll show you how to do it, I won't do it." I couldn't do nothing, so what happened, I started learning myself. I got passes every day, so I come, and first he showed me how to research. Then I was going to Jughead's legal class. It took me about eight months to learn. Once I started off learning, I did it through trial and error, by actually helping other inmates with their cases. I became an employee, snatched me a desk, and we wasn't nothing but old men back here, and there was competition. And I didn't want to make it look like, "Man, I forgot what the man taught me." So I wracked my brains day and night to answer questions, and they gave me a question, I'd wrack my brain day and night to come up with something.

Experienced jailhouse lawyers are not always eager to help novices, and sometimes a creative strategy is required to elicit assistance:

The older guys, Bee and Sancho, they'd teach me. I found out he [Bee] smoked reefer, and then he'd teach me, but if he didn't smoke reefer, he didn't. So I started smoking reefer with him [speaks in high reefer voice and imitates questions he'd ask and answers he'd receive]. And he's now teaching me civil law. And I'd go back with OJ just to confirm that I was going down the right track. And then I started taking cases. I didn't really know that much about it, but once I started taking cases, the first case I did was for the U.S. Supreme court, and I got it granted. And when I saw I got it granted, I said, "Shit, I got through that." That gave me incentive to keep on going, and guess what? I'm the best lawyer they've ever had in [here].

In some ways, experienced jailhouse lawyers resemble partners in a private law firm, and mentors may carefully choose potential junior partners:

The guys who worked over here, we'd have to see in you an aptitude. If you didn't know law, you'd have to show some aptitude to want to know law, and want to work with prisoners, because it's a hard job. It's a job that demands all your time, I'm talking about all of it. Sometimes I have to leave off taking showers. I haven't been to yard for years because of some of the cases. I have to cut television off. I can't listen to the radio sometimes just trying to develop arguments, or trying to understand some of the jarbled language that comes out of these law books, reading cases over and over and over. So when guys come here for a job, it used to be the case that we used to talk with them, and get a feed-out from them, then we'd talk amongst ourselves to see what we could do with that person, where he would fit in in this thing over here we have.

Training

In Illinois, a variety of rules prohibit civilian staff from providing legal assistance beyond directing prisoners to appropriate law books, and because most staff lack training in legal research, they tend to be less knowledgeable than most novices. Hence, mentors assume responsibility for training newcomers. Informal training, especially in institutions where there are few experienced litigants, usually entails little more than limited supervision and "rap sessions." When a sufficient critical mass of experienced litigants exists, inmates may develop rigorous training programs. When, either through attrition or institutional design, there are no longer a sufficient number of competent prisoners in an institution, critical mass is lost, and there are no longer sufficient mentors for the task.[11] Training tends to be one part of a larger process to ensure competency, and invariably requires one or more examinations. JHLs who begin as law clerks may or may not receive formal training, depending on the prison, the library system that supervises the law library, the number of clerks, staff or external support groups available to train, and the collectivist glue of clerks already employed.

Training occurs in several ways. Sometimes clerks informally train others, and sometimes clerks and freelancers will unite in sophisticated sessions that may include formal classes, instructional materials and video tapes[12]:

> I came through in '82, when Burr Oak had the library system, and one of the residents who had been familiar with [legal material] trained us, and we had like a morning session which was class time, and the afternoon session, on the job training, filing grievances, things like that. You'd always be guided by one of the more experienced clerks.

Whatever form training takes, it tends to be planned and implemented by prisoners, and structured around the specific legal needs and problems that have emerged within a given institution at a given time. The quality and extent of such training is thus dependent on the quality of jailhouse lawyers currently practicing, and when turnover of legal personnel is high, the quality of training is low. Without proper training, novice clerks are unable to satisfy the legal needs of prisoners, and the quality and success rate of petitions declines. For this reason, many JHLs perceive a "conspiracy" behind transfers, and interpret transfers as a "plot" by staff to curtail legal access.

Competition

Competition provides a third learning tactic. The pride instilled in developing a knowledge of law and in successful litigating stimulates competition between JHLs, and this competition becomes a powerful motivator, often possessing "macho" connotations. Competition tends to create a healthy environment that solidifies JHLs, giving them a sense of common purpose, promoting creative ways to expand their power and influence by recruiting others, and testing legal knowledge:

Now, the way it used to be here in the law library, the competition, we'd have an assembly line, where a case gets processed. We used to set up tables right out here on Friday nights. We'd close the library, and set up tables right out here, and have legal sessions. We'd get a guy's case. For example, Mr. Brown's case, and we'd sit here and debate legal issues. We'd all come together and do our research together, and discuss the issues, for and against. Half the guys would play devil's advocate, "How'd you come at this?" "How'd you defend it?" This is what we used to do. Those are learning skills. You know why? Because then he gave me some competition. He said, "All right, you don't know this," and it was something I didn't know, so I learned. . . . There's [currently] no competition in here. I need some competition. When I first started, there was all kinds of competition. . . . It was a healthy competition, and that's how I learned the law, through competition. Ok, if I don't know it, so-and-so knows it. And one day they show me, and I show somebody else.

Collegiality

Collegiality, normally not an adjective applied to prisoners, permeates the activity of JHLs. The need to share resources is a *sine qua non* of an enterprise where resources are scarce, and mutual problem-solving through meetings or informal discussion functions much as study groups do for law students or "brown-bags" for academics. Collegial interaction also becomes a mechanism for bringing novices into the ranks of the initiated, thereby strenthening the in-group. What do these colleagues discuss?

> We're looking for arguments of previous cases, what kinds of arguments works, what kinds were used, how do they articulate a particular idea. It's not just study, it's how to find a case that's a good case.

Connecting with networks of others involved in prisoner litigation, especially civilian legal advocates, also becomes useful in learning law. Through word of mouth, reading law journals and newsletters or corresponding with outsiders, recent legal developments, successful and unsuccessful strategies, or simply continued encouragement are imported into the institution.

Using the law is not a reflex that prisoners engage in automatically; it first requires recognition of the law as a possibility for action, and next, the arduous process of learning how to engage it. The learning process may vary, but the educational goal remains constant, and the availability of learning resources and role models pattern both career development in and application of law. Hence, the process of litigation begins with the double requirement of consciousness-raising and skill development, both of which are primary attributes of self-help, and even rehabilitation (Noblit and Alpert, 1979; Alpert et al. 1978). Learning basic litigating skills requires six to eight months, but becoming a proficient litigator takes minimally two years or longer. Within this period, JHLs pass through a series of phases.

Career Stages

JHLs pass through a series of developmental statuses, or *stages,* in which they not only learn law but also develop the requisite skills to manage clients, "cool out" tension, recognize the strategies of staff resistance and methods to cope with them, and otherwise become socialized into the career. Many of these stages are formally defined, especially for law clerks who climb the ladder from advocate to clerk. Others are less formal, but just as real. Although some freelancers may skip some of the formal organizational stages of becoming a JHL that law clerks must pass through, both share identical experiences in the learning process. The career of the JHL advances through four basic tiers or stages, which mark an inmate and define the status, tasks and opportunity for rewards. These stages have no specific name in prison argot, but are nonetheless clearly demarcated from each other. For lack of better vocabulary, these might be called the phases of faltering, hesitation, "save-the-world," and maturation.

The Faltering Phase

The first stage is that of a faltering novice, in which litigants are lost, forlorn, and totally confused. This phase is akin to "a child learning to walk":

> During this stage, the new law clerk/JHL begins to acquire the basic information and skills required to function as an effective law clerk/ jailhouse lawyer. For example, the jailhouse lawyer becomes familar with the court systems (both state and federal), available court remedies, institutional rules, regulations and procedures and acquires basic writing skills (Fuller et al. 1987).

A novice JHL resembles the member of a religious order who has not yet taken the vows of commitment to an enterprise or life style. Novices are those prisoners who come to law, often to pursue their own case, and undergo an initiation of sorts through the rites of learning, socialization, and personal change. For clerks and freelancers alike, the initiation usually requires either formal or informal training,

In Stateville, new litigants invariably participate in the inmate-sponsored legal training sessions. These include several tests, and without passing the tests, one does not advance to the next stage. Inmates hoping to become law clerks must pass these tests, as well as undergo interviews with their future colleagues, before they will be given a position. Other state institutions lack this sophisticated process, and movement from novice to litigant is more difficult. As a consequence, with but few exceptions, the state's most adept JHLs have, at some point in their careers, passed through Stateville.

If a novice successfully completes the training and is able to secure a job as law clerk, additional testing is required prior to becoming a *legal assistant,* responsible primarily for giving basic information to others in using legal materials, obtaining and completing forms, and guiding one-shot litigants to others more skilled if required.[13] If the performance in this position is satisfactory, the next step would be promotion to *legal advocate,* in which the responsibilities expand to filing complaints and taking a generally more active and responsible role in all phases of the litigation process:

> You first start by taking an exam, and they take those who score the highest on the exam. When I came, I took an exam, passed it, and then took classes, law classes, on how to file grievances, and they started off with legal assistance. They had two groups of clerks, legal assistants and legal advocates. Some people started off in the reference section and kind of worked their way around, from reference section, to legal assistant, to legal advocate.

Once novices have mastered the basics of legal research and filing procedures, if competent, they may begin filing cases for others.

The Hesitant Phase

In this stage, the novice becomes a litigant, but litigation is characterized by hesitation and timid application of the basic information learned in the previous phase.

Becoming recognized as a litigant produces a qualitative change in how one is viewed by others. Other prisoners recognize the litigant as a potential legal resource, and the requests for information or filing assistance stimulate further learning. In addition, when one begins to litigate for others, the opportunity for rewards becomes tangible, the "mind-set" changes and law begins to dominate one's existence. As a consequence, the litigant stage represents the intermediate step at which one usually decides whether to engage law as a career, or merely as a useful vocation. There are many litigants however, and the overwhelming majority—in excess of 90 percent—rarely file more than two suits during their prison stay.[14] The effort required to litigate entails further immersion in the law, for one can be neither successful nor maintain one's status without continually adapting to new case law and polishing litigation skills. Those who persevere may become acclaimed by others as "jailhouse lawyers."

The "Save-the-World" Phase

In this phase, one becomes conscious of and begins to assume an identity as a full-fledged jailhouse laywer. The "save-the-world" stage is one in which the JHL wants to charge forward, utilizing newly developed skills and abilities. There is a feeling that every problem can be solved through legal means, and this phase is often characterized by an "unrelenting crusading zeal" (Fuller et al. 1987). The transformation from the early phase is often subtle, and none are able, except in retrospect, to identify at what point the shift became obvious. For most, two primary characteristics changed their self-perception. The first, a change in life style, occurred when they recognized that their prison existence was dominated by law. They "began to walk law, talk law, eat law, sleep law," and their leisure time was spent either working on cases in their cells, discussing cases over meals, or even skipping meals to build a case. The second marker was defined by their relationship to other inmates. JHLs were no longer "that guy who works in the law library," but "the guy who filed the [significant] case." Their identities often became intertwined with an important suit, or with their ability to help others file suits, and for the more competent, their reputations spread throughout the state prison system. One JHL considered this both a reward and a motivating factor:

> I mean, a guy could jump off the bus right now, come in here and say, "You guys know Johnny Oldham?" Right away most of them would say, "Yeh, he's in the library over there." Yeh. You can go to any institution, and it's the same with other lawyers, and somebody'd get off the bus, and say, "Where's Chico?" "He's not at this institution, he's over at Stateville." Whatever, people would know certain people who are active in the law.

The Maturation Phase

In this final phase, one has "finally arrived" as a practicing JHL. This final stage is distinguished by the ability to identify those problems that can and cannot be solved, as well as the courage to refuse to pursue those problems that cannot be resolved. This stage is also characterized by the knowledge that becoming a successful jailhouse lawyer is a continuous process.

Skipping one or more stages depends largely on the availabity of mentors to guide one through the learning process. These career stages, then, not only provide a system for stratifying those pursuing law, but in practice provide a useful typology for identifying the experiences and changes through which a prisoner passes on the journey from novice to mature litigant.

Mobility

In his subtly brilliant study of career mobility in deviant careers, Luckenbill (1986) has found that the patterns of movement are as rich and complex as those in conventional careers, and mobility of JHLs is no exception. Mobility is built into the career of the JHL. Simply by attaining the position, a prisoner advances through a series of statuses. Once having attained a particular status, some JHLs, either by predilection or by ability, are content to remain. Others, however, set their goals higher and move either up or across invisible lines that shift their status or position. The three basic career paths of stability, of horizontal and vertical mobility are defined by administrative, symbolic, and compensatory factors.

Stability

The first career path may be one of relative *stability*. For JHLs with relatively short sentences (less than two years), there may be no incentive to advance once a relatively comfortable position has been attained. Such prisoners usually enter as law clerks, perform their assigned tasks, and rarely take work for others outside of their assigned clients. They maintain relatively low visibility, rarely oppose the institution by challenging rules or policies, and generally are content as legal assistants or, on occasion, legal advocates. They do not fully participate in training others, do not tend to become mentors, and although respected for their legal activity, do not elicit the same respect or rewards as do their more ambitious colleagues.[15]

Horizontal Mobility

Horizontal mobility, moving laterally across boundaries, provides a second career path. Administrative transferring from a nonlaw job assignment to another that possesses no significant increase of rewards or status, such as moving from library clerk to legal assistant, is one example of a lateral shift. A change in institutions also represents a type of administrative lateral mobility. Some JHLs, for example, have found the tasks in minimum security institutions unchallenging, even boring. One complained that the types of cases he processed in a new institution were primarily those addressing transition problems of soon-to-be-released inmates, such as taxes or divorce, and he had no opportunity to practice his civil rights specialty. As a consequence, when a transfer is requested, some JHLs may carefully consider such criteria as the nature of the institution, the availability of resources and the type of law practice possible before making such a "career move."

A symbolic lateral movement might occur when a JHL shifts from one area of legal expertise, such as tort law, to another, such as habeas law. Such a move might be analagous to a sociology professor moving from one Ivy League school to another. No career advancement (or descent) occurs, but the nature of the client, the work load, the interest areas or the pressure and environment may change.

Lateral compensation occurs when the nature of rewards shift without significant increase or decrease. For example, a freelancer might be willing to trade control of work load for the advantages of mobility available to law clerks. One might also prefer to take on difficult cases for the pride of accomplishment rather than handle less difficult cases that offer more direct compensation from clients but no feeling of professional success. Such conscious decisions and one's choice ultimately shape career advancement and future opportunities. Hence, a lateral move may be a strategic ploy by which to rise later, or it may be a decision made simply to enhance one's current mode of existence.

Vertical mobility

Vertical mobility provides a third career line. Of established jailhouse lawyers, an estimated 20 percent attempt to continue to improve their station by a combination of structural, symbolic, and compensatory ascent moves.

Structural ascent occurs when a JHL moves from one administratively defined position to another in the hierarchical ladder. For example, a litigating cellhouse electrician may move "upward" by securing an assignment in the law library, or a legal assistant may become a legal advocate. Relocating within the institutional structure may also facilitate other types of upward mobility, including symbolic advancement.

Symbolic advancement can occur in several ways, but status shifts are the most common. Nonclerks who have been filing primarily on their own behalf may begin assisting others, and with this change in emphasis comes an increase in attention and a redefinition of "self" by others. Another form of symbolic mobility ascent occurs when JHLs take on cases that are particularly difficult, or especially when they begin challenging institutional policies. This brings the litigant respect as a "fighter," as somebody "who counts." This becomes a valuable commodity in an environment where being perceived as a "fighter who can't be fucked with" is valuable currency. With only slight hyperbole, it is analogous to the move from second string status to all-star recognition, or from shortorder cook to gourmet chef. While corresponding compensation may accrue, it rarely matches the new power and prestige accruing from the change.

Compensation

When JHLs become increasingly proficient, their compensatory opportunities also improve. A skilled litigant may move from a relatively low paid status to one that commands considerable rewards, either in direct monetary remuneration or in less tangible subsidies. One's level of compensation, in fact, often indicates a new level in the JHL career.

Career advancement for JHLs is rather easy for those with sufficient talent and initiative. The nature of the prison stratification system, the unconventional reward system, and the existence of structural hierarchies all contribute to the multiplicity of ways a clever JHL may advance, both licitly and illicitly. Hence, jailhouse lawyers, like other professionals, must be recognized as members of a complex occupation that sorts out participants in ways that shape how they work and for whom.

Compensation: "What's in it for Me?!"

The possibility of compensatory rewards may not be the primary reason most jailhouse lawyers enter the career, but once in, they, like civilian lawyers, may be motivated by the opportunities for compensation. Unlike the civilian economic structure, however, JHLs operate within a closed community of litigants, thus curtailing the types of rewards available. Opportunities are further restricted by prison regulations prohibiting economic enterprise. Hence, JHLs who ply their art for money must creatively establish a reward system that does not jeopardize their enterprise; sometimes these are licit, other times not. Prisoner law, like most law, involves a transaction between the client and counsel, and compensation may take different forms. The first type of compensation takes the form of tangible rewards, such as money, commissary commodities, or services. The second is indirect, and involves symbolic compensation such as increased status or personal satisfaction, or a reward that comes from a source other than the client. In practice, both rewards may accrue simultaneously, but they nonetheless represent two analytically distinct types.

Tangible Rewards

Some JHLs do *pro bono* work, while others discourage formal compensation. Few, however, make any secret of the fact that they are compensated in often imaginative ways.[16] Corrections' officials and JHLs, when speaking "for the record," deny that such direct compensation exists. An experienced high ranking corrections official—perhaps cynically proferring the official line rather than imparting "fact"—denied all knowledge of direct compensation:

> Well, I don't think [compensation] would be allowed to happen inside the Department of Corrections, because the rules expressly prohibit any transactions.

In their candid moments, however, both staff and prisoners acknowledge that legal work entails an economic transaction, just as it does in civilian life. JHLs unanimously agree that those who charge often cannot afford otherwise, because of the limited alternative opportunities available:

> There's those who don't charge, and those who do. You have to charge. Those who charge accept the responsibility [for a case]. You're getting $45 a month, you have five kids at home. You love the law, but you have the opportunity to work in the tailor shop and make $100 a month. . . . See, [as a JHL], I'm an artist also, and it's time consuming to cultivate the talents

over the number of years that I've been involved in it. It's not to say that
. . . I can't afford to give the world the documents, or the talents that I've
developed. You have to understand also that I have to command some
respect, and the respect might be monetary reward.

Tangible rewards commonly take the form of cash payment and gift
exchange. Behind prison walls, hard currency possesses a worth higher
than its face value. Cash is stable, and highly coveted illicit goods are
usually discounted when paid for in cash rather than by barter. Cash,
however, entails risks. Staff will confiscate cash found on an inmate
during a shakedown or body search. This does not always result in a
disciplinary infraction, however, since persistent and reliable rumors
suggest that the money—the only evidence—on occasion disappears
shortly after confiscation. As a consequence, direct exchange of cash
occurs in ways that do not entail such risks. The most common strategy
of processing a monetary transaction requires a client to have cash sent
to an outside contact, and work procedes upon notification of receipt.

The second type of tangible compensation involves less risky exchanges of "favors," commissary items, or other commodities. Sometimes tangible benefits take the form of "gifts" determined by tacit
understandings evolved from the norms of the prison culture. If a client
has few resources, the gifts may be small and often given as a token of
respect or appreciation rather than for their inherent value. There may
be no set fee discussed, but the expectation is that some reward will be
forthcoming. Because most inmates have few resources, gifts may be
small, but in a society where "a little buys a lot," they are useful[17]:

> If I sit here and write your petition, I'm not going to have to ask you for
> anything. Out of the kindness of your heart, if you are a kind person, you
> are going to automatically give me something.
>
> JT: What would I want to give you?
>
> Anything. You could give me a bag of tea. If I smoke cigarettes, you can
> buy me a pack of cigarettes. If I drink coffee, you can buy me a bag of
> coffee. If I need a new typing ribbon for my typewriter, you can buy me a
> typing ribbon. If I need a legal pad, you can buy me a legal pad.

What gifts are offered, accepted or expected, however, is situational
and contingent on the resources, status or position of the client:

> Guys would give me stamps, because I'd be filing for them, and putting
> stamps on the envelopes. Stamps and coins for xeroxing . . . that's like I
> was. I don't encourage anybody to lay anything on me, but guys would
> come and say—I'd have all the crime syndicate guys come to me with books
> of three books of stamps every commissary. "Here's three books, Ricky."
> Old guys doing 20, 'cause I'd be helping them. But I never asked. That shit
> just don't settle well with me. In the situation I was in, everybody in there
> was in the same situation, and I didn't feel like taking from people who are

down and out like me. Lawyers do that on the street all the time. But it was just kind of ethics with me. Not only that, it was illegal. If you got caught doing it, you know, you could do more time. And, sure, a lot of guys I did stuff for, I could trust, but then, who knows, when a guy gets in a bind, and there's so many guys that talk, and blah, blah, pretty soon you're locked up in the hole. And you got more time tacked on.

Because of risks entailed, some jailhouse lawyers exercise caution when accepting tangible rewards, especially money:

First of all, I wouldn't take no money for a lot of reasons. It's against the rules. Secondly, they give you money, "Hey, here's $200, do the case." Now you owe them something. They're going to be bugging you, and I've got my own things to do. I gotta upset my apple cart to make sure that they get their shit done, and they got a legitimate beef, and I'm gonna get stabbed over this in the end if I don't produce? I don't need them hassles. So I wouldn't take a lot of cases. A lot of cases I would take, just for the principle.

Intangible Rewards

Some pundits have scoffed at the suggestion that JHLs are *pro bono* practitioners, but there are numerous rewards that do not require tangible exchange. Such an apparently trivial reward as "being taken seriously" may generate a variety of subsequent rewards, including increased institutional mobility or more rapport and trust with guards. Of the types of intangible compensation, symbolic rewards are the most common. In a culture in which many rewards are symbolic and define status, prestige and power, such exchanges can dramatically increase the quality of prison life. Some intangible rewards derive from the litigation act itself:

See, all the inmates respect a jailhouse lawyer, whoever he is. If you got one or two on the floor, everybody knows them, and everybody respects them, and you get a lot of [propositions] because they don't got nobody to go to with problems from in there, especially in the county jail, because nobody can rub two nickles together. In the fed system, you got guys with money who might rely on a lawyer, but a lot of guys in the county jail or in the state system, well, if you're a jailhouse lawyer, you could have everything you wanted if you wanted to hussle people. That's another thing. I never did that. I never did that shit for money. For seven years, I never took no money from anybody.

Symbolic rewards may possess a "use value" to the extent that they create advantageous situations or an ability to manipulate the environment. When, for example, a JHL becomes recognized as "serious," staff may respond accordingly, thus providing a reward:

Finally, it came to a point where they'd be searching everybody's room looking for some contraband, and they'd come to my room: "We know you ain't got nothing Ricky." Yeh, right, they'd go to the next guy. Little did they know. A couple of guys came to me, "Hey Ricky. but this in your room." I had it right underneath my bed. Some cigarettes that were stolen in the joint, I [hid them] for a guy. . . . Now I could see where E.S. was coming from, why he had his typewriter and nobody else could have one. Why he could go to the law library. Because after about a year, they realize that you're serious.

Sometimes JHLs are able to promote their frontstage image as "workaholic" as a way of manipulating their immediate environment, such as retaining a coveted single cell:

I'll get a cellie—-they'll come in, and see all those cases, and they'll just march down to the office and say, "Fuck this shit. I want out of there. The man's got wall-to-wall cases, and I ain't celling with him." It intimidates them because they think I'll be talking law all night, or with all the boxes, and there won't be room for them.

Artistic pride constitutes another intangible reward, especially for those who had few significant accomplishments prior to incarceration. Although tangible rewards may be a reflection of respect from others, the pride of "a first-rate case," especially if it sets precedent, can generate considerable self-esteem:

Ah, the gratification that you won, the gratification that you put a good document together, some guys put some shit together that won't survive in court. Now, don't get me wrong, I like money, too, but I also get gratification out of knowing that I put a document together that satisfies me. I don't care what you think about what I put together, I might be the only one that feels that way in the library, but I feel a sense of accomplishment when I get a document completed, free of grammatical errors, sentence tenses right, everything is correct. I'm telling you that I've put a document that an architect would put together. *I'm a legal architect.*

SUMMARY

Three themes emerge from the descriptions of becoming a JHL. First, becoming a JHL requires considerable effort and expertise, and the commitment and experience required to be successful, the career paths, and the reward and compensation structure resemble those of other professions. Second, although learning litigation skills is made more difficult by lack of formal educational opportunities, a variety of informal mechanisms have emerged by which skills are passed from those possessing expertise to those who have none. Finally, practicing law provides inmates with an opportunity for self-help or self-improvement. By supplementing their scarce resources, or simply by learning marketable skills, inmates are able to transform their prison experience into something reasonably productive and beneficial, both for themselves and for others.

As JHLs become further committed to their career, the compensatory opportunities increase, both because of their improved skills and because of increased knowledge of how to use their position to parlay their activity into useful returns. The return of money, status, power, maneuverability, or gifts is but one of the advantages that accrue over time, and the longer one engages the career, the greater the opportunities become. But compensation alone does not give one status; this comes from the recognition that one files "good cases." Filing good cases comes only from doing the law, to which we now turn.

NOTES

1. Shortly after, Raj was attacked by another prisoner in the law library in what was alleged to be guard-incited retaliation.
2. This chapter addresses the male experience. There are few female JHLs currently incarcerated in Illinois, and their story will be told separately (Wheeler et al. 1987; Fuller et al. 1987). The best current description of women and law remains Kates (1984).
3. All quotes but one (and so indicated) are from Illinois prisoners. The bulk of the data were obtained from 19 jailhouse lawyers, two dozen novices, and no less than 50 other inmates who have filed at least one case in the past seven years. Innumerable nonlitigating inmates also provided information. Identifying initials are used only when two or more JHLs are speaking, and have been modified to protect the identity of narrators (one *never* calls the prisoner "an informant!"). I have attempted as much as possible to use data given by persons no longer incarcerated. Brackets are used to provide more precise meanings of a word or phrase when it has been implied or previously given. Ellipses generally indicate run-on discourse, or, on occasion, removal of identifying references, and punctuation is intended to illustrate the mood and tenor of discourse rather than publisher's preferred style. Such generalizing terms as "usually," "most" or "often" may bother some readers, but statistical precision is meaningless because prisoner turnover makes precise tabulations impossible.
4. The average age of Illinois prisoners, 29.8, glosses over the statistic that most (over two-thirds) are under 30, and about one-third are 24 or younger. In the state's most heavily litigious prisons (Pontiac, Stateville) the inmate population is about 90 percent ethnic (Lane, 1985: 15; Lane, 1986b: 94–95).
5. Competent JHLs perform the same litigation tasks as a civilian lawyer, with the exception of actually arguing the case in court. On occasion, however, the more experienced litigants may represent themselves when arguing their own cases *pro se* (without counsel). For others, they typically do all the preliminary research and processing required prior to a trial, but should a bench or jury trial be required, courts usually appoint counsel for in-court responsibilities, although as noted in Chapter 5, few cases are actually tried.
6. Alpert (1978b) has provided evidence that those who seek legal aid are significantly more likely to have respect for law than those who do not.

7. For a related corroborative argument, see especially Alpert et al. (1978) and Noblit and Alpert (1979).

8. Discussions and illustrations of JHLs' commitment to law permeates this chapter, and a separate discussion has therefore been parsimoniously omitted.

9. Of the 1,309 prisoners filing civil rights complaints in the Northern District between August, 1977 and December, 1984, 40, at most, could charitably be considered jailhouse lawyers. This constitutes only 3.1 percent of all litigators. Further, not all prisoners experienced in claim-filing should be considered a JHL—although they were included in the operational defintion here. One prisoner, for example, has filed over 60 petitions between 1977 and 1986, but most of these were frivolous single-issue complaints regarding a personal health issue. This litigant was considered incompetent by other experienced prisoners, who felt that his frivolousness detracted from their own credibility. Of Stateville's 2,100 inmates, a generous maximum of 10, or less than one percent (0.47), currently fall within the definition. When litigants are asked to name currently active jailhouse lawyers, only four names occur consistently within the primary institution of study, and about 10 state-wide.

10. Since 1980, I have met only one prisoner who was an attorney in civilian life, and have heard of only one other who was an attorney prior to serving his sentence. Other JHLs have produced evidence of a law degree or legal training, but these invariably have been from mail-order diploma mills or correspondence schools. Some JHLs, however, claimed to have taken paralegal or related courses prior to incarceration.

11. In a recent tour of Joliet prison, for example, I found only two new law clerks, neither of whom were yet competent. Pontiac, with a population of about 1,800, employed three clerks, none well trained. Sheridan had no law clerk, and several inmates with legal problems were floundering in legal volumes that had no bearing on their issue and sought my assistance. Menard's population of 2,500 depended on two competent clerks. These numbers vary, however, depending on the institution's shuffling of prisoners between institutions. Dwight, the women's prison, had two clerks, one an attorney and the other well trained and proficient, but both have left the institution at the same time, making the future of adequate legal help more difficult. Stateville, by contrast, has a number of clerks and several freelancers who are reputed to be among the best in the country, and these JHLs have developed a variety of legal resources.

12. The JHLs in one Northern Illinois facility obtained about 20 sophisticated training tapes and a video cassette recorder from a sympathetic Chicago attorney. These gradually disappeared as other inmates, using the prison library for their own nonlegal ends, gradually erased these in order to tape cable movies. It was common to see a dozen or more men crowded in a small room during library hours watching these films.

13. Most civilian staff in Illinois' libraries attempt to test all applicants for basic knowledge of legal research prior to recommending or accepting a candidate as a clerk. Additional tests by prisoner-run classes provide additional gatekeeping hurdles. The process of hiring clerks and the testing required is contingent upon the knowledge and experience of the supervisor, the availability of experienced litigants and numerous other factors not easily controlled. Hence, rites of passage vary dramatically between institutions

and over time. The process described here currently exists in Stateville (Summer, 1987), and haphazardly in other institutions.

14. Prisoners who file habeas suits, as indicated in chapter 5, may do so several times. This is misleading, however, since perhaps as high as 50 percent are, in fact, related to the first suit, and are refiled because of technical errors in previous suits. This inflates the number of "multiple filers."

15. Of the law clerks assigned to Stateville's law library and other freelancers throughout early 1987, no less than half are estimated by their peers to fall into this category.

16. Some of those providing information felt uneasy about discussing or revealing rewards, since such exchanges are a rule violation with harsh consequences. I have argued that it is well known that JHLs often receive compensation, and rather than pretend it does not occur, why not explain how and why it occurs in order to give "the other side?" Many were convinced by this rationale, some were not. All, however, seemed swayed by the "intellectual integrity" argument that "science" cannot ignore facts simply because we do not like them.

17. The inmate economy, based on a mix of barter, service and currency, entails a complex system of negotiated, tacit, and shifting commodities (e.g., Kalinich, 1980). Postage stamps, for example, seemingly innocuous items, may, through several levels of exhanges, be translated into hard currency or illegal substances. This is possible because of their "fixed value," which is redeemable in many ways.

9

Doing the Law

To become a jailhouse lawyer, one must constantly engage in litigation. Viewed in this manner, active JHLs do not file simply to harass their keepers or to seek release. Instead, doing law is their vocation, and filing suits, although one small part of this vocation, is the most visible and rewarding. This *does not* mean, however, that JHLs engage in filing for its own sake. Doing law means *doing good law,* and one of the most important criterion used in judging their peers is that of avoiding frivolous filings.

THE GOOD, THE BAD, AND THE UGLY: JUDGING PEERS

Jailhouse lawyers adhere to strict unwritten professional standards by which they judge their own work and that of their colleagues. These standards define their level of commitment, separate outsiders from insiders and mere litigants from established JHLs, and provide role and case models. These standards are applied informally, but are nonetheless an effective form of peer pressure in the training of new litigants. The degree to which one consistently maintains professional standards creates a stratification system among JHLs, and this in turn enhances the opportunities for increased rewards, much as it does in the private economic sector. The most important standards are those defining good and bad JHLs and bad cases.

The Good Practitioner

JHLs find it easier to define a bad colleague than a good one, but four criteria consistently emerge when discussing most admired peers. First, a good jailhouse lawyer must "know and appreciate the law." It is not sufficient to simply file cases; one must be sufficiently and accurately informed to be a resource for others. Second, a good JHL must be able to win. Not only must cases reflect skilled artistry, but the cases themselves must possess sufficient merit to make "good law," by which is meant to set precedents that enable others to file similar suits and ultimately have a demonstrable impact. Third, the good JHL must be willing to help others by sharing information and by assisting those in need. Few, if any, JHLs remain aloof from their peers, and attempts to do so are criticized. Because of the need for collegial interaction to maintain a successful practice, those JHLs who are not willing to participate in information-sharing soon find themselves isolated, and their practice suffers. Finally, the good JHL must be attuned to the problems of the institution and be willing to litigate—often in the face of staff resistance or hostility—to change them. By these four criteria, most of those identified in Illinois prisons (by their peers, at least) are good jailhouse lawyers, with few rare exceptions.

The Bad Practitioner

Identifying a "bad" JHL generates more consensus than defining a good one, and three characteristics consistently emerge. First, bad JHLs presume a knowledge of the law they do not have; second, they put compensation ahead of law; and third, they have no hesitation in filing a legally frivolous case. Of these, frivolous case filing is most criticized, because one who files a frivolous case not only risks making "bad law," but also—by filing an unsupported case—"rips off" a client by accepting money when there is little hope for ultimate victory.

The bad JHL often falsely guarantees a victory, knowing that it cannot be attained, in order to solicit compensation: "They take you for a ride, then charge you for it!" Further, they often do incomplete research, and neither analyze the case nor obtain sufficient background to assure the suit will not be dismissed:

> A bad jailhouse lawyer is a guy who would charge you, say, "Ok, I'll take your case for five cartons of cigarettes," or somebody who gets mad, you know, something like just a harassment case. Something without a cause. Files at every opportunity. I won't do that, because it just puts bad law on the books. Then when somebody comes along with a good case, and I got this bad law, you won't get very far. That's why I always analyze my cases before I file them. Make sure they've exhausted their state remedies, their administrative remedies, all those things, before you file a civil rights suit under Section 1983.

Ugly Cases

Ugly cases, those that are not only frivolous, but reflect badly on the JHL profession, are universally condemned. An ugly case not only lacks merit but also risks making "bad law" by setting a precedent that will hamper future efforts to litigate that issue. JHLs contend that one major reason for the existence of frivolous suits is that too many novices fail to seek their assistance. Another reason stems from lack of experienced litigators to screen complaints. Another reason, and one highly criticized by most JHLs, arises from the avarice of less scrupulous litigants willing to charge clients knowing that a complaint has no legal merit. An exchange between three JHLs typifies the general views of a bad case:

M: [T]here's not really an agreed-on definition. It's something like, ah, something without evidence. Nothing to support it.

GM: Right. Without evidence. I mean, if you can prove anything that you say happened, then, to me, that is not frivolous. If you say the captain [beat you], and you have proof, like this guy witnessed it, and I have the affidavit from him to prove that he witnessed that that thing happened at such and such a time. That, to me, that wouldn't be frivolous.

AF: If you're able to provide your allegations.

JT: You're pretty much agreed on this?

Chorus! Right. Yeh.

M: If somebody was stabbed, ok, and if he had a medical record to show that he was stabbed, then you have to take it [the issue] to the security part, where they're supposed to provide security. I agree with the courts that they can't walk around with you every where you go.

AF: The court has put a heavy burden on people who've been stabbed to try to get relief. Prison security can't be absolute. Now, they've taken assault suits out of the district court. You can no longer file a [Section] 1983 on a stabbing incident, because you have a state court remedy [torts], but even in torts, you still have a heavy burden to overcome, because you have to show that, one, that the institution knew that the attack was going to take place.

M: That it was premeditated.

AF: [Two,] that it was premeditated, and, you know, that's a burden, because you can't prove that. If someone just walks up and knocks him in the head, for whatever reason, maybe you messed up your case, let's say, and you knocked him in the head. Now the courts, the burden they put on you, you have to prove that the warden on down knew that this was going to happen before hand. Of course, if the warden could read everybody's mind, there'd be no problem. "Oh yeh, so and so and so and so is goin' down to the library to knock Howie in the head. Stop him."

M: Now, if you was to have some type of premonition that something was to occur, and you informed the administration that you feared that your life was in danger because of certain incidents, that would [be different] because they knew that something could occur because of this. That's like the proof that they was aware. . . .

AF: I wouldn't say it was frivolous, but what I consider legitimate, the court would not. Like the court puts a heavy burden on you, sometimes.

GM: I think that if a guy was stabbed, and had some type of letter saying that he had previously told somebody that he was in physical danger, because something occurred, and he may have been the problem. I would say that wouldn't be a frivolous suit, no. That would be a meritorious suit.

JT: How do frivolous suits affect your jobs?

AF: It clogs the courts up, you know, the courts are crowded with a lot of cases that shouldn't be there, you know.

The view that all jailhouse lawyers are seeking the front door is belied by their view and practice of law. JHLs' professed intent to do "good law" is confirmed both by their cases and by grudging respect that at least some of them have earned from those who process their cases.[1] As a consequence, the view that these litigants are continuing their "socio-pathic activities" is not only wrong, but obscures the reality of the pride and effort put into the enterprise by those who take it seriously.

SCREENING CLIENTS AND CASES

Legal clients—whether on the streets on behind prison walls—are those who wish to settle a dispute by legal means. They furnish stories that provide the material for the legal cases. Not all stories contain equal merit, and not all clients have equal claim to the services of JHLs. As a consequence, screening clients and cases requires skill and diplomacy.

Clients

Prisoner clients, unlike most civilians seeking legal relief, tend to be undereducated, poor, and generally unable to assist themselves. In Stateville, with perhaps as high as two-thirds of the population function-ally illiterate, most clients do not have the resources that would enable them to solve even the most mundane legal problems.[2] As a conse-quence, screening clients, determining whether a valid legal issue exists, and above all, tactfully declining to take a case becomes one of the most difficult of all daily tasks.

The initial meeting with a client functions as a preliminary assessment of the merits of a case, including determination of facts and identifying appropriate legal issues. The initial screening weeds out frivolous cases, and the reputation of the JHL is critical in "cooling out" inmates who hope to cash in on a petty complaint:

> I have a reputation for being fair, so a guy would come to me and say, "Look, I'm being harassed, and I want to get these guys to treat me right." But some jailhouse lawyers would take this same guy and say, "Look, give me three packs of cigarettes, and I'll go and file it for you. . . . It might be a clerk. Everybody don't have the same integrity, you know? They would do it knowing full well he ain't got a chance. When I file a case, I always put my whole self into it.

Choosing Cases

Selecting cases may require negotiation if fees are sought or "cooling out the mark" if the case is not accepted. This requires considerable skill. For freelancers, informal discussion of case merits and perhaps possible compensation provides the necessary information for this decision. Competent freelancers rarely accept frivolous cases because of the many problems they can cause, and on occasion, they may reject a client when it becomes obvious that there will be no compensation. Clerks, however, screen cases more formally:

GM: Well, first, if you come here, you go through the filing clerk. You go to him, and he'll send you to the appropriate person who he thinks is capable of handling your case. From his knowledge of what you tell him, and various information you have.

AF: [T]he initial interview comes when you sit down and you talk to the person. You find out what he needs, and you find out if the claim is valid. Sometimes people come to you, "I want this, I want that." And it's not valid. So you have to filter the work that comes through the [law] clinic. It's an initial screening, and you have to determine what does or does not go back to the clinic.

JT: Does the assignment clerk have the final say?

AF: I don't take that responsibility upon myself. If I have doubts, if I know from the outset it's frivolous, I'll tell him. . . . If I have any doubts, I'll confer with one of the other clerks. I'll sit down and say, "Look at it this way or that way." If I see from the outset that it's frivolous, I'll tell the person. Just to satisfy, or should I say "pacify," that inmate, I'll say, "Look, it's frivolous, but if you doubt my word, go ask [him] over there." Like I said, guys get hostile toward you, they don't know that much. They don't like to be told no by anyone, especially another inmate. Everything they want, they want to get. Everything they wanted out on the streets they got, so when they come in here, they're not adjusted to the regimented routine we have to go through. And if I have to tell somebody no, I tell them no, but I'll confer with somebody else so they know I'm not just giving them a one-sided opinion. But [as] the assignment clerk, if it's a "hab" [habeas], I'll send to this person, if it's a [Section] 1983 to that person, to Hobo. If it's a court of claims, a divorce, a grievance, court correspondence, they send them to me, whatever. I get a lot of court of claims cases. Then we continue; [the next interview] is a continuation of the intitial interview. I sit down with them, say, "What's the problem?" I'm the one, now, who has your case and has to work it up. So this interview is just a continuation of the initial interview.

JT: What would I, as the plaintiff, do?

AF: OK. Give you an example. I just finished a court of claims case. First thing I would do is get the facts immediately. Then say, "Jim, I need your medical records." But with my free movement, I would just take it up front. Why send it through the mail when I can take it to the doctor? Once you get your medical records, by the time we get the medical records, I will be drafting up the complaint itself.

JT: So my role [as plaintiff] is primarily to give you information.

Chorus: Right.

A meritorius complaint provides the most compelling reason to take a client's case. Other factors, however, may enter into the decision, including monetary gain, "testing the waters," or using the cases of others to develop stronger legal strategies in pursuing one's own suits:

> Guys that had similar beefs as mine, all right? Guilty pleas,'cause I know some day I'm going to take my guilty plea, and anybody that had a guilty plea that I thought was in anyway bad, I'd attack for them. 'Cause any little issue I could see, where maybe they got some relief coming, I'd file. Let's see how the government responds, 'cause that's how they're gonna respond to mine three years away. It was like a test case, a lot of them. And a lot of guys I just felt sorry for.

Sorting out bad cases requires sufficient knowledge to determine whether a potential litigant not only has a case, but whether the alleged complaint is real, and whether the motive is merely a personal vendetta:

> Well, you can tell when a guy is just doing it to buck the system or doing it because he's got something legit and wants to get out, or wants to right a wrong. A guy comes in and says, "Listen, the doctor made me wait two days before he gave me a script for valium because I couldn't sleep at night, so I lost two nights sleep." So, like, forget about it. I tell him, "Yeh, take two aspirins, a glass of water, and walk slow." Forget about it. And if you want to make up a phony case, you could. It's fairly easy just to make up a big facade and run it into the courts. There's guys that do that. It ain't that rampant. A few guys do that, and you weed them out, and you just tell them, "Hey, forget about it. You're talking to the wrong guy."

Selecting which clients to represent and which cases to file serves several gatekeeping functions. First, it reduces the number of frivolous claims submitted to the courts. Experienced JHLs not only discourage, but actively restrict filings that they feel lack both substantive and legal merit. There is little to be gained and much to be lost by investing time and energy into a "no win" case that offers neither legal nor administrative relief, especially when there are many more deserving cases waiting. Second, the screening process provides a type of socialization for other inmates to the extent that it generates information about the correct and incorrect uses of law, suggests strategies of problem solving, and furnishes nonviolent alternatives to dispute resolution. JHLs conservatively estimate that no less than 25 to 33 percent of all maximum security prisoners seek legal assistance at least once during their incarceration, which places JHLs in a powerful position for socializing others and mediating problems.[3] Finally, the screening process provides troubled inmates with a forum to air a grievance, even when they do not ultimately litigate. The contention voiced repeatedly by JHLs that "just having somebody to talk to helps" seems to "cool out" some prisoners, thus reducing their own frustration and the probability that they will verbally or physically lash out at other guards or staff. As a consequence, the screening process should be recognized as a multi-layered activity with multiple functions, each of which helps alleviate excessive litigation as well as some of the degradation of prison life.

THE PLIGHT OF THE JAILHOUSE LAWYER

When jailhouse lawyers discuss the problems they must confront daily, those most numerous and difficult do not arise from law. Whatever the problems related to legal research, case building, interpreting complex case law, or constructing a specific legal strategy, these reflect relatively predictable and manageable snags that JHLs feel confident in ultimately resolving, either through self-learning or collegial interaction. The most difficult—and potentially dangerous—quandaries derive instead from administrative response, problems with other prisoners, and personal frustrations.

Administrative Obstacles

Jailhouse lawyers may make life difficult for their keepers, but the reverse occurs more often because of the asymmetrical power relationship in which staff have the advantage. Even when a given prison may meet mandated standards defining appropriate resources, access to them may be subverted by prison policies or staff discretion.[4] Staff obstruction tactics may include curtailing prisoners' access to legal assistance, confiscation of legal resources or hassling litigants.

Curtailing Access

One common way of curtailing access occurs through policies that limit the tasks of JHLs. Some institutions, for example, have attempted to enforce a rule preventing JHLs from assisting other prisoners in filing grievances against the institution.[5] In some institutions, particularly the newer ones in which policies have not yet been fully formulated or implemented, staff creatively interpret departmental and legal prescriptions in ways to discourage JHLs from assisting others. Creative rule interpretation includes restricting access to the library, curtailing library services and access, deprivation of formal rewards, and hassling JHLs in subtle ways not proscribed by rules. Whether by design or organizational inertia, the administration may also fail to repair office equipment, replace necessary resources, procrastinate in ordering and disseminating books, or delay in replacing personnel.

Curtailing Legal Training

Elimination of legal training on grounds of "fiscal need" and failure to promptly replace vacant clerical positions also creates problems. In a downstate maximum security institution, the law clerks have complained that not only have vacant clerical positions remained vacant, but supervisory staff load existing clerks with "make-work" nonlegal tasks that interrupt their legal work, and thus reduce their effectiveness. Even if clerks are replaced, replacements may be staff "favorites" or incompetent, and this creates additional obstacles. When there is no legal training for new clerks, older clerks must spend more time as mentors and inmate's legal problems pile up for lack of immediate attention. This contributes to the filing of suits that are not well written, that ignore court filing procedures, or fail to state legal issues. Because there is less opportunity to screen clients' cases, frivolous complaints may be filed by inexperienced clerks, which adds to the burden both of JHLs and the courts. Hence, the deleterious consequences of institutional policies may ripple beyond the walls, ultimately adding to the legal, fiscal, and processing problems rather than eliminating them.

Library Access

To become a JHL, one obviously must be able to use the law library, but for novices, access may be difficult. One is dependent upon staff for permission—given in the form of passes—that may not be easily obtained. Especially in the initial phases of litigation, staff may perceive a potential litigant to be a "troublemaker," or not take litigating seriously, for there are inmates who are known to abuse the library for questionable purposes.[6] One clerk explained his problem in obtaining a library pass for those not assigned to the library:

> If you want a pass, if you want to come to the library, if it's not your regularly scheduled day, you're shot to hell, because you're not going to get there. Because now you got to go to a counsellor, OK? But the counsellors are too busy running around playing warden. Then you go to the authority, but he's too busy, saying he's running the cellhouse.

In one midstate institution, a catch–22 situation effectively blocked many inmates from library access. In order to obtain a pass, they were first required to demonstrate they had an active suit, but in order to demonstrate a suit, they needed access to the library to obtain the appropriate forms and identify the proper resources to begin the suit. Such ad hoc policies are one of many ways that access to law can be curtailed by subverting the spirit, if not the letter, of court decisions proscribing such obstacles.

Increasing Litigation Costs

The administration may use its discretion to increase costs of litigating, which places a burden especially on those clients with few resources.[7] The burden of the increase falls particularly on JHLs or other litigants with lengthy transcripts or massive court documents that require reproduction for study or for filing. Mail costs for legal material are also subject to institutional discretion:

> They are charging us for mail going out. What they did was change the ARs [Administrative Regulations], they wanted to beat us down. The language is that [of variable policies] and it infringes upon a lot of people's rights [because they can't afford mail].

Obstructing Productivity

Lack of time, adequate facilities, research materials, free-flowing communication lines to the outside, or knowledgeable colleagues all stifle legal work. Shakedowns or spot searches of one's body or cell can effectively obstruct access to legal resources or disrupt productivity. Prisoners recognize the necessity of shakedowns as crucial to the maintenance of security, but there is unanimous feeling that staff may use discretion to prevent clerks from taking legal materials, such as books or case files, back to their cells, and require them to do all of their work during library hours. This severely reduces productivity, because much of the work (e.g., reading) can best be done in cell areas. "Taking work home," however, can create special problems. Cellhouses are noisy and such distractions as contraband hucksters, inmate counts, constant interruptions, and poor facilities (e.g., inadequate lighting, lack of work space) create distractions:

> [W]alkie-talkies of the officers [are] blasting all night, lights in the cellhouse, somebody may paint at night, they may not go off shift until five o'clock, if you have curtains you get a ticket, the light shines on ya [and many other distractions].

Hassling

The discretion of prison staff and the relative invisibility of its exercise contributes to the possibility of hassling, or intentionally creating problems for targeted inmates. JHLs all feel that they are subjected to systematic and unnecessary harassment, although not all are targeted equally. Among the most common hassles include shakedowns, removal from a library assignment, transfers, and the threat of violence.

The Threat of Discipline

There are JHLs who are either so proficient or aggressive in litigating against staff that they may be singled out for minor, but consistent, harassment. One JHL, recognized as the best and most aggressive currently in his prison, complained that he was a constant target, and a coworker described how degradation by staff created a problem for him:

> I'm talking about demeaning one verbally, in an intellectual fashion, that a policeman [staff lieutenant] would approach them in the wrong manner, saying, "Up against the wall, let me search you down." That's a humbug, no

reason, just, "We're going to harass you Sancho, because you've been filing too many law suits." [Sancho] would belittle the officer, and based on him belittling the officer, the officer would respond to that, and they would have a confrontation. And we would all the time have to go over to seg [segregation] to have to pick Sancho up and bring him out of seg. He spent a lot of time in seg because he was one of the most aggressive jailhouse lawyers we've had. Munich. Munich was another one. They transferred him from one institution to another.

Yet another way of hassling occurs when staff use their considerable discretion to attempt to curtail a given prisoner's movement, thus restricting access to the law library:

> The officer tells me, "Jake, you can't come in here," or guys can't come back after they go up for chow in the evening, thereby curtailing a guys time to do research. They write you a [false disciplinary] ticket.

Sometimes hassling can be subtle and discrete, but at other times it may be open and direct, as happened to one inmate when others overheard a supervisor ordering harassment that ultimately provided evidence for a suit:

> I've had the unit manager come up to the guard and say, "Listen. The guy that does the upper showers over there, fuck with him every chance you got." Two inmates sitting 10 feet away heard it. I filed a nice suit over that, and I fucked with this guy seriously after that.

The Shakedown

They are too often conducted beyond legitimate needs, especially when some persons are targeted more than others. Continually searching personal belongings in the cellhouse not only disrupts work, but scatters and disorganizes papers, thus requiring time and energy to reorganize the material. Searching JHLs to and from work assignment also cuts into limited time and creates psychological disruption that may stifle concentration. This is one reason for the necessity of a "strong head" and "patience" for those who hope to survive as JHLs. Some staff may overstep the bounds of their discretion by intentionally confiscating legal materials, which is not only illegal, but creates problems for which there may be no resolution. Even if one complains or litigates, the elapsed time between confiscation and return disrupts work and adds yet another case burden to the workload:

> I got a new [case] going in, but they went in and shook down my cell, and stole all my law books, and all my legal material, so I'll be initiating a new action. What happened is that the shakedown is supposed to be under the supervision of a lieutenant. They forged the lieutenant's name on the shakedown slip, and without the supervision of a lieutenant, you never know what's going to come up missing. Plus, they should have called me

out of my job to challenge anything improper that might have been found in my cell. By them not covering all the procedural bases, they made themselves liable for the shakedown. They just had an ordinary shakedown on me about three or four days ago, but see, they messed with the wrong guy.

Loss of Job

One hassle occurs when inmates are removed from their library assignment, especially when it occurs while an active suit is in progress. When a suit is filed and survives the IFP screening, substantial subsequent research is required in order to respond to defendants' motions or to file one's own motions, and such removal can be disasterous. Removal often tends to occur when staff perceive an inmate to be excessively ligitious or to willing to help others:

I was fired because I was working with people in segregation, bringing a copy of my [cases] about the faults in the procedures of the assignment committee. I've been here eight years, and I've been working in the library. How could you hassle me? You could remove me, "Don't give him any state pay." I don't get state pay. Inmates that are unassigned are supposed to get $10 a month, all right? They put the word out to every assignment, "Don't hire [me]." I was supposed to have got hired in the carpentry department. . . . I didn't. Hired in the print shop? I had to go consult with the warden first. And there's nowhere in the institution that I can get a job at. And I don't get state pay. That's one way [they hassled me]. And another way . . . they took away my typewriter [in a shakedown]. . . . I had an electric typewriter coming from another institution, and they would not let me have it in [this prison]. If you got one, and you were authorized to purchase it, and you come here, they say you can't have it.

The threat of removal does not seem to deter litigants from filing, but it does disrupt their work by adding to the personal costs of litigation and by delaying, thus jeopardizing, ongoing litigation.

Transfers

Transferring inmates from one institution to another places great burdens on JHLs in several ways. First, it increases the workloads of other JHLs by decreasing their labor force. Second, it requires filling a slot through the time consuming process of search, selection, and training. Finally, it weakens the rapport and sense of community that stimulates and improves legal proficiency.

The guy who used to teach [law], OJ, he's been in the library for six or seven years, and they sent him to the farm. I believe it's a master plan to try to break up the library. I mean, I have no proof of that, but it seems that, sure enough, they've been shipping guys out of here who meet the criteria for transfer to a different institution, but they've taken all the skilled workers. Most of the guys who they have transfered within the past year have been working in the library for five or six years, and they've taken all the experienced people.

One problem related to transfers that creates disruption for both legal activity and coping with prisons is an administrative ploy called *the circuit.* This maneuver, ostensibly a transfer, consists of a serious of "stops" along the way, which may last a few days or longer. Bits of time, personal property, energy, motivation, and will may be left behind at each stop:

> Billy, he was worse [a more active litigator] than I ever could be. At Cambridge, they finally transferred him and sent him to Tennessee. They really fucked him over. They sent him on a bus ride. That's another way to get back at jailhouse lawyers. They transfer you, but you never get to the other spot for about a year, sometimes. You go to like about 15 different places, and in the meantime, you're in transit, three weeks in the hole here, three weeks in the hole here, you never get your mail.

The Threat of Violence

Inmates often perceive a potential threat of violence exacerbated by verbal threats by staff and the occasional "mysterious death" of a prisoner.[8] Inmate lore contains the story of an inmate who died under mysterious circumstances in a Southern Illinois prison, and the guards joked about the death to litigants, telling them, "The same will happen to you if you're not careful." Whatever the actual cause of death, the message was ominously clear, and discouraged at least some litigants from pursuing the career in this institution. Others were no so easily discouraged, but nonetheless remained cautious:

> Now, at the same time, I didn't sue anybody [in my new institution] for a while. There was a lot of shit going on down there. A lot of bad things, you know, and one of them was when this black guy got killed two weeks before. Come to find out, the guy was a jailhouse lawyer over there, and he was filing for everything he seen. He had a beef with the joint, and they did something to him, and he was mad, and any little thing he seen that was wrong, he was filing against them. . . . So they took this guy, and put him in the hole for some diddly-ass reason. The guy got stabbed to death in the hole, in the shower. First of all, two people in the hole ain't supposed to be out at the same time. Now, I find out, I don't know what happened, I just knew that it happened. Years later, two years later, another guy comes rolling in from [a maximum security federal institution]. I find out the guy that stabbed this black guy was a guy named Johnny. A crazy hillbilly guy that killed like seven people in the joint already, all right? He was from [a federal institution], and he was always on lockdown [there] most of the time, and he killed several people in [it]. Well, this guy knew Johnson real good. He told me, "Yeh, I talked to Johnson." He says, "Johnson told me he does favors like that for the prison guards at times." They'd give him his little play, whatever he wanted to do, maybe they'd bring a broad in, who knows what they'd do. Maybe they give him certain leeway, or whatever. So

now I find out the lieutenant that was on duty, Lt. Beers was on duty that night. And it just all pieced together for me what happened. This guy Johnson had no reason to be in [my prison]. He was in [another institution], locked up, which he should never be out of, and they take him, they transfer him to [my prison], they put him in the hole, and just coincidentally, he and this other guy are let out at night when one guy's taking a shower, and he stabs him. And then they take him and put him back in [there] again. Now, *you* tell *me* what happened?

Whether staff actually inflict physical violence as often as rumored is irrelevant. The threat functions as a symbolic strategy of coercion that reminds prisoners of their vulnerability should staff choose to retaliate. Hence, the possibility of violent retaliation becomes quite effective in constraining the behaviors of those inmates who prefer discretion to valor.

Problems with Prisoners

Prisoners are in prison because they have committed a crime and antisocial behavior does not always cease after incarceration. As a consequence, there are some prisoners, a troublesome minority, who for reasons of avarice, predation, resentment, or ill-will, are "a pain in the ass." Problems with inmates arise from several sources. First, there are "problem inmates" who may refuse to accept that they have no legitimate legal complaint, who feel they have lost because of incompetence, or perceive that they are not receiving sufficient assistance. A second source of problems arises when those who are not serious about law lay claim to a library position or resources in ways that subvert the ability of JHLs to operate. In institutions with strong street gang membership, for example, the benefits of having access to the law library for intents unrelated to law may add incompetent clerks to the JHL staff or create competition for space and resources. Problems with other prisoners, both clients and nonclients, create touchy situations that often cannot be resolved without considerable finesse. Frustrated clients, resentful outsiders, or "prison organizations" attempting to wrest control of resources for themselves typify such dilemmas.

Problem Clients

Clients can cause problems when they want their cases done first, or attempt to circumvent procedures for preferential treatment. They may do this through intimidation, or more commonly, by appealing to avarice:

FE: They use, how shall I say it? Financial intimidation, you should it call it encouragement, really, is the word. They offer to pay you to hurry the case. Physical violence is usually not feasible, when it comes to that. They bite the hand that feeds them. Encouragement is more common.

JT: Does ["encouragement"] work?

M: Yeh, sometimes.

EF: Since we live in a capitalist society [laughs].

GM: Sometimes guys might think that because [the case] is not going quick enough, they might confront [the clerk] with it. If he feels that he's not getting [service], then he might just change clerks, you know, get a better attituded clerk, one who will work better.

M: See, one thing you got to realize, is that when they get sent down here, half of them feel they've been crossed up. So when you tell them that you're in the law, or know anything about the law, sometimes when the case comes back, and its been affirmed and they know that it should be [reversed], they say that you helped get it affirmed, and a lot of them have that animosity toward you.

JT: Would they take it out on you personally?

M: Yes. Yes they would.

JT: What would they do?

GM: A clerk might be bashed in the head because he lost.

AF: Like M. said, they gotta blame somebody [Chorus: right]. They blame the judge, they blame the police who arrested them, they blame the judge who sentenced them, they blame the jury for convicting them, and then they come down here and they blame you. You know, we don't intimidate.

Street Gangs

"Prisoner organizations," street gangs, are prevalent in Illinois prisons, and although they are involved in a variety of enterprises, licit commitments are not a top priority.[9] Poor clerks or clerks who place gang commitments above those of law makes life more difficult for other JHLs:

Of course [it's more difficult]!! Of course. Of course. That puts an additional constraint on us. [The civilian supervisor] changes the policies of the library, because he exercises more control. Before the policy was changed, the residents who worked in the library, especially the ones working on people's cases, they could go to the xerox machine and copy anything and everything they had to copy. Soupy got a gang chief, put him over the xerox machine, and said, "They only get 200 copies a year. I don't care who it is, each idividual only gets 200 copies a year, and I want you to stand on this law." And [the chief] stood on the law. He's a prisoner, now. But because he's getting $80 a month, and because he's got a title, and he gets the prestige now, and he can use the little room, and he can eat his sandwhiches back there, and he can call his little friends back in the room and have their private conference, because he's got this mechanism to deal with, he becomes oppressive to the rest of the population over that xerox machine. Soupy put him in the position, and he knew what he was doing when he put him there.

The advantages for gangs of placing members in the law library vary from mobility to increased prestige:

> Some of these guys here have the run of the institution, they can go anyplace and every place they want to go. Some of these guys are chiefs, you've got some of these guys who are chiefs of the different organizations. So people can come down and sit and talk with them, this is prestige. It heightens their strength in their organizations, because this is a prestigious job. "I work in the law library." It's the best job you can have in the institution, other than working for the warden. Lawyers can go sit and talk with the warden when they want to, they call him on the phone. "I'm coming up and talk to you." Because one, they're gang chiefs, and two, they're jailhouse lawyers, or allegedly they're jailhouse lawyers. So they can go talk to him with a problem. Now if the warden says, "Ok, so and so, I'm going to let you go to the farm. Stop that litigating. You've got some people working out there?" "Yeh, I've got a lieutenant that works down there, I've got a captain that works down there." "Well, you tell them to stop them cases, and they'll go to the farm." People who've got a 100 years. What are you going to tell them? "No, warden, I'm going to stay behind the walls, I'm not going to go for that deal." Are you going to tell him that? No!!! [In the past] we've kept gang chiefs out of here. See, to us, gang chiefs are ignorant. To us. To the average jailhouse lawyer, a gang chief is ignorant. Because he's a midget in a giant's position.

JHLs must tread a thin line when dealing with other prisoners. Despite the respect the profession receives in general, some JHLS and clients may, without careful management, conflict over resources or case processing. In a potentially volatile environment, such conflicts may erupt with unpleasant consequences. As a consequence, skirting the boundaries between "professional integrity" and "cooling out bozos" requires considerable skill and finesse.

Frustration

Despite the variety of rewards available to JHLs, there are corresponding frustrations. Those who do not possess "strong heads" ultimately leave the profession. Those who remain must confront the frustration of apparent "betrayal" by clients, ego deflating losses, and the possibility of "burn-out."

Betrayal

Frustrations occur when JHLs perceive their case has been lost because of the subsequent handling by paid attorneys, or because an inmate "copped out" and settled a strong case out of court that he believed could have been won at trial:

> He accepted $500 for his settlement, and now he comes to me and wants me to file a complaint because they only gave him $50 at a time. I told him to get the hell out of my face. I said, "You've got to be an idiot. Here

another sucker stabbed you in the head, and I get you into court, and you get a case that's winnable, and you go up there and let them intimidate you out of the damn trial, I'm gonna have nothing to do with that." And that's what makes most jailhouse lawyers really angry. All the work. I mean, your guts is in this thing, man, I mean, Jim, this is a lot of work. It's a lot of work. And it's painful work. I done cried working on some people's cases. I cried, because it hurts me to see how attorneys, because of this guys ignorance, just fuck over him.

Burnout

For JHLs who commit themselves totally to law, the risk of burnout occurs. Burnout may occur when either their caseload or the problems to be managed become sufficiently great that continued concentration or involvement becomes impossible. One JHL, for example, left the career because he could no longer invest the time required, and problems with clients and others resulted in a severe psychological drain. Most have strategies for avoiding the depression and exhaustion that accompanies overwork. For some, it may require isolation:

> I go to segregation when I get a heavy case load. I go to PC [protective custody]. Voluntarily. You can't afford to get burned out. But when you got a lot of pressure, then you remove yourself from everybody and take care of that pressure. That's why I stay over in segregation, to be able to work. I was over there for a couple of months. They let me go the first four days I was over there, but I stayed on over there because I had so much work.

How do JHLs prevent burnout? "Stress control" provides the primary means. Most avoid leisure activity such as television, which is seen unanimously as the greatest obstacle to inmate self-development. Others read voraciously, and others may take up recreational hobbies, such as chess. All, without exception, have developed some means by which to structure their existence in ways that help maintain a "strong head":

> The thing to do is pace yourself. You just can't take case upon case upon case without rest. I work out, I exercise with weights, everynight by 10:30 I was in bed, I get me sleep, I don't get high, I don't smoke no dope, I take care of myself.

All JHLs relate personal experiences in which they were tempted to withdraw from the profession because of the numerous strains, both from case-load pressures and from managing problems caused by their involvement in law. One successful JHL withdrew because of a perceived threat that his continued litigation would jeopardize his parole hearing, and another left the profession because of the time constraints his case load placed on him. Others may leave because they are not sufficiently competent to handle cases, and "burn out" in their attempts to improve, and still others exit because other assignments are, for them, more lucrative. Those who remain devise intriguing and creative ways to "stay afloat," and without such escapes, there is universal agreement that they could not long survive.[10]

"Time: My Enemy!"

One frustration repeatedly cited by JHLs is the length of time required to process a case, which can take up to five years or more. The time required to see a case from start to finish discourages many litigants and creates a problem especially when the JHL originally assisting with the case exits. Further, many cases are dismissed or returned on technicalities, not on case merits, which frustrates the inexperienced litigant and may have a "chilling effect" on further filings. Despite the view that "prisoners have nothing but time," they—as would most of us—tend to become impatient at the interminable delays that hamper a suits' resolution:

> [S]ome of our cases stay up there five or six years. They can't say we're right or we're wrong, so they just hold the suits, and that's what they do. They wear you down. They make you disgusted, until you be up in the court six years litigating, like in one of my cases, we haven't got the preliminary stage, and it's been there five years. Cooper [(*Cooper v. Pate,* 382 F.2d 518, 7th Cir., 1967)] was there eight. A long time. And they carried him through a merry-go-round. They'll carry us up, and they'll carry us down, and they'll carry us up and around, over and under, but we still would be at square one.

The Problem of Exiting

Most JHLs eventually exit the profession, either through release or "retirement." The exit can create problems when a previous reputation has earned the animosity of staff, and even after leaving an institution, other problems may arise in unanticipated ways. One JHL anticipated problems he might face upon release, and chose to drop a suit:

> Six months before I get out, they ["crime bosses"] give me a tap on the shoulder and say, "Ricky, you're suing our friend. He's with us. You've got to drop all them suits. This guy's with us. What if he gets convicted? What if all this shit that you're bringing out, these guys get convicted, and they beef on us. Then we gotta do more time." I said, "Fuck that!! I'm dropping nothing!!" I mean, sometimes I got balls this big [gestures]. A good friend of mine got killed by them back in [an Illinois city] in '77. But he was bucking them strong, and anyway, so there was misinformation too. The guy that gave them misinformation is dead now, too. They were considering doing me, too, because I knew him. That's the way they do it. They just do everybody who knows the guy. So, what happens, finally I'm thinking, I was going to go to [a city in] Wisconsin. I was going to go to the half-way house and everything, until they fucked me out of all that. I wasn't going to come back here to live in my own house that I lived in for 30 years. I ain't dropping nothing anyway, and they were pissed. Finally, I talked to a

few people, my brother, and they said, "Ah, drop all that stuff." Finally I figure why come out of jail after seven years, I gotta live in the same house, I got all the coppers mad at me, they're going to try to set me up, put a gun in my car, or dope, or something, or send me back to the joint, or kill me.

Another problem may occur even after one has left the institution when officials may attempt to set an example to other jailhouse lawyers by holding them accountable for their previous activities. One JHL faced fraud charges after release for filing as a pauper after federal officials noticed he was paying large sums for xeroxing fees while incarcerated. Case-related documents suggest a catch–22 situation for which he was to be held accountable for Freedom of Information (FOI) litigation[11]:

> The FBI comes back, and now they got to give [the documents] to me: "Well, it turns out to be 5,000 pages, send us $500." I'm *in forma pauperis* in the courts still. I tell [my client], "Listen. Send them $500." He sends them $500. "Tell Loli I need $300 here," and he has somebody send me $300 and put it on my books. So I send it to them. But it really ain't my money. And the main concern of mine is for me, I want to see their documents. That's the main thing, because I want to put this class action suit together. Now the government's coming back and saying, "Wait a minute. You're *in forma pauperis* in the courts, and all of a sudden you pop up with $500 here, $300 here, and it added up to a couple of thousand. You're defrauding us. You're not really broke. You have avenues of money out there somewhere. And it comes up when you need it for this stuff. So you're pulling a real neat one against us."

The structural and interactional problems of jailhouse lawyers' legal settings shape the background in which they conduct their work, pattern the substantive and procedural boundaries of their activities, and create the frame by which they engage their career and define their tasks and goals. Many of these problems, especially when they curtail access to law or elicit disciplinary sanctions or other staff responses perceived to be unjust, may generate further litigation to rectify the abuses. The meanings of prisoner litigation, then, extend beyond the legal cases or decisions, because the litigation experience is inseparable from the prison culture. The legal rituals and language of law impose procedural requirements on JHLs that are often incompatible with the prison context, and this tension itself symbolizes the ironic nature of prisoner litigation:

> The older group of jailhouse lawyers we had here, we tried to make this thing conducive to our needs. The lawbook is our weapon, and we use it like a weapon. We use it!! We pit the court against itself, the state court against the federal courts, some laws against other laws. We pit them.

IMPACT LITIGATION

Despite much pessimism, all JHLs indicate that one primary goal is to change prison conditions. JHLs call this *impact litigation:*

> We was talking about *impact litigation.* We was holding forums down here on Friday evenings, and we were showing [video] tapes. We were talking about the death penalty and how to fight law suits and different things. When you start practicing law on that level, you're practicing law like lawyers do on the streets, and we was showing tapes, and we were having discussions in certain areas of law, and we could challenge—we was talking about filing impact litigation. Like here, the law says you're supposed to have programs that will allow one to improve himself. You can't rehabilitate nobody. But you have to put programs here so he can improve himself. We don't have that here. We have shells. We have things on paper that they get funded for every year, but they're not "in operation," and they're not what they appear to be. So we was talking about filing a classaction law suit. This is impact litigation.

JHLs possess no delusions of great changes generated by their litigation activity, but all voice, with considerable consistency, one litigant's view of his efforts:

> Well, I'd say it breaks down those barriers that officials erect. [*JT:* Such as?]. Well, prisoners communicating. It's difficult for prisoners in this environment to communicate. If we could communicate with the populace, which we can't, for instance, I can't rightfully communicate with the media and have them come in here and talk with whoever they want to talk to. We can't do that. Impact litigation breaks down those barriers. At one time we didn't even have the right to go to federal courts. It was the case of a prisoner filing a lawsuit, and that lawsuit overturning the "hands-off" doctrine. We're going into court now. Same thing with medical needs. At one time we had no say in medical treatment. The hospital was run strictly and adminstratively, and we had no say-so. Now we have some say-so on when we can see doctors, what kinds of medications we can refuse to take, what kinds of operations we can refuse to have, we can demand to go to an outside hospital. At one time we couldn't demand none of that. We had no rights in that area, so those things have broken down. That's all based on impact litigation. But the main type of impact litigation was the overcrowding conditions. It was filed in regard to that, and the population in all the institutions in the state of Illinois was reduced because of it. Before that they was stacked on top of each other. They was in the single cells, there was three people in those cells. Over there in B house, where I'm at now, sometimes there would be four or five of us in cell, There would be four or five in the same cell. There would be four or five of us, and people would be sleeping—I used to sleep under the bed on the floor. I used to sleep on a mattress slipped underneath the bunk bed, and sleep underneath there. And the dust and stuff, they'd be sweeping the gallery [laughs] and then there'd be people sleeping outside of the beds, on the floor out there. And

we was packed like sardines. And the only reason they broke that down was because of impact litigation.

Another active litigant explained how even a single suit, if successful, can modify prison life:

[W]hat impact can a suit have? The impact [my] suit has had, *Woods v. Aldworth* [84–C–7745], is they were taking my legal mail. They wasn't following the procedures. One man is supposed to bring the legal mail around here, but they wasn't doing that. What they was doing was just bringing the mail in with the nonlegal mail, and leaving it in the sergeants office, and inmates was allowed in there, and they'd get ahold of legal mail, any officer could pick up your legal mail, so the impact this suit was, had I settled this, they gave me two grand and shipped me out of here. But the impact this had, is one man now, his name is Mr. Brown. He go around and bring everybody their legal mail, and nobody had any complaints about getting their legal mail since then.

The pride reflected in their task, the persistence despite pessimism and the standards by which peers and cases are held belie the conventional view that jailhouse lawyers are merely "troublemakers hassling their jailors." Their ability to negotiate or overcome obstacles in usually licit, and peaceful ways suggests a level of responsibility and initiative that conventional lawyers would envy, indicating that the JHL provides a service both to corrections and to society. Some JHLs argue with vehemence that perhaps their greatest service is to bring peaceful reform to prisons, albeit incrementally and haphazardly, a service that other prisoners may find Quixotic.

THE SWORD OR THE SUIT?

There are many prisoners, perhaps a majority, who believe that the best way to resolve a problem in the prison is to hit it. The sword is perceived as mightier than the pen, especially since the consequences are more cathartic, direct, dramatic, and visible. Litigation requires patience, literacy, and insight, and there is a strong feeling that law becomes a way to change not only prison conditions, but personal violence as well. For some litigants, these attributes contribute to a change in behavior:

What I think [law] does, it gives the guy who's initiating a lawsuit a protective means by which to [stop] the violence. I know some guys here who want to solve the violence, they adopt that line of attack by adopting the physical plan that they would normally use. I think a lot of the guys, though, understand the power of the pen. I'm talking about some of those guys in the institution that find that using the pen [and going to court] and use the court. But I know some guys who've got frustrated with the court, with the tedious process, and resorted to their old traits and come back on the guards with physical aggression. It's a no win situation [for them].

But not all prisoners agree in peaceful solutions to problems, and the view that "moving guards out" of a cellblock or the prison through violence or intimidation works best for resolving prison problems. An exchange between several JHLs and other prisoners degenerated into an acrimonious debate when asked, "Which works better? Lawsuits or moving guards out?"

XB: If you had an officer that was sitting in front of you that was preventing you from doing something beneficial, you could take it to your organization [street gang] and say, "Hey, look, man. Dig it, we're not going to go through all the rhetoric and red tape, we're just going to move it." You know what I'm saying? And we send him up out of here on a stretcher, and we don't have to worry about it no more. But next time we'll run the murder game down to let him know you'll have the same thing coming if we have a problem out of you. We don't do that no more.

JT: What do gangs do now?

HO: Politics]

JT: Which works better?

XB: Moving them out!!

HO: To me, law. The legal way, you get compensated, you get paid, you establish a rule that effects everybody, and everybody [not just a few people or an organization] gets the benefits. If you do it [with violence], they ain't gonna do nothing but use it against you, use it to brand you, and use it to push harder. If you do it [with violence], they say, "Hey, we've had 50 guards stabbed in the last year, so we're going to take away this privilege, that privilege, and that privilege, because this is a very aggressive environment." So they use it against you, so I'm saying it's wrong to use that way. So in Rome, do what the Romans do, so use their own means against them.

XB: But that's what they want to do, they want to get you wrapped up in that red tape, you know?

HO: It ain't no red tape.

XB: The simplist way to get through an obstacle is to remove it!!

HO: But what is the sake of it? That's what's called, uh, going back against civilization.

XB: At one time, when they was sending them studs out on a stretcher, and they was hiring new ones, and when the new ones found out what happened to the people they was replacing, they wasn't as like to fuck with you as the ones that left up out of here [on a stretcher]!

HO: What about the prisoners that get caught that gets segregation, that gets the psychological affects of being isolated in their cell? You're forgetting about that there. The sacrifice isn't necessary.

XB: It depends, you know? It depends on what you're saying. It depends who you're saying. If you got a stud that's got 60 years, a hundred years, that's laying in seg for a year for carrying out his organization's sentence, and they're taking care of him, he ain't going to care.

JT: Would he be assigned, or would he volunteer?

XB: Some of them do [it] as an organized "hit," waiting by the door with a pipe in his hand to do the hit, but this isn't done anymore. This joint is the most wide open of any institution in this state!!! For the simple reason that them studs [gangs] at one time sent them [guards] up on out of here on a stretcher to let them know that if you're down here doing time, we ain't going to tolerate anything that obstructs us. But if [guards] knew that what they did to that stud was going to be met with retaliation on both sides of the wall, they wouldn't have did it. They wouldn't have did it!! If one of their kids run into five niggers that reminded them of what they did to [prisoner recently beaten], they wouldn't do it. The assault would never have happened.

HO: This is what this institution wants. They want [our prison] to be a maximum security institution. That kind of behavior would let them do it. Every house would be dismantled like A and B house, they'll stop flow [of movement], and they won't let you go nowhere [transfer, internal movement] because of aggressive behavior and personalities in here, and everybody will stay completely locked up all the time, and the guards will bring your food to the cells. That kind of behavior, violence, doesn't work. I'll give you one good example. What if you jump a guy you think did something, and you find that he didn't, he didn't have nothing to do with it. How can you talk about brotherly love?

The relationship between litigation and reduced violence is complex and requires further examination. It would seem, however, that one indirect result of litigation is providing alternative nonviolent strategies for conflict resolution and furnishing—by example of the jailhouse lawyer—models of behavior that are quite consistent with the statutory goal of rehabilitation. If nothing else, involvement in law channels energies into more productive outlets, and turns at least some prisoners away from retaliatory violence.

SUMMARY

Several conclusions emerge from the JHL's story. First, they take their job and their career fully as seriously as do other professionals, and they adhere to a code of professional standards and competency. Second, their tasks fill both a legal and institutional void in which they serve a variety of unmet prisoner needs. Third, they clearly do not, as a group, either file or encourage the "frivolous suit," as critics charge. They attempt to carefully screen and weed out cases that have neither legal nor substantive merit. Finally, conspicuously absent from their story (and from observations) are connections with outside political activists. JHLs usually demonstrate a sophisticated political awareness, but do not in general pursue abstract political goals. Nor is there evidence that "outside activists" currently participate to a significant degree in assisting JHLs develop resources or ply their craft.[12]

Prisoners are prisoners because they have been adjudicated through the legal process, and thus by definition are bound up in the matrix of law. Further, prisoners, as a group, are more vulnerable to abuses of law, since their status is legally defined, their keepers are, in principle if not in practice, legally mandated to act as they do, and they exist in a culture that is more difficult to manage and supervise than that of most other citizens. As a consequence, they live under and with the law daily. But jailhouse lawyers not only live law; they alert others that law can be employed as a weapon in righting wrongs within this environment. The prison experience and culture create the opportunity for a legal career, but they also create problems that simultaneously nurture and jeopardize it.

There occur a number of paradoxes—or contradictions—in prisoner litigation. Among the most salient include the use of law by legal offenders to attain legal compliance by law enforcers; emancipatory action of the kept that may lead to repressive responses by keepers; structurally licit and authorized behavior that may be interactionally conceptualized in a way to redefine it as illicit and unauthorized; and above all, the ideology of law directly conflicting with the ideology of corrections and punishment. The prisoner case is conceived and constructed within the context of these paradoxes, and law becomes one weapon by which to reduce the gap between them. As a consequence, prisoner cases emerge from and are constructed in a manner which, while occasionally "frivolous" to the outsider, take on a quite different meaning to those working within the values, norms, constraints, and dangers of the setting intended to be changed. Failure to recognize the context in which jailhouse lawyers work inevitably leads to a failure to understand and appreciate their enterprise. This, in turn, only contributes to the problems that jailhouse law aims to eliminate.

NOTES

1. Interviews with civilian lawyers and state officials and a review of cases filed by JHLs indicate that, in the main, most in Illinois consistently attempt to discourage frivolous suits, and a review of their own cases further substantiates their claim. Although I have no hard statistical data, the overwhelming majority of suits lacking either substantive or legal merit seem to come from a few less scrupulous assistants who file for compensation and from one-shot litigators who are unskilled in legal procedures.
2. This estimate of illiteracy comes from discussions with state officials, educational staff, and by prison monitoring. The literacy rate varies inversely with the security level of the prison.

3. This estimate may be low, but JHLs explain that many younger prisoners do not challenge either their convictions or prison conditions, ignore preincarceration problems that could be resolved by litigation in state courts and in general have no incentive to solicit legal assistance. Alpert and Huff (1981: 318) cite 1972 data indicating that a "typical prison law office can expect to have an average of one legal problem per prisoner per year." In a study of legal contacts in a women's prison in 1986, Wheeler et al. (1987) found that in a prison population fluctuating between 500 and 600, on the average, 64 women a month sought assistance from the prison law clerks. Factoring out "repeat players" still leaves about one prisoner per year seeking legal assistance; this data is consistent with the Alpert and Huff study.

4. In 1982, a consent decree established minimal standards protecting access and defining acceptable legal resources for Illinois prisons (e.g., *Shango v. Jurich*, 77–C–00103, N.D. Ill., 1977). The American Correctional Association has also established minimal guidelines for adequate legal libraries, and most states make a good-faith attempt to meet them. Illinois prison libraries provide complete up-to-date federal and state case law and statutes, a variety of West's legal publications, one or more professional library staff with at least minimal familiarity with legal resources, "how to" manuals and prisoner law clerks, who—if not encouraged—are not directly prohibited from assisting other prisoners. Civilian staff are rarely knowledgeable in law and are not authorized to provide legal assistance. Discussions with most civilian library staff reveal considerable ignorance of legal resources, and the best law libraries (e.g., Stateville) have been developed primarily through the initiative of experienced JHLs. The legal resources available in some of the newer Illinois prisons, however, have been found severely deficient (John Howard Association prison monitoring visitations, 1984–86). Law books may be delayed in arriving at a new institution, and other delays may result from the logistics of placing and organizing volumes in the library. There can also be delays in hiring civilian library staff, in appointing prisoner law clerks, or even in determining where the legal materials should be placed. Occasionally, books are stolen and important cases are ripped out of periodicals by both staff and prisoners. Further, the legal resources in the secondary (or "satellite") facilities of some institutions, such as Stateville's "honor farm," Menard's death row, or the disciplinary and segregation units of most institutions, are substandard or nonexistent.

5. Clever inmates can create problems for the institution when they organize to file grievances. In one institution, a JHL received severe disciplinary sanctions when he organized a grievance protest over prison policy by mass-producing grievance forms and recruiting other prisoners to file them. In one medium security institution, the new law clerk was initially hesitant to speak, because he was helping inmates file grievances, a practice for which his predecessor had been dismissed.

6. Staff cogently argue that limiting access to the law library can be a useful security measure to help contain street gang activity. Some street gangs prefer the library for their meetings, because it provides relative quiet and may be the only time all members are able to congregate in a single spot. In one institution, a library clerk was removed from his position for using it as a clearing house for marketing in illicit substances, which resulted in limits and closer supervision on others, thus curtailing access.

7. One intriguing question is the extent to which some clients may engage in

illicit entrepreneurial activity, such as drug sales, to finance their case costs. If this occurs, then institutional policies that increase litigation costs may have the unanticipated consequence of generating the very behaviors that policies should reduce, thus increasing costs in other areas, such as security.

8. *Lamar v. Steele,* (693 F.2d 559, 5th Cir., 1982) dramatizes the ways by which staff may invoke both threatened and actual violence against litigating inmates. A Texas federal court ruled on behalf of an inmate who alleged that his life was endangered because of staff hostility to his litigation activity that was expressed by explicit death threats and a veiled knife attack.

9. In Illinois, prisoner affiliation with street gangs is far higher than the estimated 30 percent reported by Camp and Camp (1985a). In Stateville, well-informed prisoners place the figure closer to 70 percent, and it is certain that in the state's four maximum security prisons, at least half maintain an affiliation. The figures are dramatically lower for medium and minimum security institutions, where prisoners may be shipped back to maximum security prisons if they demonstrate gang affiliation.

10. In some ways, the "escape attempts" of JHLs resemble those of other prisoners. For a discussion of coping in prison, see especially Cohen and Taylor (1976, 1972).

11. There was no evidence of fraud, and the charges were dropped.

12. There are, however, several active legal aid offices in the Chicago area, one downstate, and several private law firms noted for handling prisoner cases. These cases tend to be dramatic class action or flagrant abuse cases, rather than the discrete case typically filed. Further, whether by accident or design, civilian attorneys consistently express difficulty in obtaining access to prisoners because of existing correctional policies.

10

Surveying the Landscape: A Beginning

How did I bring you here? Was it out of habit that you began where I must leave or did you, and why did you, reach here by way of what went before? I would understand both. Of course, there is no real end here, nor any real beginning, just a going on (O'Neill, 1972: 264).

T HE END OF OUR TOUR, LIKE THE END OF ALL TOURS, has left much unseen, much unsaid. We have visited, listened, observed, and been exposed to the litigation culture. We could not visit everybody or everything, but, with luck, we have seen enough to provide new insights into a culture alien and often misunderstood. Our journey's end provides an invitation to begin looking at prisoner litigation in a new way, one that grasps the relationships between rule-making and rule-following, social control and social resistance, justice and power, myth and reality, and stasis and change.

Of all prison topics, prisoner litigation has been plagued by poor conceptualization, lack of data, ideological obfuscation, and plain ignorance. From what we have seen, several points should be clear.

First, prisoners' rights have not emerged full-blown onto the scene, forced upon us by activist judges. Rather, they stem from centuries of legal development and social struggle, and expansion of prisoners' Constitutional protections has been one small, but visibly significant, consequence.

Second, the so-called "litigation explosion" metaphor misleads. None can deny the substantial increase in prisoner filings, but the metaphor connotes an implicit set of ideological values conveying perjorative nuances that conceal the factors contributing to litigation. Such factors include a prison population expanding at a greater rate than litigation, the changing nature of civil rights, and challenges to traditional methods of prisoner control.

Third, in the main, prisoners do not file because they are "sociopaths," to seek revenge, or to pass time. They generally file to improve their lot.

246

Most cases address substantive complaints about conditions, guard behavior, or policies, and legal relief is often the final arena of redress.

Fourth, the legal theories of habeas corpus and civil rights have evolved differently and are used dissimilarly. Further, individual states experience each type of filing differently. This suggests that there are actually two types of litigation that cannot easily be subsumed under a single category. Each must be examined as a distinct form of law, and each represents different meanings and motivations.

Fifth, the stories told by prisoners to invoke court action vary dramatically in form and content, and the readings these stories are given vary between readers. The richness of prisoner litigation begins with their story, and the processes of litigation flow from the diverse readings. As a consequence, analysis of the stories becomes an integral part of any future research on prison law.

Sixth, the processing of the prisoner story does not occur simply by one judge reading a case and then making a decision. The litigation play triggers the activities of numerous personnel, all of whom have a role in the drama. Some give predictable performances, others are scene-stealers, but all shape the denouement of the plot. Hence, litigation cannot be understood in isolation from other social factors that contribute to its unique character.

Seventh, the culture of the jailhouse lawyer is complex, subtle, and fraught with problems. Law careers are entered, maintained in much the same way as conventional careers, and the performance of law requires intelligence, skill, and commitment. Limiting our view of JHLs to only their filings conceals the complex social networks and experiences that they develop.

Eighth, JHLs, as their critics observe, are mendacious, predatory, cunning, dogmatic, hostile, selfish, and dangerous, much like the rest of us. But, also like most of us, they are vulnerable, frightened, proud, honorable, altruistic, protective, caring, and sensitive. These contradictions and ambivalences permeate the culture of jailhouse law, and the better virtues win out more often than not.

Ninth, the impact of prisoners' law, for better or for worse, has demonstrably touched courts, prisons and society in ways both direct and subtle. Even if the consequences of litigated reform have not been as profound as advocates wish, litigation has stimulated public dialogue, increased the visibility of prison conditions, shaped civil rights law, changed prison policy and, for better or worse, given some prisoners a reasonably constructive outlet for their energy.

Tenth, jailhouse law illustrates the need to examine the rhetoric of justice and how the language of cases becomes processed as an organizational activity with multiple meanings and intents. The ideology of civil rights and societal values infuses prisoner litigation with claims to be upheld in the name of justice just as judicial decisions often deny claims using similarly based rhetoric. As a consequence, prisoner litigation is as much a battle over ideological definitions and claims as over justice, and this reveals the link between law as sign and that which law signifies as a social, rather than strictly legal, act.

Finally, prisoner litigation should be recognized as a verb rather than a noun. It is a process of complex activity, an *active agent* that patterns and guides behavior and culture, codes and decodes values and shapes and becomes reshaped by social factors. Above all, it serves as an instrument of *praxis* in transforming social existence.

THE MEANING OF LITIGATION

In some ways, jailhouse lawyers resemble characters in Kafka's *The Trial*. Like Joseph K., prisoners act out a conception of justice in which conventional social rules are often inapplicable, invocation of legal lore is required but often futile, and prisoners continually operate within a surrealistic web of uncertainty and ambiguity where legal and existential reality are problematic and changing. Justice seems *mysterious,* the court's practitioners appear *profane,* but all are nonetheless bound to the *sacred* world of law through *interwoven performances* and *shared meanings.*

In short, the meanings of prisoner litigation are not to be found solely in the law they engender. Law's meanings instead are grounded in the dramas, performances, and expressions of the activity that create it. The relationship between prison structure and social organization on one hand, and prisoners' stories and litigating activity on the other, imbue prison law with a character diverse in content and rich in significance. Existential meanings are translated into legal meanings, which are in turn retranslated into organizational meanings. Prisoners, through their law, display objective conditions of the prison experience. Their symbolization of this display, constructed through story telling, expresses complex messages that must ultimately be acted upon in ways that prohibit, mediate, or permit a continuation of some performances and some dramas. The multiple realms of activity by which prisoner litigation is patterned influence a mosaic of interrelated social worlds, each with different public and private tasks, goals and needs, and each containing different criteria for constructing an appropriate performance. Occupational requisites, moral boundaries, legal myths, control strategies, and ideological preferences are but a few of the dramatic scenarios acted out through litigation, thus confounding a simple assessment of what litigation "really means."

Whatever else prisoner litigation might mean, it above all signifies *resistance.* When a dispute occurs for which no apparent resolution exists, prisoners turn to the courts for help. Sometimes they win, sometimes not, but by sheer bulk of filing, their petitioning has produced identifiable results. The impact of prisoner suits on prison reform remains contested, but there can be no doubt that there has been an impact.

IMPACT OF LITIGATION

The meaning of litigation derives partially from the impact that players' performances have had, and this impact has rippled through the entire social structure. Prisons have changed, state treasuries have been heavily touched, rights have expanded, case and statute law have been affected, and some prisoners' lives have been transformed. To what degree this has happened remains uncertain, but that it has happened is not. Three broad areas of impact include the judiciary, corrections, and the broader society.

Judiciary Impact

The most salient judicial impact of prison law has occured in the content and practice of law and in the structure and attitude of the courts.

Changes in Law

Prisoner litigation's impact on law seems obvious; through the courts, prisoners have transformed privileges into expected rights, and the courts have generally upheld these rights. Living conditions, limitations on staff power, health care, religion, speech, mail, discipline, visits, and recreation are but a few of the realms into which the courts have penetrated to establish minimal standards. As a consequence, "prison law" has emerged as a subarea of legal expertise with considerable statute and case law as the basis.

The legal impact has also extended into broader areas. Prison law has not only expanded the rights of all institutionalized persons, but has contributed—by resurrecting Section 1983—to the expansion of other civil liberties as well. The threads of the impact of prison law on broader legal issues have yet to be woven together, but the result shall surely be substantial cloth.

The expanding body of prisoner law has made corrections' officials more law conscious and has also become a sensitive area for attorneys general. In a survey of prison wardens, Champagne and Haas (1976) found that two-thirds do not believe that courts should be restricted to reviewing only the most obvious cases of abuse, and that over half have closely followed federal decisions. This suggests that prison officials may attempt to construct policies that correspond to evolving judicial norms, even if for other than humanitarian reasons. State attorneys general, too, have recognized the "evolving standards of decency" that litigation has spawned, and have reacted with a variety of strategies attempting to reduce both the flow and costs of litigation (NAAG, 1980).

Prisoner litigation has contributed to an expanded judiciary and a new way of thinking about law by promoting, through successive decisions, the right of individuals to petition courts for aid in resolving problems (McCormack, 1975). Other factors also contributed to this expansion, but the transformation of criminal procedures, "individualized rights," the obligations of state officials, and the importance of discrete relief typify a few of the legal issues prisoners' suits have helped shape. This, in turn, has led to a shift in the dominant judicial paradigm of the pre–1950s when courts rarely bothered with such issues, in part because of a limited scope of rights, and in part because few complaints were brought into court.

Changes in Courts

Court organization has both changed and been changed by prison law. The most profound transformations have occured in court structure and judicial ideology. Federal courts have met the challenge of increased prisoner litigation by expanding their bureaucracy, adding personnel solely responsible for processing suits, recategorizing statistical procedures to include such suits, and creating new rules to facilitate filing and processing. The federal system also bears a considerable burden for the costs of processing prisoner complaints. In addition to the expanded bureaucracy, there are the costs of trials, personnel, and other processing needs. In jurisdictions unable to meet these costs, judges and magistrates are faced with difficult work loads. This, in turn, may delay all judicial processing by creating a backlog of cases that often takes many years to terminate.

Judicial ideology has also shifted dramatically. The hands-off doctrine, reflecting as much an ideological as a legal positon, has been replaced with one that might be described as "responsible intervention." The degree to which judges are willing to intercede on a prisoner's behalf varies widely between judges and jurisdictions, but cautious intercession constitutes the norm. Judges have come to recognize review of prison policies as a necessary part of their judicial function, and case law has provided a body of precedents that make it difficult for even the most misanthropic of judges to totally ignore prisoners' plight. As a consequence, prisoner rights have become an integral part of judicial consciousness and have patterned the relationship between prisons, the criminal justice system, and society.

Correctional Changes

Contrary to some critics, the impact of prisoner litigation on corrections has been profound, and there is simply no foundation for dismissing prisoner litigation as ineffective, as one critic has:

It is well settled that the outcome of inmate litigation has had little impact upon prison conditions and practices. ("A prison is a prison, is a prison," Anonymous NIJ grant reviewer, 1983).

Nonetheless, several problems hamper assessment of the impact of litigation (e.g., Jacobs, 1983: 52–53).

First, what counts as an impact may be ambiguous. Should the concept be limited to reform? And if so, what constitutes a reform? Should fiscal impact or organizational changes (e.g., guard training) be included? How does one measure the changes in interaction between staff and prisoners?

Second, the cause/effect relationship may be clouded, making it difficult to determine with certainty whether a particular suit or some other factor was responsible. Some changes, such as prison construction, arguably result from bureaucratic expediency in managing increasingly large populations, rather than from suits alleging overcrowding. Changes in conditions might result from the threat of violence rather than the threat of litigation.

Third, what counts as an impact for some might be a setback for others. Dogmatic Marxists, for example, tend to argue that litigation has done little more than legalize social control and intolerable conditions rather than transform them (Ericson and Baranek, 1982; Landau, 1984; Mandel, 1986). But as McCoy (1981) has observed, people generally tend to work when nuisances do not exist, and even nuisance suits lost in courts may function to deter some forms of staff behavior.

Fourth, we have seen that prisoner litigation is recent, emerging only in the 1960s. However, the early decisions only established the right of prisoners to sue, and the initial impact was quite limited. Some observers have argued that the first real decision challenging prison conditions or discipline did not occur until the *Wolff v.McDonnell* decision in 1973 (Calhoun, 1977). Because litigation remains in its infancy, it is far too early to adequately assess the full impact of suits. Because of the institutional inertia inhibiting changes in a system not prone to reform to begin with, and because of the considerable time lag between decisions and implementation, it may be several decades before litigation's impact can be fully assessed.

Finally, prison administrators are hesitant to reveal litigations' consequences for fear that it will only encourage more. This suggests that the impact on prisons is much higher than officially acknowledged and that staff fear that visibility of results would only trigger further litigation.[1] Nonetheless, there are several areas of prison life in which the impact is visible.

Some Modest Prison Consequences
Empirical assessments of litigation's impact on prisons have generated considerable evidence to show changes, even if not all changes constitute

"improvements" (Baker et al. 1973; Champagne and Haas, 1976; Jacobs, 1977, 1983; Rubin, 1974; Vito and Kaci, 1982). Litigation has indeed brought considerable relief to some prisoners by removing the grossest excesses of captivity.[2] However, even the most ardent prison reformers are ambivalent about the role of litigation as a reform strategy, but the more thoughtful recognize the improvements that have occured (Caracappa, 1976; Champagne and Haas, 1976; Irwin, 1980; Jacobs, 1982, 1983). Singer (1980) has identified six broad areas where litigation has engendered consequential prison reforms, including: (1) expanding the constituency of prison reform to professionals and others; (2) creating grievance mechanisms at institutional and state levels; (3) liberalizing mail privileges; (4) eliminating some of the most heinous practices, such as "strip cells;" (5) decreasing the arbitrary nature of prison rules and staff behavior; and (6) increasing the availability of broad judicial remedies.

The decisions precipitating these reforms generally have been limited to individual prisons and circumstances, but in the aggregate, they have created a wave of change that has rippled through other institutions and systems. Staff training—despite its subversion in practice—has been shaped by the prescriptions and proscriptions of prison law. Guards learn that physical abuse is intolerable, discipline must be done in accordance with rules, and that prisoners do have certain rights that cannot be usurped without reason. As Jacobs (1983) has observed, litigation has created a new level of bureaucracy for corrections' systems. In some states, special offices have been established solely to process prisoner suits, and prisons may employ additional staff counsel to assist defendants. Even the private sector has found the threat of litigation a convenient stage from which to hawk insurance or such prison amenities as better lighting (Claffy, 1984).

Litigation has also led to construction or modification of prisons and influenced prison architecture as well. States under court order to reduce prison populations to rated capacity have generally tended to build more prisons or to redesign old institutions to facilitate security while simultaneously meeting program or welfare needs.[3] Expansion of inmates' rights has also removed such traditional guard strategies of control as violence, inmate overseers, and excessive discipline (Dick, 1977; Marquart and Crouch, 1985; Merton, 1980).

It is often held that, because prisoners generally do not win large, if any, monetary awards, the costs of litigation are negligible (Contact Center, 1985). This, however, is misleading.[4] Sensitizing staff to prisoners' rights has contributed to training and salary costs, implementation of prison programs requires an increase of professional staff and adds additional layers of bureaucracy and court-mandated programs and population ceilings have required additional budget allocations. In short, correctional systems absorb considerable costs in defending suits or rewarding successful litigants.[5]

Are the costs of prisoner litigation excessive? Over the long term, litigation could be fiscally responsible to the extent that it reduce others costs, such as loss of life, reduction of violence, long-term medical care upon release, and other less visible expenditures that ultimately drain social resources. Even among conservatives, the problems for prisons caused by "tough on crime" attitudes has been recognized, and prison reform has come to be seen as a fiscally responsible goal (e.g., Unger, 1980). As Rothman has observed:

> Evidence can be easily marshalled to demonstrate how irrational, costly, and dysfunctional the present system is—and public education to these facts must begin (Rothman, 1979: 55).

In sum, prisoners' law has shaped the social organization of prisons, increased the fiscal burden of states, mediated the power hierarchy, created more rational forms of discipline, smoothed the excesses of racial favoritism, and even modified prison culture to a small degree. Some cynics have suggested that prison law has merely created a "legal form" of discipline, substituting one "repressive form" for another. But as one prison reformer observed:

> Which would you rather have? Be tossed in the hole and lose some privilges, maybe some goodtime, or have the shit kicked out of you by a couple of guards, maybe lose a few teeth, and *then* be tossed in the hole and lose your privileges? The current system still sucks but I'll take it to the old!

While only the most sanguine could consider litigation and the modest corresponding reforms to be a panacea for society's prisons, only the most cynical could dismiss it as inconsequential or worthless.

Social Impact

Prisoner litigation's impact on society has been subtle, but consequential. First, it has raised the visibilty of prisons and prison conditions. Dramatic suits, especially those alleging brutality and heinous conditions, have given the public a view of life behind the walls. News media tend to cover litigation more than many other categories of prison news (e.g., Jacobs and Brooks, 1983: 108–9), and even if the attention is not always favorable, it functions to make prisons more open.

Second, if litigation's potential as a rehabilitative agent has even partial merit, then one function is that of contributing to the "resocialization" of litigants.[6] Third, nonprisoners have benefited from litigation. Jailhouse law has improved visiting conditions, thus, at least reducing some of the psychological pressure on family and friends. Enhanced and expanded prison programs, many of which have occured through litigation, increase the opportunity to learn marketable skills and ease the transition of ex-prisoners back into society. Prisoners may enter prisons with health-related problems or disabilities, or they may acquire some while incarcerated. The improved health care mandated by court decisions in the past 20 years helps reduce the burden some prisoners would otherwise confront when returning to the streets. This, in turn, lessens the burden both for prisoners' families and, ultimately, for society by proactively removing one problem some prisoners must overcome.

Negative Consequences

The dialectic between freedom and control may be seen in some of the negative consequences brought about by prisoner suits, even those that are won. Perhaps the most dramatic example of how court victories have contributed to increased difficulties for prisoners is found in disciplinary proceedings. Mandel (1986) has argued that court-mandated protections have actually increased the plight of prisoners by providing a legally sanctioned mechanism to discipline prisoners that appears to follow Constitutional procedures while, in fact, subverting them. Other research has illustrated how this occurs through the manipulation of meanings and rules that provides an effective strategy for noncompliance with court-ordered reform while appearing to implement it (Thomas, Aylward, Mika, and Blakemore, 1985).

Consent decrees prohibiting overcrowding also provide both the rationale and the resources to construct more prisons, thus creating yet a larger population likely to litigate. In addition, when guards are constrained from engaging in one form of behavior judged unconstitutional, they are likely to create alternatives no less tolerable that generate additional complaints. This has led some observers to argue that legal reforms actually maintain existing forms of objectionable power and authority rather than reducing them (Jacobs, 1977; McBarnet, 1981). These views correctly note the limitations and unanticipated consequences of legal reform, but they ignore the dialectical tension between law, social struggle and social change (Mika and Thomas, 1987). As a consequence, the utility and impact of litigation cannot be judged simply on the basis of discrete decisions or immediate consequences, but must be viewed within the larger organizational and social totality of which it is a part:

> The principles of justice are in part the ideology of the democratic state not only in their substance but in a much more fundamental way, in the very idea that there should be principles at all, that those who wield the power of the state should not do so arbitrarily but should themselves be governed by law. The idea of legality itself is an essential ideological form of the democratic state; its rule is the rule of law (McBarnet, 1981: 162).

A FINAL WORD

Clarifying the issues underlying prisoner litigation has obviously created new ones that themselves require new answers. As a sign system, prisoners' law points to meanings beyond legal decisions and immediate consequences that require decoding. Their law symbolizes a form of social activity, their complaints signify structural and behavioral nuances, and court and correctional responses reveal changing ideological and value shifts that occur continuously. The phenomenology of litigation suggests a multiplicity of experiences for all levels of society, and these experiences shape how prisons are viewed, managed, and transformed. It also suggests that society, as well as litigants, feel the impact in ways that are simultaneously obvious and subtle. Historically, both the practice and consequences of this legal activity provide a window in the changing nature of rights and social change. Those who view litigation and its impact as static and invariant ignore the ongoing transformations of law in general and its consequences in particular. The emergence of prisoner litigation is bound to the changing role of the state in mediating conflict, the expansion of the powers of the federal government, and the role of law in securing a fairly uniform ideological framework for conceptualizing values and social practices.

As *social praxis*, litigation displays the ways through which law can be used to transform social existence and the ways by which these changes can be resisted. Litigation provides a type of slippage that mediates between the formidable power of state agents and those whom the agents would control. The drama of litigation and the performances that create it decrease the historically tightly coupled link between the rules and practices of an organization, and contributes to the dialectical tension between freedom and constraint.

Prisoners have used their law to change themselves and their environment. Like the world the slaves made (Genovese, 1974), the paternalism of prison staff and even society has been slowly eroded by numerous small legal victories and even dramatic losses. The psychological impact created when a prisoner can prevent a guard from continual verbal abuse, or of requiring an institution to replace low-watt lightbulbs with ones more powerful, can only be estimated. The broader consequences, however, are more obvious. To borrow a metaphor from Thompson (1975: 197), prior to the onset of litigation, prisons resembled "banana republics" where predators fought for the spoils of power and did not agree to submit to rational or bureaucratic rules and forms. This has changed: the feudal lords have been replaced, and the new overseers submit to more powerful authorities who, for a variety of conflicting reasons, are part of a larger democratization process. The feudal domain of prisons has been reshaped accordingly.

Prison law has done little to change the structure of punishment, and prisons still loom mighty in our midst. Prisons remain an archaic social institution, but if we look more closely, we can see that, as a political movement, prisoner litigation has—in concert with other political movements—contributed to the erosion of the nonaccountable power of state officials. The institutionalized procedures by which prisoners are governed are pliant and yielding and do not constitute the direct tool of repression for which some give it credit. Through its ideological power and practical application, law becomes a weapon of action and mediating unnecessary forms of social domination:

> The rhetoric and the rules of a society are something a great deal more than a sham. In the same moment, they may modify, in profound ways, the behavior of the powerful, and mystify the powerless. They may disguise the true realities of power, but at the same time, they may curb that power and check its intrusions. And it is often from within that very rhetoric that a radical critique of the practice of the society is developed (Thompson, 1975: 265).

I have attempted to clarify prisoner law by selecting those issues usually raised by its critics. These critics tend to critique or dismiss the act or consequences of litigation with such absolute phrases as "It is obvious that . . . ," "it is well-settled that . . . " or "there is no question that . . . " litigation is a bane, useless, subversive, irrelevant, or not worth further consideration. This has added to the confusion of the topic by obscuring the origins, trends, and processes, by creating false impressions about its utility, and by using a vocabulary of certitude and clarity to obfuscate. But "clarity" can be an enemy of knowledge when it tricks us into succumbing to a feeling of a complete journey when we have taken only the first few steps (Castaneda, 1974: 85). In attempting to develop a clearer picture of the prisoners' culture, we have walked through the terrain, examined it close-up and from afar, and have advanced a few modest steps toward piecing together the broken fragments of the scattered empirical and conceptual shards in order to restore a more complete image. Much confusion remains, but (with apologies to Karl Weick) this need not be deter future journeys:

> He is quick, thinking in clear images;
> I am slow, thinking in broken images;
> He becomes dull, trusting his clear images;
> I become sharp, mistrusting my broken images;
>
> He continues quick and dull in his clear images;
> I continue slow and sharp in my broken images;
> He in a new confusion of his understanding;
> I in a new understanding of my confusion.
> Robert Graves, *In Broken Images*

NOTES

1. Both state officials and prison staff in Illinois acknowledged this rationale in interviews.
2. Among some of the notable cases successfully challenging prison conditions include *Holt v. Sarver* 300 F.Supp. 825 (E.D. Ark. 1969); *Pugh v. Locke* 406 F.Supp. 318 (M.D. Ala. 1976); *Ruiz v. Estelle* 650 F.2d 555 (5th Cir. 1981); and *Hutto v. Finney* 437 U.S. 678 (1978). For a more complete description of case trends, Palmer (1985) remains among the best.
3. In 1984, 34 new state facilities were opened in 22 states. The average cost per bed was $37,767 and $10.9 million per facility (Camp and Camp, 1985b: 22).
4. Most cases are settled out of court, and disclosure of awards is customarily prohibited as part of the agreement. Attorneys willing to divulge costs indicate that their fees can be substantial. One Chicago attorney's office provided a list of 12 "typical" cases over a four year period in which prisoner settlements totalled $66,475, or an average of $5,539.58 per suit, excluding recovery costs. Another attorney documented $250,000 for attorneys' fees alone in 1985, and one claimed $300,000 for 1984. Judges and lawyers indicate that five-figure legal fees are not uncommon in settlements. Another Chicago attorney listed five cases totalling $211,000 in legal fees (an average of $42,200 per case) and a sixth for $400,000. Attorneys claim these are not atypical and result primarily from out of court settlements or consent agreements rather than trial victories. Hence, costs can quickly escalate when the state chooses to fight a weak case and loses.
5. Chief Justice Warren Burger has estimated that the annual cost of maintaining a single federal judge, including salaries, support staff and space, averages about $250,000. In addition, the federal government bears some of the processing costs, including some housing, service costs incurred by federal marshalls, and jury per diem. The costs to states include awards and settlements, staff salaries (attorneys, clerks), trial expenditures, trial exhibits, court reporters, expert testimony, travel costs (for guards, staff, and prisoners), overnight housing, attorneys fees to plaintiffs, guard overtime, processing costs (mail, zerox), collecting and maintaining trial exhibits and numerous other "hidden" costs that, in the aggregate, are substantial.
6. I have no hard data, but I have met only one jailhouse lawyer who returned to prison after release, and that was for a parole violation. Judging from anecdotal data, even novice litigants have a better chance of not recidivating once released.

Appendixes

Appendix 1   Habeas Corpus filings for individual states,
             1970, 1975, 1980, and 1986

Year	State	No. Filed	Rate/100 Prisoners	As % of All Pvt Filings	As % All Prisoner Filings
1970	AK	7	(na)	5.34	100.00
1975	AK	2	.97	1.27	50.00
1980	AK	6	.73	1.71	35.29
1986	AK	26	1.11	5.05	40.00
1970	AL	185	4.88	12.74	85.25
1975	AL	472	10.68	21.30	69.41
1980	AL	244	3.73	9.19	31.40
1986	AL	424	3.74	11.00	32.34
1970	AR	97	5.54	15.42	89.81
1975	AR	129	5.97	11.33	40.19
1980	AR	87	2.99	7.48	32.46
1986	AR	148	3.16	7.50	26.29
1970	AZ	111	7.60	23.03	90.98
1975	AZ	99	3.71	14.18	60.00
1980	AZ	108	2.47	14.88	48.00
1986	AZ	222	2.44	12.21	24.24
1970	CA	1470	5.87	31.31	76.01
1975	CA	1254	7.25	20.30	75.63
1980	CA	456	1.86	6.61	63.87
1986	CA	616	1.12	4.87	40.18
1970	CO	122	5.91	19.65	78.71
1975	CO	31	1.52	2.88	40.79
1980	CO	55	2.09	5.10	27.50
1986	CO	69	2.05	3.57	33.17
1970	CT	48	3.06	11.24	75.00
1975	CT	63	3.41	7.98	53.39
1980	CT	57	1.32	4.67	28.50
1986	CT	51	.76	2.67	26.70
1970	DC	87	6.11	2.57	46.28
1975	DC	64	2.78	8.05	49.23
1980	DC	27	.86	2.07	36.99
1986	DC	42	.61	1.83	34.15
1970	DE	9	1.51	6.21	90.00
1975	DE	26	4.47	11.30	53.06
1980	DE	39	2.65	9.90	24.84
1986	DE	41	1.52	7.82	22.16

261

Appendix 1   Habeas Corpus filings for individual states,
1970, 1975, 1980, and 1986

Year	State	No. Filed	Rate/100 Prisoners	As % of All Pvt Filings	As % All Prisoner Filings
1970	FL	791	8.61	28.87	89.58
1975	FL	618	4.04	14.27	49.68
1980	FL	507	2.45	10.40	31.61
1986	FL	621	2.09	9.34	35.85
1970	GA	187	3.66	15.15	79.24
1975	GA	234	2.25	7.64	53.55
1980	GA	226	1.86	6.65	48.19
1986	GA	270	1.61	6.62	36.59
1970	HA	0	---	---	---
1975	HA	3	.89	1.07	50.00
1980	HA	8	.81	1.68	66.67
1986	HA	18	.84	2.21	32.14
1970	IA	26	1.49	8.00	92.86
1975	IA	50	2.80	10.29	47.62
1980	IA	44	1.77	6.30	20.66
1986	IA	78	2.72	6.22	18.75
1970	ID	4	.97	3.36	66.67
1975	ID	9	1.55	4.69	31.03
1980	ID	11	1.35	4.00	29.73
1986	ID	19	1.40	4.47	27.94
1970	IL	319	5.00	11.95	60.53
1975	IL	168	2.14	4.27	46.54
1980	IL	309	2.60	5.05	32.36
1986	IL	319	1.65	3.19	25.96
1970	IN	62	1.50	5.00	79.49
1975	IN	46	1.18	3.23	59.74
1980	IN	96	1.44	5.86	44.44
1986	IN	168	1.69	5.64	37.75
1970	KS	147	7.73	25.79	74.62
1975	KS	54	3.20	8.42	48.21
1980	KS	60	2.41	5.74	47.24
1986	KS	68	1.36	4.95	35.23
1970	KY	164	5.76	24.59	88.65
1975	KY	90	2.77	10.82	70.87
1980	KY	101	2.81	8.46	42.44
1986	KY	180	3.04	7.97	31.09

Appendix 1   Habeas Corpus filings for individual states,
              1970, 1975, 1980, and 1986

Year	State	No. Filed	Rate/100 Prisoners	As % of All Pvt Filings	As % All Prisoner Filings
1970	LA	166	3.96	4.44	90.22
1975	LA	243	5.11	5.17	70.43
1980	LA	272	3.06	4.39	37.94
1986	LA	352	2.48	4.29	32.74
1970	MA	83	4.04	6.36	85.57
1975	MA	62	2.77	1.36	53.91
1980	MA	71	2.23	3.95	55.47
1986	MA	74	1.30	2.54	45.68
1970	MD	226	4.36	20.79	78.47
1975	MD	208	2.99	17.29	55.76
1980	MD	175	2.26	9.63	31.76
1986	MD	192	1.43	6.85	27.39
1970	ME	15	2.91	10.79	83.33
1975	ME	4	.62	2.23	66.67
1980	ME	15	1.84	5.21	31.91
1986	ME	19	1.47	4.62	25.33
1970	MI	180	1.98	12.38	74.07
1975	MI	291	2.68	11.88	67.52
1980	MI	271	1.79	7.47	34.09
1986	MI	325	1.67	5.75	28.16
1970	MN	17	1.07	2.72	85.00
1975	MN	19	1.13	2.35	40.43
1980	MN	30	1.50	3.80	60.00
1986	MN	28	1.14	1.72	33.33
1970	MO	246	7.21	21.28	69.89
1975	MO	243	5.56	13.75	56.12
1980	MO	161	2.81	7.47	38.98
1986	MO	328	3.20	7.94	27.29
1970	MS	29	1.68	4.18	78.38
1975	MS	74	3.50	6.31	61.67
1980	MS	83	2.13	4.21	44.39
1986	MS	120	1.84	3.67	31.09
1970	MT	35	13.46	20.59	94.59
1975	MT	3	.70	1.28	50.55
1980	MT	24	3.25	7.19	52.17
1986	MT	54	4.66	7.11	40.30

263

Appendix 1 Habeas Corpus filings for individual states,
1970, 1975, 1980, and 1986

Year	State	No. Filed	Rate/100 Prisoners	As % of All Pvt Filings	As % All Prisoner Filings
1970	NC	222	3.72	27.44	74.75
1975	NC	277	2.52	19.62	47.84
1980	NC	285	1.84	15.55	28.44
1986	NC	232	1.32	10.61	23.48
1970	ND	0	---	---	---
1975	ND	3	1.73	3.00	60.00
1980	ND	5	1.98	3.27	55.56
1986	ND	14	3.41	5.45	51.85
1970	NE	34	3.40	11.60	54.84
1975	NE	38	3.04	8.21	62.30
1980	NE	20	1.38	3.31	33.90
1986	NE	70	3.58	5.97	22.80
1970	NH	7	2.87	5.74	87.50
1975	NH	18	7.20	5.23	20.69
1980	NH	20	6.13	4.94	45.45
1986	NH	42	5.74	8.54	45.16
1970	NJ	141	2.47	12.67	74.60
1975	NJ	141	2.48	8.63	55.29
1980	NJ	117	1.99	4.63	37.26
1986	NJ	142	1.19	3.40	24.57
1970	NM	54	7.28	17.70	90.00
1975	NM	43	4.30	8.29	56.58
1980	NM	62	4.85	9.32	51.67
1986	NM	52	2.18	5.37	26.00
1970	NV	41	5.94	23.98	97.62
1975	NV	34	4.01	9.77	59.65
1980	NV	41	2.23	8.44	46.07
1986	NV	95	2.22	7.46	26.03
1970	NY	780	6.47	11.45	71.63
1975	NY	494	3.07	6.65	51.57
1980	NY	606	2.78	6.46	48.79
1986	NY	699	1.94	5.03	35.88
1970	OH	269	2.93	15.74	96.07
1975	OH	176	1.54	7.03	63.77
1980	OH	312	2.31	9.87	49.60
1986	OH	388	1.77	6.78	48.20

Appendix 1 Habeas Corpus filings for individual states,
1970, 1975, 1980, and 1986

Year	State	No. Filed	Rate/100 Prisoners	As % of All Pvt Filings	As % All Prisoner Filings
1970	OK	165	4.53	20.65	91.16
1975	OK	195	6.22	15.49	71.43
1980	OK	100	2.09	6.29	49.50
1986	OK	190	2.12	5.10	40.08
1970	OR	39	2.17	6.69	88.64
1975	OR	48	1.94	5.49	76.19
1980	OR	105	3.31	9.41	33.98
1986	OR	75	1.60	5.02	33.63
1970	PA	665	10.57	14.07	64.44
1975	PA	260	4.35	5.50	46.02
1980	PA	249	3.05	3.87	30.22
1986	PA	448	2.98	4.25	27.84
1970	RI	13	3.71	9.77	86.67
1975	RI	8	1.96	2.70	27.59
1980	RI	12	1.48	2.48	16.44
1986	RI	5	.38	.98	13.89
1970	SC	88	3.23	10.63	79.28
1975	SC	76	1.36	5.83	49.35
1980	SC	74	.94	5.03	51.75
1986	SC	86	.75	4.82	34.54
1970	SD	10	2.56	8.55	100.00
1975	SD	10	2.96	6.45	83.33
1980	SD	22	3.46	8.09	40.74
1986	SD	25	2.30	6.39	34.25
1970	TN	195	5.97	15.80	69.64
1975	TN	184	4.03	12.08	62.37
1980	TN	131	1.87	7.10	39.82
1986	TN	301	4.22	8.85	29.45
1970	TX	440	3.07	11.83	84.78
1975	TX	767	4.05	13.73	63.81
1980	TX	692	2.32	9.69	46.98
1986	TX	784	2.08	6.58	34.71
1970	UT	105	21.38	33.65	91.30
1975	UT	8	1.22	1.93	53.33
1980	UT	8	.86	1.68	10.96
1986	UT	17	.94	1.85	17.17

Appendix 1   Habeas Corpus filings for individual states,
1970, 1975, 1980, and 1986

Year	State	No. Filed	Rate/100 Prisoners	As % of All Pvt Filings	As % All Prisoner Filings
1970	VA	528	11.36	26.75	69.84
1975	VA	375	6.82	15.24	41.07
1980	VA	421	4.72	11.20	21.10
1986	VA	325	2.61	8.50	25.06
1970	VT	13	8.02	4.33	72.22
1975	VT	4	1.64	1.83	12.50
1980	VT	7	1.46	3.27	26.92
1986	VT	0	---	---	---
1970	WA	58	2.03	8.49	78.38
1975	WA	63	1.87	6.84	79.75
1980	WA	76	1.73	7.32	35.02
1986	WA	161	2.32	8.45	34.33
1970	WI	149	5.01	21.85	80.11
1975	WI	157	5.25	16.35	40.89
1980	WI	91	2.29	9.09	30.43
1986	WI	80	1.47	5.48	27.68
1970	WV	179	19.08	30.19	96.24
1975	WV	141	11.09	13.70	58.26
1980	WV	120	9.55	10.57	34.19
1986	WV	98	5.99	7.33	39.84
1970	WY	8	3.46	12.12	88.89
1975	WY	22	7.17	14.29	59.46
1980	WY	6	1.12	2.25	9.09
1986	WY	20	2.31	5.03	24.69

Appendix 2   Civil Rights filings for individual states,
            1970, 1975, 1980, and 1986

Year	State	No. Filed	Rate/100 Prisoners	As % of All Pvt Filings	As % All Prisoner Filings
1970	AK	0	(na)	---	100.00
1975	AK	22	.97	1.27	50.00
1980	AK	11	1.34	3.13	64.71
1986	AK	39	1.66	7.57	60.00
1970	AL	32	.84	2.20	14.75
1975	AL	208	4.71	9.39	30.59
1980	AL	533	8.15	20.07	68.60
1986	AL	887	7.83	23.00	67.66
1970	AR	11	.63	1.75	10.19
1975	AR	192	8.88	16.86	59.81
1980	AR	181	6.22	15.56	67.54
1986	AR	415	8.86	21.03	73.71
1970	AZ	11	.75	2.28	9.02
1975	AZ	66	2.47	9.46	40.00
1980	AZ	117	2.68	16.12	52.00
1986	AZ	694	7.62	38.17	75.76
1970	CA	464	1.85	9.88	23.99
1975	CA	404	2.34	6.54	24.37
1980	CA	258	1.05	3.74	36.13
1986	CA	917	1.66	7.25	59.82
1970	CO	33	1.60	5.31	21.29
1975	CO	45	2.21	4.18	59.21
1980	CO	145	5.52	13.44	72.50
1986	CO	139	4.12	7.19	66.83
1970	CT	16	1.02	3.75	25.00
1975	CT	55	2.97	6.97	46.61
1980	CT	143	3.32	11.72	71.50
1986	CT	140	2.08	7.32	73.30
1970	DC	101	7.10	2.99	53.72
1975	DC	66	2.87	8.30	50.77
1980	DC	46	1.46	3.52	63.01
1986	DC	81	1.18	3.53	65.85
1970	DE	1	.17	.69	10.00
1975	DE	23	3.95	10.00	46.94
1980	DE	118	8.01	29.95	75.16
1986	DE	144	5.33	27.48	77.84

Appendix 2 Civil Rights filings for individual states,
1970, 1975, 1980, and 1986

Year	State	No. Filed	Rate/100 Prisoners	As % of All Pvt Filings	As % All Prisoner Filings
1970	FL	92	1.00	3.36	10.42
1975	FL	626	4.09	14.45	50.32
1980	FL	1097	5.29	22.51	68.39
1986	FL	1111	3.74	16.71	64.15
1970	GA	49	.96	3.97	20.76
1975	GA	203	1.95	6.63	46.45
1980	GA	243	2.00	7.15	51.81
1986	GA	468	2.78	11.48	63.41
1970	HA	1	.44	.79	100.00
1975	HA	3	.89	1.07	50.00
1980	HA	4	.41	.84	33.33
1986	HA	38	1.77	4.66	67.86
1970	IA	2	.11	.62	7.14
1975	IA	55	3.08	11.32	52.38
1980	IA	169	6.81	24.21	79.34
1986	IA	338	11.79	26.95	81.25
1970	ID	2	.49	1.68	33.33
1975	ID	20	3.45	10.42	68.97
1980	ID	26	3.18	9.45	70.27
1986	ID	49	3.61	11.53	72.06
1970	IL	208	3.26	7.79	39.47
1975	IL	193	2.46	4.90	53.46
1980	IL	646	5.43	10.55	67.64
1986	IL	910	4.71	9.09	74.04
1970	IN	16	.39	1.29	20.51
1975	IN	31	.80	2.18	40.26
1980	IN	120	1.80	7.33	55.56
1986	IN	277	2.79	9.30	62.25
1970	KS	50	2.63	8.77	25.38
1975	KS	58	3.44	9.05	51.79
1980	KS	67	2.69	6.41	52.76
1986	KS	125	2.50	9.10	64.77
1970	KY	21	.74	3.15	11.35
1975	KY	37	1.14	4.45	29.13
1980	KY	137	3.82	11.47	57.56
1986	KY	399	6.73	17.67	68.91

Appendix 2   Civil Rights filings for individual states,
1970, 1975, 1980, and 1986

Year	State	No. Filed	Rate/100 Prisoners	As % of All Pvt Filings	As % All Prisoner Filings
1970	LA	18	.43	.48	9.78
1975	LA	102	2.14	2.17	29.57
1980	LA	445	5.01	7.18	62.06
1986	LA	723	5.08	8.81	67.26
1970	MA	14	.68	1.07	14.43
1975	MA	53	2.36	1.16	46.09
1980	MA	57	1.79	3.17	44.53
1986	MA	88	1.54	3.02	54.32
1970	MD	62	1.20	5.70	21.53
1975	MD	165	2.37	13.72	44.24
1980	MD	376	4.86	20.69	68.24
1986	MD	509	3.80	18.15	72.61
1970	ME	3	.58	2.16	16.67
1975	ME	2	.31	1.12	33.33
1980	ME	32	3.93	11.11	68.09
1986	ME	56	4.33	13.63	74.67
1970	MI	63	.69	4.33	25.93
1975	MI	140	1.29	5.71	32.48
1980	MI	524	3.46	14.44	65.91
1986	MI	829	4.27	14.66	71.84
1970	MN	3	.19	.48	15.00
1975	MN	28	1.66	3.47	59.57
1980	MN	20	1.00	2.53	40.00
1986	MN	56	2.28	3.44	66.67
1970	MO	106	3.11	9.17	30.11
1975	MO	190	4.35	10.75	43.88
1980	MO	252	4.40	11.69	61.02
1986	MO	874	8.53	21.15	72.71
1970	MS	8	.46	1.15	21.62
1975	MS	46	2.17	3.92	38.33
1980	MS	104	2.67	5.27	55.61
1986	MS	266	4.07	8.13	68.91
1970	MT	2	.77	1.18	5.41
1975	MT	3	.70	1.28	50.00
1980	MT	22	2.98	6.59	47.83
1986	MT	80	6.90	10.54	59.70

Appendix 2 Civil Rights filings for individual states,
1970, 1975, 1980, and 1986

Year	State	No. Filed	Rate/100 Prisoners	As % of All Pvt Filings	As % All Prisoner Filings
1970	NC	75	1.26	9.27	25.25
1975	NC	302	2.75	21.39	52.16
1980	NC	717	4.62	39.12	71.56
1986	NC	756	4.30	34.57	76.52
1970	ND	0	---	---	---
1975	ND	2	1.16	2.00	40.00
1980	ND	4	1.58	2.61	44.44
1986	ND	13	3.16	5.06	48.15
1970	NE	28	2.80	9.56	45.16
1975	NE	23	1.84	4.97	37.70
1980	NE	39	2.70	6.45	66.10
1986	NE	237	12.11	20.20	77.20
1970	NH	1	.41	.82	12.50
1975	NH	69	27.60	20.06	79.31
1980	NH	24	7.36	5.93	54.55
1986	NH	51	6.97	10.37	54.84
1970	NJ	48	.84	4.31	25.40
1975	NJ	114	2.01	6.98	44.71
1980	NJ	197	3.35	7.80	62.74
1986	NJ	436	3.64	10.44	75.43
1970	NM	6	.81	1.97	10.00
1975	NM	33	3.30	6.36	43.42
1980	MN	58	4.53	8.72	48.33
1986	NM	148	6.20	15.27	74.00
1970	NV	1	.14	.58	2.38
1975	NV	23	2.71	6.61	40.35
1980	NV	48	2.61	9.88	53.93
1986	NV	270	6.31	21.21	73.97
1970	NY	309	2.56	4.54	28.37
1975	NY	464	2.89	6.24	48.43
1980	NY	636	2.92	6.78	51.21
1986	NY	1249	3.46	8.99	64.12
1970	OH	11	.12	.64	3.93
1975	OH	100	.88	4.00	36.23
1980	OH	317	2.35	10.03	50.40
1986	OH	417	1.90	7.29	51.80

Appendix 2 Civil Rights filings for individual states,
1970, 1975, 1980, and 1986

Year	State	No. Filed	Rate/100 Prisoners	As % of All Pvt Filings	As % All Prisoner Filings
1970	OK	16	.44	2.00	8.84
1975	OK	78	2.49	6.20	28.57
1980	OK	102	2.13	6.42	50.50
1986	OK	284	3.17	7.62	59.92
1970	OR	5	.28	.86	11.36
1975	OR	15	.60	1.72	23.81
1980	OR	204	6.42	18.28	66.02
1986	OR	148	3.16	9.91	66.37
1970	PA	367	5.84	7.76	35.56
1975	PA	305	5.10	6.45	53.98
1980	PA	575	7.04	8.95	69.78
1986	PA	1161	7.73	11.01	72.16
1970	RI	2	.57	1.50	13.33
1975	RI	21	5.15	7.09	72.41
1980	RI	61	7.50	12.63	83.56
1986	RI	31	2.34	6.07	86.11
1970	SC	23	.84	2.78	20.72
1975	SC	78	1.39	5.99	50.65
1980	SC	69	.88	4.69	48.25
1986	SC	163	1.41	9.14	65.46
1970	SD	0	---	---	---
1975	SD	2	.59	1.29	16.67
1980	SD	32	5.04	11.76	59.26
1986	SD	48	4.41	12.28	65.75
1970	TN	85	2.60	6.89	30.36
1975	TN	111	2.43	7.29	37.63
1980	TN	198	2.82	10.73	60.18
1986	TN	721	10.11	21.19	70.55
1970	TX	79	.55	2.12	15.22
1975	TX	435	2.30	7.78	36.19
1980	TX	781	2.61	10.93	53.02
1986	TX	1475	3.91	12.38	65.29
1970	UT	10	2.04	3.21	8.70
1975	UT	7	1.07	1.69	46.67
1980	UT	65	6.97	13.66	89.04
1986	UT	82	4.55	8.94	82.83

Appendix 2 Civil Rights filings for individual states,
1970, 1975, 1980, and 1986.

Year	State	No. Filed	Rate/100 Prisoners	As % of All Pvt Filings	As % All Prisoner Filings
1970	VA	228	4.91	11.55	30.16
1975	VA	538	9.79	21.87	58.93
1980	VA	1574	17.65	41.88	78.90
1986	VA	972	7.81	25.42	74.94
1970	VT	5	3.09	1.67	27.78
1975	VT	28	11.48	12.79	87.50
1980	VT	19	3.96	8.88	73.08
1986	VT	20	2.85	8.58	100.00
1970	WA	16	.56	2.34	21.62
1975	WA	16	.47	1.74	20.25
1980	WA	141	3.21	13.58	64.98
1986	WA	308	4.43	16.17	65.67
1970	WI	37	1.24	5.43	19.89
1975	WI	227	7.59	23.65	59.11
1980	WI	208	5.23	20.78	69.57
1986	WI	209	3.84	14.31	72.32
1970	WV	7	.75	1.18	3.76
1975	WV	101	7.95	9.82	41.74
1980	WV	231	18.38	20.35	65.81
1986	WV	148	9.04	11.07	60.16
1970	WY	1	.43	1.52	11.11
1975	WY	15	4.89	9.74	40.54
1980	WY	60	11.24	22.47	90.91
1986	WY	61	7.04	15.33	75.31

Bibliography

Abbott, Jack Henry. 1981. *In the Belly of the Beast: Letters from Prison*. New York: Random House.

Ackerhalt, Arthur H. 1972. "Court Orders Broad Relief to Inmates throughout Virginia Penal System Where Constitutional Rights have been Violated." *Buffalo Law Review* 22(Fall): 347–66.

Administrative Office of the United States Courts. 1986. *Annual Report of the Director of the Administative Office of the U.S. Courts: Civil and Trials Statistical Tables*. Washington: Administrative Office of the United States Courts.

Allen, Karen M., Nathan A. Schachtman, and David R. Wilson. 1982. "Federal Habeas Corpus and its Reform: An Empirical Analysis." *Rutgers Law Journal* 13(Summer):675–772.

Alpert, Geoffrey P. 1982. "Women Prisoners and the Law: Which Way Will the Pendulum Swing?" *Journal of Criminal Justice* 10(1):37–44.

———. 1978a. *Legal Rights of Prisoners: An Analysis of Legal Aid*. Lexington, Mass.: Lexington Books.

———. 1978b. "The Determinants of Prisoners' Decisions to Seek Legal Aid." *New England Journal of Prison Law* 4(2):309–25.

———. 1976. "Prisoners' Right of Access to Courts: Planning for Legal Aid." *Washington Law Review* 51(3):653–75.

Alpert, Geoffrey P., and C. Ronald Huff. 1981. "Prisoners, the Law, and Public Policy: Planning for Legal Aid." *New England Journal of Prison Law* 7(Summer):307–40.

Alpert, Geoffrey P., John M. Finney, and James F. Short. 1978. "Legal Services, Prisoners' Attitudes and 'Rehabilitation.'" *Journal of Criminal Law and Criminology* 69(4):616–26.

Alpert, Geoffrey P. and John J. Wiorkowski. 1977. "Female Prisoners and Legal Services." *Quarterly Journal of Corrections* 1(Fall):28–33.

Anderson, Debra J. 1986. *Curbing the Abuses of Inmate Litigation*. College Park, Md.: American Correctional Association.

Antieau, Chester J. 1980. *Federal Civil Rights Acts: Civil Practice*. Rochester, N.Y.: Lawyers Co-Operative Publishing Company.

Aronowitz, Stanley. 1973. *False Promises: The Shaping of American Working Class Consciousness*. New York: McGraw Hill.

Atkinson, Maxwell J., and Paul Drew. 1979. *Order in the Court: The Organisation of Verbal Interaction in Judicial Settings*. London: MacMillan.

Aylward, Anmarie, and Jim Thomas. 1984. "Quiescence in Women's Prison Litigation: Some Exploratory Gender Issues." *Justice Quarterly* 1(June):253–76.

Baker, Donald P., Randolph M. Blotky, Keith M. Clemens, and Michael L. Dillard. 1973. "Judicial Intervention in Corrections: The California Experience-An Empirical Study." *UCLA Law Review* 20:452–575.

Barrett, Edward L. Jr, and William Cohen. 1985. *Constitutional Law: Cases and Materials.* Mineola, N.Y.: Foundation Press.

Bator, Paul M. 1963. "Finality in Criminal Law and Federal Habeas Corpus for State Prisoners." *Harvard Law Review* 76(March):441–558.

Bator, Paul M., Paul J. Mishkin, David L. Shapiro, and Herbert Wechsler. 1973. *The Federal Court and the Federal System.* Mineola, N.Y.: The Foundation Press.

Becker, Howard S. 1963. *Outsiders.* New York: Free Press.

Bedau, Hugo A. 1981. "How to Argue about Prisoners' Rights: Some Simple Ways." *Rutgers Law Review* 33(Spring):687–705.

Bennett, W. Lance, and Martha S. Feldman. 1981. *Reconstructing Reality in the Courtroom: Justice and Judgment in American Culture.* New Brunswick: Rutgers University Press.

Berger, Raoul. 1977. *Government by Judiciary: The Transformation of the Fourteenth Amendment.* Cambridge: Harvard University Press.

Berkman, Ronald. 1979. *Opening the Gates: The Rise of the Prisoners' Movement.* Lexington, Mass.: Lexington Books.

Black, Donald. 1983. "Crime as Social Control." *American Sociological Review* 48(February):34–45.

———. 1976. *The Behavior of Law.* New York: Academic Press.

Blasi, Vincent, ed. 1983. *The Burger Court: The Counter-Revolution that Wasn't.* New Haven: Yale University Press.

Bloch, Charles J. 1958. *State's Rights: The Law of the Land.* Atlanta: Harrison Company.

Boudin, Louis B. 1968. *Government by Judiciary.* New York: Russell and Russell.

Braly, Malcolm. 1977. *False Starts: A Memoir of San Quentin and other Prisons.* Harmondsworth, England: Penguin Books.

Bronstein, Alvin J. 1979. "Reform Without Change: The Future of Prisoners' Rights" in A. J. Bronstein and P. J. Hirschkop, eds., *Prisoners' Rights, 1979,* pp. 19–33. New York: Practising Law Institute.

Bronstein, Alvin J., and Philip Hirschkop, eds., 1979. *Prisoners' Rights, 1979.* New York: Practising Law Institute.

Brunvand, Jan H. 1981. *The Vanishing Hitchhiker: American Urban Legends and Their Meanings.* New York: W. W. Norton.

Burger, Warren J. 1982. "Isn't there a Better Way?" *American Bar Association Review* 68(March):274–77.

———. 1976. "Chief Justice Burger Issues Yearend Report." *American Bar Association Journal* 62(February):189–90.

Burke, Kenneth. 1984. *Permanence and Change: An Anatomy of Purpose.* Berkeley: University of California Press.

Burt, Christine. 1985. "Rule 9(a) and its Impact on Habeas Corpus Litigation." *New England Journal of Criminal and Civil Confinement* 11(Winter):363–94.

———. 1969. *A Grammar of Motives.* Berkeley: University of California Press.

Calhoun, Emily. 1977. "The Supreme Court and the Constitutional Rights of Prisoners: A Reappraisal." *Hastings Constitutional Law Quarterly* 4(1977):219–47.

Camp, George, and Camille Camp. 1985a. *Prison Gangs: Their Extent, Nature and Impact on Prisons.* Washington: U.S. Department of Justice.

———. 1985b. *The Corrections' Yearbook.* South Salem, N.Y.: Criminal Justice Institute.

Caracappa, Joseph P. 1976. "Section 1983 and the New Supreme Court: Cutting the Civil Rights Act Down to Size." *Duquesne Law Review* (15):49–96.

Cardoza-Freeman, Inez. 1984. *The Joint: Language and Culture in a Maximum Security Prison*. Springfield, Ill.: Charles C. Thomas.

Carp, Robert A., and C. K. Rowland. 1983. *Policy Making and Politics in the Federal and District Courts*. Knoxville: University of Tennessee Press.

Carrol, Leo. 1980. "The Ethics of Fieldwork: A Note from Prison Research" in J. R. Mancini and F. A. M. Robbins, eds., *Encountering Society*, pp. 41–50. Lanham, Md.: University Press of America.

———. 1977a. "Race and Three Forms of Prison Power: Confrontation, Censoriousness, and the Corruption of Authority" in C. R. Huff, ed., *Contemporary Corrections: Social Control and Conflict*, pp. 49–54. Beverly Hills: Sage Publications, Inc.

———. 1977b. "Humanitarian Reform and bi-Racial Sexual Assault in a Maximum Security Prison." *Urban Life* 5(January):417–37.

———. 1974. *Blacks, Hacks and Cons: Race Relations in a Maximum Security Prison*. Lexington, Mass.: Lexington Books. Beverly Hills: Sage Publications, Inc.

Carson, Hampton L. 1971/1902. *The History of the Supreme Court of the United States with Biographies of all the Chief and Associate Justices: 1790–1902*. New York: Burt Franklin.

Castaneda, Carlos. 1974. *The Teachings of Don Juan: A Yaqui Way of Knowledge*. New York: Washington Square Press.

Champagne, Anthony, and Kenneth C. Haas. 1976. "The Impact of *Johnson v. Avery* on Prison Administration." *Tennessee Law Review* 43:275–303.

Chandler, Alfred D., Jr. 1972. *Strategy and Structure: Chapters in the History of the Industrial Enterprise*. Cambridge, Mass.: MIT Press.

Claffy, Joseph. 1984. "Lighting the Way to Less Litigation." *Corrections Today* 46(April):90, 92.

Clemmer, Donald. 1958. *The Prison Community*. New York: Holt, Rinehart & Winston.

Cloward, Richard A. 1960. "Social Control in the Prison" in *Theoretical Studies in Social Organization of the Prison*, pp. 20–48. New York: Social Science Research Council.

Cohen, Anne. 1982. "Prisons and the Law: New Limits Set on Inmate Habeas Writs." *Corrections Magazine* 8(December):37–39.

Cohen, Stanley, and Laurie Taylor. 1976. *Escape Attempts: The Theory and Practice of Resistance to Everyday Life*. London: Allen Lane.

———. 1972. *Psychological Survival: The Experience of Long-term Imprisonment*. New York: Pantheon.

Collins, Charles W. 1974. *The Fourteenth Amendment and the States: A Study of the Operation of the Constraint Clauses of Section One of the Fourteenth Amendment to the Constitution of the United States*. New York: Da Capo Press.

Colvin, Mark. 1982. "The 1980 New Mexico Prison Riot." *Social Problems* 25(June):449–63.

———. 1981. "The Contradictions of Control: Prisons in Class Society." *Insurgent Sociologist* 9/10(Summer/Fall): 33–45.

Contact Center. 1985. *Inmate Lawsuits: Report on Inmate Lawsuits against State and Federal Correctional Systems Resulting in Monetary Damages and Settlements*. Lincoln, Neb.: The Contact Center, Inc.

Cortner, Richard C. 1981. *The Supreme Court and the Second Bill of Rights: The Fourteenth Amendment and the Nationalization of Civil Liberties*. Madison, Wis.: University of Wisconsin Press.

Curry, George E. 1986. " 'Liberal Judges' Hit over Drugs." *Chicago Tribune* October 9, p. 2.

de Beaumont, Gustave, and Alexis de Toqueville. 1970/1833. *On the Penitentiary System in the United States and Its Application in France*. New York: Augustus M. Kelley.

DeWolfe, Ruthanne. 1986. "With Deference Due: Prison Law 1985." *Clearinghouse Review* 19(January):1093–1100.

DeWolfe, Ruthanne, and Alan DeWolfe. 1979. "Impact of Prison Conditions on the Mental Health of Inmates." *Southern Illinois Law Review* 4(1979):497–533.

De Zutter, Hank. 1981. "Gangs Behind Bars: How the Disciples Control Cook County Jail." *Chicago Reader* May 22, p. 3, 26.

Dick, Rebecca P. 1977. "Prison Reform in the Federal Courts." *Buffalo Law Review* 28(Winter):99–138.

Duker, William F. 1980. *A Constitutional History of Habeas Corpus*. Westport, Conn.: Greenwood Press.

Duscha, Julius. 1969. "Chief Justice Burger asks: 'If it doesn't Make Good Sense, How can it Make Good Law?' " *New York Times Magazine* October 5, p. 30.

Eco, Umberto. 1984. *Semiotics and the Philosophy of Language*. London: Macmillan Press.

Eisenberg, Theodore. 1982. "Section 1983: Doctrinal Foundations and an Empirical Study." *Cornell Law Review* 67(March):482–566.

Eisenberg, Theodore, and Stewart J. Schwab. 1986. "The Reality of Constitutional Tort Litigation." Unpublished manuscript, Cornell Law School, Ithaca, N.Y.

Eisenberg, Theodore, and Stephen C. Yeazell. 1980. "The Ordinary and the Extraordinary in Institutional Litigation." *Harvard Law Review* 93(January):467–517.

Ekland-Olson, Sheldon. 1986. "Crowding, Social Control, and Prison Violence: Evidence from the Post-Ruiz Years in Texas." *Law and Society Review* 20(3):389–421.

Engel, David. 1984. "The Oven Bird's Song: Insiders, Outsiders, and Personal Injuries in an American Community." *Law and Society Review* 18(4):551–82.

Ericson, Richard V., and Patricia M. Baranek. 1982. *The Ordering of Justice: A Study of Accused Persons as Dependants in the Criminal Process*. Toronto: University of Toronto Press.

Federal Judicial Center. 1980. *Recommended Procedures for Handling Prisoner Civil Rights Cases in the Federal Courts*. Washington: The Federal Judicial Center.

The Federalist Papers. 1961. New York: Mentor Books.

Fehrenbacher, Don E. 1978. *The Dred Scott Case: Its Significance in American Law and Politics*. New York: Oxford University Press.

Fiss, Owen. 1979. *The Civil Rights Injunction*. Bloomington, Ind.: Indiana University Press.

Friedman, Lawrence M. 1975. *The Legal System: A Social Science Perspective*. New York: Russell Sage Foundation.

Friendly, Henry J. 1970. "Is Innocence Irrelevant? Collateral Attack on Criminal Judgments." *University of Chicago Law Review* 38(1970):142–72.

Fuller, Rebecca, Jennifer Findlay, Patricia Wheeler, and Jim Thomas. 1987. "Doing Jailhouse Law in Women's Prisons." Paper presented to the Illinois Sociological Association annual meeting, October.

Galanter, Marc. 1983. "Reading the Landscape of Disputes: What We Know and Don't Know (and Think We Know) about our Allegedly Contentious and Litigious Society." *UCLA Law Review* 31(October):4–71.

———. 1975. "Afterword: Explaining Litigation." *Law and Society Review* 9(Winter):347–68.

————. 1974. "Why the 'Haves' Come out Ahead: Speculations on the Limits of Legal Change." *Law and Society Review* 9(Fall):95–160.

Genovese, Eugene D. 1974. *Roll, Jordon, Roll: The World the Slaves Made.* New York: Vintage Books.

Gibbons, John J. 1984. "Federal Law and the State Courts: 1790–1860." *Rutgers Law Review* 36(Spring):399–453.

Glazer, Nathan. 1975a. "Towards an Imperial Judiciary?" *Public Interest* 41(Fall):104–23.

————. 1975b. *Affirmative Discrimination: Ethnic Inequality and Public Policy.* New York: Basic Books.

Glick, Brian. 1973. "The Limits of Judicial Action: A Case Study" in E. O. Wright, ed., *Politics of Punishment*, pp. 281–94. New York: Harper and Row.

Gobert, James J., and Neil P. Cohen. 1981. *Rights of Prisoners.* Colorado Springs: Shepard's/McGraw-Hill.

Goffman, Irving. 1974. *Frame Analysis.* New York: Harper.

————. 1961. *Asylums: Essays on the Social Situation of Mental Patients and other Inmates.* New York: Anchor.

Goldman, Sheldon. 1975. "Voting Behaviors on the United States Supreme Court." *American Political Science Review* 78(October):911–24.

Goldman, Sheldon, and Thomas P. Jahnige. 1985. *The Federal Courts as a Political System.* New York: Harper and Row.

Goodstein, Dianne, and John Hepburn. 1986. *Indeterminate Sentencing.* Cincinnati: Anderson.

Granger, Bill. 1977. "Guard Killing is Termed P Stone Nation Revenge." *Chicago Sun Times*, December 31, p. 9.

Graves, Robert. 1961. "In Broken Images," p. 104 in *Collected Poems.* Garden City, N.Y.: Doubleday and Co.

Greenberg, Edward S. 1974. *Serving the Few: Corporate Capitalism and the Bias of Government Policy.* New York: John Wiley and Sons.

Haas, Kenneth C. 1981. "The 'New Federalism' and Prisoners' Rights: State Supreme Courts in Comparative Perspective." *Western Political Quarterly* 34(December):552–71.

Habermas, Jurgen. 1975. *Legitimation Crisis.* Boston: Beacon.

Haft, Marilyn G., and Michele Hermann, eds. 1972. *Prisoners' Rights.* New York: Practising Law Institute.

Hale, Sir Matthew. 1971. *The History of the Common Law of England.* Chicago: University of Chicago Press.

Hardesty, Monica, and Jim Thomas. 1986. "Prisoner Litigation: Boon or Bane?" Paper presented to the American Society of Criminology annual meeting, Atlanta, October 31.

Harger, Jim. 1981. "Jailhouse Lawyers." *Grand Rapids Press*, June 7, pp. 1c, 2c.

Harriman, Linda, and Jeffrey D. Straussman. 1983. "Do Judges Determine Budget Decisions? Federal Court Decisions in Prison Reform and State Spending for Corrections." *Public Administration Review* 43(March/April):343–51.

Hayek, Friedrich A. 1973. *Law, Legislation and Liberty: A New Statement of the Liberal Principles of Justice and Political Economy.* Chicago: University of Chicago Press.

Hermann, Michele G., and Marilyn G. Haft, eds. 1973. *Prisoners' Rights Sourcebook: Theory, Litigation, Practice.* New York: Clark Boardman.

Hindness, Barry. 1973. *The Use of Official Statistics in Sociology: Critique of Positivistism and Ethnomethodology.* London: Macmillan.

Hoffman, Hillel. 1981. *Prisoners' Rights: Treatment of Prisoners and Post-Conviction Remedies, Cases and Materials (1981 Supplement)*. New York: Matthew Bender.

Howard, A. E. Dick. 1980. "The Burger Court: A Judicial Nonet Plays the Enigma Variations." *Law and Contemporary Problems* 43(Summer):7–28.

Irwin, John. 1980. *Prisons in Turmoil*. Boston: Little, Brown.

———. 1970. *The Felon*. Englewood Cliffs, N.J.: Prentice-Hall.

Irwin, John, and Donald R. Cressy. 1962. "Thieves, Convicts and the Inmate Culture." *Social Problems* 10(Fall):142–55.

Jacobs, James B. 1983. "Sentencing by Prison Personnel." *UCLA Law Review* 30(December):217–70.

———. 1982. *New Perspectives on Prisons and Imprisonment*. Ithaca: Cornell University Press.

———. 1977. *Stateville: The Penitentiary in Mass Society*. Chicago: University of Chicago Press.

———. 1975. "Stratification and Conflict Among Prison Inmates." *Journal of Criminal Law and Criminology* 66(December):476–82.

———. 1974a. "Street Gangs Behind Bars." *Social Problems* 21(Winter):395–409.

———. 1974b. "Participant Observation in Prison." *Urban Life* 3(July):221–40.

Jacobs, James B., and Helen A. Brooks. 1983. "The Mass Media and Prison News" in J. Jacobs, *New Perspectives on Prisons and Imprisonment*, pp. 106–15. Ithaca: Cornell University Press.

Justice, William Wayne. 1973. "Prisoners' Litigation in the Federal Courts." *Texas Law Review* 51(1973):707–20.

Kalinich, David B. 1980. *The Inmate Economy*. Lexington, Mass.: Lexington Books.

Kates, Erika. 1984. *Litigation as a Means of Achieving Social Change: A Case-Study of Women in Prison*. Ann Arbor: University Microfilms.

Landau, Tamy. 1984. "Due Process, Legalism and Inmates' Rights: A Cautionary Note." *Criminology Forum* 6:151–63.

Lane, Michael P. 1987. *Illinois Department of Corrections: Quarterly Report*. Springfield: Illinois Department of Corrections.

———. 1986a. *Adult Correctional Center Capacity Survey*. Springfield: Illinois Department of Corrections.

———. 1986b. *Human Services Data Report, Part 1: 1984–1986, Vol III*. Springfield: Illinois Department of Corrections.

———. 1985. *Department of Corrections Annual Report, 1985*. Springfield: Illinois Public Safety and Human Services.

Legal Issues of Female Inmates. 1982. Prepared by the School for Social Work, Smith College, Northampton, Mass.

Leonard, E. B. 1983. "Judicial Decisions and Prison Reform: The Impact of Litigation on Women's Prisons." *Social Problems* 31(October):45–58.

Lewis, Walker. 1965. *Without Fear of Favor: A Biography of Chief Justice Roger Brooke Taney*. Boston: Houghton Mifflin.

Lieberman, Jethro K. 1981. *The Litigious Society*. New York: Basic Books.

Locin, Mitchell. 1981. "Prisoners Filing away with Suits." *Chicago Tribune*, October 18, p. 6.

Lockwood, Daniel. 1980. *Prison Sexual Violence*. New York: Elsevier.

Luckenbill, David. 1986. "Deviant Career Mobility: The Case of Male Prostitutes." *Social Problems* 33(April):283–96.

Luckenbill, David L., and Joel Best. 1981. "Careers in Deviance and Respectability: The Analogy's Limitations." *Social Problems* 29(December):197–206.

Lyman, Sanford, and Marvin Scott. 1968. "Accounts." *American Sociological Review* 33(February):46–62.

Maitland, Frederick. 1968. *The Constitutional History of England.* Cambridge: Cambridge University Press.

Mandel, Michael. 1986. "The Legalization of Prison Discipline in Canada." *Crime and Social Justice* 26:79–94.

Manning, Bayless. 1977. "Hyperlexis: Our National Disease." *Northwestern University Law Review* 71(Sept/Oct):767–82.

Manning, Peter K. 1987. "The Social Reality and Social Organization of Natural Decision-Making." *Washington and Lee Law Review* 43:1–21.

———. 1986. "Signwork." *Human Relations* 39(4):283–308.

———. 1979. "Metaphors of the Field: Varieties of Organizational Discourse." *Administrative Science Quarterly* 24(December):660–71.

———. 1977. *Police Work.* Cambridge, Mass.: MIT Press.

Marquart, James B. 1986a. "Prison Guards and the Use of Physical Coercion as a Mechanism of Prisoner Control." *Criminology* 24(May):347–66.

———. 1986b. "Doing Research in Prison: The Strengths and Weaknesses of Full Participation as a Guard." *Justice Quarterly* 3(March):15–32.

Marquart, James W., and Ben Crouch. 1985. "Judicial Reform and Prisoner Control: The Impact of *Ruiz v. Estelle* on a Texas Penitentiary." *Law and Society Review* 19(4):537–86.

———. 1984. "Coopting the Kept: Using Inmates for Social Control in a Southern Prison." *Justice Quarterly* 1(December):491–509.

Meese, Edwin. 1986. "The Law of the Constitution: A Bicentennial Lecture." Delivered to the Tulane University Citizen's Forum on the Bicentennial of the Constitution, October 21.

———. 1985a. "Address of the Honorable Edwin Meese III Attorney General of the United States before the American Bar Foundation." July 9. Washington: U.S. Department of Justice.

———. 1985b. "Address of the Honorable Edwin Meese III Attorney General of the United States before Old Dominion." September.

———. 1985c. "Interview: Reagan Seeks Judges with Traditional Approach." *U.S. News and World Report* October 14, p. 67.

McBarnet, Doreen J. 1981. *Conviction: Law, the State and the Construction of Justice.* London: Macmillan.

McCormack, Wayne. 1975. "The Expansion of Federal Question Jurisdiction and the Prisoner Complaint Caseload." *Wisconsin Law Review* 1975:523–51.

McCoy, Candace. 1981. "The Impact of Section 1983 Litigation on Policymaking in Corrections: A Malpractice Lawsuit by any Name would Smell as Sweet." *Federal Probation* 45(December):17–23.

Menninger, Karl. 1978. *The Crime of Punishment.* New York: Penguin Books.

Merton, Tom. 1980. "The Effects of 'Prison Reform': The Arkansas Case Study" in I. P. Robbins, ed., *Prisoners' Rights Sourcebook (Vol II): Theory, Litigation, Practice,* pp. 467–75. New York: Clark Boardman.

Meyers, Barton. 1984. "Minority Group: An Ideological Formulation." *Social Problems* 32(October):1–15.

Mika, Harry, and Jim Thomas. 1987. "The Dialectics of Prisoner Litigation." *Crime and Social Justice* 27 (in press).

Miller, Arthur Selwyn. 1982. *Toward Increased Judicial Activism: The Political Role of the Supreme Court.* Westport, Conn.: Greenwood Press.

Mills, C. Wright. 1940. "Situated Actions and Vocabularies of Motive." *American Sociological Review* 5(December):904–13.

Morgan, Richard E. 1984. *Disabling America: The "Rights Industry" in Our Time.* New York: Basic Books.

NAAG (National Association of Attorneys General). 1980. *Implementation of Remedies in Prison Conditions Suits.* Washington: National Institute of Corrections, U.S. Department of Justice.

Natale, Eugene V., and Cecelia F. Rosenberg. 1974. "And the Walls Come Tumbling Down: An Analysis of Social and Legal Pressures Bearing on the American Prison System." *New York Law Forum* 19(Winter):609–37.

Nelken, David. 1986. "Beyond the Study of 'Law and Society'? Henry's Private Justice and O'Hagan's The End of Law?" *American Bar Foundation Research Journal* 1986(Spring):323–338.

Noblit, George W., and Geoffrey P. Alpert. 1979. "Advocacy and Rehabilitation in Women's Prisons." *Law and Policy Quarterly* 1(April):207–22.

Nye, Russell B., and J. E. Morpurgo. 1970. *A History of the United States.* Harmondsworth, England: Penguin Books.

O'Neill, John. 1972. *Sociology as a Skin Trade: Essays toward a Reflexive Sociology.* London: Heinemann.

Paine, Thomas. 1974. *The Life and Major Writings of Thomas Paine.* Secaucus, N.J.: Citadel Press.

Palmer, John W. 1985. Constitutional Rights of Prisoners. Cincinnati: Anderson.

Pollack, Jack Harrison. 1979. *Earl Warren: The Judge Who Changed America.* Englewood Cliffs, N.J.: Prentice Hall.

Possley, Maurice. 1980. "Inmates Using an Out-They Sue." *Chicago Sun-Times* October 15, p. 20.

———. 1981. "5 ex-Prison Guards get 2 to 5 Yrs. for Beatings." *Chicago Sun Times* Feb. 21, p. 2.

Pound, Roscoe. 1975. *The Development of Constitutional Guarantees of Liberty.* Westport, Conn.: Greenwood Press.

Practising Law Institute. 1972. *Prisoners' Rights.* New York: Practising Law Institute.

Prison Discipline Society of Boston. 1972. *Reports of the Prison Discipline Society of Boston, Vol I: 1826–1854.* Montclair, N.J.: Patterson Smith.

"Prosecutor Gets Burglary Charge for Shoplifting." 1986. [DeKalb] *Daily Chronicle* February 25, p. 3.

Rawls, Anne. 1986. "Focusing on the Gap between Rules and Practice: A Theory of Social Problems." Unpublished manuscript, University of Wisconsin.

Reed, Anne Willis. 1980. "Guilt, Innocence, and Federalism in Habeas Corpus." *Cornell Law Review* 65(1): 1123–47.

Reinsch, Paul Samuel. 1967/1907. *The English Common Law in the Early American Colonies.* Frankfurt, Germany: Verlag Sauer and Auvermann.

Rembar, Charles. 1980. *The Law of the Land: The Evolution of Our Legal System.* New York: Simon and Schuster.

Richardson, Richard J., and Kenneth N. Vines. 1970. *The Politics of Federal Courts: Lower Courts in the United States.* Boston: Little, Brown and Company.

Robinson, Cyril D. 1984. *Legal Rights, Duties, and Liabilities of Criminal Justice Personnel: History and Analysis.* Springfield, Ill.: Charles C. Thomas.

Roby, Pamela. 1969. "Politics and Criminal Law: Revision of the New York State Penal Law on Prostitution." *Social Problems* 17(Spring):83–109.

Rothman, David J. 1980. *Conscience and Convenience: The Asylum and its Alternatives in Progressive America.* Boston: Little, Brown and Co.

———. 1979. "Decarcerating Prisoners and Patients" in A. Bronstein and P.

Hirschkop, eds., *Prisoners' Rights, 1979*, pp. 35–57. New York: Practising Law Institute.

Rubin, Sol. 1974. "The Impact of Court Decisions on the Correctional Process." *Crime and Delinquency* 20(April):129–34.

Santos, Boaventura De Sousa. 1980. "Law and Community: The Changing Nature of State Power in Late Capitalism." *International Journal of the Sociology of Law* 8:379–97.

Sharpe, R. J. 1976. *The Law of Habeas Corpus*. Oxford: Clarendon Press.

Shapiro, David L. 1973. "Federal Habeas Corpus: A Study in Massachusetts." *Harvard Law Review* 87(December):321–72.

Singer, Richard. 1980. "Prisoners' Rights Litigation: A Look at the Past Decade and a Look at the Coming Decade." *Federal Probationer* 44(4):3–11.

Singer, Richard G., and William P. Statsky, eds. 1974. *Rights of the Imprisoned*. New York: Bobbs-Merrill.

Spitzer, Steven. 1983. "Marxist Perspectives in the Sociology of Law." *Annual Review of Sociology* Vol. 9:103–24. Palo Alto, Cal.: Annual Reviews.

Stastny, Charles, and Gabrielle Tyrnauer. 1983. *Who Rules the Joint?* Lexington, Mass.: D. C. Heath.

Suchner, Robert, Jim Thomas, and Anmarie Aylward. 1986. "Politics and Cueing Theory: The Ideology of Judicial Decision Making." Paper presented at the Law and Society annual meeting, Chicago, June.

Sykes, Gresham M. 1958. *The Society of Captives: A Study of a Maximum Security Prison*. Princeton: Princeton University Press.

Sylvester, Sawyer F., John H. Reed, and David O. Nelson. 1977. *Prison Homicide*. New York: Spectrum.

Taylor, Stuart. 1984. "The One-Pronged Test for Federal Judges: Reagan Puts Ideology First in Filling Vacancies." *New York Times*, April 22, E–5.

Thomas, Jim. 1988. "The Sociology of Law: A Historical Perspective." Sociology Instructional Monograph (SAC), Northern Illinois University.

———. 1987. "Losers, Loonies, Lackies and the Law: Critiqueing Theories of Prisoner Litigation." Paper presented to the American Criminology Society annual meeting, Montreal, November.

———. 1984a. "Law and Social Praxis: Prisoner Civil Rights and Structural Mediations." Pp. 141–70 in S. Spitzer and A. Scull, eds., *Research in Law, Deviance and Social Control, Vol. 6*.

———. 1984b. "Some Aspects of Negotiated Order, Mesostructure and Loose Coupling in Maximum Security Prisons." *Symbolic Interaction* 7(Fall):213–31.

———. 1983. "Justice as Interaction: Loose Coupling and Mediations in the Adversary Process." *Symbolic Interaction* 6(Fall):243–60.

———. 1981a. "New Directions in Deviancy Research" in A. Turowetz, R. Stebbins, and M. Rosenberg, eds., *The Sociology of Deviance*. Pp. 288–318. New York: St. Martins.

———. 1981b. "Class, State, and Political Surveillance: Liberal Democracy and Structural Contradictions." *Insurgent Sociologist* 7(Fall):49–55.

Thomas, Jim, Anmarie Aylward, Harry Mika, and Jerome Blakemore. 1985. "Prison Disciplinary Proceedings: The Social Enactment of Power." Paper presented to the Midwest Criminal Justice Association, Chicago, October.

Thomas, Jim, Anmarie Aylward, Mary Louise Casey, David Moton, Michelle Oldham, and George W. Wheetley. 1985. "Rethinking Prisoner Litigation: Some Preliminary Distinctions between Habeas Corpus and Civil Rights." *The Prison Journal* 65(Spring/Summer):83–106.

Thomas, Jim, Kathy Harris, and Devin Keeler. 1987. "Issues and Misconceptions in Prisoner Litigation." *Criminology* 24(4):901–19.

Thomas, Jim, Richard Doherty, Sue Los, and Gabrielle Strohschen. 1987. "Historical Rhetoric and the Images of Law: Legal Fundamentalism as Ideology." *Journal of Crime and Justice* (in press).

Thomas, Jim, and James B. Marquart. 1987. "Dirty Information and a Clean Conscience: Communication Problems in Studying "Bad Guys" in D. Maines and C. Couch, eds., *Information, Communication and Social Structure.* Springfield, Ill.: Charles C. Thomas.

Thomas, Jim, David Stribling, Ra Rabb Chaka, Edmond Clemons, Charlie Secret, and Alex Neal. 1981. "Prison Conditions and Penal Trends." *Crime and Social Justice* 15(Summer):40–55.

Thompson, E. P. 1975. *Whigs and Hunters: The Origin of the Black Act.* New York: Pantheon.

Trubek, David M., Austin Sarat, William L. F. Felstiner, Herbert M. Kritzer, and Joel B. Grossman. 1983. "The Costs of Ordinary Litigation." *UCLA Law Review* 31(October):72–127.

Turner, William Bennett. 1979. "When Prisoners Sue: A Study of Prisoner Section 1983 Suits in the Federal Courts." *Harvard Law Review* 92(June):610–63.

Unger, Rudolph. 1980. " 'Get Tough' Attitude Puts Strains on Prisons." *Chicago Tribune,* September 22, p. 4.

Useem, Bert. 1985. "Disorganization and the New Mexico Prison riot of 1980." *American Sociological Review* 50(October):677–88.

Van Maanen, John. 1988 (in press). *Tales of the Field: On Writing Ethnography.* Chicago: University of Chicago Press.

Vito, Gennaro F., and Judith H. Kaci. 1982. "Hands on or Hands Off? The Use of Judicial Intervention to Establish Prisoners' Rights: An Examination of Sostre and other Prisoner Suits" in N. Parisi, ed., *Coping with Imprisonment,* pp. 79–100. Beverly Hills: SAGE Publications, Inc.

Warren, James, Brian Kelly, and Maurice Possley. 1986. "On the Law: An Inmate by any other Name." *Chicago Tribune* July 25, Sec. III, pp. 1, 6.

———. 1984. "On The Law," *Chicago Tribune* February 28, Sec. III, pp. 1, 8.

Wheeler, Patricia, Rebecca Fuller, Jim Thomas, and Jennifer Findlay. 1987. "The Woman Jailhouse Lawyer." Paper presented to the American Society of Criminology annual meeting, Montreal, November.

White, James B. 1984. *The Legal Imagination.* Chicago: University of Chicago Press. London: Verso.

Willging, Thomas E. 1985. *Partial Payment of Filing Fees in Prisoner In Forma Pauperis Cases in Federal Courts: A Preliminary Report.* Washington: The Federal Judicial Center.

Wolfe, Christopher. 1982. "John Marshall and Constitutional Law." *Polity* 15(Fall):525.

Wooden, Wayne S., and Jay Parker. 1982. *Men Behind Bars: Sexual Exploitation in Prison.* New York: Plenum Press.

Cases

Adamson v. California 332 U.S. 46 (1947).
Anders v. California, 386 U.S. 738 (1967).
Barron v. Baltimore, 7 Pet. 243 (1833).
Bell v. Wollfish, 441 U.S. 520 (1979).
Betts v. Brady, 316 U.S. 455 (1942).
Bivens v. Six Unknown Named Agents of the Federal Bureau of Narcotics, 403 U.S. 388 (1971).
Bounds v. Smith, 430 U.S. 817 (1977).
Brown v. Allen, 344 U.S. 443 (1953).
Calvin R. v. Lane, 82–C–1955 (N.D. Ill. 1982).
Civil Rights Cases, 109 U.S. 3 (1883).
Cooper v. Pate, 382 F.2d 518 (7th Cir. 1967).
Davidson v. Cannon, 752 F.2d 817 (7th Cir. 1984).
Delorme v. Pierce Freightlines, 353 F.Supp 258 (D. Or. 1973).
Duran v. Elrod, 74–C–2949 (N.D. Ill. 1974).
Escobedo v. Illinois, 378 U.S. 478 (1964).
ex parte Hull, 312 U.S. 546 (1941).
ex parte Kearney, 20 U.S., 7 Wheat. (1822).
ex parte Lange, 85 U.S., 18 Wall. 163 (1873).
ex parte Royall, 117 U.S. 241 (1885).
ex parte Taws, Fed Case No. 13,768, 2 Wash. C.C. 353 (1809).
ex parte Watkins, 28 U.S., 3 Pet. (1830).
ex parte Young, 209 U.S. 123 (1908).
ex rel Morris v. Radio Station WENR, 209 F.2d 105 (7th Cir. 1953).
Faheem-El v. Franzen, 79–C–2273 (C.D. Ill., 1979).
Fay v. Noia, 372 U.S. 391 (1963).
Fletcher v. Peck, 10 U.S., 6 Cranch 87 (1810).
Gideon v. Wainwright, 372 U.S. 335 (1963).
Gitlow v. New York, 268 U.S. 652 (1925).
Glover v. Johnson, 478 F.Supp. 1075 (E.D. Mich. 1979).
Haines v. Kerner, 404 U.S. 519 (1972).
Heirens v. Mizell, 729 F.2d 449 (7th Cir. 1984).
High, et al., v. Thompson, 85–C–5484 (C.D. Ill. 1985).
Holt v. Sarver, 300 F.Supp 825 (E.D. Ark. 1969).
Hutto v. Finney, 437 U.S. 678 (1978).
Jackson v. Bishop, 404 F.2d 571 (8th Cir. 1968).
Johnson v. Avery, 393 U.S. 483 (1969).
Knight v. Ragen, 337 F.2d 425 (7th Cir. 1964).
Lamar v. Steele, 693 F.2d 559 (5th Cir. 1982).
Logan v. U.S., 144 U.S. 263 (1892).
Madyun v. Thompson, 657 F.2d 868 (7th Cir. 1981).

Mapp v. Ohio, 367 U.S. 643 (1961).
Marbury v. Madison, 5 U.S., 1 Cranch 137 (1803).
McCulloch v. Maryland, 17 U.S., 4 Wheat. 316 (1819).
Miranda v. Arizona, 384 U.S. 436 (1966).
Monroe v. Pate, 365 U.S. 167 (1961).
Morgan v. LaVallee, 526 F.2d 221 (2d Cir. 1975).
Moyer v. Peabody, 212 U.S. 78 (1909).
Parratt v. Taylor, 451 U.S. 527 (1981).
Paul v. Elrod, 86–C–1867 (N.D. Ill. 1986).
Paul v. Elrod, 86–C–2718 (N.D. Ill. 1986).
Plessy v. Ferguson, 163 U.S. 537 (1896).
Powell v. Alabama, 287 U.S. 45 (1932).
Preiser v. Rodriguez, 411 U.S. 475 (1973).
Price v. Johnson, 334 U.S. 266 (1948)
Pugh v. Locke, 406 F.Supp 318 (M.D. Ala. 1976).
Rhodes v. Chapman, 452 U.S. 337 (1981).
Roe v. Wade, 410 U.S. 113 (1973).
Ruffin v. Commonwealth, 21 Gratt. 790 (1871).
Ruiz v. Estelle, 650 F.2d 555 (5th Cir. 1981).
Russell v. Franzen, 79–C–3774 (N.D. Ill. 1979).
Sanders v. U.S., 373 U.S. 1 (1963).
Scheuer v. Rhodes, 416 U.S. 232 (1974).
Scott v. Sandford, S.C. 19 Howard 393 (1857).
Screws v. U.S., 325 U.S. 91 (1945).
Shango v. Jurich, 77–C–103 (N.D. Ill. 1977).
Slaughter-House Cases, 16 Wall. 36 (1872)
Smith v. Rowe, 77–C–1029 (C.D. Ill. 1977).
Smith v. Fairman, 690 F.2d 122 (7th Cir. 1982).
Stapleton v. Mitchell, 60 F.Supp 51 (D. Kans. 1945).
State v. Cannon, 55 Del. 587 (1963).
Stroud v. Swope, 187 F.2d 820 (9th Cir. 1951).
Tenney v. Brandove, 341 U.S. 367 (1951).
Townsend v. Sain, 372 U.S. 293 (1963).
Trop v. Dulles, 356 U.S. 86 (1958).
U.S. v. Price, 383 U.S. 787 (1966).
Weems v. U.S., 217 U.S. 349 (1910).
Welsh v. Mizell, 668 F.2d 328 (7th Cir. 1982).
Wolff v. McDonnell, 418 U.S. 539 (1974).
Woods v. Aldworth, 84–C–7745 (N.D. Ill. 1984).
Wright v. McMann, 387 F.2d 519 (2nd Cir. 1967).

Index of Cases

Index